The Survival of the Adversary Culture

The Survival of the Adversary Culture

Social Criticism and Political Escapism in American Society

Paul Hollander

With a Foreword by Sidney Hook

Transaction Books
New Brunswick (USA) and Oxford (UK)

Library of Congress Catalog Number: 87-25569
ISBN: 0-88738-190-1
Printed in the United States of America

Library of Congress Cataloging-in-Publication Data

Hollander, Paul. 1932–
    The survival of the adversary culture: social criticism and political
escapism in American society / Paul Hollander, with a foreword by
Sidney Hook.
        p.   cm.
    ISBN 0-88738-190-1
    1. United States—Social conditions—1960– 2. Radicalism—United
States. 3. Communism. 4. Hollander, Paul, 1932–   . I. Title.
HN65.H562   1988
306'.0973—dc19   87-25569
                                                          CIP

Contents

Acknowledgements

I am grateful for a research grant from the Earhart Foundation which has greatly benefited my work on the domestic and foreign critiques of American society and also helped in the preparation of the manuscript for this volume.

Some of the writings here included also benefited from, or were actually completed during a stay (as a scholar-in-residence) at the Rockefeller Foundation Study Center in Bellagio, Italy in 1984; others were produced during my residence at the Hoover Institution in Palo Alto, Calif., as a visiting scholar in the summers of 1985 and 1986. Both the Rockefeller Study Center and Hoover Institution provided excellent working conditions and much intellectual stimulation and I thank both for their assistance.

My own institution the University of Massachusetts at Amherst contributed to this volume by awarding me a sabbatical semester in 1984 which I used for writing and for gathering information about the critiques of the United States found in Western Europe and Mexico.

My wife, Mina Harrison helped, as usual, to make improvements by critically commenting upon both the style and substance of most of these writings.

The author gratefully acknowledges the permission to reprint copyrighted material to the following publishers and publications:

"The Two Faces of George Kennan" is reprinted from *Policy Review* Issue No. 33 (Summer 1985). *Policy Review* is the flagship quarterly magazine of The Heritage Foundation, 214, Massachusetts Ave., NE, Washington, D.C. 20002.

"Sister City Fantasies" was originally published under the title "The Soviet people are not like us" in the *Daily Hampshire Gazette,* (Northampton, Mass.) January 16, 1984.

"Wishful Economic Determinism" appeared under the title "Wishful Determinism" in *Society*, January-February 1984.

"The Durable Misconceptions of the Soviet Union" appeared in the October 1986 issue of *World and I* magazine, a publication of the *Washington Times Corporation.*

"Trends in Western European anti-Americanism" appeared originally under the title "European anti-Americanism: Nothing New on the Western Front" in *Chronicles of Culture,* March 1985.

"A True Believer of the Old School" originally appeared under the title "Selective Affinities" in *The New Republic,* October 18, 1982.

"Romantic Communism" was an untitled review of Vivian Gornick: *The Romance of American Communism* published in *Contemporary Sociology*, January 1979.

"New Light on the Roots of Radicalism" and "A Neglected Destination for Political Tourists" (the latter under the title "The Strange Case of Taiwan") were published in *Encounter* magazine (London) in April 1984 and July 1987 respectively.

"The Anti-War Movement and Critiques of American Society" is reprinted from a forthcoming book *Vietnam: A Fresh Look at the Arguments* (ed. John Norton Moore).

"Further Explorations in the Theories and Practices of Socialism" first appeared in *Partisan Review*, vol. LII, 1985, no. 2.

"American Intellectuals: Producers and Consumers of Socialism Criticism" is reprinted from *Intellectuals in Liberal Democracies* edited by Alain Gagnon published in 1987 by Praeger Publishers in New York.

"The Appeals of Revolutionary Violence: Latin American Guerillas and American Intellectuals" is reprinted from Michael Radu ed.: *Violence and The Latin American Revolutionaries*, (forthcoming 1988) Transaction Books.

"Sojourners in Nicaragua" is reprinted from *The National Catholic Register*, May 29, 1983.

"Political Tourism in Cuba and Nicaragua" was originally published by the Cuban American National Foundation as part of its Occasional Paper Series in 1986.

Foreword

Of the many fascinating themes discussed in this impressive collection of articles by Paul Hollander, two are of central importance. The first is the recurrent phenomenon of hostility to American institutional values and practices among large segments of the American intellectual classes. This hostility goes far beyond the customary limits of criticism which is and should be endemic to any functioning truly democratic order. Indeed such criticism should be the defining role of an intellectual, and the toleration and sympathetic evaluation of such criticism the hallmark of a democratic order.

What is referred to however is a criticism that takes the form of an alienation from American society so profound that it expresses itself either in a spiritual adhesion, if not allegiance to, a form of society openly hostile to American society, or more often, in the view that there is a moral equivalence in practice between the United States and its totalitarian enemies.

Although a recurrent phenomenon, different waves of its manifestation reflect changes in recent history. In the thirties, and for some time later, when the threat of fascism in all its forms was perceived both as an effect of, and a threat to, existing capitalist democracies, large groups of intellectuals both in Europe and the United States professed open sympathy with the values and institutions of the Soviet Union. In the late fifties and thereafter when the truth about the organized repressions in Communist regimes became undeniable, many intellectuals fell back upon the view that both the U.S. and U.S.S.R. were equally repellent when viewed from the high ground of democratic morality. Since American intellectuals were living in the U.S., their function naturally was to concentrate in exposing American evils, particularly the ever present gap between promise and performance.

It is noteworthy that during the period of the rise and triumph of European Fascism when social and economic conditions in the United States were far worse than they were in the decades following World War II, American intellectuals were never beguiled into concentrating their critical fire primarily against domestic evils or drawing preposterous moral equations between the free society of the West and its totalitarian enemy. They were not impressed that Nazi Germany had solved its unemployment problem and that the real wages of the German working class had increased. When Goebbels jeered at American hypocrisy in protesting racial discrimination in Germany while

ix

practicing it against a much larger group of black victims within its own borders, it had little effect. By and large American intellectuals were aware of the price the people in Germany and Europe were fated to pay for the Nazi reforms, and they knew that in the U.S. the discriminatory practices were a violation of its own principles, and gradually being eliminated, whereas in Germany the barbaric practices—the full range of which were not yet known—were inherent in the official philosophy of government. During the late forties, fifties, and sixties although economic, social, and racial conditions had immensely improved in the U.S., with little abatement of repression and poverty in the U.S.S.R., large sections of the American intellectual classes seemed to lose faith in their own culture and political system.

In the light of the history of ideas and nations, this rather bizarre critical stance is significant. In accordance with the Marxist social and political views embraced by many of these intellectuals, one would have expected "the exploited American working classes" to develop attitudes of hostility towards and alienation from, American industrial society, and to become sympathetic to a regime that professed to be a workers' state. But the overwhelming number of the American working class had been integrated into the expanding industrial economy, ever since the adoption of the Wagner Industrial Relations Act at a time when the depression was at its worst. If anything, the American working classes turned out to be the strongest supporters of the American political system and its democratic ideals. They were critical, to be sure, of its abuses and failures, and aware of the succession of problems that had to be met. But they were just as aware of the progress that had been made in recent times. At the same time the organized American working class became the staunchest opponent of totalitarianism in all its varieties. It realized that in the absence of free independent unions in countries where there was no legal right to strike, the regime was necessarily one of forced labor.

Another odd feature in the disparity of the response made by the organized working class and the alienated intellectuals we are discussing, was the fact that the life of intellectuals, in the totalitarian cultures they were equating with American culture, was very unhappy indeed. The very vocation of the intellectual as customarily defined and lived in the U.S., was impossible to exercise in the Soviet Union or in any country organized on the Soviet model. Intellectuals in these cultures were expected to conceive of themselves as poet laureates of the status-quo. If they could not bring themselves to act in this role, at the very least, they were expected to wallow in self-criticism or become faithful servitors of the partyline. Long before the details of the Soviet concentration camps for the peasants and dissident workers became known, the world became aware of the rigorous repressions in the name of ideological orthodoxy in all fields of art and science. The intellectual classes have always been among the first victims of Communist repression everywhere, especially the critical elements among them.

How could American intellectuals, who were suffering from no manifest kind of repression or material deprivation, draw any kind of moral equation between the culture in which they had been nurtured, and one in which their lives and liberties were under perpetual threat? Professor Paul Hollander has written many illuminating pages in an attempt to clarify this phenomenon.

Many things contribute to this perversity of outlook. Much of it stems from an unintelligent idealism that understandably finds itself always in opposition to an existing evil from the standpoint of what should be, but then fails to look back and appreciate in perspective the gains made in consequences of these criticisms. Such an evaluation is not a pretence for complacency but a spur for further action.

Usually it is a sound practice in assessing either individuals, movements or institutions to judge them not merely by the position in which they are found at any particular moment, but by the *direction* in which they are moving. Even with the periodic setbacks in race relations in the United States, no one who recalls the conditions of the black minority in the United States before the Civil Rights Act of 1964, and compares them with conditions today can reasonably contest the direction and magnitude of the change towards greater justice. Yet those who morally equate American culture with that of its chief antagonists rarely ask themselves what the *direction* of change has been in *fundamental* respects within these other cultures. Has the monopoly of political power of the minority Communist Party, never legitimately acquired through a free and uncoerced electoral process, ever been breached? In assessing the significance of fundamental change in the U.S.S.R. during the current Glasnost reforms, has that monopoly been seriously affected? So far the evidence is lacking.

Whatever the explanations offered for the unbalanced hyper-criticism of American culture by the group of intellectuals who fall back upon the notion of moral equivalence—and on this question Professor Hollander's analysis is most illuminating, it is tempting to say that it simply betokens the absence of detailed knowledge of the nature and organization of Communist society. But this seems incredible. Surely it will be said, all sections of American society, and certainly the intellectuals, are well informed about Communism, not only about its domestic organization but about how Communist regimes function at home and abroad.

Long years of experience have convinced me that this is far from being true. Every season we hear from leaders of diverse peace groups, of church associations including high dignitaries among them, of legal and other professions, of organized tourists or "just plain folks" returning from visits to the Soviet Union who display not only ignorance of the facts of life in Communist societies but are totally and blissfully unaware of the history of the Soviet Union and its many changes of face and tactics in its pursuit of "peaceful coexistence." When an awareness of the systematic repression of Communist rule breaks through the protective coat of eagerness to agree, there is a tendency to discount the gravity of Communist outrage on the ground that although "they are just like us," it is too much to expect them, given their history, to act like us. They are then considered the victims of historical circumstances and traditions in a way that never holds for Americans. The Soviet borders are sensitive and permeable so that the invasion of Afghanistan or the construction of the Wall running through Germany can be interpreted as a defensively motivated aggression to preserve the peace in contrast with the actions, however moderate, of the United States in Central America.

Actually, instruction about the history and nature of communism is either non-existent or desultory in the secondary schools of the United States and even on the American undergraduate level. In the last years before I retired from teaching at New York University in 1972 many of my students were of the impression that the Communists under Lenin had overthrown Czar Nicholas II. Despite or perhaps because of the public service broadcasts of our media, evidence of the innocence of large sections of the American public concerning communist theory, practice and propaganda abounds on every hand. Nothing can be more instructive than observing the behavior of a typical rural or even small suburban center in welcoming the successive delegation of Communist visitors from all the arts and professions that keep pouring over The Bridges for Peace set up by the Kremlin and certain pacifist groups in the U.S. All of these highly trained Soviet propagandists are regarded by most of the American citizens they meet, as "ordinary nice private people just like us." It rarely dawns on them that there are no truly private persons in these delegations, that they are selected, vested, and trained by officials of the regime when they are not themselves officials. And to a man or woman, whether the subject is animal husbandry, or music, or religious practices the colloquy sooner or later turns into an impassioned defense of the internal and foreign policy of the Soviet Union, and a vitrolic attack on the policies of the American government—often but not always to the embarrassment of their American hosts.

These visiting ''private'' citizens are often given free run of American institutions—church forums, school assemblies, local media—(in a fashion never reciprocated by the Soviet regime to critical American visitors), and with no provision for adequate response by their American sponsors. Their educational mission is facilitated by a kind of misplaced American courtesy—perhaps one should call it obtuseness—in the context of crude and deceptive propaganda. As I write, I recall the incident of a visit of the assistant editor of the Soviet daily *Izvestia*, to the printing plant of a well known Vermont newspaper. The story of the technical similarities and differences between the two newspapers was given a great play in the pages of the local paper. When I pointed out to the Editor of that paper that there was no mention of the major difference, that he, the editor, could criticize the American government to his heart's content, but that at the time it would be dangerous to life and liberty for any writer in *Izvestia* to attempt to criticize the Soviet Union, he angrily replied that it would have been rude for him to have called attention to it. He did not alter his judgment when the editor of *Izvestia* delivered a tirade against the American government the next day in one of the region's high schools.

It is not only in rural and suburban centers of American life that the illusion persists that there are independent, non-official groups of citizens in the Soviet Union who are on an equal footing with their counterparts in the United States. For example, quite recently, the American Bar Association entered into a cooperative accord with the Association of Soviet Lawyers to advance the rule of law and human rights in the world seemingly unaware of or indifferent to the fact that the Association of Soviet lawyers is one of the instruments by which the repression of human rights is implemented in the Soviet Union.

Perhaps the most important source of misunderstanding even among the politically literate elements among American writers, including some politicians, about the Soviet Union is the view that the U.S. and the U.S.S.R. constitute two imperfect democracies, that the first is a political democracy and the second a kind of economic democracy, each with its own virtues and defects, both moving toward an integrated democracy of both kinds.

The classic expression of this naive, uncritical but enormously influential misperception is in Henry Wallace's famous speech on November 8, 1942 in which he declared that both countries were pursuing ''the new democracy, the democracy of the common man.''

He specified that this new democracy consists of an harmonious whole of five elements ''not only Bill of Rights (political) democracy but economic, ethnic, educational and sexual democracy.'' Of these five types of democracy, the Soviet Union is far superior in all but the Bill of Rights or political democracy. The latter, he seems to believe, have been somewhat overemphasized.

This primitive view that economic or ethnic or any other kind of democracy can exist without any Bill of Rights or political democracy is at the basis of most Communist propaganda. But how workers can participate freely in determining the rewards and conditions of work and other activities of free trade unions, how ethnic groups can express their national values and ideals without political democracy is hard to understand. Indeed the position is really incoherent, for the extent to which freely given consent is presupposed by any intelligible form of democracy, political democracy may be incomplete without other institutional expressions of democracy, but any other kind of democracy without political democracy is impossible.

Sometimes those who speak and write this way confuse democracy and equality. They ignore the blatant inequalities existing in the Soviet Union, and overlook the fact that equality by itself is only a necessary condition for a just society since it does not distinguish between a society in which all are equally free and one in which all are equally unfree.

The natural remedy for ignorance about Communism is education. But here we are brought up short by Paul Hollander's discussion of the transformation in the views of George Kennan about Communism and the Soviet Union. (One can find parallels to Kennan's development in lesser figures like Arthur Schlesinger, Jr.) Surely no one can fault Kennan's knowledge of the nature of Communism both in its domestic and international dimension. Yet the upshot of his position today with respect to American policy towards the Soviet Union is not substantially different from those who have committed themselves to the view that both powers are morally equivalent and equally repellant to anyone committed to the cause of peace. It would hardly be an exaggeration to say that George Kennan's thought has made a 180° turn from the view that the advance of communism threatened the security of Western civilization to the view that today it is the anti-communists who still oppose that advance who constitute the greater threat to peace.

It is obvious that knowledge of the nature of communism is not always enough to contain or resist it. Belief that the consequences of containing or resisting communism may be worse than enduring it, could explain the lack of resistance to communist advance by those familiar with its terror. It seems apparent that this is the key to the evolution of Mr. Kennan's thought in its shift from containment to appeasement. He does himself less than justice in offering other reasons. During the years of appeasement of Hitler, some English pacifists had maintained that so long as England tolerated the London slums, prolonged unemployment and other evils, it had no moral right to arm in defense against the Nazi legions. This position at the time was treated with well merited disdain by Kennan.

Yet in effect Mr. Kennan has argued recently that so long as drugs, crime and pornography are rife in the West there is no moral justification to organize as we do to defend ourselves from the threat of the Soviet Union which by and large is free of these vices. What he now ignores is what he stressed in the past, to wit, what we are defending are not slums or porno shops but a way of life which leaves us free to determine for ourselves how we wish to live. What is at stake in short is the existence of democratic institutions whose validity for him has become problematic.

The true reason for Kennan's shift in outlook, it seems to me, lies elsewhere. It is not merely a lapse in judgment like the incident which affected his diplomatic career.

At a plane stop in Berlin on his way to home leave when Kennan was head of the American diplomatic mission in the Soviet Union, a reporter asked him what it was like living in a Communist country. To which Kennan replied that it was like living in a concentration camp. Whereupon Stalin declared him persona non grata when the story was published. At a meeting shortly after, I commiserated with him. He carefully explained that Stalin was "laying" for him, that as the senior diplomatic officer in Moscow, he was the first person whom diplomats posted to the Soviet Union interviewed. He introduced them, so to speak, to the ropes and immunized them against the elaborate duplicities of the Soviet Foreign Office, much to the chagrin of Stalin. To my naive inquiry why, then, knowing what the situation was, he was not more cautious, he shrugged. This faux pas can be attributed to a passing lapse of judgement from which no one is immune. But the transformation of his views from containment of the Soviet Union to one of virtual appeasement is too momentous a shift to be accounted for in this way.

I am inclined to agree with Paul Hollander that the major factor in the evolution of Kennan's attitude toward Communism, as in the case of Bertrand Russell before him, is his fear of nuclear war and a universal holocaust. This was what led Russell to embrace the better

Red than Dead doctrine, which fortunately has not been embraced by Kennan, although some have argued that there is a certain ambiguity in his discussion of nuclear weaponry in the defensive posture of containment. In view of the fact that Communist Russia already under Brezhnev threatened to unleash nuclear weapons against Communist China, it should be clear that there is no assurance that a willingness to accept Communist hegemony or even Finlandization is a guarantee of peace and survival. The growth of nationalism and the likelihood of nuclear proliferation even among Communist nations does not enhance the prospects of a peaceful world. It can be plausibly argued against those who would reduce our desperate choice to becoming Red or Dead, that they do not exhaust the alternatives. "Neither Red nor Dead" is still a continuing live option.

Uncomfortable as it makes us feel, it is nonetheless true that the existence of atomic and later nuclear weapons has helped to keep the Western World free from catastrophic major wars. The paradox is that the elimination of all such weapons or their circumvention by the development of the Strategic Defense Initiative, may increase the likelihood of conventional war if one side acquires an overwhelming superiority in men and materials. In such a situation, it will no longer be true that a reasonable certainty of victory will be necessary on the part of a totalitarian power to insure its own survival. More and more the will to defend freedom and its strengthening will become central to the strategy of the West.

It is important to bear in mind that the recent tendencies towards Glasnost and restructuring in the Soviet Union—whatever their out-come—have taken place while Western defense remained in place strengthening itself only in response to the introdution of the SS20's by the Kremlin on Western borders. Kennan had anticipated that Western policy would generate greater Soviet intransigence and not the policy of Glasnost and restructuring—a policy, be it noted, not paralleled by developments so far in Afghanistan and elsewhere.

The Western world should welcome the phenomenon of Glasnost in the Soviet Union and Gorbachev's criticism of the crimes of Stalin. But we should recall that Khruschev's denunciation of Stalin was even stronger. That did not prevent Khruschev from following a foreign policy even more confrontational than Stalin's. So far Gorbachev's friendly words to the West have not prevented intense programs of Soviet disinformation alleging that the United States was behind the assassinations of Indira Gandhi and Olaf Palme as well as deliberately introducing the AIDS virus in Africa and elsewhere. This is hard to square with an authentic effort to achieve a peaceful and competitive co-existence.

To preserve and strengthen the will to freedom cannot be achieved by exhortation or by official mobilization of resources to meet emergencies. It must be part of a basic educational process within schools and without, guided by an intelligence aware of the dangers of excessive zeal and dogmatics. Although recognizing that our first priority is with keeping firm the line of defense for the free world, it must be inspired with a concern and hope for the lives of free men everywhere. The validity of that concern will be made manifest by the poignant memoir of his own life and experience in Communist Hungary with which Paul Hollander concludes this volume.

Sidney Hook

Introduction:

The Puzzle of Alienation

In 1986 I published an article in *Partisan Review* entitled "The Survival of the Adversary Culture". At the time I did not think that this title would sum up the main thrust of my writings since 1982. Subsequently it became clear that this was actually the case: almost all the writings put together in this volume focus either directly, or have close bearing on exactly this issue: the survival of the adversary culture. I was particularly anxious to launch these writings under this title because there has been so much questioning of precisely the *survival* of the ideas and the social-political forces brought into sharp focus by the term "adversary culture". These writings taken together seek to further elucidate the meaning of the concept, offer new evidence of the survival of this "culture"—and of the numerous forms this survival has taken—and examine some of the consequences of its persistence in American society.

The "social criticism and political escapism" referred to in the subtitle are, of course, major and complementary facets of the adversary culture. While the social critical impulses hardly require comment, "political escapism" covers phenomena such as the resurgence of political pilgrimages (this time to Nicaragua), the ceaseless efforts to rehabilitate and divorce Marxism from the social-political practices which have been introduced in its name, and the more general belief that "socialism" in some, sofar unrealized incarnation, will be the ultimate panacea for the ills of our times.

The writings here collected, both previously published and unpublished, span a much shorter period than those included in my previous collection *The Many Faces of Socialism*. While the latter included writings produced over a period of twenty years, (from the early 1960s to the early 1980s,) those in this volume were written (with one or two exceptions) since 1983. This circumstance helps to explain not only the topicality of most pieces but also their coherence. Unlike in most cases when shorter writings are put together between hard covers, in this instance there is little cause for concern with lack of coherence

1

and thematic unity, or widely disparate topics—frequent criticism aimed at collections of this kind. The themes and subjects of this volume are clearly focused and represent highly patterned interests of mine. The persistence of my concerns and orientation has also been noted by a critic who detected a long-standing and "astonishing consistency" in my writings.[1]

It may justifiably be asked that if my preoccupations (examined below) changed little over time is that due to a propensity to be fixated on issues, or do these enduring preoccupations mirror certain durable patterns in the world outside, which merit continuing attention? Not surprisingly I lean to the belief that enough has remained unchanged in the world to explain and justify a persistence of the questions I raise and the effort to understand the phenomena in question.

My intellectual history may be described, in a somewhat simplified way, as consisting of a movement from Soviet, and Soviet-American comparative studies to inquiries focusing on Western intellectuals and American society and its ailments. The type of "ailments" I was interested in were not, however, what sociologists call "social problems" (crime, drug addiction, divorce etc.). I have been interested in the more elusive afflictions of the social order, having to do with values, beliefs and a sense of meaning which agitate and sometimes debilitate intellectuals or aspiring intellectuals more than any other group. I have come to focus on intellectuals because they seemed to embody or exemplify with particular clarity certain trends and discontents of life in contemporary Western pluralistic societies. These were the kind of people or stratum of the population I have known best having spent most of my adult life in academic settings (see also the "Epilogue").

I came to attribute over the years considerable importance to the attitudes of intellectuals and what they have said about Western and especially American society; their utterances became a kind of a barometer or yardstick by which I was inclined to measure the social-political or psychic health of these societies. I will not claim that other indicators or measures informative of trends in Western societies could not have yielded equal or possibly superior information, but only that intellectuals have been especially adept and vocal presenting the discontents of life in the West and have invested prodiguous energies in making inventories of the ills of these societies. It is quite conceivable that had I moved in different, non-academic circles my views and interests might have developed along different lines. In all probability I would not have become concerned with matters such as "alienation", "estrangement" or "adversary culture"—concepts which have continued to preoccupy me for almost two decades.

I have been using these concepts for some time in a simple and slightly idiosyncratic way. I think of alienation (or estrangement) as an outlook or state of mind which leads to (or entails) viewing one's own society with deep misgivings and suspicion; the estranged believe that the prevailing social order is deeply flawed, unjust, corrupt and irrational, calculated to constrain or reduce human satisfactions. While it has been easy enough to discern and describe such a mindset I have found it far more difficult to explain satisfactorily its origins and uneven distribution.

Of late I encountered a different, appealingly simple yet in some ways compelling notion of alienation put forward by Bruno Bettelheim. According to him ". . . alienation . . . is an estrangement from the world we live in, and from our inner life; it is also an inability to establish harmony within ourselves and between our inner self and our way of life in this world."[2] I was especially taken by the phrase "inability to establish harmony within ourselves". These comments echoed a conversation I had with him in the summer of 1986 in which he also stressed his belief that, by and large, those who vehemently reject their social-cultural environment (i.e. are alienated, as I used the term) are not happy people, not at peace with themselves, but deeply dissatisfied both with their personal lives and social environment. Bettelheim seems to believe that personal dissatisfaction precedes or underlies the social-political kind, and becomes projected upon to the social setting. Alternatively put, personal dissatisfaction or injury sensitizes to the flaws of the social setting—an interpretation doubtless more acceptable than the former which implies that social criticism (especially of the embittered kind) is likely to be a compensatory activity for personal failings and frustrations, hence of questionable validity.

How can we combine these two interpretations for the purpose of providing some generalization to explain the behavior of groups of people such as those comprising the adversary culture? The problem of course lies in the difficulty of investigating and establishing the nature and degrees of personal happiness or unhappiness and its connection with social, or societal factors. In extreme cases, such as those of the French Marxist social critics, Althusser and Poulantzas— one of whom murdered his wife and was subsequently institutionalized while the other committed suicide—one can readily detect personal unhappiness but even in such instances it remains unclear what if any connections there are between the socially critical temper and the personal gloom. The latter, after all, need not find expression in an enlarged capacity for articulate indignation and public scapegoating. Possibly a series of biographical studies of well known social critics may shed some light on the matter—not on the validity of their criticism but on some of its sources and the circumstances which may plausibly account for its embittered, exaggerated or irrational quality. In any event it may be proposed that a sense of personal injury, disadvantage, failing or frustration, combined with the possession of higher education and high expectations is likely to create a socially critical disposition of an intense, radical and indignant variety that overlooks the positive aspects of the society in which the critic was raised.

Bettelheim's idea of the "inability to establish harmony within ourselves" is a tersely specific and clearly psychological explanation of the disposition to be harshly critical of one's society—whereas I have been trying to account for the same phenomenon by reference to social-historical trends and developments which effect individuals in different and unpredictable ways. These broader trends will not help to explain why some develop the social-critical temper and others fail to do so. To be sure we face the same problem trying to account for other variations in human behavior as well, hence perhaps it is not surprising that it is difficult to come up with a definitive answer to the question why some people become critics of society and not others?

A possible link between a more personal animus and radical (or alienated) social criticism may be found in the tendency of such critics to attribute the defects and injustices of the social order to particular groups of people in possession of great accumulations of economic and political power. It is usually implied and sometimes made explicit that human ill will or amorality (such individuals embody) plays a crucial causal part in the injustices exposed by the critics. There is in the radical critiques of American (and Western) society an unmistakable disposition to blame, facilitated by what I had called "selective determinism"[3]—one may also call it inconsistent determinism, which allows for a very different moral-ethical treatment of different protagonists in social-political conflicts.

Estrangement thus understood is most typically displayed by intellectuals or quasi-intellectuals. It has little to do with their observable material-social conditions and has long ceased to be linked to any kind of tangible deprivation or marginality. On the other hand it is coupled, especially in the United States, with high expectations as to the perfectibility of social institutions and the possibilities for maximizing the welfare of the masses and the contentment of individuals. This attitude was illuminatingly articulated by a participant at the 1986 PEN Club Congress in New York:

> Charles Rembar, a panelist and a lawyer who has been involved in a number of major First Amendment cases addressed himself to that attitude. 'People here from other countries may wonder why we—as fortunate as we are in having the freedoms we have—should still be so concerned . . . The fact that we have more freedom than other countries doesn't mean we have enough . . . Since we have more freedom . . . we have the burden that goes with it. We are the chosen people with the burden of chosen people to be a light for the rest of the world.'[4]

This then is the argument that by setting high and possibly unattainable standards for the United States offers endless opportunities and seemingly unassailable justification for its unrelenting critique. No social system can live up to such high and open-ended expectations. The adversarial critic will not be impressed by how much freedom (or material well being, or educational opportunity, or support for the arts, etc) there is, since there could always be more, especially if we are the chosen people. Hence we must forever face reproach and self-reproach. By contrast those who are not among the chosen and more fallible, escape criticism altogether since little is expected of them. Thus "selective expectations" may be added to selective determinism as attitudes helping to explain radical social criticism and the double standards it often incorporates.

Not only are such expectations directed at the social system, the American character is also subject to them. According to Tom Hayden "There are limits to outer expansion, but no limits to improving the quality of life, the integrity of our character, the breadth of our knowledge, the sensitivity of our feelings, the capacity to find purpose in life . . ." Elsewhere he chastised Americans "for refusing to explore inner frontiers [due to] . . . the fear of self-knowledge" and quoted approvingly Abraham Maslow whose comments reflect similarly outlandish expectations: "We tend, writes Abraham Maslow, 'to be afraid of any knowledge that could cause us to despise ourselves or make us feel inferior, weak, worthless, shameful . . .' ".[5] Neither Hayden nor Maslow tell us in which culture are people anxious to acquire the kind of self-knowledge that would make them feel weak, worthless and inferior or when and where human beings are intent on pursuing the kind of self exploration which results in the disagreeable feelings described. Of course there are no such societies and there have never been but that does not prevent Hayden from reproaching Americans for not indulging themselves in these forms of punitive self-examinations. Only the unrealistically high expectations of such social critics, innocent of any comparative-historical guideposts, can account for the depth of their bitterness about the perceived flaws of American culture and society.

From the moment of my arrival to these shores I was indeed puzzled by the apparent prevalence of these attitudes (at any rate among the people I got to know best) in a society I regarded as quite decent compared to most others, past or present. While I have thought and written a fair amount on these matters in an effort to answer this puzzle to my own satisfaction, a thorough understanding of the phenomenon continues to elude me.

Of late a new element has been added to this "puzzle" as the intellectual community in the United States has become more visibly divided and polarized. An increasingly well defined breach has come to divide those who view their society with doubt, contempt and hostility from those who regard the United States (and other Western democracies) as fragile and historically unique entities, worthy of loyalty, appreciation and defense, by both intellectual and military means. Hilton Kramer has recently brought into sharp focus some of the current implications of this conflicting worldview. He wrote:

> By every significant measure the Soviet Union is a far more formidable adversary today than it was forty years ago . . . Yet the intellectual class in this country which once met with intelligence and valor what was, in truth a simpler and less daunting challenge . . . has been transformed, for the most part, into a force that at best withholds its assent from American inititatives on the world scene and at worst actively argues in support of policies guaranteed to diminish our resistance to Communist expansion.[6]

I have become increasingly impressed by the well defined conflict between these two points of view (and the underlying emotional predispositions) articulated by people who often appear to be equally intelligent, educated, well-meaning and sensitive, and have equal access to information. I pondered why people of seemingly similar endowments, experience, social status, ethnic and religious background, income and occupation would hold diametrically opposed views? Why for example the "New York Intellectuals" have split, many of them persisting in left-of-center positions (entailing various degrees of professed alienation) while others became neoconservatives, defenders of American society and Western values, and confident of the moral superiority of the latter?

I found a partial explanation (which in turn raises further questions) in the way people perceive and define what threatens them. Every political-ideological stand and worldview implies conceptions of threat. Once an individual's or group's threat perception is identified we can unravel the rest of the political strands involved in their worldview.

The two types of intellectuals mentioned above are, for example, distinctly separated in their assessments of the dangers of nuclear war. Those more critical of the United States (as for example George Kennan is) are far more deeply concerned with the threat of nuclear holocaust, *and* also with the internal problems and deficiencies of American society. By contrast the neoconservative intellectuals feel far more threatened by the expansionism of the Soviet Union and its allies, by communist movements in various parts of the world; they also regard the radical critics and detractors of the United States and Western, pluralistic societies as unwholesome influences weakening the social cohesion and solidarity of these societies. They are not especially fearful of nuclear war, or worried about environmental problems, nor do they consider various domestic social problems, including poverty, profoundly delegitimating, or threatening to the survival of American society. They tend to ask what good will, say, improvements in the welfare system or reduction of unemployment do if in the meantime the global power of the United States is eroded and its political system overwhelmed by hostile forces outside. To be sure it has not been easy to specify what particular forms the Soviet threat would take in altering domestic institutional arrangements in the United States. There have been few attempts to provide the substantive details of such dark scenarios although producing them would not, in my opinion, strain one's imagination more than the far more abundant forecasts of nuclear doomsday. Of course this in itself is a value judgment, and the fruit of a particular worldview which designates one threat more plausible than another. Whether or not such threat perceptions give rise to political outlooks or the other way round is an interesting question and worthy of further thought but difficult to resolve.

One thing seems clear: threat perceptions are intimately linked to the evaluation of American society. Those highly critical of it are also the most apt to dismiss external threats to it—although there is no logical connection between these two positions. They also tend to be the same people adamantly opposed to expenditures on defense, the stationing American troops abroad, or to any American military-political intervention abroad. It is quite possible that the reason they are disinclined to sense any threat from abroad has to do with their hostility toward American society that in turn alters their perception and judgement as to what constitutes a threat. Thus for instance Soviet expansion in the Third World, or perhaps even in Europe, would not be very alarming to these critics since such developments would amount to a welcome reduction or replacement of American influence or dominance abroad. Those disapproving of a social system are not disposed to second a spread of its influence and power outside its boundaries—hence the consistent and instinctive anti-interventionism and isolationism of the adversarial critics.

These adversarial positions also tend to be associated with an overestimation, or at least overemphasis on American strength. Those who think this country and its military are far too strong (and prone to misuse their power) are not likely to display any discomfort when this supposedly excessive strength is reduced. (This attitude is also often displayed in connection with Soviet-American relations and especially disarmament.) The critics tend to regard the United States as over-assertive and aggressive—attributes clearly linked to the exaggerated assessment of its strength. More generally speaking, in any polarized worldview strength tends to be associated with evil and weakness with the forces of good, always fighting an uphill battle, always on the defensive, always victimized or close to being victimized. These stereotypes undoubtedly have religious roots in Western cultures.

As noted earlier, there are few projections regarding the possible outcomes of a continued shift in the global balance of power (favoring the U.S.S.R.) between the United States and the Soviet Union and how this might effect the status quo within the United States. The idea that anything outside the United States might have an impact on conditions inside the United States seems too absurd to contemplate for most Americans, including self-respecting intellectuals of different political persuasion. Hence, for instance critics of aid to the Nicaraguan guerillas often ridicule such policies as rooted in the fear of the Nicaraguan army advancing on Texas . . . Hence also the strong,and highly differentiated reactions to the recent television play, "Amerika"; those taking the Soviet threat more seriously tended to applaud the program, those dismissing it were enraged. For the latter the idea that the Soviet Union might impose a political system on the United States was preposterous because such a possibility implied that the Soviet Union might be a menace greater than unemployment or juvenile delinquency; picturing such an imposed system as worse, more repressive than what is currently in place was even more unacceptable to those fully persuaded of the unique ills and evils of present day American society.

The polarized threat perceptions have other consequences as well;

they determine the moral universe and the capacity for moral judgement of the groups involved. Whatever is seen as more threatening is also judged to be more evil and thus justifying greater moral indignation; whatever is seen as the lesser threat is also the lesser evil calling for lesser moral protest. Moral judgements are thus becoming increasingly contextual and divorced from the observable, immediate, measurable harm caused by whatever political force.

It is in this light that one may explain the truly striking discrepancies in the West, including the United States, between the moral protest occasioned by the policies and activities of the authorities in South Africa as against that evoked by the Soviet conduct in Afghanistan. There have been no campus protests over Afghanistan, no vigils at the Soviet embassy in Washington, no pressure to disinvest in firms which do business with the Soviet Union, no demands that we sever all ties with the Soviet Union which has for eight years engaged in an untroubled display of brutality on a grand scale. In fact diametrically opposed prescriptions for dealing with these two evils have been proposed with equal passion: contacts,—cultural, economic, grass roots, people-to-people—with the Soviet Union in order to civilise, humanize or uplift that system. Concurrently we are urged that contacts with South Africa be terminated completely to bring punitive pressure upon the rulers of that country; nothing but the imposition of economic hardship, cultural and political isolation and the harshest public condemnation will induce that system to mend its ways—so the argument runs. Thus in one instance sanctions, isolation and chastisement are supposed to yield the political behavior modification, in the other, tolerance, understanding, contacts and lack of outspoken criticism.

I trust that few would dispute that such a discrepancy in moral revulsion, political protest and the recommended response to the two phenomena exists, though many people would find it fully justified. This is so because for Western public opinion—and especially Western liberal intellectuals—it is a reflexively held article of faith that nothing could be more evil than the apartheid practiced by the South African government.

The interesting question is why apartheid (and all the injustices and repression associated with it) is seen as a self evidently greater evil than the large scale Soviet attrocities in Afghanistan?

There is ample evidence (though much of it not visual and not readily accessible to the American public) that the Soviet troops in Afghanistan have been routinely killing civilians; civilian losses have been estimated in the hundreds of thousands and one third of the population, some five million people were forced to flee the country.

Soviet troops also routinely destroy crops, civilian targets; most amazingly Soviet planes have been dropping explosive toys, aimed specifically at children.[7] The equals of My Lai are regular occurences. None of this has made much of an impact in the West and few signs of moral indignation are in evidence among Westen intellectuals (for example no resolutions were offered or passed at the 1986 PEN Congress condemning Soviet conduct in Afghanistan unlike those vehemently embraced condemning the U.S. policies in Central America). While there is a polite consensus that Soviet policies in Afghanistan are deplorable there is little discernible moral energy or passion behind it.

I believe the prime reason for the discrepancies of moral protest in these two cases is that in one, that of South Africa, it is possible to implicate the United States, the West, or capitalism, whereas in the other, Afghanistan, the blame must be placed entirely on other political actors and forces. It is the adversarial sensibility that fuels the protest and indignation about South Africa but fails to resonate to the evils of the Soviet conduct. The outrages associated with South Africa readily fit into a moral universe in which the United States (the West or capitalism) are assigned major responsibility for the evils of the world. As a recent protester against South Africa put it: "To me, South Africa is just a convenient issue that helps to expose the system. By that I mean the whole system of corporate capitalism."[8]

While a fair amount has been said so far about estrangement (or alienation) and the attitudes and (selective) moral stands it generates, the concept of the adversary culture has yet to be addressed. What exactly is it and what evidence is there to support the claim of its survival? My choice of it as a title of this book suggests that I regard it a useful and important concept. How did it emerge?

It was Lionel Trilling who introduced the concept in the early 1960s. The idea makes its first appearance, not yet fully articulated in the Preface to his collection, *The Opposing Self*. Trilling wrote: "The modern self is characterized by certain powers of indignant perception. . . . Men began to recognize the existence of prisons that were not built of stone, nor even of social restrictions and economic disabilities. They learned to see that they might be immured not only by the overt force of society but by a coercion in some ways more frightful because it involved their own acquiescence . . ." Later in the same Preface he makes reference to "selves conceived in opposition to the general culture," but the term adversary culture itself does not yet emerge.[9]

It is in the Preface to a later collection, *Beyond Culture* that the term itself makes its first appearance. The core of the concept is "The belief that it is possible to stand beyond the culture in some decisive way

. . . Any historian of the literature of the modern age will take virtually for granted the adversary intention, the actually subversive intention that characterizes modern writing . . . its clear purpose of detaching the reader from the habits of thought and feeling that the larger culture imposes, of giving him a ground and a vantage point from which to judge and condemn . . . the culture that produced him."

Trilling locates the origins of this sensibility in the late eighteenth century and in the then new idea that "a primary function of art and thought is to liberate the individual from the tyranny of his culture . . . and to permit him to stand beyond it in an autonomy of perception and judgement." By the second half of our century ". . . there has grown up a populous group whose members take for granted the idea of the adversary culture." Moreover ". . . around the adversary culture there has formed what I have called a class . . . that . . . has developed charateristic habitual responses to the stimuli of its environment . . ."[10]

Notable in Trilling's analysis is the focus on the cultural-artistic rather than political origins and implications of the adversarial mentality. Needless to say the developments Trilling refers to have been inseparable from the growth of individualism, the attribution of uniqueness and unique value to the individual which justified his desire for a detachment or liberation from his culture. It is this attitude that vindicates "an autonomy of perception and judgement" and an increasingly critical stance toward the social-cultural environment which was to take eventually a political coloration and embraced by a growing number of people, increasingly removed from the cultural-artistic ethos in which the attitude originated.

I find this an inspiring concept because, as Trilling suggests, it encompasses not only values and beliefs but also directs attention to the carriers of these beliefs. "Adversary culture" conjures up a collection of people united in certain attitudes and outlook. Moreover as in other cultures, those socialized into it, unselfconsciously take for granted its fundamental premises; most usefully the concept highlights the characteristically reflexive, taken for granted nature of the mentality, or mindset. Increasingly, in the aftermath of the 1960s, it has become a diffuse sensibility, a predisposition rather than a clearly thought out ideological or philosophical position.

John Corry's observation of television may be generalized to the adversary culture as a whole: ". . . television does not consciously pursue a liberal or left agenda, although it does reflect a liberal to left point of view. This is because the point of view is fixed and in place, a part of the natural order. The television journalist's personal beliefs (and print journalist's too, for that matter) are incidental. . . . The culture determines the point of view . . . it supplies the moral dimensions to his thinking allowing him to identify . . . just causes. . . ."[11]

It is now also possible to take an adversarial position without being strictly speaking a left-wing critic of society; in some instances the adversarial position may go hand in hand with a patrician-elitist rejection of modern (capitalist) society, or at least a deep uncertainty about its values and institutions, as in the case of George Kennan. In any event specific ideology matters less and less, as groups of people have become socialized into the adversarial position over a longer period of time which has become increasingly instinctive, intuitive, non-intellectual—as all profoundly held cultural (or subcultural) beliefs are.

The concept is also useful because it alludes to a variety of alienation quite unlike the condition of withdrawal, apathy and passivity which alienation used to signify and the adversarial groups here discussed have consistently failed to display. "Adversarial" accomodates, as I see it, a wide variety of negative attitudes toward the prevailing social-political order and institutions, ranging from passionate condemnation, reflexive rejection and smoldering hostility to a low grade aversion, contempt, condescension and ambivalence.

Irving Kristol more than anyone else gave wide currency to the concept adapting it to contemporary American conditions and drawing out its political implications. More explicitly than Trilling, Kristol has also stressed the romantic, anti-rationalistic components of the adversarial outlook and its anti-capitalist thrust. He wrote

> No sooner did the late Lionel Trilling coin the phrase 'adversary culture' than it became part of the common vocabulary . . . because it so neatly summed up a phenomenon that all of us, vaguely or acutely, had observed. It is hardly to be denied that the culture that educates us . . . is unfriendly to the commerical civilization, the bourgeois civilization within which most of us live and work. . . . The more 'cultivated' a person is in our society, the more disaffected and malcontent he is likely to be . . .

Kristol traces the adversarial disaffection to the prosaic, trivial, coarsening, commercialized nature of bourgeois society (the "cash nexus"), its unconcern with transcendence and spiritual values, its relentless secularity and finally to a reactive anti-rationalist romanticism that seized educated people from the late eighteenth century onwards and never entirely deserted them. In the spirit of Trilling he notes that this romanticism was initially "mainly an escapist aestethic mode" but gradually it has become more rebellious and political in its

implications as a confluence occurred between these romantic, individualistic, anti-rationalist impulses and the socialist critiques of the
capitalist society which provided more clear cut channels for the
expression of an initially apolitical estrangement. Hence in his words
"utopian rationalism" [associated with socialism] and utopian romanticism, between them established their hegemony as adversary cultures
over the modern consciousness and the modern sensibility. Since the
1960s the culturally and politically based critiques of American (and
Western) society have become fused in the watered down versions of
the adversarial social criticism which has claimed broader and broader
audiences especially on the campuses. Correspondingly "vulgarized
versions of modernism . . . became the mass counterculture . . . among
students who, as consumers, converted it into a pseudo-bohemian life
style."[12]

While many demonstrations and explications of the adversarial
outlook fill the pages of this book, offering examples both of its spirit
and institutional embodiments, I remain struck by the widespread
reluctance to acknowledge the very existence, the reality and persistence of the phenomenon. Perhaps not surprisingly many of those who
deny its reality, may themselves be classified as members in good
standing of the adversary culture. They dispute its existence presumably in part because their notion of what constitutes an adversarial
position or outlook is quite different from those who notice this
mindset; those within the adversary culture have increasingly taken
their own positions and worldview for granted and self-evidently correct, seeing it not so much as adversarial, but rather as descriptive of
the prevailing state of affairs. Moreover the spread of these views and
their predominance in many social settings and their partial adoption
even by members of elite groups (politicians, journalists, religious
functionaries, professionals of various kinds) also help to obscure their
distinctive, adversarial character.

The significance and survival of the adversary culture has also been
called into question in the context of the political changes of the 1980s
and in particular the election and reelection of Ronald Reagan for
President. The perception has increasingly gained ground (as also
noted on pp 143–144) that the values, beliefs and movements associated with the 1960s have been swept away by the social-political
changes of the 1970s and 1980s and little remains of the radical
critiques and rejections of American society that emerged during the
1960s. For all these reasons it seems appropriate to add a few more
words here to my discussions of the *survival* of the adversary culture
and further elaborate on some of the unmistakable indicators of this
survival.

While it is true that many radical movements and organizations created during the 1960s disappeared or changed their character, others survived and continued their activities very much in the spirit of the 1960s. A notable example of remarkable continuity and dedication has been the Institute for Policy Studies which has been since the early 1960s a major producer of adversarial social criticism as well as a purveyor of policy recommendations designed to implement its political philosophy.[13] Many other prominent social critics and protestors who emerged a quarter century ago have also remained active today in pursuit of the same values. Moreover the adversary culture continues to command substantial organizational, institutional, financial and demographic resources, entailing foundations, think tanks, a wide range of publications, publishing houses, radio stations, colleges and churches.

The major single resource of the adversary culture remains the campus. Even if the majority of the students in the nation today do not subscribe to an adversarial mentality, large and vocal portions of their teachers do, especially in the humanities and social sciences. My own discipline, sociology, has, for example been quite thoroughly politicized and probably a majority of its practicioners take an adversarial disposition for granted. Irving Louis Horowitz recently observed that ordinary crime in these circles is still redefined as political protest, as was done during the 1960s and treated sympathetically as principled defiance of the "power structure". He also noted that among these adversarial sociologists it has been axiomatic that "every reform measure in the United States since the New Deal is doing little more than staving off the inevitable collapse of capitalism . . . [that] welfare operates as a form of social control." Likewise ". . . the existence of conspiratorial elites remains a fixed point of faith" for those perceiving "American society . . . [as] a cleverly rendered political conspiracy to maintain bourgeois power . . ." A substantial portion of sociologists are self-proclaimed Marxists of one kind or another and "the sacred texts of yesteryear are pored over with a sobriety and affectation that could well inspire religious zealots." The discipline is permeated by "a thinly disguised anti-Americanism that uses the rhetoric of social sciences to express animosites that would otherwise be quickly challenged or readily repudiated."[14] Perhaps the current prominence of these attitudes should not come as a surprise when one recalls that Lipset found in the early 1970s (in his study of "the politics of American sociologists") a "general tendency of achieving intellectuals to support a politics of social criticism" and a well-defined left-of-center disposition.[15]

Such attitudes are not confined to sociologists. The Latin American Studies Association, for example, routinely passes resolutions supportive of Marxist-Leninist movements, guerillas and governments in Latin America and even sent a delegation to sympathetically observe and certify the probity of elections in Nicaragua.[16] In turn a recent resolution of the Modern Language Association (MLA) resolved that

> The MLA of America condemns our government's unjust and frequently illegal assaults on the people and government of Nicaragua. We urge our colleagues in all fields to speak, educate and act against these policies . . .

The rationale offered for this resolution read in part:

> *When a government persistently follows a cruel and undemocratic course of action . . . and when it violates even the meager restraints it has imposed upon itself,* scholars and teachers have a special responsibility to protest . . . the government of the U.S. is pursuing in Central America a murderous course of action . . . [my emphasis][17]

Not to be outdone the 1982 national convention of anthropologists adopted motions

> urging anthropologists not to undertake work for the CIA or the U.S. military . . . a motion condemning a video game called "Custer's Revenge" for its celebration of "the historical oppression of the Native Americans by the U.S. government"; and a motion calling upon the U.S. government to "freeze the development, production and deployment of nuclear weapons" and "dismantle its existing arsenal" (an amendment to include the Soviet Union, and urging bilateral and verifiable freeze was defeated) . . . there were two resolutions denouncing Israel . . .[18]

In the same spirit the anthropologists expressing deep concern for the plight of Guatemalan peasants refused to extend the range of their compassion or show any corresponding interest in the problems of the Misquito Indians of Nicaragua or the peasants of Vietnam, Laos or Cambodia.[19]

The spread of the so-called Peace Studies in colleges and high schools may also be cited as institutional echoes of the adversarial mentality since such studies frequently support either a unilateralist attitude or tend to blame the United States for global tensions and often suggest that there is a connection between the deficiencies of American domestic institutions and an alleged American militancy abroad.[20]

Interestingly enough even the U.S. Air Force Academy felt it useful to acquaint its students with a prominent representative of the adversary culture by inviting Josep Heller to preside over a conference organized to celebrate the 25th anniversary of the publication of his *Catch 22*. As will be recalled the message of this book was that "love of country is a naive delusion . . . the military is both evil and insane and . . . nothing on earth is worth dying for."[21] Also, in the early 1980s the former Stokely Carmichael (more recently known as Kwame Ture) still toured the elite college circuit assuring his audiences about the virtues of "scientific socialism" ready to sweep the world while students at Hampshire College in Massachusetts continued to resonate to a regular parade of radical social critics, including Alexander Cockburn, the journalist, who disclosed that "they can never be radical enough", while Leonard Boudin, perhaps the most prominent radical critic in the legal profession, was guest professor at Stanford University Law School and reverentially profiled in the student newspaper.[22]

Famous "activists" of the 1960s like Abbie Hoffman (assisted by the daughter of former President Carter) continued their triumphant tours of the campuses reviving the style of protest of that period and getting acquitted by a sympathetic jury for obstructing CIA recruitment[23]. Mark Rudd too "decided to step up his visible political activities" eager to apply what he considered the lessons of Vietnam to educating the American public about Central America.[24] The editors of all but one Ivy League student newspapers went on record opposing American military aid to El Salvador and called on Americans "to participate in grass-roots demonstrations" against U.S. policy in El Salvador.[25] It was still, or again, possible for draft evaders to win at once "indictment and celebrity"[26].

Generally speaking there has been an upsurge of political activism and protest on the campuses in the 1980s focusing on South Africa and Central America, but underlying it were the familiar and long standing adversarial impulses and sentiments which found new causes and targets. As Todd Gitlin, himself a former leading activists of the 1960s (currently professor of sociology at Berkeley) put it, "there has been a free floating moral energy" on the campuses finding expression in these protests which, he approvingly noted, "reinvent the history of the 1960s".[27] Sidney Lens, the lifelong radical activists continued on the pages of *The Nation* to hold forth against "infantile anticommunism" and "leftist timidity" recommending to "try radicalism" while James Mitchner the popular novelist designated the 1980s on the op-ed page of the *New York Times* "The Ugly Decade" tainted by the policies of the Reagan Administration[28]. Since 1980, according to information provided by the publisher, "there have been 85 college adoptions of [Michael] Parenti's textbook, *Democracy for the Few*,"[29] a violent denunciation of American society.

Enormous organizational resources came to be devoted in the 1980s to causes like the support of Marxist-Leninist Nicaragua as tens of thousands of Americans went on political sightseeing tours of that country and thousands volunteered their labor in support of its government, while others collected funds and various supplies for it at home. Hundreds or organizations and their local or regional affiliates offered lectures and lobbied in support of Nicaragua. Norman Podhoretz observed that "private American citizens raising money and lobbying for the Communists in Central America do so with impunity, while private citizens raising money and lobbying for the anti-Communist democrats are treated as criminals."[30] While the parallel is imperfect since the Iran-Contra hearings were called in response to such activities on the part of government officials, not private citizens, the fundraising of the pro-Sandinista groups (and those supportive of the communist guerillas in El Salvador) have yet to be subject of Congressional curiosity or the searching exposés of the media.

Another notable phenomenon of the 1970s and 1980s, at once a symptom and source of the persistence of the adversary culture, has been the development of what might be called political-administrative enclaves of estrangement. These were the towns and municipalities ran, or dominated by radicals or left-of-center groups and individuals presumably enjoying the support of the people electing them. Such towns and municipalities included Berkley, Santa Monica and Santa Cruz in California, Ann Arbor in Michigan, Madison, Wisconsin, Burlington, Vermont and Amherst, Massachusetts—among others.

In such settings it was possible to lead a life almost fully sheltered from the impact of the surrounding society. A resident of one such enclave, (and veteran 60s activist) Derek Shearer wrote:

> Many of the alternative institutions of the 1960s have survived—food cooperatives, printing collectives, bookstores, alternative schools, restaurants, research centers, progressive foundations, publications and so on . . . In our hometown of Santa Monica, California, my family shops at Co-Opportunity, a food cooperative, where we . . . purchase health food and see our friends while we shop. Our children attend the Santa Monica alternative School (SMASH), which is a public school, but run in a democratic manner, with student and parent participation. I shop for books at the Midnight Special or Papa Bach, both run by political activists. The Liberty Hill Foundation, located in the nearby Ocean Park Church, gives donations to a variety of community action groups in the Los Angeles area. We take our children to hear benefit concerts by

artists like Pete Seeger for *In These Times*, or Jackson Brown to raise money for the statewide nuclear freeze campaign. *Mother Jones, Working Papers, Democracy* and other publications regularly arrive at our house with news and political information.

In Santa Monica we are also fortunate to belong to a local political organization—Santa Monicans for Renters Rights (SMRR)—that has won five successive elections, put numerous activists into political office, won majority control of the city council and brought the city the honor of being dubbed by the press as the People's Republic of Santa Monica.[31]

This phenonomenon, yet to receive the social scientific and public attention it deserves, is among the most telling and tangible indicators of the survival of adversary culture and its institutionalization. As in the case of the towns mentioned, academic institutions located in or near these towns have served as catalysts or magnets for the emergence of these enclaves, offering "resource people", activists and a critical mass (even if a minority of the entire academic population was involved) ready to support an adversarial, left-of center town government. A remarkable document mirroring the sentiments which often move and motivate members of these communities (and that of the adversary culture as a whole) was published as a paid political advertisement by a group of citizens of Amherst, Massachussetts to coincide with Thanksgiving. It read:

We Mourn on Thursday for GENOCIDE

1763—General Jeffrey Amherst intentionally orders smallpox infested blankets to be given as 'gifts' to local native American Indians, causing fatal epidemic.

1983—United States corporate and military presence exists in many countries, often supporting the exploitation and murder of indigenous people. Consistently these are Third World countries where people of color reside.

TODAY—On Thanksgiving we ask you . . . to join us in mourning this racist U.S. history and policy . . . We are committed to uncovering these truths and to creating a world free from genocide.
We yearn and hope for a day when we can celebrate life. [A list of 174 names followed][32]

While the story about the vile misdeed of the general may well be true, the text cited exemplifies the use of the past as a delegitimizing device and the effort to link its sins to far more dubious allegations about the present. The advertisement also reflects a sense of guilt often demonstratively displayed (by adherents of the adversary culture)—as its public embrace implies a moral superiority on the part of those confessing to it. These attitudes also coincide with the "tendency to read our history solely for its unhappier features, and . . . to see the nation's adversaries around the world as islands of virtue besieged by the United States."[33]

Among the characteristic activities of these towns and muncipalities has been the establishment of "sister city" ties with towns in Nicaragua or the Soviet Union, the declaration of themselves as nuclear free zones and divestment of shares of companies doing business with South Africa, sometimes even of those who contribute to the production of military supplies. These activities have not been limited to towns run by leftists, many others, numbering in the hundreds have taken similar steps. Another characteristic activity associated with left-leaning municipalities (but again not limited to them) has been the profer of sanctuary to refugees from El Salvador and Guatemala, but not from Nicaragua or any other country making clear that these offers were less inspired by charity than by the wish to make a political statement.

Adversarial sensibilities are also reflected in the refusal of some 120 municipalities to participate in civil defense measures such as planning or practicing relocation in the event of nuclear war—an attitude not reciprocated by Soviet cities.[34]

The 1986 PEN Congress in New York City was another occasion that provided an abundance of examples of the vigorous survival of the adversarial mentality among leading intellectuals. It was, in the words of Walter Goodman, "an opportunity to attack American policies" and revealed "a kind of community of indignation".[35] Not only was there strong objection to Secretary of State Schultz addressing the Congress (symbolic of the deep distaste felt for leading figures in the government of the U.S.), but representatives of the Nicaraguan government were treated with reverence and deference. The spirit of the adversary culture infused both the unstated assumptions and programmatic statements of the Congress and its agenda. As Edward Rothstein put it:

> And so the presumptive political lines of the congress were drawn, again and again making out the boundaries of what might be called the international counterculture. The volume of assumptions, the absence of genuine argument, the indifference to other positions . . . were stunning. Would any speaker have dared to praise Reagan as Schlesinger and Gaddis and numerous others condemned him? Would any panel speaker have openly condemned the left as consistently as its positions were praised? The congress as a whole was not simply a literary congress . . . On display were the manners of contemporary literary culture . . . with . . . its own hidden assumptions.[36]

It should also be noted that in this, as in other instances, the adversarial sentiments of American writers and intellectuals were effectively bolstered by the outspoken and emotional anti-Americanism of some of the foreign visitors such as Gunter Grass or the Nicaraguan delegation.

The American writers congress in 1982 was no different; there too hostility to American institutions was much in evidence. James Atlas observed:

> The old familiar themes came up again and again: the malevolent activities of the CIA; the ominous power of the corporations; the government's oppression of the poor . . . And the panels—'Feminist Literature', 'The Media and United States Foreign Policy', 'Whatever Happened to the Labor Press?'—were avowedly radical . . . Whatever its original intent, the congress soon became a spontaneous welling up of resistance to the reactionary forces perceived to dominate the country, the first real opportunity in a decade for those on the left to protest out loud.[37]

Last but not least one also finds manifestations of the adversarial worldview in American political institutions, including the U.S. Congress, often revealed in a persisting isolationism of many of its members and the unwillingness to support anti-Soviet guerillas in Africa and Central America. Such isolationism is associated with a tendency to hold the United States responsible for most ills of the world and a corresponding distaste for asserting its power. It has been rightly said of these, usually adversarial isolationists that "Paralyzed by their suspicions of power and of national self-assertiveness, they have been unable to come to terms with the fact that every cherished liberal value, be it liberty, democracy, peace or national independence, depends ultimately upon American power."[38] As was also noted earlier, there is an unmistakable connection between highly critical views of the American social-political system and disapproval of a projection of its power abroad.

Perhaps in the final analysis the disposition to overlook the survival of the adversary culture in all these settings is related to broader shifts in American public and elite opinion over the last quarter century, to the changes in the general climate of opinion which itself has been sufficiently influenced by the adversary culture to make its discernment more difficult.

This volume is organized to reflect major expressions and some of the social-cultural roots of the adversary culture.

Part I examines the impact of this culture on approaches to Soviet-

American relations and on perceptions of the Soviet Union. As will be clear to the reader I have been quite unhappy with these perceptions and critical of them. In particular I criticize, in several of the pieces, the attribution of moral equivalence (or symmetry) to the United States and the Soviet Union, a school of thought (identified by Jean Kirkpatrick) that is based on either plain or willful ignorance of the very substantial institutional-structural differences between the United States and the Soviet Union. It is an approach that obliterates moral distinctions between the two social systems and countries typically subsumed under the term "Superpowers".

The cultural pervasiveness of the moral equivalence thesis is demonstrated by its appearance in such unexpected places as James Bond movies which over the years have increasingly come to present Western (and American) and Soviet spies and intelligence services and their governments as quite similar. In these films great care is taken not to present the Soviet Union in a negative light; the forces of evil are usually represented by political entities not connected with either East or West, often greedy, and/or power hungry capitalists (merchants of death) or deranged fanatics of no discernible political affiliation.

The moral equivalence school is generally supported by all those who regard the lack of amity between the United States and the Soviet Union as a regrettable result of mutual misunderstandings and misperceptions aggravated by "hawks" or "hardliners" on both sides—a point of view extremely congenial to many Americans. This attitude also finds expression in the Cult of the Summit Meeting. The latter seems to rest on the belief that if the two leaders get together and have a heartfelt exchange of their true feelings they are bound to reach agreement on most issues and sweep away the corrosive accumulation of misunderstandings and misperceptions due to faulty communications and lack of direct, face-to-face contact. Of late Senator Paul Simon of Illinois (seeking the presidential nomination of the Democratic Party) made a memorable contribution to this school of thought as he suggested that if "Ronald Reagan had once been an exchange student in Moscow . . . we would be living in a different world today."[39]

Appearances notwithstanding the attribution of moral equivalence tends to conceal a posture far more critical of the United States than the Soviet Union. In fact, as I argue below, the negative views of America condition those of the Soviet Union; the more negative is the assessment of the United States, the more benign, or at any rate the less critical, are the views of the Soviet Union. In Western Europe aversion to the United States (stemming from many diverse cultural, political-nationalistic, ideological, economic etc. sources) creates pressures for a more benevolent assessment of the Soviet Union. By contrast in Eastern Europe hostility toward the Soviet Union creates a highly favorable attitude toward the United States. "My enemies' enemies are my friends" thus remains the single most powerful axiom explaining political attitude formation in various parts of the world.

The first essay in this section examines the influential views of George Kennan which, it seems, have been increasingly shaped by his disenchantment with his own society. "Sister city fantasies" is a critique of a popular movement that seeks to diminish the prospects of nuclear war by grass roots exchanges and informal links between "ordinary" Russians and Americans; it rests on ill informed and unrealistic assumptions about the ability and willingness of Soviet citizens to put pressure on their government and influence its policies. In "Wishful Economic Determinism" I criticize what seems to be an exaggeration of Soviet economic weaknesses and their (hoped for) impact on Soviet domestic and foreign policy. In "The Durable Misconceptions" I examine more systematically what appear to me the most enduring mistakes in thinking about the Soviet political system. I have been especially impressed by the resilience of wishful thinking in the American (and Western) conceptions of the Soviet Union. It is an attitude that feeds on an uncertainty about the desirability of defending the West, (leading to convenient denials of the presence of any threat). Such a collective indifference to public affairs, including national defense, conjures up notions of decadence. A student of decadence posed the question: "Does America have any deadly enemies? May be yes, maybe no. But where the possibility exists, one form of decadence may well consist of being too nice to envisage the possibility. In the new symbol-intoxicated Brahminical caste of America—disdainful of the few constraints in the least constrained society on earth, unable even to conceive of societies based on class struggle, class dictatorship, and the systematic reign of terror—I sense a willfull naivete . . ."[40]

The two concluding pieces in Part I are brief forays into the field of anti-Americanism abroad, sampled in Western Europe and Mexico respectively. It is hoped that taken together this group of writings will also shed some light on the confluence of the domestic and foreign critiques of American society.

Regarding my own views of the Soviet system, especially in the current Gorbachev period, I find it difficult to be as hopeful and expectant as many Western commentators have been. On the other hand unlike Hilton Kramer I am not *entirely* certain that the Soviet

Union is a more formidable enemy today than it was forty years ago. I readily see, as he does, the ceaseless expansionary dynamics (probably compensating for domestic social-economic failures) supported by the huge military- political machine but on the other hand I also detect a slight loss of political will within the Soviet Empire which has allowed a modest decline in coherence, cohesion and political discipline in parts of the Empire and perhaps, in some degree even inside the Soviet Union.

How much Gorbachev really differs from his predecessors and colleagues (besides a greater energy and capacity for some new initiatives) and how consequential these differences will be for either the domestic or foreign policies of the Soviet Union remain to be seen. In the meantime an occasional remark of his reveals the limitations of his outlook and a mindset forged in the same political culture as those of his predecessors and no better informed of the world ouside than his less innovative colleagues. Thus it is worth recalling that Gorbachev advised a group of visiting U.S. Congressmen in 1987 "that the United States solve its race problems by setting up separate states for blacks and other minorities . . ." As one congressman correctly observed, Gorbachev's comment echoed the old idea, championed by the U.S. Communist Party in the 1930s "to carve out an all black state to encompass Mississippi and Alabama." Gorbachev also suggested that following the Soviet model the U.S. should provide such autonomous areas for blacks, Puerto Ricans and even Polish-Americans.[41]

As far as the applicability of the concept of totalitarianism is concerned—an issue that preoccupied me in my earlier writings on the Soviet Union—I certainly agree that changes over the past decades (and not merely since Gorbachev) should give us a pause regarding the usefulness of the concept for the understanding of many aspects of Soviet society. Yet I remain at a loss as to the best characterization of the Soviet system since it still is significantly different from other, non-Marxist dictatorships. There is still a distinctiveness to Soviet ways of governing and organizing society that call for explicit conceptual recognition and some appropriate, distinguishing terminology.

It should be noted here that East European analysts and critics of Soviet-type societies do not share the hesitation of Western specialists about the applicability of the concept of totalitarianism. Thus for example Feher, Heller and Markus of Hungary while conceding that since Stalin's death the Soviet Union ceased to be a "terroristic totalitarian state" designate the outlawing of pluralism as the central defining characteristic of totalitarianism—which of course has survived in the Soviet Union and similar systems.[42] More recently Vaclav Havel, the Czech author described the Soviet style totalitarianism in his own country in terms reminescent of the misplaced characterization of the late Herbert Marcuse who located such a "repressively tolerant" yet not overtly violent social system in the West. Havel wrote:

> . . . our totalitarian system is less openly or directly based on violence, even though it certainly rules society by means of an enormous police force, army and bureaucracy . . . In the system we live in you won't normally encounter . . . street battles between citizens and the police or direct violence . . . from the regime. What one does encounter however is something that Orwell saw, and that is more dangerous in certain respects. Totalitarian regimes get under the society's skin. Their complex forms of manipulation penetrate every sphere of life. . . . The regime leaves its mark on everything . . . In our system, the violence is spiritual rather than physical."[43]

Part II may be considered a collection of short case studies in the varieties of the adversarial sensibility. In particular I try to trace here the long shadow cast by the ethos of the 1960s over the present and recent past. Unlike those impressed by change I tend to be struck by the resistance to change and especially the reluctance of groups or individuals to significantly revise their political worldview. An interesting example of this is provided by Corliss Lamont who, unlike most other critics of American society and institutions, persevered not only in an adversarial position toward American society, but in an affectionately tolerant attitude toward the Soviet Union. While atypical of much of the adversary culture that emerged since the 1960s Lamont's case is important in classically exemplifying the combination distress over the flaws of his own society with a predisposition to admire uncritically others which claim to have overcome such flaws. The type of attitude is still with us, as witness the outpouring of admiration directed at Nicaragua. In a letter protesting my comments of his writings, Mr. Lamont insisted that his attitude toward the Soviet Union "has always been one of *critical sympathy*" and concluded by suggesting that my review "constitutes a warning to the public that we may face a revival of the vicious Red-baiting of the McCarthy era."[44]

It may be noted here that the concept of "Red baiting" and allusions to McCarthyism have, since the 1960s been incorporated into the key ideas of the adversary culture and became major justifications of its anti-anti-communism. ("Red baiting" itself has been an intriguing concept implying at once that there is nothing wrong with being "red" while at the same time signaling profound indignation over being called just that.) As to the general phenomenon of anti-anti-communism among distinguished intellectuals, this too remains something of a puzzle since the refusal to being counted as an anti-communist combines, in most of these instances with an attitude in fact critical of cummunist systems, movements, their policies and practices. Why then the visceral recoil from the anti-communist appellation? The persisting after-effects of McCarthyism and the fear of being identified with the disreputable anti-communists of the extreme right is a major explanation, as I had argued elsewhere. Yet it is not self-evident why the same people are less anxious about being associated with similarly disreputable elements on the extreme left, or why in fact these elements are less disreputable? The climate of the 1960s and the Vietnam war may provide further explanation for the growth of anti-anti-communism. Many of the intellectuals in question were deeply effected by the turbulence on the campuses and were apprehensive about distancing themselves from the young by holding on to what the young regarded as suspect and antiquated beliefs.

Other essays here included examine the recent attempts at retroactively romanticising the American communist movement—an effort also encouraged by the anti-anti-communist feelings which surfaced since the 1960s. Further writings discuss the confluence of the Vietnam war protest and generalised social criticism, the less obvious roots of the radicalism of the 1960s and probe the persisting appeal of socialism among intellectuals. Two of the essays here included offer more detailed analyses and indications of the adversarial attitudes and activities of American intellectuals and the paradox of the gradual transformation of the adversarial, dissenting mindset into a new, increasingly established and entrenched pattern of conformity

In Part III I provide examples of what I call political escapism, a concept similar to utopia-seeking but somewhat broader. By political escapism I mean a disposition—very much a part of the adversarial worldview—to transcend the imperfections experienced in the familiar social setting by giving every benefit of doubt to new social-politicl systems and their supporting ideologies which make appealing humanitarian and egalitarian claims. This mindset need not operate with any clear cut utopian blueprint, rather its hallmark is a diffuse susceptibility to the appeals of political-revolutionary reorganization which seeks to infuse society with a new sense of purpose and a spirit of community missing from the familiar and much criticised social setting. Of course this is the same mentality I had described at some length in *Political Pilgrims* and which found astonishing revival in the political tours of Nicaragua in the 1980s. Two of the five pieces here included deal with the tours and perceptions of Nicaragua; one is a case study of particularly egregious misperceptions of the prison systems of putatively socialist societies including those of the Soviet Union, China, Cuba, Vietnam and Nicaragua. Another piece examines the attractions left-wing guerillas of Latin America have been exerting on American intellectuals—their idealized images offering excellent examples of yet another form of political escapism. The last essay raises the question as to why Taiwan—a great success story of material progress in the Third World—has failed to attract Western intellectuals ostensibly interested in and supportive of rapid modernization.

The Epilogue was originally written for a collection of writings (yet to be published) by various American sociologists exploring the relationship between their life and work. It traces the connections between particular experiences of my life and the evolution of my professional-intellectual orientation. Those pages should also make clear why I have not been tempted by the adversary culture despite its pervasive influence in the settings where I lived and worked over the past decades and the tangible and intangible advantages conferred by signalling one's affinity with it. This is not to suggest that being a professed critic of the adversary culture always exacts a heavy price in the predominantly liberal academic setting; I am happy to say that my critiques have elicited little discernible animosity, perhaps they were dismissed as an eccentricity ascribed to my exotic background. On the other hand I have been keenly aware of another, potential prize one may have to pay for such a critical stand, namely a drift into an adversarial, polemical and politicized position of one's own. This is the problem of balancing committment and support for certain ideas and ideals with a determined refusal to allow matters political to dominate one's outlook on life. It is an extremely difficult balancing act since on the one hand we cannot fail to recognize that political attitudes and ideas are consequential and often deeply destructive of human freedom and happiness, while on the other we must insist that the political dimension not be allowed to invade and overwhelm the whole range of human experiences, values and aspirations.

Notes

1. A Review of *The Many Faces of Socialism* by Ivan Szelenyi in *Contemporary Sociology*, May 1984.
2. Bruno Bettelheim: "Alienation and Autonomy" in his *Surviving and Other Essays*, New York: Knopf, 1979, p. 337.
3. "Sociology, Selective Determinism and the Rise of Expectations" in *The Many Faces of Socialism*, New Brunswick: Transaction Books, 1983 pp. 241–251.

4. Edwin McDowell: "PEN Talks on Freedom of the Word", *New York Times*, January 16, 1987, p. C17.
5. Tom Hayden: "American Identity: The Frontiers of Custer and Thoreau" in Mark E. Kann ed.: *The Future of American Democracy—Views from the Left*, Philadelphia: Temple University Press, 1983 p. 71; Tom Hayden: *The American Future: New Visions Beyond Old Frontiers*, Boston: South End Press, 1980, p. 32.
6. Hilton Kramer: "The Importance of Sidney Hook", *Commentary*, August 1987, p. 24.
7. See for example George Urban: "Turn Spotlights on Afghanistan and Romania", *Wall Street Journal*, July 16, 1978; John Corry: " 'Battle for Afghanistan' on CBC Reports", *NY Times*, July 29, 1987; "Requiem for a Nation" (Editorial), *NY Times*, December 30, 1984; "The Toy That's Making A Lasting Impression on Thousands of Afghan Children" (Advertisement), *NY Times*, June 5, 1987.
8. Robert Lindsey: "1960s Activists Jailed in New Causes", *NY Times*, May 19, 1987.
9. Lionel Trilling: *The Opposing Self*, New York: Viking Press 1955, pp. X, XIV.
10. Lionel Trilling: *Beyond Culture*, New York: Viking Press, 1965, pp. XII, XIII, XV–XVI.
11. John Corry: *TV News and the Dominant Culture*, Washington, D.C.: Media Institute, 1986, p. 1.
12. Irving Kristol: "The Adversary Culture of Intellectuals" in *Reflections of a Neoconservative*, New York: Basic Books, 1983, pp. 27, 28, 30, 39, 38.
13. See for example Joshua Muravchik: " 'Communophilism' and the Institute for Policy Studies", *World Affairs*, Winter 1984–85.
14. Irving Louis Horowitz: "Disenthralling Sociology" *Society*, January–February 1987, pp. 49, 50, 51, 52.
15. Seymour Martin Lipset and Everett Carll Ladd Jr.: "The Politics of American Sociologists", *American Journal of Sociology*, July 1972, p. 85.
16. Alfred G. Cuzan: "LASA spreads disinformation on Nicaragua", *Times of the Americas*, January 30, 1985.
17. "The MLA", [Correspondence], *Commentary*, April 1987, p. 13; see also James Atlas: "MIA at the MLA", *New Republic*, January 26, 1987.
18. Stephen H. Balch and Herbert L. London: "The Tenured Left", *Commentary* October, 1986, p. 49.
19. Wilcomb Washburn: "Leftist academics and ethnic minorities", *Washington Times*, December 30, 1982.
20. See for example Herbert I. London: *Armageddon in the Classroom—An Examination of Nuclear Education*, Washington , D.C.: University of America Press, 1987; also Philip Gold: "Academe at War over Peace Studies", *Insight*, April 6, 1987 and "Teaching About Nuclear War", *Newsweek*, July 18, 1983.
21. Norman Podhoretz: "Air Force plays bad joke on itself", *New York Post* October 14, 1986.
22. Marcy Larmon: "Socialism the answer, black activist claims", *Daily Hampshire Gazette*, December 6, 1983; Meredeith Carlson: "Radicalism promoted—Hampshire Graduates hear reporter's talk", *Daily Hampshire Gazette*, January 23, 1984 p. 1; Barbara Schuler: "Basic rights concern lawyer", *Stanford Daily*, June 5, 1985.

23. Matthew I. Wald: "Hoffman Sees Himself as a Radical for All Times", *NY Times*, February 1, 1987; Brenda Elliot and Deborah McDermott: "Amy Carter, Abie Hoffman go on Trial", *Daily Hampshire Gazette*, April 6, 1987.
24. David E. Pitt: "To '68 Leader, Columbia Is Still Lively", *New York Times*, March 28,1987, p. 31.
25. William G. Blair: "Ivy Editors Unite on Salvador", *New York Times*, March 24, 1982.
26. Stuart Taylor Jr.: "A Draft Evader Wins Indictment and Celebrity", *New York Times*, July 14, 1987.
27. Todd Gitlin: "Divestment Stirs a New Generation", *Nation*, May 18, 1987, p. 585; see also Larry Bohter: "Protests Indicate Activism Is Stirring on Campuses", *New York Times*, April 25, 1985.
28. Sidney Lens: "Old Ideas for New Socialists", *Nation*, April 6, 1985, p. 393; James A. Michener: "You Can Call the 1980s 'The Ugly Decade' " *New York Times*, January 1, 1987, op-ed.
29. Balch and London *cited*, p. 45.
30. Norman Podhoretz: "Reverse McCarthyism" *New York Post*, May 12, 1987.
31. Derek Shearer: "Foreword" in Mark E. Kann: *The American Left— Failures and Fortunes*, New York: Praeger, 1982, p. XI-XII.
32.. "We Mourn on Thursday for Genocide", *Daily Hampshire Gazette*, November 22, 1983.
33. "The Loss of Hart", *New Republic*, June 1, 1987, p. 10.
34. "Municipal Hue and Cry Makes Foreign Policy Waves", *Insight*, April 6, 1987.
35. Walter Goodman: "At PEN a Feeling of Community", *New York Times*, January 20, 1986; see also Edwin McDowell: "PEN Congress to Open Without Soviet Writers", *New York Times*, January 11, 1986, and Cynthia Ozick: "Literature Lost", *New York Times*, January 22, 1986, op-ed.
36. Edward Rothstein: "Lead Me Not Into PEN Station", *New Republic*, February 24, 1986, p. 22.
37. James Atlas: "Writers Joining the Working Class", *Atlantic*, January 1982, p. 82.
38. Joshua Muravchik: "Maximum Feasible Containment", *New Republic*, June 1, 1987, p. 24.
39. Fred Barnes: "Pee-Wee's Big Adventure" *New Republic*, October 5, 1987, p. 27.
40. Robert M. Adams: *Decadent Societies*, San Francisco: North Point Press, 1983, p. 173.
41. Bill Keller: "Gorbachev Urges Minority States", *New York Times*, April 18, 1987; see also "Gorbachev's Remarks Are Denied", *New York Times*, April 2, 1987 and "Separate But Equal Soviet Style" (Editorial), *New York Times*, April 21, 1987.
42. Ferenc Feher, Agnes Heller and Gyorgy Markus: *Dictatorship Over Needs*, New York: St. Martin's Press, 1983, p. 146, 162.
43. "Between ideals and utopias—A conversation with Vaclav Havel", *East European Reporter*, No. 3, 1987 p. 13.
44. Letter by Corliss Lamont, *New Republic*, November 8, 1982, p. 2.

PART I

"Moral Equivalence" and Critiques of America

1
From Containment to "Understanding": The Evolving Views of George Kennan

George Kennan used to be an unapologetic critic of the Soviet Union and an advocate of a firm U.S. response to its expansionism. Now he seeks to understand and accommodate Soviet behavior. What accounts for this remarkable change in one of the most influential voices in American foreign policy since World War II?

In 1947, Mr. Kennan published a pseudonymous article in *Foreign Affairs* that called for a U.S. policy of "long term, patient but firm, and vigilant containment of Russian expansive tendencies. . .by the adroit and vigilant application of counterforce at a series of constantly shifting geographical and political points, corresponding to the shifts and maneuvers of Soviet policy." The "Mr. X" article became the blueprint for the policy of "containment" that was generally adopted by five presidents, from Truman to Nixon. Mr. Kennan argued that containment should be a global strategy, not one restricted to a few areas, and that it was a means to defeat the Soviet system. Without expanding, the Soviet empire would collapse.

Since his "Mr. X" article, Mr. Kennan has gone on to become one of the nation's most respected diplomats and experts on Soviet affairs. He was U.S. ambassador to the Soviet Union in 1952, and to Yugoslavia from 1961–1963. He has had an enormous influence on the Soviet studies establishment, and is regarded as the patriarch of Sovietology in the West. No longer are his opinions confined to the pages of scholarly magazines or rarefied meetings of academics; they are amplified in the pages of the *New York Times, Washington Post, New Yorker, The Atlantic,* and other popular journals. Indeed the propositions advanced by Mr. Kennan have become, with the passage of time, less and less distinct, more and more part of the conventional wisdom. Paradoxically, Mr. Kennan's current set of views converges with those of other public figures profoundly ignorant of Soviet politics, Russian culture, and the history of U.S.-Soviet relations, and animated by an adversary posture toward their own society. Though himself a critic of American foreign policy, Mr. Kennan is distinguished from these numerous advisors of a conciliatory position toward the Soviet Union by his first-hand knowledge, experience, and insight into Soviet conduct and the mentality of Soviet leaders.

Mr. Kennan is reluctant to admit it, but his understanding of the nature of the Soviet Union and the Soviet threat has changed remarkably over the years. His writings in the 1940s and 1950s reveal an urgent sense of the dangers posed by the Soviets and the need for a firm U.S. response. In 1946, Mr. Kennan wrote that the Russians "have no conception of permanent friendly relations between states"; for them, "all foreigners are potential enemies." The United States was advised, "Don't act chummy with them," "Don't make fatuous gestures of goodwill," and "Don't be afraid of unpleasantness and public airing of differences." In his *Memoirs*, Mr. Kennan recalls a statement he made in 1951, in which he voiced skepticism about arms control because "armaments are a function and not a cause of political tension" and "no limitation of armaments on a multilateral scale can be effected as long as the political problems are not tackled and regulated in some realistic way."

Perhaps the line of argument most continuous with his early thought is Mr. Kennan's claim that the Soviet Union is a chronically insecure regime that seeks to project its power in pursuit of an elusive security. But in the past Mr. Kennan regarded the Soviets' insecurity as a source of aggression and conflict; now he seems to regard it as something to be understood and accommodated.

He argued in a *New Yorker* article last year that the Soviets suffer from a "siege mentality," that their expansionism results from a "state of mind that assumes all forms of authority not under Soviet control to be, or to be likely to be, wicked, hostile, and menacing." Mr. Kennan lapses into a clinical vocabulary as he describes Soviet leaders as possessed of a "congenital sense of insecurity" and a "neurotic fear of penetration"—he frequently characterizes them as frustrated, secretive, defensive, fixated, troubled, and anxious. Quite recently he ascribed to them "dark suspicions of everything and everyone foreign . . . obsession with secrecy . . . compulsion to conceal." (At the same time, in the context of arguing for agreements with the Soviets to diminish the nuclear risk, he presents the same Soviet leaders as sober, conservative, responsible, stable, and cautious.

Of late he has stressed that these insecurities and neuroses are best alleviated by understanding and tolerance. Mr. Kennan seems to share the therapeutic perspective of scholars such as Jerry Hough, Stanley

Hoffman, Theodore von Laue, Marshall Shulman, and Stephen Cohen, who regard insecurity, of an almost pathological kind, as the principal driving force in Soviet politics, foreign and domestic. Correspondingly, Soviet aggression is often perceived as epiphenomenal, inconsequential, and inspired by weakness—not strength. Hostile Soviet statements are treated as harmless rhetoric, the domination of neighboring countries as measures of understandable insecurity, the projection of military power across the globe as muddled adventurism, or perhaps as a peculiar mixture of motives involving traditional Russian geopolitical goals and the tiresome necessity of competing with China in the Third World.

Moral Accommodation

In his pursuit of accommodation, and to reduce the menacing aspects of Soviet policies, Mr. Kennan is eager to de-emphasize the distinctive and often unpleasant attributes of Soviet leaders. In a February 1985 *New Yorker* article, Mr. Kennan noted that "these Soviet Communists with whom we will have to deal are flesh and blood people like us," an assertion not likely to be doubted. He went on to concede that they were "misguided, if you will, but no more guilty than we are of circumstances into which we all were born—and that they, like us, are simply trying to make the best of it." What is one to make of such Olympian perspectives, such a resolutely non-judgmental stance? Can't we apply the same lofty and generous considerations to any political system, or group or individual, thus foreclosing moral judgement over any behavior? Weren't the Nazis born into circumstances beyond their control?

While Mr. Kennan does not hesitate to pass moral judgments about American society on subjects ranging from pornography, crime, pollution, Watergate, the CIA, and Vietnam, he recoils from being judgmental about Soviet politics. Following the Polish military takeover in December 1981, Mr. Kennan advised the American government "to reserve judgment in the face of a rapidly moving and unpredictable situation." He was equally unable to muster indignation when the Soviets invaded Afghanistan, viewing the event primarily as a matter that "has created serious international complications." Generally speaking, Mr. Kennan's concern with Soviet transgressions has been that they disturb Western public opinion and make rapprochement between the superpowers more difficult.

Over the years, Mr. Kennan has come to believe that the negative image of the Soviet Union is "a monster of our own creation." He intends to provide a corrective in the form of a more judicious and balanced image. For example, in *Nuclear Delusion*, he views the Soviet attempt to build missile bases in Cuba as "an unwise effort . . . something [either] forced upon Khrushchev by his own colleagues or . . . a last desperate gamble on his part with a view to restoring his authority." Recent Soviet advances in the Third World are "no more far-reaching or. . .any more successful than those they had put forward in earlier decades." The Soviet adoption of "a rhetorical and political stance of principled Marxism [was] designed to protect them from charges by the Chinese Communists that they were betraying the cause of Marxism-Leninism." The Soviet invasion of Afghanistan he described as "bizarre" and "an ill-considered" act of "incredible clumsiness." Mr. Kennan was eager to give the benefit of the doubt to the Soviets for a probable violation of the ABM treaty; in a Winter 1985 article in *Foreign Affairs*, he argued that the construction of the Krasnoyarsk radar "becomes understandable" when you consider that it "fills an important gap in Soviet warning systems." What is troubling is Mr. Kennan's apparent difficulty to deem illegitimate any manifestation of the Soviet determination to cling to or project power. Wherever he looks he finds exculpatory reasons for Soviet expansionism.

When the argument requires it, Mr. Kennan can move very swiftly from the realm of understatement about the Soviet Union to vivid language to caricature the view of those who see the world and the Soviet leaders differently. Thus he talks about "professions of determination to grind the Russians into the dust economically to exploit the resulting misery," a characterization difficult to match with any U.S. policy. In the view of those who disagree with him, according to Mr. Kennan:

> The Soviet leaders appear as a terrible and forbidding group of men: monsters of sorts . . . men who have all internal problems . . . essentially solved and therefore free to spend their time evolving elaborate schemes for some ultimate military showdown—men who are prepared to accept the most tremendous risks, and to place upon their people the most fearful sacrifices, if only in this way their program of destruction or domination of ourselves and our allies can be successfully carried forward.

Mr. Kennan's own view of Soviet leaders is one of "a group of quite ordinary men, to some extent victims . . . of the ideology on which they have been reared, but shaped far more importantly by the discipline of the responsibility they and their predecessors have borne as rulers of a great country in the modern technological age." They are seen as men who share the horror of major war . . . who have no desire to experience another military conflagration and have no intention to launch one—men more seriously concerned to preserve the present limits of their political power and responsibility than to expand those limits—men whose motivation is essentially defensive and whose attention is riveted primarily to the unsolved problems of economic development within their own country . . . men who suffer greatly under the financial burden which the maintenance of the present bloated arsenals imposes on the Soviet economy.

Mr. Kennan seems convinced that the Soviets' choices are drastically limited by historical necessity, of which the Soviet leaders are merely "victims." A most telling expression of this is the way that Mr. Kennan reacts to Soviet persecution of dissidents. "I am far from approving of the treatment these people are receiving," he has written. "I feel almost sorry for a regime whose sense of weakness is so great that it cannot find better ways than this to cope with differences of opinion between itself and a relatively small and helpless band of intellectuals." Here Mr. Kennan seems to narrow the distinction between victimizer and victim. Why should anybody feel "almost sorry" for a regime so intolerant and repressive? By Mr. Kennan's criteria, one is unable to censure South African whites who repress and murder blacks because they feel threatened by the prospect of revolution and loss of power, or the Nazis who were paranoid about the possibility of a Jewish takeover of the world.

Benevolent Determinism

Another thread in Mr. Kennan's thinking is the belief that the Soviet Union, sometime after World War II, shed its menacing and ideologically conditioned peculiarities. From then on, he wrote in *Nuclear Delusion*, "The Soviet Union would behave in the main as a normal great power, the traditional concerns and ambitions of Russian rulers taking precedence over ideological ones." The men in the Kremlin, Mr. Kennan said, were acting "in the tradition of nationalist Russian rulers of earlier periods. Their predominant and decisive concern ran to the protection of their own rule within Russia, and also to the security of the Russian heartland." And Mr. Kennan seeks to refute those who argue that Soviet leaders place political objectives above the welfare of their people. Indeed, he seems hopeful about Soviet intentions to reduce armaments because "the program of social and industrial development on which the Soviet leaders have set their hearts . . . is still far from complete and its completion . . . could not be reconciled with the preparation for any major military undertaking.''

Occasionally Mr. Kennan writes about Soviet repressive practices as if they were anthropological curiosities that unreasonably disturb ethnocentric Americans and constitute one of the unnecessary impediments to better relations.

> The Soviet authorities will no doubt continue to adhere to internal practices of a repressive nature that will continue to offend large sections of American opinion. They will continue to guard what they consider their right or their duty, to subject the United States to periodic rhetorical denunciation and to give anti-American political factions in Third World countries support . . . None of this will be helpful to the development of the relationship.

In recent writings, Mr. Kennan has increasingly displayed a historical determinism combined with an effort at a sympathetic understanding of Soviet policy. ''The Soviet leaders view Western Europe, we may be sure, with a troubled and unhappy eye. Its military association with the U.S. has always been disturbing. Its high living standards provide an uncomfortable comparison.'' Mr. Kennan finds some justification for Soviet imperial ventures in the Near and Middle East. ''This is, let us first remember, a region much closer to the Soviet borders than it is to ours. It would be idle to expect the Soviet leaders not to feel their interests seriously affected by whatever happens in that area.'' Mr. Kennan fully understands Soviet reluctance to ease its grip on East Germany. ''East Germany remains, for various reasons,the kingpin of the entire Soviet position in Central Europe. For this reason Moscow is *obliged* to cling to positions, with relation to Berlin, to the Wall, and the division of Germany.'' In the Third World, ''Political necessity *obliges* Moscow to try to keep its hands as a supportive force for left-wing and national liberationist efforts of every sort.'' Soviet expansionism in Africa is explained by the Chinese challenge. The Soviet Union ''has *no choice* but to keep up its involvement.'' After dismissing the invasion of Afghanistan as ''bizarre'' and ''ill considered'', Mr. Kennan discerns a Soviet eagerness to withdraw, just as it is eager to withdraw from other areas under its domination. Yet, ''Moscow might *feel itself compelled* to hang on even though it would like . . . to withdraw,'' Mr. Kennan wrote in the *New Yorker*. (Emphases mine.)

This benevolent determinism provides the basis for the uneven application of moral judgments to the U.S. and Soviet systems. Mr. Kennan seems to say that while both commit reprehensible actions, the United States is to be held accountable for its evils, while the Soviet Union is excused because its actions lie outside its control. Mr. Kennan also argues as though the Soviet Union were a political system that exercised power with utmost reluctance and inefficiency. A look at the map of the world since World War II, and particularly since the end of the Vietnam War, does not sustain this image of Soviet reserve.

Curiously, Mr. Kennan overlooks the perennial link between defensiveness and insecurity on the one hand, and aggressiveness and power-hunger on the other. In the case of generations of Soviet leaders, these two sets of attitudes are inextricably interwoven. Stalin felt threatened by Trotsky, for example, even when Trotsky removed himself to Mexico—we all know how Stalin assuaged this sense of insecurity. And the fact of the matter is that ruling groups or individuals intent on expanding their power at home and abroad will sooner or later be bound to feel more threatened on more occasions than those with more limited aspirations.

Here is Mr. Kennan's version of the domino theory applied to the Soviet empire. He explains why Moscow cannot bring itself to improve relations with Japan by returning the islands it seized following World War II.

> Moscow could no doubt appreciably improve its relations with Japan were it able to yield on this point. But there is apparently fear on the part of the leadership that to do so would be to make itself vulnerable to similar demands for readjustment of borders in Europe, where the Soviet Union also appropriated several areas which other governments do not regard as historically or otherwise natural parts of Russia.

By this logic no aggressor can ever cease to aggress, and no conqueror relinquish any of it conquests. Perhaps the Soviets do feel that to yield to Japan would also mean yielding to Romania and Lithuania and Afghanistan. Perhaps the Soviet leaders also fear that to permit 20 dissenters to gather in Red Square would be to risk mass demonstration of thousands or hundreds of thousands of people whose popular discontent would sweep the regime from power. But if this is the case, why does Mr. Kennan have so much empathy for the regime? Why should the desire to retain the fruits of conquest be treated as a respectable impulse? By the same token, one may absolve of responsibility any power which ever conquered any land, or any group which ever subjugated others: concessions are always dangerous and may lead to further demands.

The Reasons Why

It is not easy to account for Mr. Kennan's gradual change of heart and mind about the Soviet Union. One obvious explanation is that the Soviet Union today is less barbarous than it was under Stalin. But the essential nature of the Soviet regime has not changed; indeed in some ways Stalinism has been institutionalized. Mr. Kennan himself, while noting changes in the Soviet Union over the years nevertheless wrote recently, "The traces of Stalinism, while today much faded and partly obliterated, are still not wholly absent from the Soviet scene."

Perhaps a more significant factor is Mr. Kennan's apocalyptic fear of environmental disaster and "the growing darkness of the nuclear shadow." In *The Decline of the West* Mr. Kennan writes:

> We are faced with two conceivable versions of catastrophe. One is a possible . . . catastrophe in case we should militarily clash with the Russians. The other is an absolutely certain ecological and demographic disaster which is going to overtake this planet within the next, I would say, 60–70 years, but the effects of which will probably make themselves very plainly felt before the end of this century . . . compared to the dangers which confront us on the ecological and demographic front, the possibility of Soviet control of Western Europe . . . would strike me as a minor catastrophe.

In *Nuclear Delusion,* Mr. Kennan argues, "We have been putting the emphasis in the wrong places. We talk of saving Western civilization when we talk of a military confrontation with Russia—but saving it for what? In order that 20 or 30 years hence we may run out of oil and minerals and food and invite upon humanity a devastating conflict between the overpopulated and undernourished two-thirds of the world and ourselves?"

Perhaps we can share Mr. Kennan's concern for the earth's limited resources, but it is hard to see why tackling that problem and keeping the Soviet Union from expanding its influence should be mutually exclusive. Mr. Kennan seems to feel either that the ecological-demographic situation is so bad that it warrants turning attention away from all other threats, or he does not view the other threats as so bad after all. Perhaps a key to Mr. Kennan's changed views is his growing conviction that American claims of moral superiority over the Soviet Union are dubious, at best. In 1983, he wrote, "If what we want to achieve is liberalization of the political regime prevailing in the Soviet Union, then it is to example rather than precept that we must look; and we could start by tackling with far greater resolution and courage than we have shown to date, some of the glaring deficiencies in our own society." Earlier, in 1976, Mr. Kennan wondered "what use there is in trying to protect the Western world against fancied external threats when the signs of disintegration within are so striking. Wouldn't we be better advised if we put our main effort into making ourselves worth protecting?" These are baffling arguments if taken at face value—surely Mr. Kennan does not believe that, say, the reduction of air pollution, juvenile delinquency, and other social ills in the United States would motivate the Soviet regime to relax censorship, stop incinerating Afghan villages, and cease confining their dissidents to psychiatric wards.

Mr. Kennan does believe, however, that the flaws and defects of American society disqualify its representatives from dwelling on the evils of the Soviet system. In one memorable passage in *the Decline of the West,* Mr. Kennan writes:

> Isn't it grotesque to spend so much of our energy on opposing Russia to save a West which is honeycombed with bewilderment and a profound sense of internal decay? Show me first an America which has successfully coped with the problems of crime, drugs, deteriorating educational standards, urban decay, pornography, and decadence of one sort or another—show me an America that has pulled itself together and is what it ought to be, then I will tell you how we are going to defend ourselves from the Russians. But, as things are, I can see very little merit in organizing ourselves to defend from the Russians the porno shops in central Washington. In fact the Russians are much better in holding pornography at bay than we are.

Mr. Kennan seems to have arrived at this conclusion from an elitist, aristocratic point of view, somewhat similar to the fulminations of Herbert Marcuse against a debased mass society. Unlike most social critics of contemporary America—of the radical, radical-liberal, or quasi-Marxist persuasion—Mr. Kennan is not primarily troubled by inequalities, a phenomenon he probably considers endemic to all societies. His main concern lies with standards: moral, cultural, educational, aesthetic, or environmental. Their decline is at the root of his critique of American society.

These sentiments are also evident in Mr. Kennan's account of a small Danish port he was visiting: "swarming with hippies—motorbikes, girl friends, drugs, pornography, drunkenness, noise—it was all there. I looked at this mob and thought how one company of robust Russian infantry would drive it out of town." These recollections reveal with special force his visceral distaste for the many hedonistic elements of contemporary Western culture and youth culture, and a deep-seated revulsion from disorder, crowds, and cheap escapism. His wishful allusion to a clean-up operation by robust Russian soldiers also suggests that he would favor the heavy-handedness of authoritarian moral purpose and purification over the permissive, dissolute hedonism of the declining West. In his *Memoirs,* Mr. Kennan readily admitted to "a preference for hierarchy and authority over compromise and manipulation" and a "distaste amounting almost to horror for the chaotic disorder of the American political process." By contrast, he has developed a grudging respect for the Soviet exercise of authority to deal with social problems. Soviet leaders, when they recognize the debasement of modern society, "would have the political authority and the economic controls necessary to enable them to take the practical consequences of their insights," Mr. Kennan writes.

What set Mr. Kennan apart from many other critics of American society was his aversion to the rise of the New Left in the 1960s. He found the rhetoric and tactics of antiwar activists extremely distasteful, although he shared many of their concerns about U.S. foreign policy. But while opposition to the New Left helped prod many liberals into becoming neoconservatives, Mr. Kennan's disapproval of the radicals further alienated him from the West. He treated the cultural radicalism of the New Left as a symbol for new attitudes that were becoming widespread in the West—loose living, hedonism, and il-mannered behavior—and he began to ask the question of whether this decadent society was worth preserving, after all.

Left Out

Mr. Kennan admitted to an alienated sensibility as early as 1951, when he wrote of travelling to the heartland of the country and being repulsed by the dirt, desolation, and ugliness of large midwestern cities. He wandered around them in a daze, feeling totally estranged. "Even the language [of children playing in the streets] was unfamiliar to me."

In 1952, Mr. Kennan complained that "our country bristles with imperfections," including racism, graft, slums, juvenile delinquency, decline of community, inflation, mass media culture, deterioration of the soil, and lack of spiritual purpose. These problems seem to introduce a deep pessimism in him, even causing him to doubt "whether America's problems were really soluble at all by operation of the liberal democratic and free enterprise institutions traditional to our country." These worries about the West were compounded by a personal sense of loneliness and failure. In his *Memoirs,* Mr. Kennan recollects, "I returned to Princeton [from Washington] extremely lonely. There was, it seemed to me, no one left in Washington with whom I could discuss matters fully, frankly, and hopefully against the background of a common outlook and understanding." Despite his enormous influence, Mr. Kennan has always felt under-appreciated, and once remarked on a feeling of declining "public usefulness over the course of the years."

A final explanation of Mr. Kennan's current views may lie in his nostalgia for pre-industrial life and values. In his *Memoirs,* we have a striking passage where Mr. Kennan remembers, in his early trips to the Russian countryside, a sort of rural utopia, presumably free from all the by-products of technology and progress.

> I knew, in fact, of no human environment more warmly and agreeably pulsating with activity, contentment, and sociability than a contemporary Russian dacha on a nice spring morning . . . Everything takes place in a genial intimacy and informality: hammers ring, roosters crow, goats tug at their tethers, barefoot women hoe vigorously . . . small boys play excitedly at the little streams and ponds, family parties sit at crude wooden tables in the gardens under the young fruit trees. The great good earth of Mother Russia . . . seems once more to exude her benevolent and maternal warmth . . . I realize, as I look back on it today, that the magic of this atmosphere was derived not just from the fact that this was Russia but also from the fact that it was a preindustrial life . . . a life in which people were doing things with their hands, with animals, and with Nature, a life little touched by any form of modernization . . . how much richer and more satisfying was human existence, after all, when there was not too much of the machine.

Mr. Kennan once described himself as in "an impossible situation between two worlds." His views of both worlds—that of the Soviet Union and the United States—have changed substantially over time. He has not forgotten some of the grim facts he learned about the Soviet Union several decades ago, but those sets of images have come to coexist with a new set of beliefs—often this does not make for a very consistent amalgam. Also, Mr. Kennan has become increasingly critical of American society, and less hopeful about it finding solutions to its various social problems.

He has concluded that Americans should not criticize Soviet behavior or propose ways to improve the Soviet system. "Such a country [as the U.S.] ought to follow a policy of minding its own business . . . we have nothing to teach the world."

So Mr. Kennan's views of American and Soviet society and their

respective political systems and foreign policies, are inextricably connected and mutually reinforcing. They are not mirror images of each
other, as some have suggested. It is more like a seesaw: as Mr.
Kennan's appreciation for American society goes down, his esteem for
its adversaries rises.

2
"Sister City" Fantasies

Taking the first step to launch the sister city program, Mayor Mulsante of Northampton* wrote to the Mayor of Yelabuga on Dec. 7, 1983:

> "Your city, Yelabuga of the U.S.S.R., and our city of Northampton, Mass., USA, have much in common. We are about the same size and we are located in an attractive area. More importantly, we are united in our love for our children and hopes for their futures."

While the goodwill underlying these sentiments is not in doubt, the attribution of any meaningful commonality borders on the surrealistic. To be sure, we are united with the residents of Yelabuga in our love for our children and hopes for their futures. These feelings, however, also unite us with the residents of every other city of similar size anywhere in the world, indeed with mankind as a whole. As to the attractiveness of the area where Yelabuga is located, this remains a matter of conjecture since neither of us have been there or know anybody who has been. We are left with a slender basis for fervent espousals of commonality.

Now let us take a look at the differences which are a good deal more specific and consequential. Provincial cities, small towns and rural areas in the Soviet Union are depressing and deprived places characterized by scarcities of many kinds. There is a chronic shortage of most consumer goods and even essential foods. Peasants and other residents of such towns and cities often take trains to go to major cities to buy food and other essentials. There are hardly any catering establishments, recreational facilities, cultural amenities. I doubt that there is a single place of worship in Yelabuga. Few residents have telephones or cars. Professional people do everything they can to avoid assignment to such places. These small towns or cities are often used as places of exile, as was the case with a famous Soviet poet whose

*Northampton, Mass. is the hometown of the author

43

life ended in Yelabuga. Incidentially, Yelabuga (and much of the Tatar Republic, and the Soviet Union as a whole) is off limits to foreigners.

More important to note is, for example, that the citizens of Yelabuga all work for the state, the only employer in the U.S.S.R. They don't belong to dozens of different churches, civic groups, political organizations. If there are any gays in Yelabuga, they would not hold rallies or marches since homosexuality is a criminal offense. If there are any critics of government policy they don't charter buses to make their displeasure known at the seats of power in Moscow. If they have any notion about the magnitude of Soviet military expenditures (which is unlikely) and believe that resources should be shifted to areas more closely related to human welfare, they refrain from revealing such sentiments. If Yelabugans are unhappy with the Soviet intervention in Afghanistan, they don't make their feelings known.

Thus, the least we have in common with the citizens of Yelabuga has to do precisely with those areas which matter most to war and peace and the actions informed citizens can take on such public issues. We can make known our displeasure with the policies of our government in a wide variety of ways, ranging from expressions of such sentiments in the press, over radio, television, to marches and rallies, voting or not voting for certain politicians, blockading military bases, entering submarine yards in symbolic protest and many other actions which are either totally legal and risk free, or unlawful but largely free of any serious risk and carry limited penalties.

The citizens of Yelabuga (and the rest of the Soviet people) can in no way express their disagreement with prevailing official policies, or propose alternatives in a legitimate and risk-free manner. Even more important, they would not even dream of doing such a thing, since they do not expect to influence official policies in any way, formally or informally. On the other hand, Soviet citizens are given ample opportunity to express their approval of Party/government policies and are regularly called upon to do so.

All this is relevant not only to underscore the obvious, namely that people are everywhere, to a great degree, products of their environment (and if these environments are very different so will be the outlook and attitudes of the people), but also because such facts erode the major premises of the sister city project. One such premise is that if ordinary people ("small people," one advocate of the project put it) somehow make contact and get together at the grassroots level, they can exert pressure on their respective governments to avert the dangers of war.

We have extremely little in common with the people of Yelabuga as far as political freedoms, ways of making a living, material living standards, historical and cultural tradition, opportunities for political participation, organization and expression are concerned. That still leaves us with certain things we unquestionably have in common. For example, we all prefer pleasure to pain, health to sickness, money to spend on welfare to money spent on weapons; we all wish the best for our children, prefer a good diet to a poor one, fresh air to polluted air, and would rather make love than war. All this we already know. One may ask what these commonalities have to do with the preservation of peace? What if somebody in the Soviet Communist Party's Agitation and Propaganda Department decides that Yelabuga should get the green light to respond, and its representatives designated by the authorities confirm that health is preferable to sickness and love to death?

It must be realized—and this seems to be the most difficult to those who sincerely believe in the sister city idea—that there is no such thing, as far as Soviet citizens are concerned, as a spontaneous, informal, non-governmental, grass-roots contact with groups of Americans or other Westerners. From its earliest beginnings the Soviet regime had abhorred this kind of spontaneity and has done everything in its power to extinguish such initiatives. If and when Soviet citizens get involved in any program of any political relevance involving contact with Westerners, they always do so in some official capacity; they are chosen by the authorities, they have political tasks to perform or they are to begin with "professionals" or specialists in such matters. Along these lines it is also important to remember that the only peace movement that exists in the Soviet Union is the official one, the origins of which go back to the days of Stalin and post World War II period. The handful of Soviet citizens, the true peace activists, who tried to create a spontaneous, unofficial peace movement have been harassed, jailed, put into psychiatric hospitals, barred from contact with Western counterparts.

At the recent meeting at City Hall devoted to the sister city idea, much was said about the importance and redeeming qualities of communication between us and them. But what exactly should or could be communicated? As several of the speakers suggested, such communications on our parts should be "completely innocuous" and non-political. "Praise them. Forget about advertising ourselves;" they should find out "that we are people too." We should highlight similarities and not dwell on differences.

What would this leave us with? If we were to deemphasize anything that is distinctive of our culture, society, political institutions or narrower social setting, what of any possible significance can be communicated? If we are earnestly advised not to reveal anything of importance about the way we live—since such revelations would tell them for example something about our higher living standards and greater political and religious-spiritual freedoms—what is left that is worth communicating? We cannot tell them of our homes since we have a lot more square yards per family than they do; we cannot tell them much about our recreational or leisure time activities since that would reveal how many more possibilities and choices we have; we cannot tell them of our organizational-associational life, since this would truly bewilder or confuse Soviet citizens used to participating only in the mass organizations provided by the party and the state. Moreover, in Soviet eyes far more things have political-ideological meanings. What then are the "innocuous" topics of uncontroversial commonality and total political insignificance which are supposed to pave the way to mutual understanding and peace?

Since most topics of any substance are "delicate," one way or another we are likely to be reduced to sharing information about matters such as the weather, or the waterways near our homes, the ballgames our children play and the programs of the Hampshire Choral Society. Or, as a non-invidious revelation about our diet we might introduce the topic of peanut butter, always fascinating for foreigners. Then there is always the possibility of sharing with our potential interlocutors our criticisms or misgivings about our government and its policies. Here a substantial common ground might indeed be found since Soviet citizens need not be apprehensive about criticizing the government and policies of the United States. On the other hand, Americans should not expect their Soviet "counterparts" to reciprocate by criticizing their government, or suggest in public ways in which its performance could be improved.

Even if such contacts and communications were to be established, it is unclear how exactly they would contribute to a lasting peace, how the exchange of benign platitudes, generalities and assorted trivia would percolate into the realm where political decisions are made. There is a long way to go from peanut butter, borsch, ball games, the love of one's children or the program of local choral societies to nuclear disarmament.

The path to peace lies elsewhere. As a group of distinguished Soviet emigres put it recently (calling themselves Committee for Detente) in a public letter addressed to Andropov:

"If your appeal for peace and detente is not to be met with cynicism you must first establish detente with your own citizens, and make peace with the people of the Soviet Union by loosening and hopefully eliminating the shackles that bind them." (Committee for Detente, *New York Times,* May 15, 1983).

As long as these shackles are in place and weigh especially heavily on those citizens of the Soviet Union who seek peace in ways other than those approved by the government, sister city projects and other attempts at informal, non-governmental contacts between Soviet and American citizens remain wishful fantasies at best, possibly, opportunities Soviet propaganda might seek to exploit.

3
Wishful Economic Determinism

Marshall Goldman has accomplished, a remarkable feat: he offers in this issue of Transaction/SOCIETY (Jan./Feb. 1984) an article about Soviet economic problems that does not discuss the military and its impact on the Soviet economy. This is all the more noteworthy since Soviet military expenditures, always huge, have in the past twenty years been steadily and significantly rising. (They have also represented a far greater proportion of the gross national product than in other industrial societies.) How, then, can an economist, who is also a certified Soviet specialist and longtime observer of Soviet affairs, make a considered statement about Soviet economic difficulties without one word about the part played by the military? This deserves extended analysis as either a riddle in the sociology of knowledge or a parable of our times and a reflection of the climate of American opinion in the post-Brezhnev period.

We can hope to understand this peculiar omission only by placing it in the context of an emerging conventional wisdom in the United States, regarding both the state of the Soviet Union and its role in world affairs as well as the relationship between the U.S.S.R.'s foreign and domestic policies. In turn, the current climate of opinion in the United States and the new conventional wisdom alluded to must be understood against the following broad background. American society is not and has not ever been a militaristic society, not even when vast sums of money were spent on the military-industrial complex. This is a society where military conscription has been rare and never fully legitimate, and where, most recently, even draft registration is viewed as having questionable legitimacy and necessity. This is also a country where public opinion carries perceptible weight in the political process, and where politicians prefer to follow, rather than lead or mold (let alone defy), such opinion. Thus, the Reagan administration has antagonized much of America's public, opinion leaders, and national media by shifting resources from civilian to military expenditures. Moreover, we live in a time of growing antinuclear fervor, which has increasingly gripped the most vocal segments of public opinion and gradually expanded into opposition to all military spending, including conventional, nonnuclear weapons and forces. Last but not least, attempts to redress what was earlier seen as a significant military imbalance between the United States and the U.S.S.R. have coincided with economic recession in the United States and especially high unemployment.

It is the state of affairs just sketched that has lately given rise to growing efforts at redefining the Soviet Union as no longer strong and threatening but, rather, weak and unthreatening—a process that paralleled the mounting unwillingness to allocate resources to counter what used to be seen as a hostile power. So the "paper tiger" image of the Soviet Union was born (in some instances a descendant of the perennial underdog, a pathetic, impoverished, besieged, and encircled country, forever preoccupied with external threat). This image has a number of manifestations, and Marshall Goldman's article is one of them. It is persuasive in most of its details, but seriously flawed in its implications and questionable in some of its major premises.

What are the components of the paper tiger argument? Some of them appear to be projections of American weakness, past policy failures (such as Vietnam), and sensitivity to world and domestic public opinion. Take Afghanistan. We have been assured by a chorus of experts and influential media voices that Afghanistan has been an unmitigated disaster for a Soviet Union "bogged down" just as the United States once was in Vietnam. Actually, the Soviet involvement caused hardly a ripple in the USSR—where daily casualties suffered by the armed forces abroad are not televised during the evening news—and posed few problems for the Soviet regime in international relations, apart from cautious and ritualistic disapproval in the UN and elsewhere. At the same time, the military has acquired a new training ground for troops and weapons and a new string of strategic bases and depots. Moreover, far from making the Soviet Union seem like a paper tiger, or a weak-willed and irresolute superpower, hanging onto Afghanistan enhances the Soviet image of toughness, "meaning business," and having contempt for world public opinion (such as it is) and creates a certain grudging respect.

Another example of the paper tiger myth (also used by Marshall Goldman) concerns the recent Israeli-Syrian war, which supposedly proved the inferiority of Soviet weapons against American-made ones. Goldman, like many other commentators, neglected to consider that it might have been the inferior performance and training of the Syrian troops, rather than deficiencies in Soviet military technology, that accounted for their defeat, not to mention the superior training of the Israeli forces (as well as improvements made by Israel to the American weapons).

Nor was Poland such a disaster for the Soviet Union, as many wishful thinkers would have it, either in reputational or political-economic terms. It was a "moral defeat" all right, but the Soviet Union has managed to live with such moral defeats for a long time. No serious interference with trade or technology transfer occurred; the Soviet government did not have to bail out Poland economically, as Western creditors were assisted by Western governments. It was not even necessary to use Soviet troops to crush Solidarity; the well-trained Polish security forces were equal to the task, thus saving the U.S.S.R. what might have been a far greater (if temporary) embarrassment.

Soviet domestic economic difficulties have been the other major area lately where the paper tiger image has been invoked most eloquently and most persistently. We have heard innumerable times—from TV commentators, *New York Times* and *Washington Post* columnists, politicians, disarmament activists, and academic experts on international relations (occasionally even specialists on the Soviet Union)—that Soviet economic problems in the past few years (or during the entire Brezhnev era) have been so severe as to constrain the build up and/or use of military force; or that, even if such a buildup did occur, it caused great pain and unhappiness to a Soviet leadership eager to transfer resources to the civilian realm and gratify the pent-up desires of grumbling consumers. How could a country that has such acute and chronic economic problems be a threat to the world (or NATO or the United States)? Surely a system that cannot produce a predictable supply of onions, toilet paper, or plumbing fixtures, or an adequate quantity of windshield wipers or refills for ballpoint pens or whatever goods and services are taken for granted in most industrial nations, cannot be a menace to peace or an active and willing participant in international intrigue, let alone an expansionist power! And if this is the case, why should the West squander its resources on armaments—nuclear or conventional—especially during a recession?

Such thinking reached a crescendo after the passing of Leonid Brezhnev and his succession by Yuri Andropov. This can be explained partly by the ingrained American tendency to look at change as generally good or at least as promising. Surely Andropov is anxious to put an end to whatever is unseemly or irrational (in the eyes of the Western beholder) in Soviet behavior or policies. He cannot possibly wish to perpetuate a situation in which a country, suffering from chronic economic difficulties and shortages in essential food supplies, must maintain immense armed forces and expend huge resources on weaponry. If the image of the Soviet Union has been reconceptualized as the "paper tiger superpower," Andropov's image has also undergone interesting transformations. Some have seen him as a man of Western tastes—rational, pragmatic, interested in good relations with the West, efficient and reasonable—complementing in certain ways a Soviet image that was born out of growing American reluctance to continue the military buildup which began under President Carter. Redefining the Soviet Union as a country overwhelmed with economic difficulties, but now headed by a more dynamic and sensible leader who wants to put his house in order, leads inexorably to the conclusion that concern over the military imbalance, or Soviet aggression, is delusory (especially given the recently proved inferiority of Soviet weapons). Marshall Goldman's statement and its omissions may be interpreted in this context.

More surprisingly, Professor Goldman also appears to entertain what might be described as an ethnocentric image of Soviet political behavior. Indeed, if the Soviet government were like the American (or West German or Dutch or Danish) government, it could not preside over a greatly mismanaged and underperforming economy and continue to nourish the military establishment. But, unfortunately, the Soviets do not have such a government. What is failure for us is not the same sort of failure for them; what is intolerable here is tolerable there; what is "the wrong product mix" here need not have the same consequences there. To say, as Goldman does, that "the Soviet economic system . . . has outlived its usefulness" invites us to ask, From whose point of view, from what point of view, and by what criteria? To argue that the "structural deformities" of the Soviet economy are "incurable" again invites questions: In whose judgment and by what criteria and, even if true, what are the results? Basically, these deformities have been in place for sixty-five years, yet the regime has been a going concern, certainly from the point of view of its leaders and elites. Over time, the Soviet Union has unquestionably increased its global influence—most spectacularly during the very years of economic stagnation ascribed by Goldman to the Brezhnev era. Hence, Soviet-style economic mismanagement, extension of military power, and political influence have been compatible.

Professor Goldman says that "the challenge [for the Soviet leaders, that is] is to find some way to make the economy more responsive." To what, one may ask? Popular preferences? To Western models of economic rationality? The Soviets have been eminently successful in building an economy responsive to their political and military needs, an economy subordinated to the military machine and quite efficient in producing weapons of great variety and in great abundance. Incurable defects notwithstanding, the Soviet economy has been strong enough to produce several times the numbers of tanks, planes, artillery pieces, and so forth manufactured by the United States. Moreover, the weaknesses of the Soviet economy also appear somewhat overstated in light of a recent CIA report that found earlier estimates of Soviet production to be low. We need not insist on calling the Soviet system totalitarian to know that "responsiveness" has not been one of its prominent characteristics. It is certainly not responsive to popular pressures or Western conceptions of rationality and reasonableness.

I have no quarrel with Professor Goldman's analysis of the Soviet economy as such (apart from his refusal to comment on the military sector). The problems of low productivity, mismanagement, rigidity, neglect, red tape, and waste are all there. He fails to note, however, that the source of such problems is to be found, to a very large degree, in the dogged and long-standing determination of the regime to favor the military sector over all others. The Soviet military buildup over the past twenty years (and before) was accomplished largely at the expense of the nonmilitary sectors. The most qualified people are claimed by the military economy, and scarcities prevail because of such resource allocation. To the military expenditures one may add the economic burden created by the generously financed state security services (KGB) and the costs of various global aid and agitprop activities.

What in fact is truly remarkable about the Soviet Union found no expression in Marshall Goldman's statement: Moscow has been capable of pursuing both vigorous rearmament and material military support of its client states abroad *while neglecting* domestic needs; its initiative and dynamic have not flagged in the international arena despite all the economic difficulties Goldman described. This capacity to ignore (or suppress) domestic needs and discontent and press ahead with its foreign policies and military "adventurism"—as Western analysts prefer to call such maneuvers in order to deprive them of a patterned, premediated character—has been precisely the strength and the unusual feature of the Soviet system as an imperial power.

Perhaps one could even argue that the expansion of Soviet global initiative and influence has not been altogether detrimental to domestic stability and has even performed certain legitimizing functions. It is not at all impossible that as Soviet citizens learn about the far-flung Soviet empire—its outposts or client states no longer limited to Eastern

Europe but also being found in Southeast Asia, Africa, the Caribbean, and Central America—they may take nationalistic pride in such global ascendance and, as the "Socialist commonwealth" expands to distant places traditionally untouched by Russian influence, come to feel that the regime "must be doing something right." Moreover, the bureaucratic elite clearly benefits from such expansion: experts in the military, the KGB, and various economic organizations enjoy foreign assignments and the privileges that go with them.

Among the flaws of the statement here criticized is the implication that the Soviet regime must turn inward to repair its "incurable" economic defects. Even more questionable is the assertion that "what happens to the Soviet economy in the years ahead will determine the limits of future Soviet domestic and foreign policy." It is hardly surprising for an economist to be an economic determinist—it is more unusual that a longtime student of Soviet affairs would overlook the fact that political and ideological decisions have almost invariably preceded and conditioned, if not determined, Soviet economic policies. After all, it has been the political will (and objectives) of Soviet political leaders which created the type of economic situation that prevails today: an economy geared above all to heavy industry and military requirements at the expense of Western-style rationality and the needs of the civilian sectors. Whatever the current and long-standing ailments of the Soviet economy, it will be a similar political will and the ideological perspectives of the leadership (combined with their responses to what Western powers do) that will in the future determine Soviet policies, domestic and foreign. The time is yet to come when Western observers or public opinion can take comfort in the contemplation of Soviet economic disarray and when such disarray might be expected to exercise any significant restraining influence on Soviet international conduct. Soviet priorities are not the same as ours.

4
The Durable Misconceptions of the Soviet Union

. . . in our haste always to assign malicious motives to anything the Soviets do, or do not do, we often miss the fuller, more complex and more human story.

E. Chivian M.D. and John Mack M.D.[1]

We live with the scenario that Russia is an evil force. Now, the world is on the edge of destroying itself. Can we afford abhorrence any longer?

Norman Mailer[2]

How can I save my little boy from
Oppenheimer's deadly toy
There is no monopoly of common sense
On either side of the political fence
. . . We share the same biology
Regardless of ideology
What might save us me and you
Is that the Russians love their children too

Sting, rock singer[3]

The Western peace movement could do worse than find an occasional KGB agent in its midst.
Letter in NY Times[4]

Perceptions and Predispositions

I have been teaching courses on Soviet society since 1963 and have also published books and articles on Soviet affairs during the same period. From the very beginning of my life in the United States it made a deep impression on me how difficult it was, even for educated Americans, to grasp the fundamentals of the nature of the Soviet system and how little help they were getting from their schools,

54

colleges, mass media and opinion leaders. Of late I came to the depressing conclusion that, as far as I could tell—looking at the media, my students and various reflections of public opinion—there has been little, if any, progress in public understanding of the Soviet Union. In fact there has been a persistence of misconceptions and wrongheaded stereotypes, modified, to be sure, by occasional semantic innovations or trendy concepts.

Certainly, it has never been easy to learn about the Soviet system. Language barriers, the secretiveness of the regime, lack of opportunity for field studies, inadequate or limited scholarly contacts have all combined to restrict the flow of information. Even today only a handful of social scientists specialize in Soviet studies, or teach courses about Soviet society. However I slowly realized over the years that the main problem has not been the lack of information *per se*, especially as under Krushchev and Brezhnev it became easier to learn about aspects of Soviet reality, with Soviet social scientists and journalists also contributing to the growth of knowledge and providing occasional revelations that had formerly been proscribed.

After all, many authentic accounts of Soviet concentration camps were published in the West before Solzhenitsyn's Gulag series but not much attention was paid to them. Likewise there was information about the less genial aspects of Stalin's personality well before Khrushchev addressed himself to that topic at the 20th Party Congress, yet public awareness of such matters remained negligible. Curiously enough even before anti-communnism had acquired the unsavory reputation (in liberal circles, at any rate) as a consequence of the activities of the late Senator McCarthy, a thorough grasp of the Soviet system was rare to behold. Anti-communists were not invariably better informed than the sympathizers, or those inclined to give the Soviet authorities the benefit of doubt.

Gradually I came to realize that the understanding of the attitudes toward the Soviet Union in the United States have far more to do with domestic political-cultural conditions and climates of opinion than with the actual state of Soviet society, the access to information, the funding of centers of research, the existence of scholarly journals or the requisite language skills, although of course all these are also important.

American (and Western) misconceptions of the Soviet Union have a long and remarkable history, as long as that of the Soviet Union itself. Many of them I documented and analyzed in a study entitled *Political Pilgrims*.[5]

To be sure there is little today that matches the bizarre misconceptions and grotesque misperceptions common in the 1930s and early 1940s (excepting perhaps Billy Graham's praise for Soviet religious freedoms and the supply of caviar provided for distinguished visitors like himself).[6] The misconceptions of the past were associated with some of the most revered intellectuals and public figures of the times. They included writers, philosophers, scientists and journalists such as Louis Aragon, Henri Barbusse, J. D. Bernal, Bertolt Brecht, Malcolm Cowley, John Dewey, Theodore Dreiser, W. E. B. Dubois, Lion Feutchwanger, Louis Fisher, Julian Huxley, Harold Laski, Pablo Neruda, Romain Rolland, Jean-Paul Sartre, G. B. Shaw, Upton Sinclair, Anna Louise Strong, H. G. Wells, Edmund Wilson and many others.

It is significant that the admiration of the Soviet Union in the West peaked between the late 1920s and the mid 1930s, that is in the period of the forced collectivization of agriculture and the attendant famines, the Purges, the establishment of the cult of Stalin, and the Moscow trials. That such could be the case suggests that the connection between the nature of a political system and its evaluation by outsiders can be wholly independent of the actual characteristics of that system. Generations of Western visitors, especially during the 1930s, managed to tour the U.S.S.R. seeing only a fairyland, carefully assembled by their hosts anxious to shield them from unpleasant impressions and experiences.

Western intellectuals visiting the Soviet Union in the 1930s came with an overwhelmingly favorable predisposition projecting upon the Soviet Union many hopes and expectations. They were particularly impressed by the sense of purpose and community they discovered, the sense of justice and social equality, the dedication and sincerity of the leaders, the spirit of popular participation, the rise of the New Soviet Man and the humaneness of the political system, including its enlightened penal policies.

That such beliefs and perceptions—so completely at odds with prevailing reality—could exist suggests a close connection between predisposition and perception, and in turn between the state of Western societies and the expectations they generated in some of their members. American intellectuals and opinion leaders flocked to the Soviet Union in the 1920s and 1930s because they were looking for alternatives to the economic and social bankruptcy of the Depression years. The Soviet Union with its planned economy, full employment and (seeming) political stability presented an appealing antithesis to the crisis-ridden societies of the West.

The phenomenon was to repeat itself in the 1960s, 70s and 80s. In the 1960s the attention of American intellectuals was drawn to Cuba, a new revolutionary society of great apparent vitality presenting a striking contrast to the racial problems, social injustice and empty affluence the critics deplored in the United States. Involvement in the Vietnam war intensified the quest for other, more just and peaceful societies some found in Cuba, North Vietnam, or Mao's China. Sympathy for yet another Marxist-Leninist society sprang up in the 1980s when the Reagan presidency inspired a new wave of social criticism and political estrangement that found emotionally satisfying expression in championing Nicaragua, which was seen as a victim of the Reagan administration as well as past American policies. In each instance the idealization and misperception of Marxist-Leninist societies were conditioned by domestic discontents.

Pragmatic Status Quo Power

Among the recurring misconceptions of the Soviet Union has been the belief that it is on the verge of recognizing the advantages of the free enterprise system and about to embrace the benefits of the capitalistic methods of production and distribution, stimulated by vigorous trade with the United States. By doing so, Soviet leaders would gracefully preside over the gradual transformation and humanization of their system, as the new capitalist techniques would irresistibly bring with them growing liberalization effecting both the cultural and political realm.

The readiness to attribute such propensities to Soviet leaders—besides being a manifestation of wishful thinking, a major and most enduring influence on American attitudes towards the Soviet Union—is also rooted in a pragmatic disposition that balks at accepting that political leaders can take ideas and ideologies seriously. Claude Cockburn, the English author commented on these attitudes as early as the late 1920s: ". . . Wall Street Men . . . looked upon the U.S.S.R. . . . as in effect just another fast developing area with a big trade potential . . . as though the Revolution and the doctrines of Marxism-Leninism were puerile incidents, temporary deviations from the ultimate forward movement of the world alongside businesslike American lines."[7] In turn William Barrett observed in 1946 that "The fellow travelers . . . would love to believe that Russia is capitalist at heart, and so no worse, and therefore just as good—by God!—as anybody else."[8] More recently Joseph Finder paraphrased a current version of this outlook: "a taste of capitalism would turn the old men of the Politburo from increasing military stockpiles to improving the Russian way of life."[9]

Of late the pleading for more trade (and the desire for more profit) acquired an uplifting moral justification, namely, that trade will not only be profitable but will assure lasting peace. As Donald M. Kendall of the Pepsi Corporation put it "We should give the Soviet Union a stake in peace which we are best prepared to give through trade" [Kendall 1983].[10]

Generations of American business leaders such as Cyrus Eaton, Armand Hammer, Averell Harriman and David Rockefeller entertained such ideas finding it genuinely difficult to believe that Soviet leaders' calculations of cost-benefit ratios could be significantly different from their own and their thinking fundamentally different from that of any self-respecting head of a major business corporation. The desire to assimilate the image of the Soviet Union to that of a modern business corporation have also been assisted by occasional scholarly efforts— as for example Alfred G. Meyer's conception of "U.S.S.R. Incorporated"—focusing on the allegedly universal characteristics of modern bureaucratic organizations, transcending political-ideological boundaries.[11]

Probably the major source of these and other misconceptions of the Soviet system and the conduct and aspiration of its leaders may be found in the related processes of projection and wishful thinking. They have both been with us for a long time, but of late they have been given new impetus by fear of nuclear war. Wishful thinking regarding Soviet foreign policy typically manifests itself in the denial, or the minimizing of Soviet aggression when it occurs and in the questioning of any aggressive intent when it can be inferred from ideology or policy statement. For the wishful observer Soviet statements are accepted at their face value when they convey benevolent attitudes, but disbelieved when they reflect hostility or belligerence. In the latter case they are viewed as mere "rhetoric" produced for domestic consumption, or dismissed as ideological windowdressing, put out to please a few aged "diehards" or "hawks" left over from the days of Stalin. The combination of pragmatic and wishful thinking enables many Americans to play down simultaneously both the Soviet expressions of hostility and its ideological underpinnings.

It is not hard to understand why so many American businessmen, journalists, politicians and peace activists have been disposed to deny or belittle the ideological foundations and determinants of the official Soviet attitudes and policies. If they were to be taken seriously they would make Soviet expansionism more plausible and more highly patterned—the very phenomenon these groups seek to avert their eyes from. The more serious Soviet leaders are about their ideology, the less likely to accommodate the West, the less likely to behave like heads of another status quo power, the less likely to put domestic shortages ahead of foreign policy objectives. Crediting them with serious ideological commitments would also clash with the image of a team of pragmatic, technocratic manager-types that wishful Americans have been trying to conjure up for decades. Even a perception of the Soviet Union as merely obeying the imperatives and dynamics of great power status and filling the gaps left by the other retreating great power is more comforting than the image of a political system propelled, *to any degree,* by a messianic urge to spread the true belief and export the institutions supporting it. Hence even when Soviet expansionism is grudgingly acknowledged, it tends to be viewed by the wishful thinkers as limited in its objectives, capable of satisfaction (or appeasement) and a mere continuation of the age-old Russian quest for security. Nor has there been a willingness, generally speaking, to recognize the connections between Soviet domestic problems—much discussed in the last few years—and a global assertiveness and activism recognized of late by Severyn Bialer[12] and earlier by Helen d'Encausse.[13]

Wishful Thinking and the Therapeutic Approach

Wishful thinking irresistibly makes its appearance on occasions when Soviet conduct is particularly painful to contemplate and its realistic interpretation likely to lead to the conclusion undermining the observer's sense of security. Thus Vladimir Bukovsky, the Soviet dissident, observed:

> Even the most undeniable facts—like the shooting down of the Korean airliner . . . or the invasion of Afghanistan—failed to change public opinion in the West. Instead . . . Soviet behavior in both cases has prompted many to look for more "rational" [that is to say, more benign and reassuring–P.H.] explanation of Soviet motives . . . And more often than not, these explanations tend to blame the Western governments rather than the Soviet. . . .
>
> In general, whenever a person is confronted with something mindboggling . . . horrible and beyond his control, he goes through a succession of mental states ranging from denial to guilt, from fantastic rationalizations to acute depression.[14]

Wishful thinking often appears in combination with, and apparently produces, the efforts to "understand" Soviet behavior. Long before the earnest present day appeals to goodwill and understanding on behalf of peace and friendship, William Barrett spotted and criticized this attitude in 1946: " 'We must be neither for nor against Russia, but we must try to understand her.' Analogously, we should have been neither for nor against Hitler, but simply have tried to understand him.' "[15]

Barrett's comment is a reminder that the appeals to "understand"— and thereby regard with a measure of sympathy the behavior of either individuals or political entities—are always selectively made. Just as few pleaded to understand the Nazis, few today argue, in the name of reason and fairness, that it is absolutely vital to understand the Africaners and their abhorrent policies of segregation and discrimination. Quite obviously, such arguments are not made because doing so would blunt the edge of moral indignation toward the South African whites. By contrast appeals to understand the Soviet leaders and their policies have proliferated in the 1980s giving rise to what I called the therapeutic approach toward (or school of) Soviet behavior. For example, George F. Kennan wrote:

> . . . These Soviet Communists with whom we will now have to deal are flesh-and-blood people like ourselves, misguided if you will but no more guilty than we are of the circumstances into which they were born. They too, like ourselves, are simply trying to make the best of it.[16]

Elsewhere Mr Kennan lapsed into a revealing clinical vocabulary in describing the Soviet leaders and the grounds on which they deserve understanding and sympathy. Thus he saw them possessed of "a congential sense of insecurity" and a "neurotic fear of penetration", "easily frightened", and characterized them repeatedly as frustrated, obsessive, secretive, defensive, fixated, troubled and anxious.[17] He also perceived them

> . . . as a group of quite ordinary men [viz. "the banality of evil" thesis of Hannah Arendt–P.H.], to some extent victims . . .
> of the ideology of which they have been reared, but shaped far more importantly by the discipline of responsibilities . . . as rulers of a great country . . . more seriously concerned to preserve the present limits of their political power than to expand those limits . . . whose motivation is essentially defensive . . . whose attention is riveted primarily on the unsolved problems of economic development within their own country . . .[18]

Kennan and his followers see the Soviet Union as being in the grip of necessity and without alternatives—constrained or propelled by a form of selective historical determinism that deprives it of sensible choices, but allows great freedom of action to its adversaries; a historical destiny that compels it to act sometimes imprudently, to expand, conquer (or not to relinquish conquests), repress dissent at home, and generally speaking, conduct itself in ways Western observers ought to view with some regret and distaste but more importantly, with a measure of non-judgmental understanding. Thus, for example, Jerry Hough warns against a "rush to judgment" of the Soviet invasion of Afghanistan and generally appreciates the influence of "feelings of anger and grievance on Soviet policy."[19]

The therapeutic approach is discernible to various degrees in the work of scholars such as Steven Cohen, Stanley Hoffman, Jerry Hough, Theodore von Laue, Marshall Shulman and their younger colleagues of the "revisionist" school of Soviet historiography.[20]

The major premise of this approach is the insistence that Western scholars and politicians improve their understanding of Soviet affairs by avoiding the imposition of their culturally conditioned Western criteria in interpreting and evaluating Soviet attitudes. They must be aware, for instance, that what may seem aggressive behavior to us might be no more than an acting out of historically conditioned insecurities and apprehensions. In the therapeutic perspective, unattractive forms of Soviet behavior, including abusive rhetoric and hostile propaganda, must not be taken too seriously but ascribed to a difficult past. In turn such tolerance will generate trust and better international (or Soviet-American) relations.

A number of associated premises bolster the therapeutic approach. For instance the proposition that the Soviet Union is a status quo power; that there is a basic symmetry between the Superpowers; that many, or most of the tensions between them result from mutually reinforcing misperceptions and misunderstandings; that anti-Soviet or anti-communist attitudes are basically irrational; that the cold war was the reflection, for the most part, of such attitudes rather than a genuine conflict of interests; that when the relations between the Superpowers are more warm and friendly, Soviet domestic policies become more liberal. (Of late such components and correlates of the therapeutic approach have been given increasingly vocal expression and assimilated into the ideology of the peace movement, which insists that only the kind of understanding sketched above will avert nuclear holocaust).[21]

A culmination of the non-judgmental, therapeutic approach was reached by the historian Theodore von Laue in his quest to restore the image of Stalin to the proper moral-historical place.

Von Laue's vision of Stalin is inseparable from a conception of Russia, the underdog, eternal victim, which produced Stalin as tough-minded redeemer of his victimized nation. As is often the case, Von Laue's reticence to judge Stalin or the Soviet Union is more than balanced by his animosity towards the United States and his indignation toward his more judgmental colleagues:

> American and Western historians have sat solemnly and self-righteously in judgment of Stalin. One wondered by what right, by what standards, by what power of their imagination? How can the bookish tribe of scholars judge the harsh realities which shaped Stalin and his judgment? . . . Our sights cleared at last, we are left to praise Stalin as a tragic giant set into the darkest part of the twentieth century. . . .Praise then to the strength and fortitude of mind and body that raised Stalin to such heights—and compassion too for his frailties [Von Laue 1981].[22]

In similar statements Von Laue has undertaken the task of saving us from the "guilt of moral imperialism." His reassessment of Stalin represents a bizarre culmination of a one-sided historical determinism that froze, once and for all, the Soviet Union in the role of the underdog-nation, and that also sought to explain and excuse every aspect of Soviet conduct as an outcome of the imperatives of modernization in the face of supposedly insuperable odds and obstacles. In turn the halo of this uphill struggle came to be extended to Stalin himself.

The therapeutic approach may give rise to therapeutic appeasement. It differs from ordinary appeasement by circuitously offering justification based not, as is more customary, on the overwhelming strength of the power to be appeased, but on its weakness. This type of appeasement is far more acceptable psychologically (and thus politically) than one that legitimates similar policies by the superior strength of the adversary and by doing so implicitly acknowledges one's own weakness or fear, or both. By contrast, when appeasement is vindicated by the weakness, insecurity or folly of the other side, the appeaser assumes a superior, mature, and rational role. Why fight over banana republics, tribal countries in Africa, sundry "quagmires", remote, unimportant places like Angola or Afghanistan. Let them have Grenada or Benin or the Malagasy Republic if that will make them happy. Let them gratify their childish, irrational, grabby impulses, bred by their historical insecurity. We understand it all.

Projection

Some of the attitudes here discussed are not limited to relations with the Soviet Union and are linked to what Irving Kristol called "the liberal theory of anti-social behavior" (in international affairs). In his view, the State Department has for some time "implicitly subscribed to what Philip Rieff called the 'therapeutic ethic', according to which undisciplined nations would be chided for their transgressions . . . and would thereby learn to behave in a 'proper' and 'socially responsible' way. Even the strategy of containment of the Soviet Union had this theory behind it. . . ."[23] While such a theory applies to the Soviet case insofar as its transgressions are seen as temporary and to be outgrown, there has been less emphasis on "chiding" and more forebearance and understanding.

As was briefly noted before, projection is yet another mechanism that, in conjunction with wishful thinking and therapeutic understanding, tends to create a distorted picture of the Soviet Union. It comes into play when, for example, Soviet policies, institutions, or leaders are cast into shapes familiar to and deriving from the American experience. They have their hardliners and we have ours; their military lobbies for a bigger slice of the budget pie and so does ours; they have their self perpetuating bureaucracies and so do we; their leaders are under pressure to satisfy a public that demands more consumer goods and has no stomach for military adventures, while Americans put pressure on their elected representatives to spend more on human welfare and less on arms; their leaders believe no more in their ideological pronouncements than the American politician making speeches on the stump; they are as interested in the balance of power and global peace as we are (perhaps even more). We blundered into Vietnam, they got "sucked" into Afghanistan. Similar projections led to the attributions of Western economic rationality to Soviet political leaders on the part of our business tycoons.

Richard Pipes noted an aspect of American culture that has strongly influenced the perceptions and misperceptions of the Soviet Union along the lines discussed above. He wrote

> Nothing is more difficult to convey to an American audience [than the idea] . . . that Soviet society and its political culture are significantly different from those familiar to Westerners. . . .
>
> Americans feel uncomfortable when told that other people are "different' . . . because it is a basic premise of American culture . . . that people are everywhere the same and only conditions under which they live differ. This belief in the identity of human nature and human interests and the view that conflict is rooted in ignorance, prejudice and misunderstanding is the source of the widespread belief that if the American and Soviet leaders only got together they could solve all the problems dividing their countries.[24]

These comments also help to explain why every new Soviet leader is greeted with effusive expressions of hope and confident anticipation that he will act like an American politician. American comments about Andropov illustrate this point:

> Andropov's accession to power . . . was accompanied by a corresponding ennoblement of his image. Suddenly he became in *The Wall Street Journal* "silver haired and dapper." His stature, previously reported in *The Washington Post* as an unimpressive "five feet eight inches", was abruptly elevated to "tall and urbane." *The Times* noted that Andropov "stood conspicuously taller than most" Soviet leaders and that "his spectacles, intense gaze and donnish demeanor gave him the air of a scholar." . . .
>
> Soon there were reports that Andropov was a man of extraordinary accomplishment . . . According to an article in *The Washington Post*, Andropov "is fond of cynical political jokes with an anti-regime twist . . . collects abstract art, likes jazz . . . swims, plays tennis and wears clothes that are sharply tailored in West European style . . ." *The Wall Street Journal* added that Andropov "likes Glenn Miller records, good scotch whisky, Oriental rugs and American books." To the list of his musical favorites *Time* added "Chubby Checker, Frank Sinatra, Peggy Lee and Bob Eberly" and . . . said that he enjoyed singing "hearty renditions of Russian songs" at after-theater parties. The *Christian Science Monitor* suggested that he has "tried his hand at writing verse . . . of a comic variety."
> . . . According to *The Washington Post* Yuri Andropov is a "perfect host" . . .[25]

More recently similarly excited expectations were generated by Gorbachev's rise to power, an even more suitable target of wishful projections (being younger than his predecessors and boasting a well-dressed wife).

Members of a recent U.S. Congressional delegation in Moscow came away with highly favorable impressions of Gorbachev, perceived (as virtually all of his predecessors) as a man "we can do business with".

Speaker of the House, Thomas O'Neill, was impressed "not only with his politician's informality but also with a solid grasp of the issues and of American politics." O'Neill also found him ". . . easy and gracious. He is like one of those New York corporation lawyers . . ." Senator Paul S. Sarbanes, a Maryland Democrat, suggested that the way Mr. Gorbachev "makes his points, as a lawyer does in reasoned fashion," made the Americans wonder whether he could be argued into compromises. Silvio Conte, a Massachusetts Republican thought that ". . . he would be a good candidate for New York City . . . a sharp dresser . . . [a] smooth guy . . .'' Robert Byrd, Senate Minority Leader, noted that "He is a younger man, educated, clever and trained as a lawyer . . ." As Hedrick Smith summed it up, "Mr. Gorbachev's mixture of wit and argument and his informal manner left several Senators feeling as if they had met an American-style politician in the Kremlin."[26]

Clearly, Americans are anxious to see Soviet politics and politicians in a highly personalized manner, as counterparts of American politics and politicians, which is the way American politics tends to be portrayed by the American media. The emphasis on the personal characteristics of Soviet leaders helps to humanize them, and assimilate them into the familiar American political-cultural context, making them less threatening, and by implication diminishing the significance of their ideological convictions and political values.

It should be pointed out that these and other projections are not merely or invariably the products of wishful thinking. Projection is also encouraged by simple ignorance. It becomes a device helping to fill the gaps in one's knowledge about Soviet behavior, policies or institutions. In the absence of information to the contrary, it is often tempting to assume that people all over the world have social-political arrangements, beliefs and values basically similar to one's own. This tendency is strengthened by what is left of an optimistic American universalism and belief in progess: that countries all over the world will gradually and naturally gravitate toward some kind of political democracy; that it is difficult to rule people against their will; that basic human nature is good and sooner or later finds expression; that material improvements and political liberalization go hand in hand as does universal education and demands for liberty. Some of these beliefs also found their way into the so-called convergence theory of modern industrial societies, which predicted the gradual liberalization of Soviet society. The hope that each new Soviet leader will be an improvement over his predecessor can be linked to another American cultural belief that change is usually for the better.

The major source of projection thus remains an ingrained inability or difficulty to conceive of political arrangements and institutions, cultural and historical traditions, and conditions of life as very different from one's own. At the same time, people may also project their fantasies upon distant countries, their conceptions of ideal social arrangements that only exist in their imagination or in the literature of utopia. As noted earlier, this form of projection is no longer a major source of the misperceptions of the Soviet Union.

Academic Revisionism

The more benign images of the Soviet Union here examined stretch over a period of decades and had their roots both in genuine political change, such as followed Stalin's death, and the kind of wishful thinking to which reference has already been made. Among the scholarly reflections of the more favorable conceptions of the Soviet system has been the rejection of the concept of totalitarianism that had earlier been widely used to characterize the Soviet Union. This author wrote in 1973:

> "[the concept of] Totalitarianism . . . has come under heavy criticism both by those who have come to believe that it has *never* been a useful concept and by those who think that it has been rendered obsolete by social change in the Soviet Union. The applicability of pluralism to American society in turn has been questioned most forcefully by C. Wright Mills and his numerous followers. Note that the growing denial of pluralism in American society by one group of social scientists has been paralleled by an increasing imputation of pluralism to the Soviet Union by another group. Indeed the search for signs of pluralism (however feeble or minor) in the Soviet Union has been just as determined and purposeful as the pursuit of data to prove its non-existence in the United States! These two endeavors have been carried out by different groups of scholars, yet they spring from the same underlying "Zeitgeist", which prompts many American intellectuals to approach their own society in the most critical spirit and other societies fearful of being critical—increasingly haunted by the specter of self-righteousness"[27]

The state of affairs described 14 years ago is still with us. In the 1980s the pursuit for signs of pluralism in the Soviet Union continues and the skepticism about pluralism in American society also persists. For example Jerry Hough stated that the Soviet leadership (under Brezhnev) "almost seems to have made the Soviet Union closer to the spirit of the pluralist model of American political science than is the United States." He also discerned political participation in the U.S.S.R. as meaningful as in the United States and a striving for the creation of constitutional restraints within the Soviet leadership.[28] Hough's perception of political participation in the Soviet Union is colored by a reluctance to clearly distinguish between pseudo-participation, performed under some degree of duress and official pressure, and a participation that is voluntary and can influence the political process rather than represent a ritualistic endorsement of high-level decisions.[29]

The concept of totalitarianism remains by and large discredited (at any rate as applicable to the Soviet system), and a new school of revisionist scholarship has arisen seeking to redefine, sometimes even retroactively, the character of the Soviet system. The main thrust of this revisionist historiography has been aimed at minimizing centralized authoritarianism in Soviet social and political transformations. Commenting on such endeavors, Peter Kenez wrote:

> In the writings of the revisionists there is no ambiguity. Denying the extraordinary nature and importance of state intervention in the life of society is at the very heart of their interpretation of the 1930s . . . Stalinism disappears as a phenomenon. In their presentation the politics of the 1930s was humdrum politics: interest groups fought with one another; the government was simply responding either to public pressure or . . . [that] of circumstances, such as the bad harvest . . . the Soviet government was just like any other government operating in difficult circumstances. This view is utterly contrary to all available evidence . . .[30]

There has arisen even a revisonist view of the Purges, so far the most ambitious attempt to rehabilitate the Soviet system by removing the stains of the past from the present by, in effect, denying or bypassing the past and its greatest moral outrage. This was attempted in a book entitled *The Origin of the Great Purges*.[31]

> The very title . . . leads one to expect an explanation for one of the bloodiest terrors in history. It soon turns out, however, that for Getty the purges meant above all a revision of party rolls . . . He then proceeds to devote far more space to the 1935 exchange of party cards than to mass murder. He adds, rather disingenuously, that he will not discuss in detail the bloody aspects of his story, for that has been done by others. . . . His choice of subject matter reminds one of a historian who chooses to write an account of a shoe factory operating in . . . Auschwitz. He uses many documents and he does not falsify the material. He decides not to use all available sources and dismisses the testimony of survivors as "biased." Instead he concentrates on factory records. He discusses matters of production, supply and marketing. . . . He does not notice the gas chambers.[32]

According to another such revisionist ". . . general fear did not exist in the USSR at anytime in the late 1930s."[33]

The Peace Movement

In the 1960s and early 1970s perceptions of the Soviet Union were indirectly conditioned by the Vietnam era rejections of the United

States. Those preoccupied with critiques of American society were not in the mood to dwell on the flaws of its foreign critics and adversaries, including the Soviet Union. In the 1980s other influences have come into play. At every level of American society—from grassroots nuclear freeze activists and promoters of "sister cities" and "nuclear free zones", to members of Congress and State Department officials—the spectre of nuclear war has become a determinant of the images held of the Soviet Union. As a rule, the more fervent the desire for peace (at any price) and the more vivid the visions of the nuclear holocaust and its imminence, the greater the internal pressure to redefine the nature of the Soviet system and discard its critical conceptions. Insofar as the totalitarian image of the Soviet Union entailed strong criticism, as it undoubtedly had (stressing the uniquely repressive characteristics of such societies) it had to be jettisoned, first by experts, later by media and the educated general public.

A survey taken in 1984 illustrates the relationship between the fear of nuclear war and the changing conceptions of the Soviet Union and what were considered appropriate attitudes towards it. First of all, and underlying the other attitudes, it was found that ". . . Americans have come to believe that nuclear war is unwinnable, unsurvivable." Moreover "The public now is having second thoughts about the dangers of . . . an assertive posture at a time when the United States is no longer seen to maintain nuclear superiority . . ."

The Vietnam defeat too made a distinctive contribution to the development of these attitudes: "From our Vietnam experience, voters draw the lesson that we must keep uppermost in mind the limits of American power . . . we must avoid being provocative and confrontational." Clearly there has been an upsurge of fear about nuclear war with 38% of all those surveyed and 50% of those under 30 believing that such a war is likely to occur within the next ten years. It may be noted here that such fears suggest a connection between trust in deterrence on the one hand and American nuclear superiority on the other. In other words, it appears that people felt less threatened while the superiority of the U.S. was unquestioned than at the time when a new balance of power established itself.

The Yankelovitch survey revealing these attitudes also found a growing readiness on the part of Americans to blame their country for poor relations with the Soviet Union: "Huge majorities (76% of those surveyed) feel that America has been less forthcoming in working things out with the Russians than it might be and that we have to share some of the blame for the deterioration in the relationship." It is of some significance that, according to the findings of this survey, younger and better educated Americans are more willing to give the benefit of doubt to the Soviet regime and indicate more trusting attitudes: ("They are almost totally free of the ideological hostility that the majority of Americans feel toward the Soviet Union.") Even more significant, these younger Americans are more skeptical in some ways of their own authorities than of those of the Soviet Union: ". . . young Americans . . . believe the degree of Soviet cheating is overstated by those who oppose negotiating with them . . ." (59% of those under 30 expressed this view).

Remarkably enough, while on the one hand most respondents expressed great fear of nuclear war, the Soviet Union itself has come to be seen as less threatening, a country not interested in expanding its influence or imposing its social-political systems on others. Thus for example ". . . by a margin of 67% to 28%, people agree that we should let the Communists have their system while we have ours, that 'there is room in the world for both.' " Likewise "by a margin of 59% to 19%, Americans also say we would be better off if we stopped treating the Soviets as enemies and tried to hammer out our differences in a live-and-let-live spirit."[34] Evidently neither survey designers nor repondents have given much thought to the possibility that it is the Soviet Union that may deeply be committed to a hostile view of the United States and that such an attitude has deep ideological and political roots.

What exactly is the connection between the peace movements and the fear of nuclear war? The most plausible answer is that these movements emerge in response to such fears and reflect them. At the same time the peace, and especially the anti-nuclear movements themselves, stimulate such fears by constantly dwelling on the horrors of nuclear destruction and their likelihood unless the policies they advocate are introduced. In fact much of what goes under "peace studies" proposed, or already adopted in schools and colleges, consists of the vividly detailed depiction of the gruesome consequences of nuclear war.[35]

If, as suggested before, the peace and anti-nuclear movements have become in the 1980s a major influence on the perceptions of the Soviet Union—and a major source of its reinvigorated misconceptions—it is important to better understand the characteristics and origins of these movements and the broader cultural and political context in which they function. The most immediate cause for their resurgence appears to be the installation of intermediate range missiles by NATO in Western Europe, which in turn stimulated vigorous Soviet efforts to thwart such action by a combination of diplomatic, political and propaganda campaigns. While the Soviet Union sought to stimulate and infiltrate Western peace movements in order to achieve such specific goals[36] such activities were probably also conditioned by a changed vision of the West, and especially the United States, in the post-Vietnam era. In the words of two Hungarian emigree scholars:

> They [Soviet leaders] are more and more convinced especially after Vietnam and the Watergate affair (which for them was the ultimate proof of the contemptible lack of authority in this unruly society) that the West has very weak knees and that a combination of menacing gestures and peace-loving phrases will force Western countries into important political and economic concessions.[37]

At the same time it is of some interest to note that Western susceptibilities to apocalyptic fears have deep roots and had preceded the invention of nuclear weapons. It is today largely forgotten that, as Malcolm Muggeridge recalls, similar sentiments were widespread before the outbreak of World War II:

> We had all been talking about war, for literally, years past. It would be the end of civilization . . . Our cities would be razed to the ground in the twinkling of the eye; . . . there is no defense against aerial bombardment. Many thus held forth with great vigour and authority at dinner tables, in clubs and railway carriages; as did leading articles, sermons . . . after dinner speeches at gatherings like the League of Nations Union and the Peace Pledge Union . . . Books appeared interminably on the subject with lurid blurbs . . . films were made about it, garden fétes dedicated to it, tiny tots lisped rhymes about it. All agreed that another war was unthinkable, unspeakable, inconceivable and must at all costs be averted . . .[38]

Such a sense of impending doom, before World War II, followed closely upon the heels of the Depression and the economic crisis and social dislocations it had produced; it was a time conducive to a vision of the West as decadent and deserving to be judged severely, deserving, perhaps to be destroyed. Similarly unflattering images of the West and especially of the United States, are rife today: heedlessly immersed in an irrational and lethal arms race, misusing its science and technology, polluting its environment, appropriating the resources of the world for purposes of frivolous consumption, exploiting the Third World, becoming increasingly impersonal, bureaucratized and dehumanized—it is hardly surprising if such images inspire (or reflect) loathing and the attendant anticipation of impending, well deserved punishment. As Feher and Heller put it "The Doomsday atmosphere

... has to be understood in a literal sense ... The ultimate content of this anxiety is the emphatic feeling of a New Fall ... the conviction that 'progress' was poison".[39]

As if to counteract such terrifying visions, which the peace movement itself has helped to stimulate and perpetuate, spokesmen and activists of the movement have increasingly turned to emphasizing the unity of mankind, the common humanity and basic goodness of ordinary people. As John Corry of the *New York Times* observed, "The problem of course is that these ordinary people do not invade Afghanistan, negotiate arms treaties or impose hegemony over Eastern Europe; their Government does."[40]

Notwithstanding such truths the peace movement has of late dedicated itself to propagating what it sees as redeeming grassroots contacts between American and Soviet citizens and the widest variety of exchanges between them, ranging from "peace cruises and peace treks" to jointly climbing mountains, riding bicycles, singing folk songs, attending storytellers' conferences, playing volleyball, eating hamburgers, exchanging photos of their children, women sharing their special concerns about peace and war—any activity seen as potentially enhancing mutual understanding and trust. Such attitudes were not limited to peace activists. Charles Wick, head of the U.S. Information Agency, said: "The exciting thing about this [exchanges] agreement is that it will promote the kind of understanding and mutual trust . . . on which can be built a genuine foundation for genuine arms control. When people understand each other, governments cannot be far behind."[41]

In fact a curious duality permeates the peace movement, a readiness to oscillate between profound gloom and child-like optimism. On the one hand the imminence of nuclear holocaust is endlessly reiterated, its horrors conjured up in the darkest colors. On the other hand it is constantly stressed that the conflict between the "Superpowers" has, in effect, no objective basis, but is a product of irrational, mutually reinforcing fears, misunderstandings, misperceptions, stereotypes and mistrust, which can be dispelled by personal warmth and an abundance of contacts and meetings of the citizens of the two countries set in the context of apolitical goodwill. It follows that critical views of the Soviet Union harm the cause of peace and impede mutual understanding because they engender or reinforce mistrust and suspicion, which in turn fuel the arms race. What need emphasis are the similarities, not the differences, e.g., "people who cultivate wheat can't possibly want war."[42] A member of an American women's delegation seeking a "dialogue" wrote: ". . . what we lacked in knowledge we made up for in enthusiasm, and we shared a sort of innocent faith that the women of our two countries were probably more alike than different."[43]

The proposition that a major source of tension between the two countries has been due to misperceptions and misunderstanding was also adopted by such specialists on Soviet affairs as Marshall Shulman of Columbia University (formerly also of the State Department). He wrote: "The hostility did not grow out of any natural antipathy between the peoples of the two countries [an idea easy to refute since few people have ever maintained it!—P.H.] but with the passage of time each has come to be so persuaded of the malign intent of the other that it has become difficult to distinguish what is real and what is fancied in the perceptions each holds of the other."[44] Richard Barnet, author of *The Giants,* argued that "The cold war is a history of mutually reinforcing misconceptions" and that "monumental misunderstandings" occurred in Soviet-American relations.[45]

Peace activists took it upon themselves to dispel such misconceptions and prevent the rise of new ones. A much favored method that became highly popular in the 1980s has been the establishment of ties between American and Soviet communities in the framework of the "sister city" program. The latter firmly embraced, in effect institutionalized the major American misconceptions and illusions about Soviet society and especially its political institutions.

In my own town, Northampton, Massachusetts, prompted by a vocal group of peace-loving citizens, the mayor addressed the following letter to his presumed counterpart, the mayor of the Soviet town of Yelabuga which was selected for Northampton by the Ground Zero Pairing Project, a national organization promoting sister cities:

> Your city of Yelabuga of the U.S.S.R. and our city of Northampton, Mass., USA have much in common. We are about the same size and we are located in an attractive area. More importantly we are united in our love for our children and hopes for their future.[46]

While the goodwill underlying these sentiments is hardly in doubt, the attribution of meaningful commonality borders on the surrealistic. To be sure the mayor could have added that we are also united with the citizens of Yelabuga (and of other Soviet cities, or for that matter non-Soviet cities and citizens!) in preferring pleasure to pain, health to sickness, a good diet to a poor one, fresh to polluted air, and most of us would rather make love than war.

At the town meeting devoted to discussing the establishment of sister city ties much was said about the importance of communications between Americans and Soviet people. But what exactly should or could be communicated? Several speakers suggested with commendable candor that the communications on our part should be "completely innocuous" and non-political. "Praise them"; "Forget about advertising ourselves"; "they should find out that we are people too." In other words, highlight the similarities, play down the differences.

Yet it is the differences that matter most, especially in the context peace activists are most concerned with, namely the citizens' access to government and their influence on its policies. Thus for example if Soviet citizens have any idea about the magnitude of Soviet military expenditures and believe that the money could be better spent on human welfare, they refrain from revealing such sentiments; if they are unhappy with Soviet intervention in Afghanistan, they don't make their feelings publicly known; and if they are not unhappy, that too reveals a profound asymmetry between their attitude and those of many Americans vocally opposed to any American military intervention abroad.

If they had better understanding of the nature of the Soviet system, peace activists would realize that there is no such thing, as far as Soviet citizens are concerned, as spontaneous, informal, and risk-free protest against or criticism of the official policies, or a similar, unauthorized, grassroots contact with groups of Americans free of governmental supervision and manipulation. From its earliest beginnings the Soviet authorities abhorred these and other kinds of spontaneity in political life and have done everything in their power to extinguish such initiatives. Only by wishfully projecting upon the Soviet system characteristics it does not have can American peace activists believe that they will do business with their Soviet "counterparts".[47] And worse, the vast majority of Soviet citizens probably do not even believe that they should be in a position to influence government policy.

Such misunderstandings may help to explain why only 26 Soviet towns responded to the invitation of 1000 American towns to join hands in the pursuit of peace and why, in at least one instance, an American town (Greenbelt, Md.) was "paired" with its Soviet "counterpart" boasting a forced labor camp and KGB prison.[48]

At the confluence of the peace movement and the adversary culture, a new set of factors came into play contributing to the misconceptions of the Soviet Union.

While peace activists generally refrain from criticism of the Soviet Union, for the reasons stated earlier, they show a marked propensity to criticism of the United States—not only its foreign policy but also domestic institutions, prevailing values and policies. It is hard to know whether or not those attracted to the peace movements are predisposed, to begin with, towards a critical view of American society, or such attitudes develop in the course of involvement in such groups, subcultures and the associated organizational activities. Whichever is the case—and I am inclined to believe that it is the former—there is a striking contrast between the willingness to give the benefit of doubt to Soviet policies and the readiness to hold American government responsible for a wide range of global problems, including, of course, the arms race and Soviet-American tensions. Following the Chernobyl disaster, two American peace activists offered a benign interpretation on the withholding of information by the Soviets and excused it on the grounds of an apparently laudable "tendency on the part of the Soviet leadership to downplay catastrophes and instead offer reassurance to the Soviet people so as to prevent emotional distress." They also argued that such withholding of information ("this practice of governmental and media protection") was beneficial for mental health and made Soviet youth more optimistic about world peace.[49] It is not hard to imagine their response if the American authorities had attempted to conceal, in the interests of public emotional welfare and mental health, a malfunctioning of American nuclear plants.

Peace activists and social critics alike tend to find the source of Soviet-American rivalry and conflict (and a host of other problems) in the nature of American society. Ramsey Clark for instance argued that "We need a revolutionary change in values, because we glorify violence and want 'things' inordinately . . . Money dominates politics in America and through politics, government." He also favored unilateral disarmament on the part of the United States.[50] A professor of "medical-psychiatric anthropology" argued on the op-ed page of the *New York Times* that the United States has become so militaristic that even the type of music played on classical-music radio stations was "intended to rouse a martial spirit." Not only music but also ". . . cinema, fashion all express that toughness, defiance, eagerness for unbridled action, truculence, that lie at the heart of the . . . 'national mood.' They are part of a great national preparation—for war."[51] A book-length study was dedicated to the proposition that belief in a Soviet threat (in an "illusory enemy") was nothing but a product of the American domestic political process and of the groups dominating it.[52]

Such views have been widespread in the 1980s and associated with the cross fertilization between the anti-nuclear peace movement and the survival of the adversary culture, that is to say, elements and activists of the protest movements of the 1960s.[53] It was not surprising that "The nuclear disarmament rally . . . expected to draw hundreds of thousands of people into Manhattan . . . has been conceived and organized by groups with a history of protest reaching back to anti-Vietnam War days and by a new set of protesters."[54]

Vaclav Havel, a Czech dissident, captured the roots of the connection between the Western peace movements and a broader agenda of protest and aspiration:

> . . . for them the fight for peace is probably something more than simply a matter of certain demands for disarmament [but]—an opportunity to build unconforming, uncorrupted social structures, an opportunity for life in a humanly richer community, for self-realization outside the stereotypes of a consumer society, and for expressing their resistance to those stereotypes.[55]

Although the self-critical sentiments that foster the more favorable, or benefit-of-doubt attitudes towards the Soviet Union are predominantly produced by conditions within American society, there have also been Soviet contributions to these attitudes. In particular, expressions of hostility and guilt-inducing techniques have been widely used, for example, accusations of American warmongering combined with constant reminders of the number of Soviet people killed in World War II, far exceeding the number of Americans killed, a reminder apt to make most Americans guilty and at the same time impress them with the sincerity of the Soviet desire for peace. Expressions of hostility by themselves can lead to characteristic, good-natured American soul searching, which ultimately yields the conclusion that amends must be made and critical judgments of the Soviet Union revised. Richard Pipes observed that ". . . a strong residue of Protestant ethic causes Americans to regard all hostility to them as being at least in some measure brought about by their own faults . . . It is quite possible to exploit this tendency . . . Thus is created an atmosphere conducive to concessions whose purpose is to propitiate the allegedly injured party."[56]

Moral Equivalence

Many of the trends and tendencies associated with the misconceptions of the Soviet system discussed above have found support and new expression in the currently popular moral equivalence thesis first brought into critical focus by Jeane Kirkpatrick.[57] The core of the idea is that there are no important differences between the United States and the Soviet Union—usually referred to as the Superpowers—and certainly none that would justify giving any moral credit to the United States over the U.S.S.R.

The moral equivalence thesis allows those embracing it at once to appear objective and detached (they don't favor either of the rival Superpowers), and at the same time provides a respectable retreat for those who had earlier sympathized with the Soviet Union, which is now seen as neither any better nor any worse than the United States. Most importantly, by obliterating important distinctions between the two societies, it allows for more effective denigration of the United States.

In fact, contrary to appearances, the moral equivalence school is far from truly neutral or objective but usually harbors some degree of hostility toward the U.S. Those subscribing to it tend to be far more critical of the U.S. than the U.S.S.R., as their critiques of the latter are perfunctory while their critiques of the U.S. are intense, passionate and specific. Thus on close inspection the moral equivalence thesis reveals an asymmetry: an adversarial disposition toward the U.S. nurtured by a moral passion and indignation wholly absent from the critiques of the U.S.S.R.

The moral equivalence thesis reflects developments noted earlier: the passing of the idealization of the Soviet Union (which, however has not necessarily been replaced by a seriously critical understanding of it); the rise of the peace movement and the pressures it has exerted against critical views of the Soviet Union; and the survival and institutionalization of the adversary culture that does not take kindly to regarding the United States as better than an other country, and especially one that continues to claim socialist credentials. The moral equivalence position also appeals to those anti-anti-communist intellectuals and opinion-makers who remain apprehensive about the possibility that a strongly critical stand towards the Soviet Union might put them in the unsavory company of "cold warriors" and "right-wingers."

A social scientific precurser of the moral equivalence school may be found in the convergence theory that used to be fashionable in the 1960s and postulated growing similarities between the United States and the Soviet Union due to the imperatives of modernization.[58] This however was an essentially optimistic view: the Soviet Union was to become more liberal and democratic, gradually adopting the practices and values of advanced pluralistic societies (such as the United States); the message of the moral equivalence is more cynical, stressing the unappealing attributes both societies have in common—a state of affairs that should discourage the United States and its champions from assuming airs of moral superiority.

Thus Richard Barnet points out—in what might be regarded as a definitive handbook on moral equivalence, *(The Giants)*—that "The CIA and the KGB have the same conspiratorial world view," that "in both countries leading military bureaucrats constitute a potent political force . . . ," and "the military establishments in the United States and the Soviet Union are . . . each other's best allies," that "Khrushchev and Dulles were perfect partners," that "both sides have a professional interest in the nostalgic illusion of victory through secret weapons," that "Both societies were suffering a crisis of legitimacy," that "both are preoccupied with security problems," that "military bureaucracies are developing in the Soviet Union that are mirror images of American bureaucracies," that "the madness of one bureaucracy sustains the other," and that "each [country] is a prisoner of a sixty-year-old obsession . . ."[59]

The affinity towards the moral equivalence thesis also feeds on a generally diminished capacity to make distinctions that have been with us since the 1960s, a legacy of the anti-intellectualism of that period. Other examples of this attitude include the propensity to dilute distinctions between mental health and mental illness, religion and therapy, learning and entertainment, political freedom and repression, art and politics, what is private and what is public.

Thus in the final analysis we are led back to the suggestion that conditions within the United States are the most important determinants of American perceptions of the Soviet Union. It is unfortunate that these conditions, more often than not, predispose to misconceptions rather than to insight.

Notes

1. E. Chivian and J. E. Mack: "Soviet Minds Sheltered from Catastrophes" (Letter), *New York Times*, May 15, 1986.
2. N. Mailer: "A Country Not a Scenario," *Parade Magazine*, August 19, 1984.
3. Sting: "Dream of the Blue Turtles," Lyrics (text with tape), 1985.
4. J. Wehling: "KGB Agents, Welcome to the (Peace) Club!" (Letter), *New York Times*, August 5, 1983.
5. P. Hollander: *Political Pilgrims: Travels of the Western Intellectuals to the Soviet Union, China and Cuba 1928–1978*, New York: Oxford University Press, 1981.
6. P. Hollander: *The Many Faces of Socialism*, New Brunswick, N.J.: Transaction Books, 1983, pp. 278–279.
7. C. Cockburn: *Crossing the Line*, London: McGibbon & Kee, 1958, p. 123.
8. W. Barrett: *The Truants—Adventures Among Intellectuals*, Garden City, New York: Anchor/Doubleday, 1982, p. 247.

9. J. Finder: *Red Carpet*, New York: Holt, Rinehart & Winston, 1983, p. 316.
10. D. M. Kendall: "Give Moscow 'Carrots,' " *The New York Times*, Op-Ed, February 9, 1983.
11. Hollander, *cited*, 1983, pp. 66–77, 105–114.
12. Severyn Bialer: *The Soviet Paradox: Eternal Expansion, Internal Decline*, New York: Knopf, 1986.
13. Helene C. d'Encausse: *Confiscated Power: How Soviet Russia Really Works*, New York: Harper & Row, 1982.
14. V. Bukovsky: "The Peace Movement and the Soviet Union," *Commentary*, May 1982; see also Edward N. Luttwak: "True Secrets," *National Interest*, Fall, 1985.
15. Barrett, *cited*, p. 254.
16. G. F. Kennan: "Historian Says Soviets Are Like Americans," *Daily Hampshire Gazette* (Northampton, Mass.), November 19, 1983.
17. G. F. Kennan: *The Nuclear Delusion—Soviet-American Relations in the Atomic Age*, New York: Pantheon, 1982, p. 153.
18. Kennan, *cited*, 1982, pp. 64–65.
19. J. Hough: "Why the Russians Invaded," *The Nation*, March 1, 1980.
20. For a discussion of the latter see P. Kenez: "Stalinism as Humdrum Politics," *Russian Review*, 1986.
21. P. Hollander: "Therapy for the Kremlin," *Wall Street Journal*, December 24, 1985.
22. T. Laue: "Stalin Among the Moral and Political Imperatives, or How to Judge Stalin?" *Soviet Union* (Part I), 1981, pp. 2, 17.
23. I. Kristol: "Foreign Policy in an Age of Ideology," *National Interest*, Fall, 1985, p. 11.
24. R. Pipes: *Survival Is Not Enough*, New York: Simon & Schuster, 1984, pp. 278–279.
25. E. J. Epstein: "The Andropov File," *New Republic*, February 7, 1983.
26. H. Smith: "Impressions of M. Gorbachev," *New York Times*, September 12, 1985.
27. P. Hollander: *Soviet and American Society: A Comparison*, New York: Oxford University Press, 1973, p. 110.
28. D. E. Powell: "In Pursuit of Interest Groups in the USSR," *Soviet Union* (Part I), 1979, pp. 111–112.
29. See also J. Hough and M. Fainsod: *How the Soviet Union Is Governed*, Cambridge: Harvard University Press, 1979, pp. 297–298.
30. Kenez, *cited*, pp. 4–5.
31. A. J. Getty: *The Origin of the Great Purges*, New York: Cambridge University Press, 1985.
32. Kenez, *cited*, pp. 8–9.
33. W. T. Thurston: "Fear and Belief in the USSR's 'Great Terror': Response to Arrest, 1935–1939," *Slavic Review*, Summer, 1986, p. 730.
34. D. Yankelovitch and J. Dole: "The Public Mood: Nuclear Weapons and the USSR," *Foreign Affairs*, Fall, 1984, pp. 34, 35, 37, 38, 39–40, 43, 44–45.
35. J. Adelson and C. E. Finn, Jr.: "Terrorizing Children," *Commentary*, April, 1985; A Ryerson: "The Scandal of 'Peace Education,' " *Commentary*, June
36. See for example Bukovsky, *cited*, 1982; Ronald Radosh: "The 'Peace Council' and Peace," *New Republic*, January 31, 1983.

37. F. Feher and A. Heller: "On Being Anti-Nuclear in Soviet Societies," *Telos*, Fall, 1983, p. 148.
38. M. Muggeridge: *Chronicles of Wasted Time: The Infernal Grove*, New York: William Morrow, 1974, p. 73.
39. Feher and Heller, *cited, p. 161*.
40. John Corry: "Comrades Examine Soviet Life," *The New York Times*, July 2, 1986.
41. P. Samuel: "Mr. Wick Goes to Moscow," *National Interest*, Spring, 1986, pp. 102–103.
42. J. Howard: "American and Soviet Women—Are We Really So Different?" *New Woman*, April, 1986, p. 122.
43. A. Russell: "Reaching Beyond Politics," *Foundation News*, November-December, 1983, p. 41.
44. M. D. Shulman: "What the Russians Really Want," *Harpers*, April, 1984, p. 63.
45. R. J. Barnet: *The Giants—Russia and America*. New York: Simon & Schuster, 1977, pp. 95, 14.
46. P. Hollander: "What Northampton and Yelabuga Have in Common?" *Daily Hampshire Gazette*, January 16, 1984. (See also p. 43–47 in this volume)
47. See also A. Ryerson: "Small Town Freeze," *New Republic*, October 15, 1984.
48. A. M. Eckstein: "Greenbelt's Ugly Sister-City: Rezekne, USSR Has a Secret," *Washington Post*, June 15, 1986.
49. Chivian and Mack, *cited*.
50. C. Bohjalian: "Former Attorney General Says Greed Fuels Violence, Arms Race," *Daily Hampshire Gazette*, October 7, 1981.
51. H. F. Stein: "Dum, Dum, Dum, Dum, Dum," *New York Times*, Op-Ed, September 22, 1980.
52. A. Wolfe: *"The Rise and Fall of the 'Soviet Threat'—Domestic Sources of the Cold War Consensus*, Washington, D.C.: Institute of Policy Studies, 1979.
53. P. Hollander: "The Survival of the Adversary Culture," Partisan Review (No. 3), 1986.
54. R. Herman: "Protesters Old and New Forge Alliance for Anti-Nuclear Rally," *New York Times*, June 4, 1982.
55. V. Havel: "Peace: The View from Prague," *New York Review of Books*, November 21, 1985, p. 28.
56. R. Pipes: "Some Organizational Principles of Soviet Foreign Policy," Memorandum for the Subcommittee on National Security of the U.S. Senate, Washington, D.C., 1972, p. 14.
57. See example in L. Roche, Ed.: *Scorpions in a Bottle: Dangerous Ideas About the United States and the Soviet Union*, Hillsdale, Michigan: Hillsdale College Press, 1986.
58. B. D. Wolfe: "A Historian Looks at Convergence," in *Revolution and Reality*, Chapel Hill: University of North Carolina Press, 1981.
59. Barnet, *cited*, pp. 93, 106, 111, 119, 168, 169, 171, 173, 175.

5
Trends in Western European Anti-Americanism

I visited Western Europe recently to learn more about the critical attitudes of intellectuals and other opinionmakers (primarily academics and journalists) toward the United States. I was especially interested in how such European critiques resembled those produced by American intellectuals. I also wanted to learn something about the connections between animosity toward the U.S. and the social-critical impulses of Western European intellectuals toward their own society. I suspected (partly on the basis of some earlier work) that there was a confluence of social criticism focused on particular Western European societies, a broader rejection of the West and the designation of the United States as a major source of evil and corruption in our times.

I do not equate specific criticisms of American society or foreign policy with hostility toward the U.S. By contrast I regard anti-Americanism as a broad predisposition to blame the U.S. for a wide variety of evils in the world today, a diffuse hostility which does not reduce to specific criticisms of the U.S., and is more than the sum of its parts. Such a hostility is not simply a response to the misdeeds or errors of American political leaders or to the greed of American businessmen or the vulgarity of American mass culture. The phenomenon I have for some time been interested in is the readiness to designate the United States as a global symbol of evil, destructiveness, injustice, and irrationality—a scapegoat for a wide range of problems in different parts of the world. To be sure, such a predisposition can be activated or intensified by particular policies of American politicians or the behavior of particular individual Americans (including ordinary tourists) or by exposure to particular products of American culture.

Although intense hostility toward the U.S. has been a cornerstone of the Soviet view of the world and a major component of its policies, I do not believe that Soviet efforts have been responsible for the hostility here discussed, though, of course, Soviet policy seeks to enlarge such sentiments.

While much is written these days about the intensification of anti-Americanism in West Germany and the sharp decline of corresponding sentiments in France, less attention has been paid to other Western European countries which may exemplify more enduring attitudes toward the U.S., or perhaps more enduring varieties of animosity. I decided to take soundings of such attitudes in England, Holland, and Sweden. In the course of my travels I had conversations or more formal interviews with TV and newspaper journalists, prominent columnists, newspaper and magazine editors, educators and academics (primarily in the social sciences and humanities), and lawyers active in labor and liberal politics. My informants included peace movement activists (leaders as well as rank and file), a member of the House of Lords (in England), English and Dutch specialists in both Soviet and American studies, both detractors and friends of the U.S.

One of the first things I found out was that at the present time animosity toward the U.S. tends to take the form of equating the U.S. and the Soviet Union as "The Superpowers." This seemingly detached and objective formula accommodates attitudes far more critical toward the U.S. than the U.S.S.R. as it allows for equating the actions and policies of the two countries which bear only the most superficial similarity. Thus, for example, many English, Dutch, or Swedish intellectuals find the Soviet intervention in Afghanistan and American intervention in El Salvador equally deplorable—a comparison that overlooks the difference between an intervention with 55 military advisors (who are not even allowed to go into the battle zone) critically scrutinized by the mass media and the intervention of 120,000 Soviet troops using every nonnuclear weapon available in an indiscriminate onslaught on a country which no foreign journalist is allowed to cover, an intervention not subject to public opinion nor to any legal, constitutional, or moral restraint. Not only are these two forms of intervention equated; in fact the American one generates far greater critical publicity and moral outrage.

The Superpower equation conceals a profound incapacity or unwillingness to make distinctions. Protestors at Greenham Common in England compared the local authorities of the nearby Newbury to the KGB for seeking to restrain their protest activities. According to a Dutch sociologist, the television program on Poland produced by the U.S. Information Agency elicited more fervent criticism than the military coup which the program sought to protest. A young English sociologist described these attitudes more generally as a feeling that "there is little to choose between the two Superpowers" (a feeling he himself shared). He thoughtfully observed that there were no concentration camps in the U.S. but hastily added that when it came to foreign policy there was little to choose between.

Notwithstanding such "evenhandedness," disapproval of Soviet misconduct (e.g., in Afghanistan) tends to be perfunctory and lacking in emotional force or moral indignation. A leader of the Campaign for Nuclear Disarmament in England may admit that the Soviet-inspired repression in Poland is regrettable but will not dwell on such a topic and move rapidly to a truly heartfelt denunciation of American policies in Central America or Grenada. Even when such equations are made there is a quality of understanding reserved for the Soviet side and a respectful appreciation of the Soviet concern with security.

On closer inspection the equation of the Superpowers reveals peculiar double standards. Peace activists and leftwing intellectuals who are extremely judgmental about American policy claim that they expect more of the U.S. But, one may ask, if they expect more why are they so hostile to begin with? Why should one be *predisposed* to criticism and disapproval toward a country or political system more highly regarded? There are two possible answers. One is that these critics don't really expect more of the U.S. but it is a convenient rationalization of their double standards. Secondly, it is possible that what they mean by "expecting more" translates into ambivalence.

That the equation of the Superpowers conceals a profound asymmetry of standards and sentiments is also shown in the nature of political protest emanating from the Peace Movements of Western Europe. When pressed on the one-sidedness of their protest, which rarely is addressed to the Soviet Union (although it long ago deployed the intermediate missiles NATO is seeking to deploy in the years ahead), peace activists usually admit that it is no use directing any protest at the U.S.S.R. Yet the U.S. gets no credit for being a political power which even its critics perceive as more responsive, more reasonable, and tolerant of protest. When I inquired about the apparent unconcern with the SS-20, I was repeatedly told that little was known about them and little information was provided by the media. Dutch critics of the peace movement brought to my attention a recent opinion poll which revealed that 25 percent of those polled expressed doubts about the existence of the Soviet intermediate missiles.

It does not take a lengthy investigation to reach the conclusion that animosity toward the U.S. and professed concerns with nuclear war are hard to separate in Western Europe. A similar relationship between critiques of American society and antinuclear protest can also be observed in the United States. As a matter of fact, critics of the U.S. tend to oppose all forms of military spending on the part of the U.S.

and NATO. The Campaign for Nuclear Disarmament in England, in particular, is more than a movement organized for the purpose of averting nuclear war. The CND is a classic protest movement—not unlike the Vietnam antiwar movement of earlier times—which brings together a variety of causes and grievances and a wide range of groups and individuals held together by a diffuse sense of discontent with their society. According to a Dutch academic, what members of the peace movements, and especially the activists, have in common is "a sense of the sinfulness of the West." Such a generalized social criticism—which sees Western nuclear arms and military policies as the culmination of the evil or folly of Western societies led by the U.S.— echoes the critiques of the 1960's and early 70's. Consumerism, materialism, impersonality, excessive individualism (or, the stunting of genuine individualism)—the old themes are all there, at any rate, in a residual form. Under the broad umbrella of the antinuclear or peace movement one finds assembled, first, the radical-left-wing critics of capitalism and bourgeois democracy (providing the leadership and activist core), radical feminists, homosexuals, crusaders for the physical environment, contingents of teachers and social workers and, in ever-increasing numbers, clerics. They are especially important as they bestow upon these movements spiritual purpose and respectability.

Another asymmetry in the Superpower equation is that many who subscribe to it claim to feel far more threatened by the U.S. than the U.S.S.R. They claim that the Soviet Union is self-evidently less bellicose and more of a status quo power, because of the losses it suffered in World War II. The personality of President Reagan is also frequently invoked to explain the sense of threat the U.S. today represents. A mild-mannered, generally reasonable and thoughtful English sociologist said to me that "the U.S. under Reagan is the most dangerous country in the world," that "every escalation in the arms race came from the U.S." and unlike the U.S. "the Soviet Union is encircled." Soviet bases in Cuba are totally different from American bases in Turkey.

The perceived attributes of Reagan are significant factors in the recent upsurge of hostility toward the U.S. In the eyes of actual or potential critics of the U.S., Reagan has come to stand for most of the things generations of critics disliked about America, including his background as an actor. Such objections go well with a more traditional elitist cultural anti-Americanism which sees incompetence and inexperience in high places. Reagan is also seen as the symbol of everything inauthentic about American culture and society: Hollywood, public relations, the manipulation of the media, crass commercialism, the love of luxurious consumption, support of the rich and indifference to the poor, an old-fashioned, hollow patriotism, the defense of capitalism and American power.

Reagan is also regarded as trigger-happy, aggressive, and provocative toward the Soviet Union. His "evil empire"characterization of the Soviet Union was repeatedly mentioned with great consternation. (Even in Hungary, where hostility of any type toward the U.S. is rare, the cowboy image appeared to be imprinted in the minds of people suggesting the possibility that we may here also confront an example of a highly successful Soviet propaganda campaign that shrewdly capitalized on images and predispositions in search of a personified scapegoat. I should add that my visit to Hungary was unrelated to my interest in anti-Americanism.) On the whole, Reagan's power and influence is vastly overrated both among the critics and friends of the United States. Highly educated people appeared to entertain a view of the American political system more appropriate to the personal dictatorship of Quadaffi of Libya or Kim Il Sung of North Korea than to a system in which "the chief executive" is subject to a vast network of controls, restraints, and countervailing forces.

While much of the animosity toward the U.S. is ostensibly focused on its foreign policy, there are deeper layers of sentiment and historical memories which undergird the current criticisms. In particular, Vietnam and Watergate loom large, the first symbolizing recklessness and brutality in foreign policy, the second corruption and the abuse of power at home.

My conversations also confirmed that specific critiques of the United States almost invariably rest on a bedrock of anticapitalist sentiments. Critics of capitalism in Western Europe (and elsewhere) are bound to be hostile to the U.S., the guardian of the "world system" of capitalism, the most powerful capitalist country. Anticapitalism is also congenial with the peace activists who readily fix the blame for every political conflict upon profit hunger and the lucrativeness of the arms business ("weapons manufacturers seeking to expand their multibillion dollar market," as a booklet of the British Campaign for Nuclear Disarmament puts it). By contrast, the Soviet contribution to the arms race is unknown or unappreciated or legitimized by the honorable motives of self-defense. That motives other than profit could play a part in the militarization of a society and its rise to a military superpower status eludes such critics of the U.S.

It appears that CND has abandoned even a pretense of evenhandedness as far as American and Soviet contributions to the arms race and a possible military conflict are concerned. Its publications overflow with undisguised hostility toward the U.S. The women of Greenham Common "recognized with horror that Britain was becoming a nuclear dump for a foreign power." The base itself "is a small American town in which the U.S. dollar is the currency and the British criminal law counts for little" *(Greenham Women Against Cruise Missiles*—apparently an American publication of the Center for Constitutional Rights in New York City).

In another pamphlet discussing life at the U.S. bases in England one can read:

> Luxury is cheap and abundant . . . In the officer's mess at Mildenhall a champagne brunch is laid on. . . . A young pilot clad in a very zippy flying suit festooned with bright badges, flashes, emblems, decals, numbers and bars, sits at a table covered with fine linen eating a giant cream puff with a silver fork. He has champagne there and three other types of cream cake and, as he quaffs away at both, he is deeply absorbed in the pages of a child's comic (*Sanity,* May 1984).

It is all there: the childlike American technological savage with the pea-brain and vast power luxuriating on British soil. Only the theme of drug addiction is missing (I was also told by CND sympathizers that one reason Americans should not be trusted with nuclear weapons is because drug-taking is rampant among the troops). The U.S. air base, according to CND literature, is not only the setting of such bizarre contrasts (as the infantile American guzzling champagne over comic books), but "a major U.S. air base is a strange, different, alien and menacing world." Presumably, military air bases of other nations are warm, friendly, and familiar spots.

American reconnaissance planes "aim to provoke" the Warsaw Pact countries. On the whole, "The use of U.S. troops around the world has a number of consequences, chiefly the stifling of the rights of people to determine their own destinies. . . . This tendency to intervention has an added sinister dimension. By multiplying confrontations of conventional forces, it multiplies the opportunities for conventional confrontations to turn into nuclear ones." The booklet also asserts that "currently more than half the U.S. Federal tax dollars are spent on the military." It is in fact less than a third.

While the part played by the churches in the peace movements and their highly critical attitudes toward the U.S have been analyzed before, some new light was shed on the matter in my conversations. Virtually everybody I talked to observed that the peace issue and the activism it generates has been a great boon to the churches anxious to retain or regain their flock. A Dutch historian suggested that for the churches the nuclear issue is especially congenial as it represents "the exploitation of fear." After all, he added, "the churches don't like truly liberated people; they need people with fear." Perhaps even more to the point is that the peace movement offers an easy path to virtue and a set of new certainties. Such strongly moralistic movements also need an image of evil which can conveniently be projected upon the U.S. In addition, it appears that it is much easier for Western European peace activists, including intellectuals, to imagine—with the assistance of the media—the horrors of nuclear war (accidental or other) than the disagreeable aspects of life under a Soviet-type political system. And even if that could be imagined, it is hard to see the connection between unilateral nuclear disarmament, shifts in global power relations, and the approach of Soviet domination. But I also heard—especially in Holland—that "Finlandization" is not such a terrible fate, after all.

It did not take long to recognize that the critiques of American society and policies voiced in Western Europe were almost identical with the major strands of social criticism directed at American institutions and policies at home. While such a convergence is presumably largely a matter of osmosis, I was also given examples of situations in which American social critics instructed their European counterparts or provided them with cues to follow. A Swedish professor of economics insisted that "all Swedish Marxists learned their Marxism in America." A Dutch historian told me that not long ago Stanley Hoffman of Harvard lectured a Dutch academic audience on the perils and flaws of American foreign policy. An English journalist noted that, when in London recently, Gloria Steinem dwelt on "the lack of freedoms in America" and referred to President Reagan as a "smiling fascist." *The Missing* was a huge success in Western Europe. Western European critics of the U.S. readily refer to American sources and supporting material. Indirectly, the products of American mass culture also support denigration of the U.S. more at the cultural than political level. "They look at *Dallas* and their heart swells," said an English intellectual, commenting on the kind of confirmation such programs provide of the stereotyped, negative views of life in the United States. A leader of the CND told me that on his visit to the U.S. he was surprised at the vehemence of criticism directed at American policies from the pulpits of the churches in this country. According to an English educator, many critics of the U.S. in England rely heavily on the Bowles-Gintis critique of American education and society.

In trying to understand why the temptation to criticize and disparage the U.S. in Western Europe seems so irresistible, one is led to ponder the impact of the available visual images of this country. There are documentaries and pictorial reports (on television) which offer vivid, visual images confirming and substantiating in concrete detail the various critiques and negative predispositions. Western Europeans (like Americans) can readily call upon mental pictures of American slums, the homeless, victims of assassinations or crime, lines waiting for unemployment assistance, photos of American machines of war, and many other unappealing images of American society and power. By contrast, the muted and perfunctory criticisms of the Soviet Union can at least in part be explained by the almost total absence of any visual image of the ills and injustices of Soviet society which could provide vivid and powerful emotional substantiation and support for the typically lukewarm disapproval of Soviet domestic policies and exercise of power. The victims of war in Central America are prominently displayed on the evening news in the U.S. as in Western Europe; Afghan villages daily obliterated by Soviet air power or artillery are not to be seen. Soviet poverty, in the absence of visual documentation, remains an abstraction. Thus, in the final analysis, the Soviet Union reaps considerable benefits from its elaborate policies of censorship (and the self-censorship it imposes on resident Western correspondents). It allows her to present a seamless monolithic and somewhat mysterious facade which interacts with the high levels of Western public ignorance and lack of interest. It is difficult to muster moral indignation against something about which one knows very little and of which one has no conceptions, visual or other.

Several conclusions might be drawn from these impressions and experiences. The first one is that hostility toward the U.S. is, in large measure, independent of what this country does; it is not necessarily a response to identifiable policies or actions, although the latter may and often do deepen or aggravate the negative predispositions noted. If so, there is a limit to what the U.S. can do to make itself popular or well liked in many parts of the world.

Second, critics of the U.S. in Western Europe also tend to be critics of their own society and its real or imaginary defects. Whatever they find wrong with their own society has its counterpart in the U.S. multiplied severalfold. In the words of a Dutch student of American society, "the disaffection with America [is] part of a much wider disaffection with the complexities and contradictions of modern society."

Underneath such animosities lurks at least the memory of high expectations. Anti-Americanism in its virulent, irrational form may only cease when unreasonable expectations are laid to rest. My landlady in Budapest asked me, "Have the Americans found a solution to the food smell in refrigerators?" Such concerns illustrate the evolution of expectations in Hungary. While the U.S., as Hungarians see it, is neither any longer the powerful champion of human freedoms around the world nor paradise on earth, it may still hold the key to the solutions of problems vital to the new generation of consumers in Hungary. Needless to say, there is no animosity toward the U.S. in Hungary. Nor do Eastern European intellectuals harbor high expectations about the perfectability of social systems and human beings. By contrast, many Western European (and American) intellectuals blame the United States for the discomforts of living in a world which has not only become an increasingly dangerous place, but also one which cannot gratify their longing for a sense of purpose and meaning.

6
Mexican Intellectuals and the United States

A trip to Mexico in 1984 fully confirmed the observations of Octavio Paz about Mexican attitudes toward the United States. He wrote: ''The United States is always present in our midst even when ignoring or turning its back on us; its shadow falls on the whole continent . . . the United States is the image of everything we are not.''

I went to Mexico to begin collecting information for a study that will compare the attitudes of intellectuals in various countries (Mexico, Canada, Western Europe) toward the United States. My impressions and experiences in Mexico strongly suggest that, notwithstanding the proper social scientific caution about generalizing from a limited sample, the perceptions of the United States are so highly patterned as to allow for a few generalizations.

To begin with one must keep in mind that attitudes toward the United States have to be viewed against the background of a vast fund of historical grievances and inequities. A sense of such grievances has become a pivotal part of Mexican political culture and is reinforced by the system of formal education and the peculiar revolutionary mystique institutionalized since the early part of this century.

The recognition of ambivalence is the first step in any effort to understand the feelings of Mexican intellectuals toward the United States and things American. Again, as Paz puts it, there is ''. . . an ambivalent fascination: the titan had become the enemy of our identity and the secret model of what we wanted to be.'' Or, according to one of the numerous Mexican intellectuals I talked to (himself very critical of the United States), a blend of envy, resentment and imitation is the major common denominator of the attitudes toward the United States. To these I would also add curiosity, pervasive suspicion, and reflexive rejection. A highly critical stance toward the United States remains an established part of Mexican political and intellectual life. (I was also reminded of the saying: ''Poor Mexico, so far from God and so close to the United States.'') Moreover, the critical attitudes toward the United States appear to be largely static based on a correspondingly frozen image of the United States. The only change some of my interlocutors detected in American policy toward Mexico was that, of late, American manipulations of and controls over Mexico have become more subtle—a view that echoed the late Herbert Marcuse.

The sense of grievances, as might be expected, is quite deeply embedded in the national psyche and kept alive by many historical reminders and references. There are giant monuments commemorating the ''children heroes'' who, in 1847 literally draped in the Mexican flag, resisted to the death the American invaders; also a subway station and other public places were named after them. The major thoroughfares of Mexico City are called ''Insurgents'', ''Revolution,'' and ''Patriotism,'' as well as ''Reform.'' A troubled and conflict-ridden history replete with foreign invasions helps to explain the nationalism of Mexican intellectuals. The longstanding historical confrontation with the United States was bound to produce the type of nationalism Isaiah Berlin likened to the ''bent twig,'' forever ready to lash back at the oppressor. Berlin's definition of nationalism ''as an inflamed condition of national consciousness . . . usually . . . caused by wounds, some form of collective humiliation'' perfectly fits the Mexican case. Besides the momentous and well-known historical-political grievances of the past, there is also the persisting phenomenon of American economic domination greatly resented by intellectuals—a resentment that finds the embrace of some variety of Marxism particularly congenial.

There is, furthermore, the powerful American cultural presence conveyed by the mass media and embodied in the products of mass culture. All of these factors create a predisposition to blame the United States for a wide range of Mexican economic, social and cultural problems. Not that Mexican intellectuals are unaware of the indigenously rooted problems of their society such as, say, corruption, economic mismanagement or environmental deterioration (nobody can ignore, for instance, the air pollution in Mexico City). Yet they are allergic to outside criticism especially from their northern neighbor and, when offered, they react defensively. (Mexican intellectuals are not prone to the type of collective breast-beating common in the United States particularly among academics in the humanities and social sciences.) As one of them put it: ''I know I have an idiot child but you cannot say that I have an idiot child.''

While Mexican intellectuals (as well as non-intellectuals) are ready to admit that the Mexican work ethic could not have provided the model for Max Weber's theory of the Protestant Ethic, they turn the issue around and ask what is so great about the Protestant work ethic (although I was also told the ironic adage that Mexicans want to live like Americans and work like Mexicans). The outdated stereotype of the joyless, work-obsessed American unable to relax, persists among many Mexican intellectuals. I was told a number of jokes, much enjoyed by the Mexicans listening to them, which culminated in the message that Americans are highly standardized, homogenized, robot-like interchangeable creatures (also naive, simplistic, crude, uncouth and materialistic) deformed by technology and divorced from the capacity for genuine feeling and good fellowship. The difference between a typical American and Mexican—I was told—is that if the American is offered a job 3000 miles away with a five percent pay raise, he will pack and move without hesitation whereas the Mexican would not, loath to disrupt his social-familial ties and roots. (Such views bear a surprising resemblance to the counter-cultural critiques of American life and values which proliferated in the 1960s in the United States.)

The negative views of the United States are not without their paradoxes, or, as a resident American put it, Mexican intellectuals can live with a high tolerance of ambiguity. Thus, it was brought to my attention time and again that even the most vocal radical-Marxist critics of the United States are fond of visiting our decadent yet efficient land of capitalistic contradictions, and that they also enjoy the many dubious products of American mass culture and take pride in the possession of American consumer goods. At the same time, I was also told that many intellectuals and students refuse to learn (or to speak even if they know) English, "the language of imperialism." And while it is nationalism rather than Marxism which is the root of many of these attitudes, Marxism is a handy stick with which to beat American capitalism, economic or cultural expansionism, "neocolonialism" and other evils imputed to the United States. Although Marxism-Leninism of some variety colors the outlook of many Mexican intellectuals and has become a form of conventional wisdom, I was often told that much of it is shallow and opportunistic, a rhetorical device or a form of conformity to prevailing subcultural values in many academic circles (e.g. the gigantic National Autonomous University of Mexico, the most heavily and one-sidedly politicized). This obligatory Marxism, it was pointed out to me, was also often a tribute to feelings of guilt intellectuals experience when they contemplate the contrast between their relatively privileged position and the condition of the impoverished masses especially obvious in Mexico. Hence Mexican intellectuals, not unlike many of their counterparts in the United States and other parts of the world, are subject to the familiar conflict between the elitist and egalitarian impulses; in a country like Mexico, it is particularly tempting to look down upon the unwashed hordes while at the same time wishing to uplift and save them. (It was also alleged by middle class Mexicans I met that Mexican domestic servants prefer working for Americans who treat them with less condescension and on the whole more generously.)

"Toleration of ambiguity" also properly characterizes the attitudes of Mexican intellectuals toward Cuba. There is, to begin with, an impulsive and highly emotional identification with a country which successfully defied the United States and freed itself from American economic, cultural and political domination (never mind that it slid subsequently into political-economic dependence on the Soviet Union). At the same time, I was also told that "we are not prepared to have that kind of political system"—a remark reflecting a recognition of the constraints on free expression which prevail in Cuba. Yet others dismissed the issue of intellectual and political freedoms (not unlike their less numerous counterparts in the United States) insisting that what truly matters are the improvements in public health, education and literacy. Pro-Cuban sentiment among many intellectuals is so strong, I was told, that for example it would be unthinkable for an anti-Castro Cuban to be invited to UNAM (National Autonomous University of Mexico) to give a lecture. When I asked about Huber Matos, I got blank looks or it was noted that nobody talks about him. Valladares, the poet, who spent over twenty years in Castro's prisons got very mixed reviews in the Mexican press with the left trying to discredit him.

It goes without saying that pro-Cuban sentiments also translate into vigorous support for the Sandinista regime in Nicaragua and the guerrillas in El Salvador. Would people be bothered by having a pro-Cuban and pro-Soviet regime on Mexico's southern borders I asked? No, they would not, said most of my informants, but some wavered. A few people said that whatever the Mexican rhetoric against United States interventionism, they harbor the secret belief that the United States would not allow a communist takeover of Mexico, which they don't wish for their own country though applaud elsewhere.

As regards Soviet influence or penetration in Central America or the Caribbean, my interlocutors were uniformly skeptical of such possibilities; indeed, they were totally incapable of grasping the reality of Soviet power and global aspirations such was the degree of their preoccupation with and overestimation of American power. Correspondingly, not unlike their fellow intellectuals in the United States (or Western Europe), they could not entertain the possibility that Soviet-Cuban attempts to extend political-military influence in this hemisphere and the indigenous roots of social unrest (including native guerrilla movements) are *not* mutually exclusive. The idea that the Soviet Union and Cuba could or would exploit such unrest was rejected as a pure CIA-bred fantasy. Generally speaking, attitudes toward the Soviet Union, while not necessarily warm, were lacking in the sharp critical edges reserved for the United States. This was generally justified by the distance separating the Soviet Union from Mexico as opposed to the proximity of the United States. In addition, some degree of benevolent neutrality was also reserved for the U.S.S.R. on account of its perceived role in restraining American imperialism.

It should also be emphasized that the attitudes sketched above do not apply, I was told repeatedly, to the technocratic segments of the Mexican intelligentsia. Among the latter, traditional anti-American sentiments are far less in evidence; they look to the United States as a model in modernization and efficiency as they often had been educated there and are more conscious of the problems of Mexican society and of the governmental mismanagement of the Mexican economy than academic intellectuals. At the same time, Mexican intellectuals on the whole are more likely to be involved with the government and its many bureaucracies than their American counterparts, and such involvements taint less perhaps because the governments ever since the 1920s can claim a socialistic legitimation and commitment to social justice and the uplift of the masses. For this reason bureaucracy per se is not generally viewed by Mexican intellectuals as an unmitigated evil or even as a serious problem but rather as an instrument of social-distributive justice.

In conclusion, it should also be pointed out that the anti-American sentiments discussed above are quite unevenly distributed in Mexican society as a whole; that is to say, the Mexican middle classes are more pro than anti-American and so are probably the masses of the "ordinary" people, especially those living closer to the American border.

In the final analysis, Mexican intellectuals are in many ways not so different from their American counterparts; they certainly share many specific criticisms of the United States, its domestic and foreign policies, social and economic institutions and culture. Where they differ significantly is that while American intellectuals tend to focus their discontent on their own society, the circumstances of history made it possible for the Mexicans to channel a good deal of their critical impulses outside their society, north of the border.

PART II

Subcultures of Criticism

7
A True Believer of the Old School

Although Corliss Lamont's life was reasonably interesting—a fair balance of good breeding, wealth, political activism, worldwide travel, warm family ties, and friendships with many famous people—his memoirs are not by themselves especially absorbing. *Yes to Life* is nonetheless one of those books that are thought-provoking and significant in ways quite independent of, or even contrary to, their authors' intentions. It is a case study of sorts that allows readers so inclined to pursue various interesting and consequential sociological and social-psychological phenomena of our times.

Corliss Lamont was born into a wealthy family of Scottish descent. His father "became in 1911 a partner in J. P. Morgan & Co., the leading banking firm in the United States, and in 1943 Chairman of the Board." He describes both of his parents as "highly cultured and politically sensitive." He acknowledges that he "inherited from his parents more money than I could put to intelligent personal use" and consequently gave much of it away for what he considered "the good of [his] fellow human beings." He attended Phillips Exeter Academy, Harvard College, and Columbia University. After teaching at Columbia for four years, he resigned and devoted his life to the moral and material support of various radical causes, writing, and travel; and he served on the board of the American Civil Liberties Union between 1932 and 1945. He wrote or edited twenty-one books, among them *Russia Day by Day* (1933, with Margaret Lamont), *The Peoples of the Soviet Union* (1946), and *Soviet Civilization* (1952 and 1955). He describes himself as "an independent, free-wheeling radical," "a left liberal or moderate radical," an opponent of "all theories of universal determinism," a fighter for freedom, one engaged in "permanent rebellion" (even as he is approaching eighty). He ends this book by averring that "we should continue to resist and combat misguided men and evil institutions as long as our hearts go on beating."

Such are the bare outlines of Corliss Lamont's life and aspirations. I think there are several circumstances that make Mr. Lamont's musings and recollections—and his entire life—emblematic. A man of wealth and comfort turned social critic, he personified a social-psychological process that we still don't properly understand, widespread as the phenomenon has been in the United States and elsewhere. The life and beliefs of Corliss Lamont also exemplify the paradox of high-minded and gentle individuals ending up as apologists of, or at least sympathizers with, exceedingly brutal political systems. Mr. Lamont's public life and utterances also illustrate the phenomenon of double standards in political judgment so striking in our times among people who are finely tuned to the defects of their own society yet regularly overlook the flaws and outrages of political systems they designate as superior to their own. And last, this book provides many occasions to reflect on the inability (or limited ability) to learn from the past and the tremendous weight of past political commitments.

Although Mr. Lamont now claims that his attitude toward the Soviet Union "has *all along* been that of critical sympathy [my emphasis]," it is hard to find that critical component in his earlier books. On the contrary, he had no patience with critics of the U.S.S.R.; in 1933 (in his *Russia Day by Day*) he claimed that American tourists critical of the Soviet Union merely converted minor discomforts into social criticism. As for him, there was hardly any facet of Soviet society he did not find admirable. It was in 1933 that he explained that people had no savings in Russia because there was no need for them, so well did the state provide for all their needs.

To be sure, Mr. Lamont was far from singular in so perceiving the Soviet system in the early 1930s; what is more remarkable is his reluctance to go beyond the grudging and qualified admission of his misjudgments. Indeed, his visit in 1959 (a time by which most earlier pro-Soviet enthusiasts had fallen by the wayside) and his account of it in this book could have come out of a travelogue of the 1930s.

To give Mr. Lamont his due, he does admit in this book that while Stalin was in power the U.S.S.R. was "one of the most cruel and violent dictatorships in history, culminating in the judicial frame-up of Soviet leaders in the Moscow Trials (1935–38)." But, like the Soviet authorities, Mr. Lamont doesn't seem to think that the Soviet system has been at all compromised by what went on under Stalin or, for that matter, before and after Stalin. As far as post-Stalin conditions are concerned, he brings himself to admit that the Soviet Union "still falls short of being a true democracy," a statement somewhat similar to one which would claim that Nazi Germany fell short of according complete respect for all ethnic groups. As others before him, he finds mitigation of the lack of civil liberties in the missing democratic traditions of Russia (and China and Vietnam), a courtesy he would certainly not extend to South Korea, present-day Turkey, Taiwan, Argentina, and a host of other right-wing dictatorships similarly lacking in democratic traditions. Like other sympathizers with Marxist one-party states, he too feels that since the United States is

> far from having attained the democratic ideals that our forefathers wrote into the Declaration of Independence and the Bill of Rights . . . an element of hypocrisy taints our criticism of the failing of democracy in foreign lands.

Naturally this is said in the context of criticizing Soviet authoritarianism. Mr. Lamont and those of his persuasion never faltered in their criticism of, say, South Africa or Spain under Franco (and other non-Marxist dictatorships) because of the imperfections of American political institutions. Mr. Lamont would not visit Spain under Franco but he had no scruples about visiting Russia under Stalin and China under Mao. This consistent selectivity in moral indignation and compassion is revealed throughout the book, as in the dismissive aside about the Chinese refugees in Hong Kong "naturally . . . bitterly anti-communist."

Mr. Lamont's visit to China in the spring of 1976 was close replay of his Soviet visits. All was well in China, including the hotel accommodations ("first rate") and food ("quite good on the whole"). Few Chinese were ill-fed, the school visited was splendid and the children "staged a marvellous ballet" for his party which consisted of twenty-three other American "political activists." But in the Sino-Soviet dispute Mr. Lamont comes down on the Soviet side although despairing of the friction between the two. He mused, "Perhaps we need an American Association for Chinese-Soviet Friendship." Again, as one reads his criticism of China for its aggression against Vietnam, it is hard to avoid thinking how he managed to overlook the Soviet aggression against the East Germans in 1953, the Hungarians in 1956, the Czechs in 1968, the Baltic people after World War II, the Afghans in the present, etc. I suppose that, if pressed, he may admit that none of those actions were especially commendable but were necessary to defend socialism from CIA intrigues (or the misguided, nationalistic demands of inhabitants of these nations)—but the point is that such matters just would not come up. Perception is indeed selective. Is it possible to establish the roots of such a world view, such a predisposition? What looms in the background of all these one-sided moral concerns?

We can probably eliminate the motive of rebellion against familial background; his family was apparently encouraging, directly and indirectly, the author to head in the direction of social criticism and well-intentioned armchair radicalism. Mr. Lamont tells us that his father took a "vital interest in the Soviet Union" when he was still a schoolboy. The Depression certainly played a predictable part in his political development, prompting him "to explore systematically the possibilities of the Socialist alternative." Well before, while at Harvard College in 1924, he proposed inviting speakers such as Eugene V. Debs, William Z. Foster, and Scott Nearing. Whether any conscious or subconscious unease about having so much unearned money around entered into the evolution of his political ideals we shall never be able to establish conclusively. Mr. Lamont, for one, is assured that "the deciding factor in my being won to Socialism was not some emotional urge but the uncompromising use of intelligence."

Once the attraction of the ideals of socialism was firmly in place, the mistaken identification of specific countries (notably the U.S.S.R.) as socialist followed, and he no longer had any great difficulty ignoring or screening out evidence that would have suggested that the societies calling themselves socialist, foremost among them the Soviet Union, represented little if any improvement over Western capitalist democracies. Indeed, one of the most remarkable aspects of these memoirs is their indication of how little their author's views have changed over half a century, and how deeply they remain permeated by the perspectives of the 1920s, and in some respects of the nineteenth century. Thus, for example, he tells us that socialism "can unlock to the fullest extent the economic potentialities of the machine age with its scientific techniques"; that "socialist planning for abundance, democratically administered, permanently overcomes the contradictions of capitalism"; that "socialist planning would release and coordinate frustrated talents"—without stopping to pause once to ask where these appealing developments have taken place. In the countries of socialist realism where people are routinely jailed for their ideas, the countries of curtained limousines, special stores, and special clinics, in the lands of massive corruption, bribery, and stealing "public" property? One can only marvel at this resolve to avoid juxtaposing the ideal to reality, which alone makes it possible to retain, to hang on to, the ideal.

Familiar as many of these attitudes are in their general outlines, certain particulars of the case remain baffling. How could this man of good will—a "foremost exponent of civil liberties" and a free thinker whose major belief had been "that men's minds should be critical and free from control by any authority whatsoever"—feel so much warmth toward societies which crushed the slightest manifestations of the critical spirit and concentrated unprecedented resources on controlling men's minds, political systems where authority was not only intolerant of criticism but insisted on fawning adulation? Surely such contradictory attitudes do not emerge and persist so stubbornly through "the uncompromising use of intelligence."

It may well be true, as Mr. Lamont proposes, that "The factors that bring people to or toward the Left are human sympathy and compassion plus reason or intelligence. . . ." However, when this magic "Left" remains identified with countries like the Soviet Union, China, or Vietnam, one has reason to wonder how great a part remains to be played by "reason and intelligence" in the maintenance of such commitments.

8
Romantic Communism

Those who study political movements have for some time been familiar with the notion that political commitments often spring from non-political sources. Likewise, it has often been noted that political commitments may engulf and thoroughly transform people's attitudes and behavior. The book being reviewed here provides a series of miniature case studies in the dynamics of political commitment and its decline. It probes the connections between the political and non-political spheres of life of a group of American Communists between the 1930s and late 1950s. By the end of this period, most of them had left the Communist Party due to the revelations of Khrushchev at the twentieth Party Congress. Notwithstanding the flaws discussed below, this study should be of interest to social scientists concerned with political participation, commitment, disillusionment, extremism, and political morality, as well as those with an interest in recent American social-political history.

There is something deeply dissatisfying about a model of political involvement with an organization like the American Communist Party, which is built upon the metaphor of "romance" and intends to conjure up the images and emotions associated with this concept. It is from this fundamentally flawed perspective that so many of the shortcomings of this potentially informative book follow.

A major objective of this undertaking has been to persuade the reader that those attracted to the American Communist Party were a diverse group of ordinary Americans. Gornick appears concerned with rebutting stereotypes about American communists, including the belief that most of them were Jews from New York or, in any event, immigrants and generally neurotic. Since neither she nor the American Communist Party provides data on the socio-economic and ethnic characteristics of former (or current) party members, the reader must take her word for the proof of diversity.

Gornick's second "thesis" is that American communists harbored political passions of unusual intensity and gravitated to the Party because of their passionate longing for justice and need for community. The desire for community and the need for identity through political action, rather than more specific and clearly political goals, explain best the commitments of these people.

A third and somewhat more ambivalent message of the book is that overall, these people did well. They neither wasted their lives nor sank into ignominy in the unquestioning service of the Party. Rather, they retained an enlarged sense of humanity and whatever their errors, prepared the way for a new wave of better and wiser radicalism in America. She writes in the last two paragraphs: "For better or worse, radical politics—full of sorrow and glory—embodies the stirring spectacle of human beings engaged, alive to the beauty and rawness of self-creation. American Communists were caught up in the magnificent sorrow. They gave themselves to it passionately, with a wholeness of being. For this I honor them, and I am grateful to them" (p.265). Such an assessment of the contributions of American communists is placed in the context of the author's view of the unfolding of left-wing radical politics. She envisions a chain leading from the utopian socialists in the nineteenth century to the organized and power-conscious Marxists rallying around the Soviet Union and from there to the contemporary "unaffiliated Marxists" who represent a fine synthesis of the unsatisfactory polarities of the past. Gornick writes: "Would it [i.e., the current generation of Marxists] have been able to recover with such sure knowledge the *idea* of socialism if the Communist had not lived out for them the bitter-as-gall lessons of a visionary idea subordinated to the political apparatus?" (p. 264). Therein lies the major premise of the salvage operation and soul searching conducted by Gornick and her informants. The mistakes and misdeeds of the past are part of a chain of glorious (and less than glorious) historical developments from which they derive meaning and absolution. The hard work, self sacrifice, and anguish were not in vain.

The author's compulsion to romanticize her subject matter is most revealingly shown in her descriptions of the physical attributes of her informants. Arnold Richman's body is "full of easy grace" while his wife "moves with the grace of a high-strung cat" (p. 215); Diane Vinson at 62 "is a remarkably beautiful woman" (p. 227); Anthony Ehrenpreis's face "is commanding—marked by strength, dignity and intelligence" (p. 235). And so on. Virtually every one of them looks much younger than his actual age. What is one to make of this? How did Gornick stumble upon such an extraordinary collection of athletic, graceful, vigorous, and impressive looking people?

Two possible explanations occur. One is that her informants were selected on the basis of their looks and those who fell short of certain standards of attractiveness were excluded. The other, more likely possibility is that Gornick's perceptions became captive to the intended message of the book. It seems as if the bodies and faces of people as well as their politics become idealized, a part of the romance. The author's reticence to reveal how she went about selecting her approximately two dozen informants gives further substance to such speculations. Regrettably, the combination of these concealed identities and Gornick's style creates a quality of fuzziness in the narrative and an uneasy sensation of confronting a mushy mixture of fact and fiction.

The fact that those interviewed are either old or well into their middle age poses another problem in that the recollections of their political past and their youth coincide. It takes superhuman effort not to obscure the difference between the charms and exhilaration of being young and the charms and exhilaration of working for the Communist Party of the United States. Gornick does not seem to consider the possibility that people in their advanced age try to salvage their major commitments and are disinclined to write off a large part of their lives as wasted, futile, and tainted by service to an organization of rather dubious ethical principles. At the same time she finds the self-reproach of ex-communists (not that there are many in her "sample") "dismaying in the extreme," and "everything in [her] rises up in protest" when ex-communists such as Lionel Trilling or Richard Crossman subject their former enthusiasm to cold, rational, and critical analysis (pp. 18–19). This is a strange position to take considering the fact that she is quite aware of the many unappealing attitudes and activities associated with the service to the Party.

She recognizes, for example, that "Thus among the Communists . . .who gained the courage to plunge after freedom were in the end not free. Men and women who had great intelligence were in the end in no position to use that intelligence. . .who were eminently reasonable. . .were in the end a caricature of reason. . .who sought to control the cruelties of social relations through the justice of scientific analysis in the end used scientific analysis to impose new cruelties" (p. 15). She has few illusions about the ruthlessness, deceit, doublethink, arrogance, and authoritarianism the Party embodied and transmitted to its adherents; she knows that means routinely took precedence over ends. The ultimate test of political rectitude becomes the depth of feeling associated with the stand taken. This position may provide the key to the principal flaw of the book, specifically the imposition of the sensibilities of the 1960s upon another era and another set of actors and attitudes. Gornick projects onto the former supporters of the American Communist Party a set of attitudes and beliefs—and sometimes even a vocabulary—which proliferated in the 1960s. Presumably her informants also furthered this tendency by echoing and reflecting what was trendy in the 60s and applying some of it retroactively to their earlier attitudes.

Gornick unwittingly offers support to those detractors of left-wing radicals (past or present) who disparage the depth and authenticity of their commitments by linking them to unresolved personal problems and to forms of neurosis. The political core of Party affiliation recedes as we learn from the author and her informants about the feelings which accompanied working for the Party. The latter was said to be a "most amazing humanizing process" (p. 9), "an awesome move toward humaneness [and] an immense and tormented effort of the heart" (p. 23) which filled people with "love, laughter and wisdom" (p. 50) as well as "tremendous surges of comradeship" and "the mad, wild joy of revolutionary expectation" (p. 57). Many informants confessed to having been made "a human being" by the Party and privy to "a visionary life." All the benefits of "the Communist experience" were summed up as follows by one of the informants:

> Right, wrong, errors, blind pro-Sovietism, democratic centralism, the lot notwithstanding. In our lives, as Communists we had community. We had integration. We had the civilising sense of connectedness. . . . It wasn't just good wine in our veins, that life, it was ambrosia [P. 116].

The author never seriously entertains the possibility that such craving for and abject submission to "community" (real or imagined) may not be a good thing and that such abnegation and abandonment of self (Fromm called it "escape from freedom") exact a high price. "The inability . . . to make reason dominate emotion" (p. 22) was not peculiar to the Communist experience in the United States or elsewhere. Political commitments of great intensity produce highly patterned and not altogether admirable forms of behavior commonly designated as fanaticism and intolerance. There is welcome evidence at the end of the work that these propositions are not totally foreign to the author. There she reveals how, in the course of confronting dogmatism and intolerance among radical feminists, she fully realized the perniciousess of these attitudes, and more generally, the problem of ends and means in politics. It is unfortunate that these insights failed to inform the book as a whole.

9

New Light on the Roots of Radicalism

The " '68 Generation" Analysed

Almost twenty years have passed since the beginning of the student protest movement and the upsurge of political radicalism in the United States (and, shortly thereafter, elsewhere in the West.) The passage of time has not provided a consensus in the interpretation of these events, nor have historians or social scientists found convincing and widely accepted explanations for them. What most people mean by "the sixties" started in 1964 and faded away around 1972–73; not surprisingly, what has been written about this period tends to reflect an author's predisposition towards and experiences of it. In the United States at any rate, the closest thing to a conventional wisdom about radical student protest and the 1960s has been that it was a time of "lofty ideals", "youthful idealism", and an exhilarating if transient sense of "community."

If in retrospect the anti-intellectualism and intolerant self-righteousness of many of the student radicals (and of their mentors) have been deemed less appealing and acceptable than they seemed in the heat of the political action and drama, their attitudes and politics are still defended in much of the media and academia as honourable. Of all those reminiscing, in recollections and appraisals of the '60s, some were then in their prime, others outright young, in college or graduate school. Hence, in many minds, the politics of the 1960s and being young, youthful, and hopeful are irresistibly associated—an essential factor for the analysis of that era.

Whatever the "mature" judgment of history or social history, one thing already appears clear; that the *discontinuity* between the '60s and '70s (and early '80s) has been vastly exaggerated. The '60s were not some isolated eruption without antecedent and after-effects. Although Tom Wolfe was not incorrect in labelling the 1970s as the "Me Decade" in seeming contrast to the public-spirited '60s, the differences were not quite so pronounced, and were not simply matters of self-centredness-versus-public-spirited generosity. Individualism already flourished in the '60s, with millions of young people insisting on "doing their own thing", bent on instant gratification, and propelled by a wide range of hedonistic impulses. It is possible to some degree to differentiate between the political and apolitical aspects of that decade by employing the concepts of cultural-versus-political radicalism; but the two strands were in practice intertwined. Some of the political-militant radicals might well have been puritanical radicals, but most also found it important to smoke dope, listen to rock music and engage in some variant of unconventional sexual behaviour. It is the savage rejection of Western political institutions and social order *and* a determined individualism and hedonism that ties together the '60s and the '70s. The level of political activism has declined, but the attitudes and beliefs giving rise to such activism have clearly persisted into the 1980s.

Moreover, many wrong lessons have been learned. For instance, although it has become increasingly difficult to persist in entertaining illusions about the good-natured humanity and popularity of Uncle Ho's North Vietnamese Communists and the good life they brought to the masses, it is still obligatory in many circles to profess deep shame about the U.S. opposing a régime that was to give us the "Boat People." Furthermore, losing a war against one of the most repressive and militaristic régimes in our times led many to conclude—including high-level policy-makers—that the U.S. should retreat from virtually all global involvements and refrain from using military force to defend its interests. Today what President Carter scornfully called "the inordinate fear of Communism" has receded so far that American élites are no longer disturbed even by the rise of pro-Soviet and pro-Cuban régimes on their very doorstep, their "backyard" in Central America and the Caribbean. Many of the same activists who idealised the Viet Cong and the North Vietnamese now protest against American involvement in Central America and idealise the Marxist guerrillas of that region. "Grenada" becomes "another Viet Nam." Much of the media follows suit. On the American campuses the spirit of the 1960s persists in the virtual institutionalisation of estrangement, and in the habits of self-censorship exercised by professors and university administrators to avoid disruptions by radicals. Hence the drastic constriction of subjects in courses of studies, in topics for visiting speakers, and of the whole range of controversial opinion in academia.

Accordingly Stanley Rothman's and Robert Lichter's *Roots of Radicalism*[1] is a major contribution to understanding the social and political movements and the spirit of the 1960s. There is nothing quite like this massive, ambitious, and thorough study, which combines and successfully integrates social-historical, sociological, social-psychological, and psychoanalytic perspectives in an attempt to come to grips with complex social phenomena. If read with an open mind it will change many preconceptions and stereotypes about the period and its major protagonists. It will also confirm certain impressions with a formidable array of data, both quantitative and qualitative.

The authors' research procedures included a survey questionnaire administered during 1971–73 at four large American universities, to over 1,100 students drawn from both random and probability samples; they were also given various "projective" tests. A small group of students were given additional "intensive clinical interviews" and further projective tests. In 1974–75 the authors administered similar questionnaires to 120 non-student radicals or former student activists (early New Leftists). These radical adults were compared to a sample of non-radicals—"business and professional people active in community affairs in a small northeastern city." There was a European counterpart to the American study, involving 230 students at two West German universities. The authors supplemented such data with an abundance of printed source materials about the period and its major protagonists (although they overlooked the writings of the American historian D. M. Potter, on alienation, changing authority relations, and problems of identity formation in recent times, which are highly relevant and complementary to their work).

It is impossible here to enumerate, let alone discuss, all the interesting and sometimes striking findings and propositions of this study and its sophisticated methodology. Broadly speaking, its major contributions lie in providing new insights and data about the relationship between politics and personality, family background and political-attitude formation, the sources of alienation and rejection of society, and attitudes towards political power, violence, and authority. It will surely compel a rethinking of the social history of the 1960s and of the conceptions of American society which arose at the time (and are still with us). More specifically, it represents a new departure in understanding the roots of both Jewish and non-Jewish radicalism, the differences and similarities between them, and how they were welded into a single (if ultimately fragmented) social-political movement.

Rothman and Lichter have not been the first to note that radical movements on the left tend to attract a disproportionate number of Jews. Thus, for example, in 1970 a survey in the U.S. found that 23% of all Jewish college students considered themselves "Far Left" when only 4% of Protestants and 2% of Catholic students defined themselves as such. They found in their samples that Jewish students "were three times as likely as non-Jews to engage in frequent protests and twice as likely to lead or organize protests . . . by every measure we employed. Jews made up a majority of the New Left on these campuses."

Children of Jewish academics were found to be "by far the most radical group studied, much more so than the children of non-Jewish academics."

Even after the Protest Movement had peaked. Jews continued to be disproportionately represented during the 1970s in a wide variety of "counter-cultural" or "anti-Establishment" organisations such as the various anti-nuclear groups, anti-DNA-research, and Gay-Liberation movements, and were prominently represented in consumer groups, radical jurists, and in Left-wing research organisations (e.g. the Institute of Policy Studies). The combination of liberal-Left leanings and a concentration in certain key occupations and élite colleges and universities helps to explain the Jewish influence on the protest movements of the 1960s (A 1968 study found that they accounted for 20% of the faculty in élite colleges and universities: 12% of the faculty of law schools, but 38% of élite law schools; while 25% of all social scientists were Jewish at élite schools.) Their role in the mass media was equally significant. A 1969 study found that 27% "of those working for the most influential media outlets . . . were of Jewish background." They also played an important role in the so-called underground press of the 1960s.

Two major questions must be asked about the protest movements of the 1960s, indeed about the protest movements of any period. The first is why they erupted at a particular time (given the endemic nature of some of the ostensible targets of protest). The second is what exactly motivated the participants, or in what measure one should look for explanation in the socio-political setting as distinct from certain shared characteristics of the protestors or revolutionaries. At both the beginning and the end of *Roots of Radicalism* the authors note—and it is gradually becoming more and more evident—that neither concern over "racial injustice" nor American involvement in the Viet Nam war by themselves offer satisfactory explanations of the 1960s, and especially of the steadily widening nature of the social criticism and estrangement which emerged.

A third major question about the radicalism and radicals of the '60s involves the sources, the genesis, of social criticism. Was it primarily a response to visible and self-evident evils of the socio-political environment? Or was there something in the nature, make-up, and the conditions of life of the critics? Considering the fact that, if not the absolute majority, the vanguard and leadership of the radical student movement were "children of privilege", it is certainly tempting to subscribe to the still widely accepted view that theirs was a wholly idealistic outpouring of action and emotion, since they themselves had little to gain either from the anti-War protest (they enjoyed college draft deferments) or from the struggle for civil rights (they were white) or from the protest against inequality (they were well-off).

The most influential assessments of the radical students of the period were highly positive and laudatory. They included social-scientific studies which

> "agreed that the student movement represented the best in their societies. . . . Researchers concluded early that radical students were dedicated to free speech and the rights of minorities. In many cases they came to this conclusion simply by asking students whether they believed in free speech. . . ."

Students were, however, rarely asked about their willingness to extend such rights to groups they despised on ideological grounds. Rothman & Lichter thoroughly examine and expose the weakness of many such studies carried out by authors sympathetic to the students in the first place (the best-known being Kenneth Keniston); and they point to the typical confusion of "idealistic political pronouncements with personality traits" characteristic of much of this research and of the liberal-Left perceptions of the student radicals. They note in passing that even the notorious Felix Dzerzhinski, the founder of the *Cheka* and of what subsequently became the *KGB*, was given to pronouncements about loving people and flowers. They might also have added Stalin's famous statement about the importance of carefully nurturing the masses like plants in a nursery.

Perhaps the most striking among their propositions—and one likely to provoke the greatest controversy—is that (among the Jewish radicals, at any rate) a major component of the idealism, the identification with "the underdog", rested on other than disinterestedly idealistic motives.

> "Many white radicals supported 'black power' as a surrogate expression of their own hostility against the Establishment. The black underclass was finally fulfilling the role in which it had been long cast—as the vanguard of a revolt *against* the American Dream."

Nor was the phenomenon entirely new.

"The identification of some Jewish males and females with the Russian proletariat during the Soviet revolution, with Irish and Italian workers during the 1930s, and with the black underclass or Third World nations during the 1960s may have reflected motives beyond mere sympathy with the underdog . . . in both the 1930s and the 1960s many Jewish radicals were projecting their own needs and desires upon those groups."

They go on to observe:

"For some Jewish radicals, then, it is not only the oppression of Third World nations that attracts them as they move from cause to cause but, rather, the imagined virility of these nations and their powerful leaders. . . . As Abbie Hoffman described Fidel Castro: 'Fidel sits on the side of a tank rumbling into Havana. . . . The tank stops in the city square. Fidel lets the gun drop to the ground, slaps his thigh and stands erect. He is like a mighty penis coming to life. . . .' "

"As agents of the oppressed, and the justly violent oppressed in particular, they could treat their own aggressive urges as morally legitimate. . . . This identification helps [the radical] deny his own aggressiveness. He speaks and acts not for himself but for the worthy cause whose emissary he has become. . . . The projection of positive feelings onto the 'people' or 'the oppressed' is matched by the negative emotions projected onto the oppressors. . . ."

"Students, too, could be victims, could enjoy the righteousness that comes from persecution."

In short, "many radicals identified with black and third world militants as a psychological means of incorporating their power."

These findings, which fly in the face of the conventional wisdom about the motives of the young radicals,[2] derive from a more general and far-reaching theory of Jewish radicalism and of the authors' new perspectives on Jewish marginality and an associated estrangement. For one thing, unlike many other Western intellectuals they do not believe that alienation automatically confers a clearer view of social realities:

". . . marginality can also serve to narrow one's vision. The oppressed may see only the worst side of a culture or social system."

As the authors see it, then, political radicalism, as far as such American Jewish groups are concerned, stems from a broader and more basic hostility toward the social order, from a *predisposition* to reject a social system which defines them (or had defined them) as outsiders. This attitude explains both the attraction of universalistic ideologies such as Marxism, and the interest in other oppressed groups victimised by the system.

What gives such ethnic radicalism a unique character—besides the long history of Jewish persecution and marginality—is, according to Rothman & Lichter, the Jewish family structure and its impact on attitudes toward authority and the handling of aggression. Two aspects of the Jewish experience and character-formation appear to be of particular significance.

> "Faced by persecutors too powerful to resist physically, Jewish families of the diaspora gradually came to place tremendous emphasis upon inhibiting the direct expression of physical aggression, particularly by male children. . . . Survival called for the creation of controls that became an integral part of character structure."

The corresponding presence of weak fathers became typical of many Jewish families, and "Jewish radicals were the only group to perceive their families as matriarchal."

In other words, the Jewish radicals' identification with the tough Third World guerrillas (especially the Viet Cong), rioting Negroes, Black Panthers, and other victimised yet assertive groups, had a strong compensatory flavour. Some groups like The Weathermen quite consciously cultivated toughness, and modelled (or imagined they had modelled) themselves on such groups. The investigations reported in this study revealed the radicals' preoccupation with power and authority, again contrary to widespread belief among liberals that authoritarianism is the preserve of Right-wing elements.

> "The traditional authoritarian [the image of which was enshrined in studies like that of Theodor Adorno's *Authoritarian Personality*] deflects his hidden hostilities onto outsiders and outgroups. The inverse authoritarian [i.e., the New Left radical] unleashes his anger directly against the powers that be while taking the side of the world's 'victims' and 'outcasts'."

Moreover, the widespread rejection of authority during the 1960s was highly *selective* rather than reflecting a generalised mistrust of *all* authorities. The same radicals who felt the mildest academic regulations intolerable and repressive (and parental authority altogether intolerable) were capable of extreme submissiveness toward groups, authority figures, and symbols that they admired, e.g., Blacks, the Viet Cong, Castro, Ho Chi Minh, Chairman Mao, and the repressive systems which they represented. As Rothman & Lichter shrewdly point out,

"Their temporary opposition to authority is part of a quest for a new authority that can command their wholehearted loyalty."

Presumably an authority that is not hesitant, ridden with doubt, and lacking in strength and determination.

The broader implication is, of course, that political attitudes and beliefs often stem from non-political sources. None of this reduces the radicals to "a bunch of neurotics" or "spoiled brats" as the hostile stereotype had it. None the less, the findings make it clear that there is a difference between what is manifest and what is latent, between professed intentions and underlying motives. The authors, however, are fully aware that it is under particular historical circumstances that the psychological or personality variables assume causal significance in explaining mass movements:

"As political and cultural authority declined in the 1960s, so did the authority of the family and ego strength. Such is always the case in revolutionary (or pseudo-revolutionary) eras. At such times people seize the opportunity to act upon fantasies that they normally keep under control. All such fantasies contain universal elements, but their content is also partly determined by the cultural norms of the society in which the individual lives."

Another major contribution of this volume is the systematic delineation and explanation of the differences between Jewish and non-Jewish radicals. Until now, the lack of a clear understanding of these highly patterned differences had led to wildly contradictory theories about radicalism and the part played in its development by family background. Here are some of the findings concerning these two groups:

"About half the Jewish students were raised in a liberal or leftist political milieu. . . . By contrast only 1% of the non-Jews rated their fathers as 'Radical democrats,' and not a single non-Jew subject came from a socialist background."

"Jewish radicals were more than twice as likely as non-Jews to see radical publications [in their homes when they were growing up] while non-Jewish radicals were three times as likey as Jews to see conservative journals."

"Among Jews, the more radical the child, the more radical he or she perceived the father. Among non-Jews, this pattern was reversed: the more radical the child, the more conservative the father."

The inquiry into the family background of adult radicals turned up similar results, i.e., "the tendency of Jewish radicals to come from relatively politicized and leftist family backgrounds.'' Furthermore, ''Jewish radicals [again, in the adult sample] were drawn primarily from intellectually and economically privileged backgrounds, while non-Jewish radicals were drawn more heavily from the bottom of the status hierarchy.'' There were also suggestive differences between Jewish and non-Jewish radicals in regard to participation in dangerous contact sports (Jewish participation being far more limited) and even in driving habits, with ''non-Jewish radicals driv[ing] aggressively'' whereas their Jewish peers were ''less likely to use automobiles as instruments of self-assertion.'' All in all, it appeared from the accumulated data that

> ''Non-Jewish radicals seemed most likely to lack impulse control and to express aggression directly. Jewish radicals on the other hand were more timid physically. Their participation in the Movement may have provided a means of gaining strength by uniting with a powerful force.''

Participation in the radical activism of the 1960s, therefore, had different functions and meanings for Jewish and non-Jewish radicals. Certainly Jews constituted initially the major force and much of the leadership in the Movement, diluted, as time went by, by the influx of the non-Jewish element. These two types of radicalism were in turn related to different patterns of child-rearing and family background, and after reading *The Roots of Radicalism* we can better comprehend the peculiarly personal element often observed in 1960s politics. I refer to the self-conscious orientation toward self-transcendence, self-expression, personal problem-solving through political action and immersion, and the conversion of public issues into highly personal concerns.

The findings of the German study were similar to the American, especially in regard to the development of radicalism among non-Jewish students. Thus,

> ''German radicals gave little indication of continuing family traditions of leftist ideology or behaviour. Instead they seemed to be actively rebelling against parents who were either genuinely conservative or insufficiently radical to satisfy their more fervent children. . . . The most important finding is that radicals had significantly greater power needs and conflicts than non-radicals. . . . The German radicals closely resembled their American non-Jewish counterparts in both their social diversity and psychological homogeneity. They exhibited the same political and personal rejection of their parents and the same power complex which they apparently resolved by adopting the negative identity of the social outlaw. . . . An emotional alliance with the third world served the same

needs some American radicals fulfilled by attaching themselves to the Black Panthers."

In conclusion the authors point out that the current "absence of overt protest has not meant a return to 1950s quietism. Elite campuses have become bastions of Left-liberal and radical social criticism. . . . "Moreover, many of the views and values of the 1960s have become institutionalised, and absorbed by groups other than college students as a general shift to the Left has occurred.

I should note, finally, that since the book was written, overt protest and street politics have revived—without quite reaching the level of the late 1960s and early 1970s. This resurgence of protest, focused on U.S. aid to anti-Communist regimes in Central America and on Western efforts aimed at restoring the military balance between NATO and the Soviet Union, is in some ways more ominous than that of the earlier vintage. Today the elements of wilful self-delusion are even stronger than they were in the 1960s, and the issues more singularly focused on international affairs. The upsurge of "Unilateralism" is a far more devastating symptom of Western alienation and loss of collective will than protest against American involvement in faraway Viet Nam. Likewise, treating the rise of pro-Soviet régimes in Central America as inconsequential is a related form of collective self-delusion rooted in wishful thinking. Until other writers, equally sensitive and thoughtful, follow Rothman & Lichter in examining carefully the current crop of activists (including members of the clergy), we shall not authoritatively know what blend of idealism, self-delusion, alienation or fear (this time of manifest Soviet power) presents itself as a wholly rational and highly ethical protest against "American imperialism . . . wasteful military expenditures . . . and the risk of nuclear war."

Notes

1. *Roots of Radicalism: Jews, Christians, and the New Left.* By Stanley Rothman and S. Robert Lichter Oxford University Press, $27.95. £21.50.
2. Perhaps, in part, because it is in general so difficult for Americans to be critical of the young, because of the Rousseauian tendency in American culture to connect the young and youthfulness with many human virtues: idealism, nobility, selflessness, candour, purity, sincerity, authenticity. . . .

10
The Antiwar Movement and the Critiques of American Society[1]

A most striking aspect of the debate on Vietnam—both while the war was going on and since it has ended—has been the confluence of the critiques of the American involvement with domestic social criticism. It took some time to recognize that the war mobilized powerful political-emotional energies and discontents within the United States which were largely unrelated to the American involvement and the methods of warfare although the latter were the ostensible focus of the protests.

My vantage point for observing the antiwar protest was the campus: between 1963–68 Harvard, after 1968 the University of Massachusetts at Amherst (which in 1986 distinguished itself by awarding an honorary degree to Mr. Mugabe, Prime Minister of Zimbabwe to honor his contributions to human rights and social justice.)

By the late 1960s the merging of antiwar protest and domestic social criticism was complete: a binding consensus was established and entrenched on most campuses, certainly the major ones, and was, if need be, enforced by violence, or its threat. As a member of the 1960s student generation recalled ". . . the notion that it took some special sort of courage to protest the Vietnam conflict utterly ignored the campus realities that prevailed at the time. By 1969, the all-but-unanimous antiwar sentiment among students and faculty at our elite universities had become so strong that it took far greater courage to defend our role in the war . . . than it did to follow 10,000 others to a protest demonstration."[2]

It was widely held that American participation in the war was not merely wrongheaded, but immoral, indeed a height of immorality, representing a historically unique manifestation of evil, matched only by the misdeeds of Nazi Germany. The American involvement in the war symbolized virtually everything that was wrong with American society in the eyes of antiwar activists. According to the prominent war-critics Richard Barnet and Marcus Raskin "The [Vietnam] war itself was not an accident but the logical extension of a 'national security' policy of permanent war on a global scale. U.S. forces, agents, and spies operate in every country on the planet trying to make the world conform to an American vision of order that serves our pocketbook and our pride."[3] Tom Hayden saw "The real lesson of Vietnam . . . [in] what it may yet teach us about our genocidal history, about the real identity of American civilization as understood by its victims."[4] American conduct in the war was routinely described as genocidal and it became popular to spell America with a letter "k" (Amerika) to stress symbolically the kinship between the U.S. and Nazi Germany.

Such were the beginnings of a new habit of willful carelessness in foregoing distinctions and making historical and political equations, the beginning of a period (which has yet to end) marked by the decline of the powers of discrimination. As I have argued before[5] such an impaired capacity to make important distinctions has been one of the enduring legacies of the 1960s displayed by many intellectuals, politicians and opinion leaders who lump together unhesitatingly various forms and degrees of social evil and moral-political corruption. A major current manifestation of this phenomenon has been the moral equivalence school, so designated by Jeanne Kirkpatrick, which is at a loss to discern any significant and morally relevant differences between the United States and the Soviet Union.

In the mid and late 1960s a tidal wave of moral indignation swept the campuses which was both reflected in and fanned by the sympathetic media. The impassioned and unqualified rejection of U.S. policies in Vietnam rapidly became the entrenched conventional wisdom of the times. (I think it remains to date in the same circles although less vocally expressed.) Even those reluctant to share it were impressed by the outpouring of moral passion and silenced by its intensity. The phenomenon was an excellent example of an effective social movement, which as Barrington Moore points out, requires a combination of both moral and material interests since ". . . moral passions without material interests rarely if ever suffice to move large bodies of men and women in a way that leaves a deep mark upon the historical record."[7]

In the case of Vietnam the "material interests" involved was the draft: students passionately protesting the immorality of war also protested the possibility of being drafted and thus risk their lives although their privileged draft deferments reduced this eventuality. As I had written elsewhere "Although for most college students the prospect of being drafted was remote, it enraged the sense of security enjoyed heretofore. Brought up during and impressed by the tranquility of the 50s, tired of the 'cold war rhetoric' of their elders, seeing the cold war (that is, anti-communism) discredited by its most vocal American representatives on the Right (McCarthy in particular) and familiar with the powers of American technology, foreign threats were neither real nor credible for this generation."[8] It has often been pointed out that after the end of the draft the campus protests sharply declined.

Neither the protection of such tangible group interests nor the horrors of war, and the allegedly uniquely immoral means used by the U.S. explain satisfactorily the intensity of the protest among middle class students, academic intellectuals, journalists and other elite groups. The moral indignation unleashed by the war tapped deeper reservoirs of discontent and hostility toward the established institutions and dominant values of American society. The warmth and receptivity toward the claims and virtues of the enemy (the Vietcong and the North Vietnamese regime) displayed by so many of the war critics, further suggests, that there was more to the antiwar protest than revulsion against the use of napalm or the relocation of peasants in "strategic hamlets". The major objection to the war coincided with deeply felt objections to the nature of American society and the attendant protest against the assertion its political will and military power.

Alienation, that much abused concept, goes a long way to explain the attitudes here discussed. I am using it here to refer to the belief that society and its major political-economic institutions are unjust, irrational, deeply and irremediably flawed. Such a disposition also entails a pervasive distrust of and suspiciousness toward the political decision-makers and the feeling that existing institutional arrangments are a sham, that hypocrisy and inauthenticity prevail in public life and even personal lives are infringed upon and threatened by the defective institutional arrangements.

It is hardly surprising that those holding an exceedingly unfavorable view of American society would vehemently disapprove of any assertion of American political-military power as they find much unwelcome continuity between the rotten domestic institutions and the expansion or maintenance of American power and influence abroad. Thus certain forms of isolationism, certainly the post-Vietnam variety, rest on the conviction that a deeply flawed social system ought not be allowed to influence others and that the world would be a much better place if the U.S. exercised as little influence as possible. To be sure, isolationism has other sources as well, including the opposite feeling, that of superiority which prescribes detachment from the demeaning squabbles of other countries. Both types however tend to be combined with a form of excess security—the tacit or vocally held conviction that nothing seriously, if at all, can threaten us from the outside.

Susan Sontag provided a tersely precise description of the attitudes I am trying to convey when she said ". . . Vietnam offered the key to a systematic criticism of America."[9] In a similar spirit Jerry Rubin observed at the time: "If there had been no Vietnam, we would have invented one. If the Vietnam war ends,we will find another war."[10] Richard Barnet and Marcus Raskin proposed that "The Indochina War is not the chief cause of the American crisis but a symptom of that crisis . . . a visible manifestation of a systemic disorder . . . if the war were to end this afternoon most of the problems that are tearing away at American society would remain.[11]

The current U.S. involvement in Central America has come to provide, in some measure, an analagous target for the kind of political energies and sentiments Vietnam used to mobilize: the Vietnam era war protest has come to serve as a model for emulation and a convenient point of reference for renewed social criticism made more acceptable by its association with (another) anti-war protest. Opponents of American aid to El Salvador and the Nicaraguan guerillas constantly draw parallels between these involvements and Vietnam.

Almost a decade ago I wrote, noting the connection between domestic social criticism and the anti-war protest:

> . . . indignation about American intervention in Vietnam had sources other than the aggrieved concern with the consequences of the war per se. Vietnam mobilized the rejection, criticism or hatred, as the case maybe, of American society that had been dormant or partially articulated earlier. The war gave new vehemence and assurance to the social critics who languished during the . . . 50s without major issues or causes that could have [in the words of Sontag] 'offered the key to a systematic criticism of America.' Vietnam was more a catalyst than a root cause of the rejection of American society in the 1960s. It confirmed all lurking apprehensions about the United States among the critically disposed and the estranged.[12]

I am not suggesting that all war critics displayed an estranged sensibility, or were profoundly alienated. There were many who were able and willing to separate the critiques of the American involvement from the sweeping rejection of the entire American social-political system and its basic values. But for many influential critics, and certainly for those whose views increasingly dominated the public discourse, there was an irresistible temptation to find an instrinsic connection between an unjust war and an unjust society. For Daniel Berrigan "The American ghetto and the Hanoi 'operation' were a single enterprise—total war in both cases."[13]

Such perceptions became highly influential in part because they were expressed with great moral passion and emotional fervor and because they were embraced by the educated young whose views are often given special authenticity and grace in American culture. In turn the mass media gave prominence to the most dramatic denunciations of U.S. policy.

What were the themes of social criticism which converged with the critiques of American involvement in the war?

In all strongly felt social criticism—and even in the deterministic and allegedly scientific varieties of Marx and his followers—some evil entity must be identified, personified and exposed. Impassioned social critics are not in the habit of invoking impersonal social forces, unintended consequences or errors made in good faith. Some form of ill will, malice or deformity of character must be uncovered and the perpetrators of evil not allowed to escape into the realm of historical determinism,—in short, personal responsibility must be established (and magnified) otherwise the critic and his audience could not rise to gratifying moral indignation. By contrast, opposed to the wrongdoers fully responsible for their behavior are those who "have no choice but . . ."—groups or individuals looked upon with favor, as for example the student rebels of the 1960s setting fire to ROTC buildings in order to get some attention, or the hard pressed Vietcong reluctantly murdering civilians in government employ. When the favored political actors engage in questionable actions such determinism provides instant moral insurance and absolution. The 1960s was a period rich in examples of selective moral indignation and the associated selective social determinism.[14]

In the opinion of many antiwar critics American policymakers were not merely misguided but malevolent. Conor Cruise O'Brien among others, suggested that civilian casualties were willfully inflicted. Discussing the condition of a North Vietnamese child severely injured in a bombing raid he wrote:

> From the type of weapons . . . used against the North Vietnamese and the conditions in which they are used, as reported by observers like Mr H. Salisbury and Mr Gerassi, and from Mr McNamara's statement, it becomes evident that the fate of this child is not a by-product of military necessity but is an intended result, satisfactory to those who make policy in Washington.[15]

He also suggested that it was the self esteem of high American officials—and the injury to it—that led them to resort to such repugnant means of conducting the war.[16] In turn Richard Barnet and Marcus Raskin suggested that the Vietnam war was a manifestation of "the disease of an entire ruling class"; they too were persuaded that it was deliberate American policy "to create widespread civilian casualties."[17]

Such assessments were common at the time; many war critics viewed the American political-military establishment as harboring singularly depraved and amoral individuals, comparable to the Nazi war criminals of World War II. Only a profoundly flawed social system could produce such people and elevate them into positions of power— so the argument ran.

There were other important themes of social criticism borne along the tides of the war protest. Capitalism was certainly implicated. Stokeley Carmichael, for example earnestly argued that "the 'real' reason the United States was fighting the Vietnam war was 'to serve the economic interests of American businessmen who are in Vietnam solely to exploit the tungsten, tin and oil . . .' "[18] More commonly it was held that the war—as always—was good for business, thus favored by the military-industrial complex. Social critics who found competition and competitiveness a particularly abhorrent trait of capitalism and American culture argued that war was the supreme and most deadly expression of such impulses.

Feminists in turn claimed that the war was an age old expression of machismo, intimately tied to the sexist nature of American culture.

It was also possible to link racism to the war by pointing out that a high proportion of casualties were black and by claiming that the brutal ways in which the war was fought reflected a latent racism since the victims, the Vietnamese were not white people, hence could be treated ruthlessly.

The critiques of modern technology and applied science were also easily integrated with the critiques of the war as it was often claimed that American technology—by providing highly destructive weapons— played a particularly odious role in the conflict. This proposition was usually combined with the idea that American culture in general was singularly prone to misuse technology and allow it to destroy the physical environment and even impair both work satisfaction and personal relationships through its standardized impersonality. Norman Mailer provided a memorable formulation of this criticism as he linked packaged bread to the technology of war:

> The sliced loaf half collapsed in its wax paper was the embodiment . . .
> of corporation land which took the taste and crust out of bread and . . .
> was, at the far extension of this same process, the same mentality which
> was out in Asia, escalating, defoliating . . . the white bread was also
> television . . .[19]

The critiques of technology were frequently joined to the rejection
of bureaucracy, impersonality and hierarchy—aspects of American life
felt to be especially intolerable and stifling during the 1960s and
plausibly associated with the military establishment. (In the memorable words of a highly articulate draft resister of the times: ". . .
America as bully . . . taking everybody's natural resources, bleeding
all these little countries and shit like that, imperialism et cetera,
building cars so they will fall apart, the whole waste-greed trip, you
know, was a drag."[20]

The heightened anti-authoritarian attitudes of the times also played
a part in the antiwar movement intensifying its anti-militarism. The
characteristics of military service defied every countercultural value
and attitude as they required subordination, discipline, obedience to
authority, impulse control, deferred gratification, a tightly routinized
existence, specialization, mastery of technology and restraint over
individualistic self expression—all of them unacceptable infringements
of personal freedom and individual choice from the point of view of
the war critics and protestors.

What of the moral judgments of the adversary? It is to say the least
that the critical impulses and sentiments radiating from the war protestors invariably by passed the Vietcong or the North Vietnamese; there
was little if any moral and intellectual energy left for scrutinising their
methods of warfare, their political values and objectives, their civilian
victims, their treatment of prisoners of war, their propaganda and
conception of ends and means. There was either silence about these
matters or outright idealization and support: Ho Chi Minh chants,
Vietcong flags reverentially carried, friendly delegations touring North
Vietnam and returning with glowing reports of the humanity of the
regime and its leaders. Ramsey Clark returned with the news that there
was no crime and "no internal conflict" in North Vietnam[21]; Sontag
was surprised to find an absence of "existential agony [and] alienation
. . . among the Vietnamese . . ." and was struck by their "grace,
variety and established identity."[22] The visit to North Vietnam induced
in Daniel Berrigan a "dreamlike trance" (his words) and he discovered
"a naive faith in human goodness . . . powerfully operative in North
Vietnamese society."[23] Staughton Lynd and Tom Hayden were most

impressed by "the unembarrassed handclasps among men, the poetry and song at the center of man-woman relationships . . . [and they] began to understand the possibilities for a socialism of the heart."[24] For Barnet and Raskin "The 'communist menace' turned out to be old ladies and young boys in black pajamas fighting for their homes."[25] Mary McCarthy, more candid than many others, stated her *preference* not to believe that the communist forces had anything to do with the Hue massacres.[26] Orwell had anticipated these attitudes when he wrote: "Actions are held good or bad, not on their own merits but according to who does them, and there is almost no kind of outrage— torture, the use of hostages, forced labor, mass deportations, imprisonment without trial, forgery, assassinations, the bombing of civilians—which does not change its moral color when it is committed by 'our' side."[27]

It was the determined and single-minded preoccupation with the ills of American society that has given rise to these double standards and to the illusions about the moral and cultural superiority of the North Vietnamese. The media made it easier to harbor such attitudes by not reporting or paying little attention to Vietcong atrocities which were, to be sure, more difficult to "cover". But even when information was available, as in the case of the Hue massacres, it had little impact on the critics of American policies. Such incidents, if noted, were regarded regrettable, a part of the war and especially civil war, and somehow still the responsibility of the U.S. In the same spirit the Pol Pot massacres were blamed on American bombing of Cambodia.[28] Although these raids predated the massacres by several years they supposedly made the Khmer Rouge tense, nervous, beleagured and hence (?!) genocidal, as was for example suggested in the film "Killing Fields".

The persistence of these attitudes was also revealed in the exceedingly hostile critical reception of a movie "The Hanoi Hilton" which documented the mistreatment of captured American pilots.[29] Such a vivid visual evocation of the inhuman behavior of the communist side was unacceptable for many erstwhile war critics since their attitudes were built in part on the premise (illustrated above) that our enemies were decent people and that it was the American not the communist side which conducted itself in a dishonorable way. If it were to be admitted that the other side was cruel and inhumane, (for instance in its treatment of captured pilots) the unconditional condemnation of American involvement in the war would have been shaken, the critiques of American conduct somewhat neutralized. The high intensity antiwar criticism could be sustained only on the assumption that the enemy was basically good and honorable (defending their homes bravely against our unwarranted, immoral assault) and the American side evil and unscrupulous. It was not easy to find war critics while the war was waged who maintained simultaneously that the United States had no business to fight a war in Southeast Asia although admittedly its enemies were quite despicable and represented a highly repressive political system.

Not surprisingly the boatpeople and the reeducation camps which were among the consequences of American withdrawal also failed to arouse the moral passion and compassion of those who remained fixated on the shortcomings of American foreign policy and domestic institutions; they retained the conviction that the U.S. was responsible for all the evils of the Vietnam war and its aftermath. There were both indifference toward and outright denial of communist atrocities as in the memorable *NY Times* advertisement signed by the most ardent supporters of North Vietnam (such as Richard Barnet, David Dellinger, Richard Falk, Corliss Lamont, Paul Sweezey and Cora Weiss.) The advertisement asserted, among other things that "The present government in Vietnam should be hailed for its moderation and extraordinary effort to achieve reconciliation among all its people . . ."[30] Two years later a much diminished group of diehards still insisted, in a macabre fashion, that "Vietnam now enjoys human rights as it has never known in its history."[31]

Not only have many former war critics and sympathizers given their continued moral support to the communist authorities in Vietnam after the war ended, some of them journeyed there to partake in conducted tours. Thus a group of (mostly Methodist) church officials were taken to a model "reeducation camp" and returned greatly moved by these humane institutions—as were their predecessors by the model camps and prisons in Stalin's Russia and Mao's China.[32]

Those like the visiting churchmen who continued to give every benefit of doubt to the Vietnamese authorities remained relentless critics of American society—a disposition which still functioned to provide the major emotional underpinning for their sympathy toward countries, governments or movements they saw as victimised by the United States. As at other historical junctions, hostility toward American society and sympathy toward its foreign critics and adversaries, (and putative victims) were inextricably interwoven.

Vietnam also provided a major boost and legitimation for the anti-anti-communist persuasion: more than ever before it was plausible to maintain that anti-communism leads to ruinous foreign policies and military involvements. More than ever before it was possible to argue that opposing communist movements and systems is foolish, imprudent or worse and that anti-communist policies are immoral and lead to a destructive outcome. Thus a major result of American participation in the Vietnam war was not merely the upsurge of isolationism but also the strengthening of the anti-anti-communist impulse by now deeply rooted in the intelligentsia and influential in the political culture at large.

To be sure the revival of anti-anti-communism has also been associated with the peace and anti-nuclear movements which too were ready to conjure up and dwell on the dangers of anti-communism and its deadly consequences, that is, increasing tensions with the Soviet Union that could ultimately lead to nuclear catastrophy.[33]

The alternation of moral absolutism and moral relativism—the former aimed at American society the latter reserved for its adversaries—provides the best explanation of the attitudes here discussed. This alternation in turn is predictably regulated by political values which underlie the ebb and flow of moral impulses and judgements.

Thus in the final analysis the committment to high-minded social criticism such as displayed by the antiwar protestors may bring about unintended consequences including indifference to political repression—if perpetrated by those who share the aversion the critics harbor toward their own society, and if the critics' own professed moral standards are violated in the name of a higher morality or the alleged imperatives of historical necessity.

Notes

1. Based on a paper presented at a conference on "The Debate on Vietnam" at the Center for Law and National Security, Law School, University of Virginia (Charlottesville), in October 1986
2. Michael Medved, "60s Generation Should't Be So Smug", *Wall Street Journal*, 1986, (April 28).
3. Richard J. Barnet and Marcus Raskin, *An American Manifesto*, New York: New American Library, 1970, p. 24.
4. Tom Hayden, *The Love of Possessions is a Disease with Them*, New York: Holt, Rinehart & Winston, 1978, p. 98.
5. Paul Hollander, "The Survival of the Adversary Culture", *Partisan Review*, 1986, (No. 3., July).
6. See for example Lissa Roche, ed. *Scorpions in a Bottle*, Hillsdale: Hillsdale College Press, 1986; and Melvin J. Lasky, "The Doctrine of Moral Equivalence", *Encounter*, 1985, (December).
7. Barrington Moore Jr., *Reflections on the Causes of Human Misery*, Boston: Beacon Press, 1972, p. 3.
8. Paul Hollander, *Political Pilgrims*, New York: Oxford University Press and Harper & Row, 1981, 1983, pp. 182–183.

9. Susan Sontag, *Trip to Hanoi*, New York, Farrar, Giroux & Straus, 1968, p. 87.
10. Jerry Rubin, *Do It*, New York: Simon & Schuster, 1970, p. 105.
11. Barnet and Raskin, *cited*, 1970, pp. 23–24.
12. Hollander, *cited*, 1981, 1983, p. 198.
13. Daniel Berrigan, *Night Flight to Hanoi*, New York: Macmillan, 1969, XIV.
14. On the latter see Paul Hollander, "Sociology, Selective Determinism and the Rise of Expectations", *American Sociologist*, 1973, (November).
15. John Gerassi, *North: A Documentary* With an Introduction by Conor Cruise O'Brien, Indianapolis; Bobbs-Merill, 1968, p. 14.
16. Gerassi, *cited*, 1968, p. 15.
17. Joshua Muravchik, "The Think Tank on the Left", *New York Times Magazine*, April 26, 1981, p. 42.
18. Stokeley Carmichael, "Carmichael to Take Part in War Protest April 15th", *New York Times*, 1967 (March 30).
19. Norman Mailer, *The Armies of the Night*, New York: New American Library 1968, p. 77.
20. Roger Neville Williams, *The New Exiles—American War Resisters in Canada*, New York: Liveright, 1971, p. 154.
21. Ramsey Clark, "Clark's Hanoi Comments", *New York Times*, October 25, 1974.
22. Sontag, *cited*, 1968, pp. 69. 77.
23. Berrigan, *cited*, 1969, pp. 45, 79.
24. Staughton Lynd and Tom Hayden, *The Other Side*, New York: New American Library 1967, pp. 58, 62.
25. Barnet and Raskin, *cited*, 1970, p. 25.
26. Joan Colebrook, "Prisoners of War", *Commentary*, 1974 (January) p.36.
27. George Orwell, *The Collected Essays*, New York: Harcourt, Brace Jovanich, 1968, Vol. 3.: p. 369.
28. William Shawcross: *Sideshow: Kissinger, Nixon and the Destruction of Cambodia*, New York: Simon & Schuster, 1979.
29. *Insight* "The Suppression of the Hanoi Hilton," 1987, (June 8).
30. Advertisement I.: "Vietnam: A Time for Healing and Compassion", *New York Times*, 1977, (January 30).
31. Advertisement II.: "The Truth About Vietnam", *New York Times*, 1979, (June 24).
32. *Mainline Churches and Radical Social Witness*, Institute on Religion and Democracy, Washington, D.C., 1983.
33. William Philips, "Intellectuals and Politics", *Partisan Review*, No. 4, 1983, p. 600.

11
Further Explorations in the Theories and Practices of Socialism

Books on the theories and contemporary incarnations of socialism continue to come forth in a seemingly endless stream. They fall into several categories. There are, to begin with, authors limiting themselves to the theories of socialism (usually Marxism of some variety and interpretations) and averting their eyes from existing socialist societies, or at any rate, societies which claim to be socialist and have succeeded, by and large, in making Western public opinion accept the claim. Writers of this type are capable of discoursing on the fine points of theory and its conflicting interpretations, as if the practices followed in the name of the theory raised no questions whatsoever about the validity or relevance of the theory in our times. Books in this group are permeated by at least an implicit belief in socialism which, however, need not have an identifiable historical or geographical focus or incarnation. At the same time, many authors of this persuasion are motivated by fervent anticapitalist sentiments, take the desirability of socialism for granted (undisturbed by the problems of its attempted introduction) and seek the transformation of their own Western society along socialist lines.

Another approach, by contrast, focuses on particular countries or social systems which claim the socialist credentials and seeks to understand the degree of correspondence with or divergence from the original socialist ideals, and it may offer explanations of the gap between theory and practice.

There are several explanations of the persisting interest in the theories and ideals of socialism associated with Marxism. The first may well be the continued, nagging discontent felt by many Western intellectuals with their own societies and their recurring attempts to transform them, to find alternatives. The second explanation is the very existence of societies which are supposedly socialist and the disputes generated by their characteristics, and especially their deviations from the ideals of socialism. Ever since the establishment of the Soviet regime in 1917 until the recent rise of "Nicaraguan socialism," the expectation has been that the latest incarnation of the socialist ideals will be *the* authentic one; each time the collapse of such hopes has led to a renewed search for a new incarnation. This point leads to the most likely explanation of the persisting appeals of socialism: the search for faith or redeeming values in Western societies. Evidently neither the return to more traditional religious values nor the various innovative spiritual gropings of recent times have provided intellectuals with lasting satisfaction and met their needs for meaning, sense of community, and social justice. Hence socialism, a much bedraggled ideal (and the associated secular humanism) is all they are left with.

The two books by Feher, Heller, and Markus[1] (Hungarian emigres of comparatively recent vintage) and *Confiscated Power*[2] by d'Encausse are enlightening additions to the literature on socialist, or, as some of these authors call them, "Soviet type" societies. Thất a reviewer in 1985 should praise books for providing essential information about such societies is a good indication of the surprisingly limited progress which has been made in understanding such political systems in the West. Thus grotesque stereotypes and profound misunderstandings, embedded in vast undifferentiated ignorance, are still plentiful today in the media and among the educated public and politicians.

Let me mention here only two recent and related developments which tellingly illustrate the continued public misapprehension of the nature of Soviet type societies. One is the spread of the unilateralist sentiment and the other, less well known but even more revealing, is the so-called Ground Zero Pairing Project in this country. The major flaws of unilateralism have been dissected often enough (among others, by Sidney Hook in parts of his volume here reviewed). It should suffice to say that it is wrong because: *a.* it assumes that *Western* disarmament will, once and for all, remove the threat of nuclear war (ignoring the possibility of such a conflict between Communist regimes); *b.* it invites the alternative of nuclear war or submission to Soviet power (better red than dead).

The Ground Zero Pairing Project seeks to match American towns and cities with what are (mistakenly) assumed to be their Soviet counterparts and establish informal, nongovernmental contacts between citizens of such "matched" communities in the belief that they will discover their common humanity and shared interest in survival through such apolitical contacts. It is further postulated that once this happens, each in their own country will start exerting pressure on their respective governments to disarm or reduce their nuclear arsenal and pursue more peaceful policies. The Ground Zero Pairing Project has released across the United States (including academic communities with a highly educated population) vast reservoirs of ignorance and naivete about the Soviet Union, providing fresh evidence of how little progress has been made over the years in understanding the character of Soviet society. (Four major flaws of this approach may be noted here briefly. They include the belief that ordinary Soviet citizens can engage in informal, nongovernmental contacts with citizens of the United States; that they can bring to bear pressure on their government to modify its policies or propose new policies; that they would be willing to propose policies different from those already publicly embraced by their government; and that the "discovery" of common human characteristics such as love of one's children, the interest in certain recreational activities, the preference for peace over war, etc., will transcend historical-political-cultural differences between the two political systems.)

The fear of nuclear war as a factor in the current development (or stagnation) of public and even elite understanding of the Soviet Union cannot be underestimated. Unilateralists, freeze supporters, and pairing project enthusiasts are at one in their desire to redefine—overtly or subliminally—the nature of the Soviet system in order to justify their hopes and wishes. For those bent on such a wishful redefinition of the Soviet regime, it is essential to substitute for the image of a system expanding its political and military influence that of a political system which responds to the needs and wishes of its citizens.

There have been echoes of the popular wishes and fears among Soviet specialists too. It will be recalled how, for example, Andropov's rise to power prompted a wave of wishful speculation about the enlightened and rational policies this supposedly Westernized political figure was to initiate; more recently we were assured by Mr. Armand Hammer (on the op-ed page of *The New York Times*) that the new leader, Chernenko, is the one "we can work with." (Mr. Hammer managed to work with them all.)

One of the major accomplishments of *Dictatorship over Needs,* perhaps the most substantial of the volumes here reviewed, is its serious and sustained effort to come to grips with the question: Are the contemporary societies generally considered socialist, socialist indeed? It is hard to overestimate the importance of systematically confronting this question since there has always been a tendency in the West to go along with the self-characterization of societies which assert that they are socialist. But terminology matters. Even when critics of such societies observe their shortcomings while bestowing on them the "socialist" label, they concede something of importance, some basic if limited legitimacy and moral virtue which by implication capitalist democracies are devoid of. And even those who dispute the "socialism" of these societies seem to acquiesce in their usurpation of the appellation.

This state of affairs, in turn, allows these countries to harvest at least the residual goodwill of Western idealists and become beneficiaries of their benefit of doubt. Displaying the socialist label thus becomes at least a proof of good intentions—if not results; in turn such intentions tend to disarm Western intellectuals, who rarely devote to the analysis of societies so labelled the same emotional energy and determination to locate the gaps between theory and practice they display in the study and criticism of their own societies.

Feher, Heller, and Markus go a long way toward demolishing the self-serving claims of putatively socialist societies. Moreover, they suggest that there is *some* connection between the deformations of practice and the theories which inspired them:

> . . . since socialism does not exist except as the sum of its historically existing varieties, nineteenth and early twentieth-century socialist doctrines are at least co-responsible for the "real socialism" of today, even if we reassert our statement that the upshot is not socialism in any meaningful sense of the term.

They locate, as a key problem in the realization of socialist ideals, ". . . a very wide gap between an uncritically maintained idea of human perfectibility . . . as the public doctrine and that of virtue in minority, a desperately pessimistic view of human substance, as the secret doctrine."

While regarding themselves as "radical socialists," they tell the reader in the first sentence of the book that "the emotional and intellectual motivation for writing this book was the exact obverse of the French maxim: *tout comprendre, c'est tout pardonner*. By contrast . . . we sought to understand the whole of 'real socialism' in order critically to expose this new and formidable system of internal and external oppression. . . ." In particular, they sought to speak to Western leftists whom they correctly regard as harboring illusions and misconceptions about existing "socialist" regimes. Not surprisingly, central to the argument of the authors is the link between socialism and democracy ("we cannot conceive of socialism without democracy"). Correspondingly, one of the goals of the study is to strip regimes calling themselves socialist of their "socialist facade"; hence the term "dictatorship over needs" is useful in reminding the reader that they *are* dictatorships and that they are dictatorships of a novel kind, more ambitious and more comprehensive than the many other varieties of repression history has produced. Here one should also note that the authors do not recoil from using the concept of totalitarianism. They point out that:

> . . . in a totalitarian society the identification of public and private goes hand-in-hand with the definition of the obligatory creed and politics of the subject by the state. . . . All present East European societies are totalitarian, independently of the degree of their pluralism-tolerance. In them pluralism has been outlawed to just as great an extent as before and this is precisely what totalitarianism by definition means.

Unlike many Western students of Soviet type societies, Feher, Heller, and Markus do not confuse the patterns of domination in such systems with bureaucratization per se. They are cognizant of the uniqueness of Soviet type bureaucracies, "not characterized by formal rationality." Moreover, "the Soviet bureaucracy *has* to be inefficient in order to accomplish its true aim: to stem the tide, to defer the satisfaction of the population's needs. . . . Its function is primarily to practice dictatorship over needs. . . . " Along these lines they also shed new light on the matter of rationality many foreign observers and sympathizers have mistakenly associated with supposedly socialist regimes:

> Anyone entering these societies from the world of calculative rationality has, as first impression, the feeling that he has arrived in Bedlam. Nothing functions, or at least nothing does in the way one would expect having been brought up in the spirit of rationalist standards . . .

Elsewhere they observe:

> . . . one of the basic experiences familiar to any citizen of an Eastern European society—the experience of impotent rage when confronted with the sheer irrationality of this acclaimed logic of planning, expressed in the production of waste . . . and in a staggering overdevelopment of the unproductive apparatus of organization and control. Both are organic features of an economic structure where the only connection between consumption and production is realized through the administrative decisions of a centralized and hierarchical bureaucracy.

In short, these regimes are characterized by the "simultaneous production of waste and scarcity"; they "systematically produce and reproduce artificial shortages."

Full employment, the major accomplishment of these societies, is also subjected to critical scrutiny:

> According to the formulation of the constitution, "right to work" means guaranteed employment. It entails however something else too, namely compulsory employment. . . .
>
> . . . the right to work coexists in these societies with the legal obligation to work enforced through punitive measures . . . it does not mean the obligation to earn a living through one's own labor . . . but the obligation to earn it in administratively recognized jobs and places of work, and in this way it is an important element of the general social-political control over the population.

Unlike many American commentators on Soviet domestic problems, our three authors do not believe that the economic weaknesses observed exert pressure on the Soviet Union to scale down its global involvements and aspirations:

> It is no exaggeration to say that the Soviet empire's leap forward has been taken to escape from internally unresolvable problems. . . . The real motivating force of Soviet imperialism is the utopia of Soviet leaders, that by eliminating world capitalism they could eliminate "dissenting wishes" from the minds of their subjects. . . . in the last fifteen years . . . the Soviet Union has launched a type of foreign politics practically unknown in its preceding history, that of political imperialism. . . . The goal is to increase political influence and gain dominance in new spheres all over the world . . . the perfection of the army is the main target: only a strong army can back imperial politics.

They also note an affinity between the Soviet regime, its foreign policies, and many Third World dictatorships:

> . . . the "export of revolution" means largely the export of the oppressive technology of government perfected by the Soviet apparatus, which certain local power elites are only too eager to take over. . . . They are Bolshevik in the important sense that the Bolshevik technology of oppression appeals to them. . . .

It is worthy of note that the authors of a study which so illuminatingly and mercilessly catalogues the defects of political systems claiming to have been inspired by Marxism continue to see themselves as Marxists or "radical socialists." Moreover, unlike many other intellectuals in the West, they don't flinch from entertaining the possibility (as indicated in an earlier quote) that there may be *some* connection between the theory and the practices it had unwittingly inspired. If so, their clinging to a Marxist identity is at least mildly puzzling. Perhaps Sidney Hook's observation[3] (in his writings here reviewed) may apply to their case as well:

> . . . today when a person characterizes himself as a Marxist, we no more know what he really believes than we do when a person claims to be a Christian.

Hungary 1956 Revisited by Feher and Heller is a short study of a recent revolutionary attempt to redress the huge imbalance between theory and practice. It is also a reinterpretation of the 1956 revolt and its aftermath with more than a few references to the new order which replaced both the aspirations of the revolution and its Stalinist antecedents.

The authors do not share the Western euphoria over the accomplishments of the Kadar regime ("an enlightened police state" they call it) or what Khrushchev called "goulash communism" and caution against "confusing pacification with legitimation." They believe that its Western popularity is in part connected with guilt feelings over the failure of the West to do anything constructive in 1956 (yet things did not turn out that badly) and in part a product of a condescending attitude toward Eastern Europe which must not expect anything significantly less authoritarian. I would add yet another reason. The Western celebration of Kadar's Hungary is also, at least unconsciously, motivated by the desire to conjure up a less threatening image of the Soviet Union and its domain. Surely, if the Soviet regime allows within its empire as much political and economic freedom as Hungary has obtained, this shows that it has become a more reasonable power with which the West can do business and coexist in détente happily ever after.

The new element in their interpretation of the revolt is somewhat strained and appears to be a product of the desire to apportion blame for its defeat evenhandedly between the Soviet Union and Western powers. Needless to say, the Western powers share responsibility for the Yalta and Potsdam agreements which delivered Eastern Europe into the Soviet orbit. But it is a rather big leap from this proposition to suggest that "despite the 'false consciousness' of many Hungarians in revolt, their rebellion was directed against *all* signatories of the Yalta and Potsdam agreements, against the Western protagonists as well as the Eastern." The authors also argue—perhaps again in order to blame both superpowers for the defeat of the Hungarian Revolution—that the latter presented unique opportunities for the United States to enter into negotiations with the Soviet Union and "end the cold war."

Such reservations notwithstanding, this is basically a judicious reassessment of what the revolution did and did not try to accomplish and what its impact has been on Hungary and the rest of the world.

Confiscated Power is one of the more ambitious overviews of the Soviet system to appear in recent years. It represents a rewarding combination of political, sociological, and historical perspectives, and it makes use of a great variety of Soviet sources, including sociological data. The volume strikes a careful balance between approaches which stress the vulnerabilities of the Soviet system and those which treat it as virtually immutable. Yet, for good reasons, the author emphasizes the factors which make for the stability of the system, preeminent among them the bureaucracy and the techniques of socialization. She writes:

> The improvements made in the system of government have transformed a bloody personal tyranny into the administrative dictatorship of an oligarchy. But this transformation has not changed the basis of the system . . .

It is among the virtues of this volume that it offers both sweeping generalizations (well-grounded in data) about Soviet political institutions and practices and specific details about the workings of the system. Of particular value are the discussions of the Party, the problem of succession, the function of elections and popular "participation," the success and failure of political socialization, the dimensions of dissent, the rise of religious and nationalistic feelings—all of which add up to a carefully drawn and persuasive balance sheet of the strengths and weaknesses of the system. It is a remarkable book because of the author's ability to grasp and articulate the contradictory facets of Soviet society. Thus, for instance, on the one hand:

> . . . 8 million people in all are permanently charged with supervising and instructing Soviet society. In this network of convergent training systems and activities, all of which spread the same ideas and values, the life of the ordinary citizen . . . leaves little room for personal reflection and the search for other sources of information.

At the same time:

> In a survey carried out in the early seventies in a Leningrad factory 75% of the workers questioned about what motivated their attendance as political training sessions answered that they attended meetings because they were forced to. . . .

Young people in particular ". . . seem to brush aside everything that has to do with politics," and their occupational aspirations significantly diverge from the prescriptions of the authorities. Data from readership surveys also attest to the apolitical disposition of the majority of Soviet people.

Although social mobilization replaced coercion, the authorities will not accept "associations established outside their control." Social mobilization, or what I prefer to call pseudo-participation, is designed to occupy "the totality of social space in order to leave room for no possibility of mobilization or organization foreign to it."

While much has been made among some Western Sovietologists about the rise of interest groups in Soviet society sometimes leading to the attribution of pluralism to the system, d'Encausse reminds us that although the Politburo has become "the place where the various bureaucratic apparatuses were represented," this does not mean that the Soviet power "has evolved toward institutional pluralism" since "the Party remains the integrating element . . . the Party exercises . . . arbitration."

What has certainly not changed is the "will to power [that] allows the political system to survive, to impose itself on rebellious or sceptical societies. . . ." It is the will to power that links domestic and foreign policies and seeks to compensate for domestic stagnation by foreign initiatives:

> Domestically, the authorities have encountered nothing but increasing difficulties . . . to which they have opposed an inflexible attachment to the foundations of the system and total immobility. But in foreign affairs the same authorities have demonstrated a flexibility and dynamism that have enabled them to raise the U.S.S.R. to the rank of the United States. . . . In foreign affairs the prudent septuagenarians of the Kremlin have been audacious and innovative statesmen taking all governments by surprise with their untold initiatives.

Many Western policy-makers have been unable to grasp the fact that the Soviet Union has, for a long time, pursued a "dual policy— 'détente' on the one side, destabilization on the other." Hence there is a corresponding duality to the Soviet system, at once "a vulnerable country . . . and a triumphant power." The dynamic foreign policy pursued under Brezhnev (himself an undynamic person) served, among other things, the purpose of "derive[ing] legitimacy from external successes. Is the progress of communism in the world not irrefutable evidence of the Party's historic mission?"

Last but not least, the character of Soviet policies, indeed of the nature of the system, is also related to the policies and postures of the Western powers. The book ends on this somber note:

> Simulataneously weak and powerful, the U.S.S.R. has based its power above all on the impotence of the capitalist world, and it justifies the continuation of a weakened and challenged system by invoking the weaknesses and challenges to the alternative system. . . . Who will be the first, the U.S.S.R. or the West to be defeated by its own decline?

Written before the death of both Brezhnev and Andropov, there are only two brief references to the current leader, Chernenko, neither suggesting his possible rise to power.

The translation often does not do justice to the rich substance of this study; as some of the quotes also show, the style is often awkward and unpolished.

The Forward March of Labour Halted?[4] is an uneven collection of scholarly and political commentaries over the failure of the English working class and the Labor Party to transform society along putatively socialist lines. Of the twenty contributors, three are academics, two journalists, and the rest assorted political and union activists and functionaries; the best known among the latter group is Tony Benn, leader of the left wing of the Labor Party. The volume is organized around the title essay by Eric Hobsbawm, which is discussed by other contributors who also include several functionaries of the British Communist Party. An air of left wing-popular front attitudes hangs over these writings, often colored by the agitprop jargon of olden times which evidently survives in these circles. For instance, thus writes Mike Le Cornu, identified as a shop steward at Heathrow airport:

> I believe we should face up to the possibility that it is the failure of our party and the left consciously to inject the necessary political content into the struggle which has largely contributed to the "forward march of labour" having halted, though I agree with Kevin Halpin that to describe the movement as having "halted" appears to be a negation of the Marxist concept of constant change.

The same author chastises another contributor for lacking "that deep analytical content based on a scientific approach to the problem." A key and recurring idea of the volume, and especially of Hobsbawm's piece, is "the period of world crisis for capitalism." The authors take many things for granted. Thus the question is hardly raised, let alone answered: Where precisely would labor march forward, or what exactly would socialism in Britain seek to achieve, and what if any lessons have been learned from existing systems which claim to be socialist? Even Raymond Williams talks about "imperialism" as if the concept would self-evidently and singularly apply only to the United States and former Western colonial powers, and sees the world as ". . . the deadly military confrontation between the imperialist alliance [presumably NATO—P.H.] and now powerfully established socialist states. . . ." although of the latter he adds "most of these new states not of our own kind of foreseeing or desire." Still he calls them socialist. Hobsbawm by contrast evinces greater sensitivity to the problems of socialism in practice as he mentions "the crisis of bureaucratization in the Soviet Union and Eastern Europe." In this and a few other fleeting references, he succeeds at least occasionally to rise above the singularly British concerns of the volume.

Marxism and Beyond is a collection of eighteen pieces, some of which directly address the most crucial issues in the interpretation and application of Marxism, while others range over topics which include the Frankfurt School (an especially outstanding piece), "Lenin and the Communist International," "Communism and the American Intellectuals from the Thirties to the Eighties," "A Critique of Conservatism," "In Defense of the Cold War, *Neither Red Nor Dead,*" as well as critiques of authors dealing with problems of Marxism, Stalinism, and American society. Such diverse pieces are held together by an uncommon degree of lucidity, a profound knowledge of Marxism and political theory in general, and the author's commitment to what are the most important and enduring Western values. Especially impressive is Hook's capacity to write about abstruse issues of Marxism without the ponderousness and opaqueness that attend mosi similar discussions. A major thrust of the volume and of the lead essay is the clarification of the divergence between the Marxism of Marx and that of Lenin, and of the political practices of all those legitimating their rule by invoking Marx's name in our times. Hook is particularly insightful and enlightening in explaining why Marxism has retained and even increased its appeals of late, notwithstanding its inapplicability to the modern world, its numerous erroneous predictions and blind spots.

He suggests that "Marxism is a monistic theory that offers an explanatory key to everything important that occurs in history and society. . . . It provides a never failing answer to the hunger for explanation among those adversely affected by the social process. . . ." To which one might add: and increasingly also for those not adversely affected—such as prosperous Western intellectuals—who nonetheless also hunger for such explanations and a coherent worldview. Secondly, all the more welcome at a time when the condition of mankind as a whole and of individual societies offers little to be cheerful about and the problems of secularization are far from overcome. While he fully understands the contemporary appeals of Marxism, he has little patience with those who seek to transform it into a theory of alienation on the basis of the early writings of Marx which his later mature work thoroughly contradicted. ("The doctrine of alienation . . . violates the entire historical approach of Marxism which denies that man has a natural or real or true self from which he can be alienated.")

Besides the various discussions of Marxism and its contemporary uses, misuses, and interpretations, there are also topical essays on current political controversies (such as disarmament and the cold war). The great value of these pieces lies in, among other things, their capacity to remind the reader what are the truly important differences between the Western world and Western values on the one hand and the multitudinous forms of authoritarianism in the world today. Few people have been more persuasive and forceful than Sidney Hook in arguing against the false alternative between nuclear war and Western surrender. He has for decades been a rare voice of reason in a chaotic world of changing intellectual fashions and dubious political commitments.

Sidney Hook is not only a defender of the humanist legacy of Marx against those who sought to legitimate their inhumane policies by his ideas; he also teaches us how to distinguish the liberating, democratic ideals of socialism from the wide variety of misuses they have been subjected to in our times, both as vindications of tyranny and escapist fantasies of limitless "self-realization."

Notes

1. *Dictatorship over Needs.* By Ferenc Feher, Agnes Heller, and Gyorgy Markus. St. Martin's Press; *Hungary 1956 Revisited.* By Ferenc Feher and Agnes Heller. Allen & Unwin.
2. *Confiscated Power.* By Helene Carrere d'Encausse. Harper & Row.
3. *Marxism and Beyond.* By Sidney Hook. Rowman and Littlefield.
4. *The Forward March of Labour Halted?* Ed. by Martin Jacques and Francis Mulhern. Blackwell Press Ltd.

12

American Intellectuals: Producers and Consumers of Social Criticism[1]

> *. . . judging by the rage and contempt emanating from books, paintings and films—never before have so many people taken up indictment as a pastime.*
>
> Czeslaw Milosz[2]

I.

For the past quarter century influential and vocal segments of the American intellectual community have been predominantly critical of American society. These attitudes entail a rejection or reflexive disparagement of the major American institutions and values, an aversion to the status quo and the powers-that-be as well as receptivity to the foreign critiques of the United States. Such a state of affairs has prevailed despite the decline of movements and activities associated with the 1960s, the rise of the so-called neo-conservative intellectuals and the continued employment of many intellectuals by the government as experts, advisors, consultants. The critiques of society also survived (indeed coexisted with) the "yuppies" and the "me-decade". In the words of Peter Berger (writing in 1976)". . . many of the radical impulses of 10 years ago have now become firmly institutionalized . . . within the intellectual milieau there has been a far-reaching delegitimation of some of the key institutions and values of American society . . ."[3] These attitudes have persisted notwithstanding the widespread belief that the Reagan years have been marked by the retreat or virtual disappearance of the adversarial dispositions associated with the social and political protests of the 1960s.

Whether or not one accepts or rejects these assessments depends in a large measure on how we define intellectuals and what we mean by social criticism? If intellectuals are defined broadly so as to include all those with higher qualifications and education, or all those involved with the production of ideas[4] without reference to the nature of the ideas involved, then clearly we cannot insist that all such people—geologists, accountants, computer programmers, zoologists, astronomers, therapists, entomologists, higher civil servants, industrial designers etc—are social critics. It is nonetheless possible to identify certain occupations associated with the production or interpretation of ideas which tend to have a high concentration of social critics and I will do so below.

Not only will our definition of who is an intellectual obviously determine our estimate of the incidence of social criticism among intellectuals, just as important is our understanding and perception of what constitutes social criticism. Such perceptions are significantly colored by ideological and psychological factors. This becomes especially clear when we talk about "*radical* social criticism" and estrangement (or alienation), or about "middle class radicalism" which rest on a moralistic discontent with the state of society and especially the divergence between social ideals and realities. Radicals of this type " . . . demand that their society . . . be judged by the highest possible standards and . . . expect it to adhere in international affairs to the kind of strict moral code relevant to the conduct of individuals . . ."[5]

There are many forms of social criticism or assertions about the state of society which seem so self evidently true and widely held that we take them for granted and hardly regard them as social criticism, let alone radical or estranged criticism. We have different thresholds for perceiving and identifying social criticism depending on our own view of the social world. Those generally content with the status quo will judge more statements as critical or strongly critical than those deeply hostile towards it. For those in the latter group few critiques will appear radical enough. One person's self-evidently true descriptive statement is another's alienated social criticism. In short our definition of what constitutes social criticism has an obvious bearing on our estimation of how much there is of it.

It should be noted here that since the 1960s, and the intense social discontent generated in that period, the political-ideological discourse has undergone considerable change in the United States: much of what had once been considered to be novel and radical social criticism has become assimilated (with or without some modifications) into mainstream social-cultural values. Notions of "moderate", "liberal", "radical" or "conservative" have been redefined in the light of the extremes of criticism and the "center" shifted toward the left. For example, while most American intellectuals today would not go on record claiming that American society represent a historically unique evil comparable to Nazi Germany—as many did in the 1960s—probably they would readily assent to the more moderate proposition that it is a deeply flawed society and not much, if at all, superior or preferable to other social systems.

These developments make the critiques of society which have been with us for decades less noticeable; we are so used to them we barely register them, just as we barely notice the billboards lining the road along a familiar route we take to work every day.

In evaluating the nature or quality of social criticism—and especially in trying to decide whether or not it is "radical" or "alienated"—it is also important how one views its origins or precipitants. It is one thing to regard social criticism a product of high and by implication unrealistic expectations, and quite another to see it as a rational response to the observable and indisputable malfunctioning of existing social institutions and the avoidable ills of society.

In the following my points of reference will not be all those who might, by some of the criteria noted above, be defined as intellectuals, but rather the more vocal and creative minority among them whose views and beliefs reach the general public through their publications and other public statements. We can only learn about the social criticism of intellectuals as it becomes disseminated in some observable and enduring manner. Social criticism voiced during private conversations, at cocktail parties or in the classroom is not without significance but we have little if any access to it.

Occasionally the beliefs of segments of the intellectual community, including those who do not publish (or make other public statement) become accessible through public opinion polls or survey research. Reference will be made to such data. However such investigations are rarely directed at "intellectuals" as such, this being an imprecise occupational category.

The more restricted conception of intellectuals here employed follows in part from the topic in question (which is the social role of American intellectuals as critics) and also from the traditional view of intellectuals, seen, among other things, as social critics and value-formulating elites.[6] In this perspective intellectuals are envisioned as both producers and interpreters of ideas, but ideas of a more general social, cultural or political nature. Intellectuals can be legitimizers, or servants of the status quo, but more often than not, they are critics, especially when they have a choice in the matter. They don't have much of a choice when the alternative to being a legitimizer (or supporter of the status quo) is the certitude of punitive sanctions which may range from the loss of occupation (relevant to training), to exile, imprisonment, and other forms of deprivation. Given such risks one cannot expect intellectuals to embrace the social-critical role in large numbers, especially in the Marxist-Leninist one-party regimes of our times which treat ideas as weapons. In these societies the social-political roles of intellectuals are determined to a far greater extent by the existing institutional structure than in Western, pluralistic societies such as the United States, where there is a real and risk free choice between becoming critic or legitimizer. (In some subcultural settings, i.e. some campuses, being a legitimizer may be a more difficult and risky role than being a critic.) Moreover in Western societies it is also possible to combine the roles of critic and "servant" of the status quo; many intellectuals may work for the government in some specialised capacity without being significantly inhibited or curtailed from expressing critical sentiments of a more general nature.

The evolution of intellectuals in Western societies as a critical and moralising elite (social criticism must have a moral basis) is in part a byproduct of secularization, of the decline of the virtual monopoly of the moralising functions by the clergy, or at any rate a decline of the credibility of such functions on the part of the clergy.

Today people who used to be called philosophers are called intellectuals; they do what philosophers used to do, or were supposed to do: reflect, meditate or pontificate in private and in public (or for public benefit at any rate) on a more or less full time basis on the great issues of life and death, society and the individual, things timely and timeless. As Michael Novak put it they are "a class of thinkers who comment on everything, who are in themselves in need of large general ideas and a vision of an ideal future."[7] Moreover they are supposed to be engaged in these activities in a disinterested, idealistic manner.

Sociologically speaking I locate the social-critical intellectuals in American society primarily in the institutions of higher education and especially in the schools and departments of the humanities and social sciences; other concentrations of such intellectuals can be found in the media, foundations, publishing houses and welfare related branches of the government and in church organizations; also among the so-called helping professions and among unaffiliated writers and literary critics.

A development which contributed to the current disputes regarding the nature and definition of intellectuals has been the proliferation of people who can claim intellectual status due to the expansion of higher education and other structural changes. As two American social scientists, Douglas and Wildavsky described the process:

> The United States produced more educated people than could be absorbed in industry; their talents tended to mobilize words and people.

As the size of the government expanded with the size of the economy, positions were created . . . Vast new cadres of employees in the arts, social sciences, and humanities generally, as well as in government, were set apart from those involved with industrial production . . . A larger proportion of the population of working age was disengaged from the production process than had been before. The economic boom and the educational boom together produced a cohort of articulate, critical people with no commitment to commerce and industry . . .[8]

These are people to whom the appellation "intellectual" is often congenial since it confers a somewhat elevated moral and social status, a basis for claiming membership in an elusive elite of the socially conscious and responsible.[9] Given the original conception of intellectuals as a small, nonconformist, often beleaguered minority on the battlefield of ideas—such as the French Encyclopedists or the 19th century Russian intelligentsia—it is hard to think of them as numbering in the millions. Such a quantitative change has also led to other transformations in the character of American intellectuals to be discussed below.

The social critical propensities of American intellectuals were not borne in the 1960s, although it was a period in which the critical temper was most strikingly and massively displayed. In the 1920s and 1930s there were similar outpourings of social criticism related to the economic crises of the period. Social historians will have no difficulty finding other, chronologically more distant manifestations of social criticism among American intellectuals connected with their unhappyness about living in a highly commercialized society that did not take ideas seriously enough.[10]

Even in periods of relative calm, such as the last decade, when the pendulum has swung away from militant protest and political unrest, a reflexive disparagement of American society has maintained itself and become, a new form of conventional wisdom, more or less taken for granted among the strata of population here discussed.

It is in fact one of the propositions of this essay that the contrasts between the 1960s—seen as the period of the most vocal rejection of American society in recent times—and the decade that followed (sometimes called the "me decade") as well as the 1980s, have been greatly overdrawn. To be sure the rejection of the status quo in the 1980s has been less frequently reflected in street demonstrations, uncompromising rhetoric, dramatic political gestures or the colorful proliferation of "alternative lifestyles". Recent manifestations of estrangement and social criticism tend to be more restrained and circumspect. Thus for example the suggestions and tone of a leaflet circulated in 1968 and endorsed at the time by Tom Hayden (who himself exemplifies the process of adopting a more restrained political behavior while retaining his old values from the 1960s)—seem somewhat inappropriate by the standards of the current forms of social criticism: "Burn your money . . . Break down the family, church, nature, city, economy . . . What is needed is a generation of people who are freaky, crazy, irrational, sexy, angry, irreligious, childish and mad. People who burn draft cards, burn high school and college degrees, people who say 'to hell with your goals!' People who . . . redefine the normal . . . who . . . have more in common with Indians plundered than they do with their own parents. Burn your houses down and you will be free."[11]

Today many people who harbor strong negative feelings about the prevailing social order work "within the system" but without any sense of allegiance towards it. It is not the basic values and attitudes of the critics that have changed but more typically their overt behavior and the methods advocated for radically changing the system. Thus for instance it is quite unlikely that Bernardine Dohrn, a former leader of the Weather Underground, who joined a prestigous law firm in New York has seriously modified her views of "the Establishment" still held when she surfaced from her underground life in 1980. At the time "She accused the U.S. of 'unspeakable crimes' and said she still believed 'in the necessity of underground work.' "[12] Likewise Staughton Lynd has switched from being a more or less full time anti-war activist and Vietcong sympathizer to the role of labor lawyer "helping workers in struggles with corporations and union leaders. His philosophy and confrontational tactics have not changed." Nor, one may add, his sympathy towards Marxist-Leninist regimes. He wrote in 1979: "I believe that Vietnamese communism, like Communism in the Soviet Union, China and Cuba, has improved the life of the majority . . . while repressing minorities." He as other social critics of the same (1960s) generation, has also retained a propensity to give every benefit of doubt to countries or political movements locked in conflict with the United States, having shifted his support from the Vietcong to Marxist Nicaragua.[13]

Examples of similar continuities in political belief could be readily multiplied.

II.

What are some of the main themes and characteristics of social criticism which span the period from the 1960s to the 1980s and continue to animate and command the agreement of a large numbers of American intellectuals?

Prominent among the traits of social criticism that has flourished since the 1960s has been an incapacity—willed or genuine—to discriminate between various symbols and symptoms of social evil and political-moral corruption. The polemical attribution of fascism to the United States was typical of this approach, as was the equation of My Lai with the Nazi death camps. Similar unwillingness or inability to differentiate is displayed when the temporary dispatch of American troops to Grenada—welcomed as liberators from the rule of a violent police state—is equated with eight years (as of this writing) of exceptionally brutal and secretive Soviet warfare in Afghanistan involving at least 120,000 troops and producing millions of refugees and hundreds of thousands of civilian casualties and the deliberate devastation of the countryside.

An impaired ability to discriminate is displayed in another context when New York literati, led by Norman Mailer, misidentifies a violent criminal, Jack Abbot as a great creative artist and authentic witness to the inhumanity of American society[14]: when Gore Vidal equates the military take-over in post-Solidarity Poland with the "occupation" of the United States by corporations[15] and (in the words of Lehman-Haupt) blames "the Chase Manhattan Bank for everything that is wrong in the contemporary world."[16] Nor were the powers of discernment in evidence when Arthur Miller asserted that the controls (exercised by the *NY Times*) over what is produced in American theatres are tighter than the censorship in Poland, Rumania, Czechoslovakia or the Soviet Union.[17]

The powers of discrimination were also overwhelmed by the social critical passion when George Wald, Nobel Prize winning scientist declared that "we Americans . . . are the most brainwashed people in the world"[18] and when Raymond Hunthausen, archbishop of Seattle observed ". . . that Trident [the American nuclear submarine] is the Auschwitz of Puget Sound."[19] Not to be outdone, Noam Chomsky referred to American schools as ". . . the first training ground for troops that will enforce the muted, unending terror of the status quo in the coming years of a projected American Century . . ."[20] In turn James Baldwin, the black writer wrote that "The educational system of this country is . . . designed to destroy the black child. It does not matter whether it destroys him by stoning him in the ghetto or by driving him mad in the isolation of Harvard."[21]

Reflecting on the enfeeblement of the powers of discrimination it may also be recalled that in the 1960s and early 70s not a few academic intellectuals entertained the opinion that college students were a new class of "Niggers" (for a prominent exposition of this viewpoint see Farber)[22] while Louis Kampf (former head of the Modern Language Association) deemed the Lincoln Center such a source of elitist corruption that he urged—in his "Notes Toward a Radical Culture" (!)—its defacement with substances rarely mentioned in polite conversation.[23]

Critiques of the evils of technology have also endured and flourished since the Vietnam war up to the present. The propensity to misuse technology was said to be a characteristic defect of American culture and society predisposing to the gratuitous and massive use of violence as argued, among others by Susan Sontag and Loren Baritz, the historian.[24] Other critics such as Richard Barnett and Marcus Raskin, (founders of the Institute of Policy Studies, a major producer of critiques of American society and foreign policy) preferred to look upon the Vietnam war as a manifestation of "the disease of an entire ruling class" and viewed it as genocidal, suggesting that it was deliberate American policy "to create widespread civilian casualties."[25] Some critics succeeded in blaming the United States for the economic difficulties and repressive policies of the Vietnamese communist regime ten years after the war ended. John McAuliff, Director of the Indochina program of the American Friends Service Committee ". . . suggested that American hostility toward Hanoi after the war might have contributed to the Communists' policy of imprisoning large numbers of former South Vietnamese soldiers and officials . . ."[26]

For Noam Chomsky the United States stood for a "commitment to a social order that guarantees endless suffering and humiliation and denial of elementary human rights."[27] and he faulted American foreign policy for the killings by the Pol Pot regime in Cambodia (while viewing these attrocities as greatly exaggerated by the American media).[28] Moreover he believed, in the words of a reviewer, that ". . . the U.S. Government favors client states with bloody-minded dictators over Third World democracy . . ."[29]

Critiques of the domestic defects of the United States also continued through the 1980s. Expanded conceptions of the underprivileged retained credibility not only in academic but also political circles; a member of the U.S. House of Representatives, Ronald V. Dellums asserted (in the *New York Times*) that: "America is a nation of niggers . . . If you are black, you're a nigger. If you're an amputee, you're a nigger. Blind people, women, students, the handicapped, radical environmentalists, poor whites, those too far to the left are all niggers."[30]

In less colorful language college texts in sociology have identified the United States as the singular respository and exemplar of social problems, including racism, which, according to one, "... has positive consequences for the maintenance of the status quo."[31] Crime too has been seen in a similar light "sustain[ed] . . . as a highly visible component of the American experience since "for many Americans criminals serve as a negative reference group whose violations of common decency render such decency uncommon and praiseworthy." Accordingly inequality or "the continuing victimization of the disinherited" has also been deliberately maintained for the social-psychological benefit of those better off.[32] *Crisis in American Institutions,* a popular college level sociology text, now in its sixth edition, took an encyclopedic inventory of all defects of American society ranging from the family to foreign policy.[33] Generally speaking textbooks on social problems treated the latter as singular products of American society and capitalism.

The horrors of technology continued to haunt the 1980s now perhaps more in the context of public health and damage to the physical environment than in connection with military violence, although the renewed fear of nuclear war helped to replenish the pool of fears linking technology and political conflict. Marge Piercy, the feminist writer said: "Technology is monstrous . . . because our values are monstrous . . . They are killing us . . . with cancer, drugs, contraceptives, food, asbestos . . . bad schools and television." She saw American society teeming with " 'oppressed' peoples—women laborers, blacks, the poor, native Americans, older people—whose lives are controlled by the 'ruling class' ".[34]

E. L. Doctorow, the popular writer entertained an equally gloomy vision of the state of American society in the 1980s: "Our psychic deterioration goes beyond intellectual life. In the past ten years there has been a terrible loss of moral energy in art, in politics, in social expectations . . . In the name of rugged individualism, we celebrate greed, gluttony and social coercion . . . We've got to watch out for . . . the constrictions of public debate . . . the rising levels of irrationality in our group relations . . . the tendency of our elected government to abridge our political liberties . . ."[35]

The abridgement of civil liberties was also very much on the mind of Ira Glasser, head of the American Civil Liberties Union, who in 1984 warned against the "subtle but unmistakable" signs of an emergent reign of repression "Using the threat of terrorism as today's excuse", averring that "Today, the signals of that danger are once again clear, unmistakable" and concluded "It is tragically ironic that this new, ominous information gathering and government invasion of privacy would reach such dangerous heights during 1984—a year that is almost a cliche here at the ACLU.''[36]

Ira Glasser was not alone in seizing on the metaphor of 1984 for launching new critiques of American society. A host of commentators took the occasion to insist or imply that the insights and predictions Orwell incorporated into *1984* are applicable to American society today. Walter Cronkite, former anchorman for CBS News and probably the most influential and widely known "media intellectual" wrote:

> Would Smith [of the novel] recognize the origins of his world in a democracy such as ours where . . . educational performance is on the decline; where the result is a growing number of functional illiterates, barely able to cope in their personal lives and clearly unfit to consider competently the affairs of the nation? . . .
>
> Could Smith see the seeds of his Oceania in our society, in which the Federal Government tries to shroud more and more of its activities with 'security' classifications; in which scientists keep the Government informed of their research . . .
>
> . . . in our world, where a Vietnam Village can be destroyed so it can be saved; where the President names the latest thing in nuclear missiles the 'Peacekeeper'—in such a world can the Orwellian vision be far away? . . .
>
> The two-way telescreen may have been a fantastic idea in 1948; the technology is here for 1984.[37]

Not one word in the article suggested that there might be any other country in the world which could have provided the inspiration for *1984*, or which in its contemporary aspects has anything in common with the vision of the novel.

At an academic conference on *1984* (financed in part by the National Endowment for the Humanities) ". . . the basic theme of most of the papers . . . was that the totalitarian nightmare of *1984* has been, or at least is about to be, most fully realized in America . . . Paper after paper attacked the United States for the highly oppressive character of its culture, society and government . . . there was not a single presentation on Eastern Europe, 'Socialist' Asia or the Soviet Union.''[38] Similar themes were sounded at another scholarly gathering organized by the Modern Language Association in New York city. According to Prof. Gene Bell-Villada of Williams College ". . . Orwell's vision . . . could already be seen in such phenomena as Watergate, urban slums, multinational conglomerates and sophisticated techniques of surveillance." In the opinion of Prof. Cripsin Miller of Johns Hopkins University ". . . the United States bore deep similarities to the totalitarian 'Oceanic State' of Orwell's imagination."[39]

The increasingly popular idea of a moral equivalence between the "Superpowers" has been yet another vehicle for expressing criticism of the United States. While on the surface this doctrine equates these two political systems in a seemingly neutral way stressing areas of symmetry or similarity, more often than not it succeeds in combining aversion toward the United States with a benefit of doubt posture towards the Soviet Union. While the critiques of the former tend to be passionate and specific, the reproaches of the latter are general and perfunctory lacking in moral fervor and indignation.[40]

Upholders of the moral equivalence thesis range from prominent scholar-diplomats like George Kennan to full time social critics (such as the associates of the Institute of Policy Studies), journalists taking pride in their objectivity and uncounted millions of educated Americans who are not friendly towards the Soviet Union but uncomfortable with the idea that their own society may have a moral edge over it. The latter tendency has been strengthened by the peace movement concerned with what it sees as the adverse effects of American arrogance and sense of superiority on resolving disagreements between these two nations.

Kennan's observations typify the attitudes associated with moral equivalence and the policy recommendations drawn from it:

> Isn't it grotesque to spend so much of our energy on opposing Russia to save a West which is honeycombed with bewilderment and a profound sense of internal decay? Show me first an America which has successfully coped with . . . crime, drugs, deteriorating educational standards, urban decay, pornography and decadence of one sort or another . . . then I will tell you how we are going to defend ourselves from the Russians. But, as things are, I can see very little merit in organizing ourselves to defend from the Russians the porno shops in central Washington. In fact, the Russians are much better in holding pornography at bay than we are.[41]

At an altogether different level the popular conception of moral equivalence much heard on college campuses was accurately captured by a Smith College student:

> On the moral issues of war and peace it is important to realize that the United States is not perfect and the Soviet Union is not evil. American citizens should . . . realize that we are not a perfect society and therefore have no right to take a moral stance against the USSR. . . .

> Until our country is perfect, we should refrain from proclaiming our-
> selves judges of "human rights" in other countries. It is blatant hypoc-
> risy.[42]

E. L. Doctorow's version of moral equivalence has also been frequently heard since the 1960s:

> Each of the superpowers has the demonic *other* to justify its espionage,
> its assassinations, its interventions and its invasions. We and the Soviet
> Union have actually created an unholy alliance, a gargantuan intimacy,
> in which, by now, our ideological differences are less important than the
> fact that we think the same thoughts, mirror each other's responses, heft
> the same bombs and take turns committing crimes and deploring
> them . . .[43]

The belief in moral equivalence is not limited to a handful of
prominent academic or literary intellectuals. In a survey of 3500
readers of the magazine *Psychology Today*, (of whom 75% completed
college or graduate school) the researchers were led to "the conclusion
that a 'mirror image' exists between Soviet and American military
conduct and posture". They also found that "for every man or woman
who said that the Soviet Union had been more aggressive, four others
pointed the finger at the United States."[44]

Manifestations of the moral equivalence posture (blended with social
criticism) can also be found in high school texts of American history.
A study of six popular and widely used texts published in several
editions during the 1960s and 70s concluded that "With the exception
of one paragraph in textbook A, none of the textbooks can be said to
present an overly favorable view of U.S. foreign policy. On the
contrary, there is a tendency . . . to give the Soviet Union greater
benefit of doubt than is given to the United States."[45] Another study
of American Government textbooks found more indirect evidence of
the same approach in the reluctance of the textbook authors to recognize any distinctive merit in democratic political arrangements such as
found in the United States: ". . . if students are taught to see everything
as almost equally imperfect, they are ill-prepared to distinguish those
areas which, in fact, constitute legitimate grounds for shame from
those which are causes for legitimate pride."[46]

The rise of the doctrine of moral equivalence and the diminished
capacity for making distinctions discussed earlier has been a simultaneous development possibly stimulated in some instances by ". . . the
frustration of inveterate ideologists, who, if they can no longer be pro-
Moscow, can at least go on hating Washington all the more; for if

Russia is no longer an attractive Utopia then American must become an even worse source of reaction and counter-revolution."[47]

While libraries could be filled with the impressionistic and qualitative reflections and recent examples of social criticism such as were cited above, these statements and a widespread receptivity to them are supported by the findings of studies of attitudes and opinion among American elite groups.

Reviewing studies of faculty elites since World War II Lipset reached the conclusion that they "have been disproportionately critical of society, and more disposed than other strata to support forces that reject the status quo." He also found—and thereby disposed of the notion that failure or frustration explain the social critical disposition—that "the higher the achievement, the more liberal faculty members are politically" and that "the more successful are the most left-inclined."[48]

In their studies of media elites (involving "240 journalists and broadcasters at the most influential media outlets, including the NY Times, the Washington Post, the Wall Street Journal, Time magazine, Newsweek, U.S. News and World Report, and the news departments of CBS, NBC, ABC and PBS . . .") S. Robert Lichter and Stanley Rothman found similar evidence of a strong social-critical disposition.

54% in their sample "place[d] themselves to the left of center, compared to only 19% who chose the right side of the spectrum". 46% believed that the "U.S. exploits Third World, causes poverty"; 57% that "U.S. use of resources immoral"; 51% that "Goal of foreign policy is to protect U.S. business"; 49% that "structure of society causes alienation"; 86% that "Big corporations should be publicly owned". 81% of them voted for McGovern in 1972.[49] It should also be noted that once more the socially critical attitudes were not associated with an underprivileged background or current disadvantage but with elite positions and "socially privileged upbringings. Most were raised in upper-middle class homes."

In another study the same authors probed the attitudes of leaders or top staffers in 74 public interest organizations including the American Civil Liberties Union, Center for Law and Social Policy, Common Cause, Consumers Union, Environmental Defense Fund, Public Citizen, etc. as well as major public interest law firms. They concluded among other things that

> The liberalism of public interest leaders shades into profound dissatisfaction with the American social and economic order . . . In fact their alienation was one of our most striking findings . . . Three out of four

believe the very structure of our society causes alienation, and over 90%
say our legal system favors the wealthy. . . . Only about half the public
interest leaders believe the system can be salvaged.

As was the case with the media elite, the public interest elite also
favored McGovern, with 96% of those sampled voting for him. They
too come from comfortable backgrounds and possess impressive educational credentials, 72% having attended private colleges or universities, most went to law school and belong to what may be called the 60s
generation. They have also been very well paid.[50]

In yet another study of elite groups the same authors examined the
political values and attitudes of moviemakers. Their random sample
included 149 writers, producers and directors of the fifty top grossing
films from 1965 to 1982. They were found to be "primarily white males
with very large incomes, moderate to liberal economic attitudes, and a
low regard for our institutions." 82% of them voted for McGovern.
While not anti-capitalist (perhaps not surprisingly, with two third of
them reporting family incomes in excess of $200,000 per year) "they
are alienated from society in other ways. Almost nine out of ten believe
that the legal system favors the wealthy, over 60% agree that the very
structure of our society produces alienation. . . . over half think that
American institutions need a complete overhaul." They would prefer
to see intellectuals rank first among the groups which exercise leadership.[51]

In a corresponding study these authors addressed the same questions to "the cream of television's creative community" which included 15 presidents of independent production companies, 18 executive producers, 43 additional producers, 10 network vice-presidents
responsible for programming and other highly placed individuals involved with programming. Once more the results led the authors to
conclude that "Given their widespread rejection of both American
social institutions and their guardians, one would suspect that many in
the television elite would like to see substantial changes in our society.
In fact, a substantial minority of 43% endorses a complete overhaul of
American institutions . . . their acceptance of the economic system is
tempered by a deep-set alienation from the social-political system."
Moreover ". . . the television elite is deeply dissatisfied with the
direction our society is taking and would like to alter it in profound
ways." Their critical attitudes apparently lead them to a desire ". . .
to move their audiences toward their own vision of the good society"
through the programs they devise.[52]

Reviewing the findings of all the elite studies carried out sofar

Rothman concluded that "While some commentators believe that the 1980s have been characterized by a revival of more traditional values, my research thus far indicates that appearances are deceptive. The rate of change may have slowed, but the patterns which emerged in the 1960s have been incorporated into American culture, to a considerable extent."[53]

Rothman's and his associates' research was not the first to highlight the social-critical attitudes of the elites associated with the film and television industry. An earlier study arrived at similar conclusions through the analysis of both the programs produced and the attitudes of the producers. "All of them, even those with millions of dollars, believed themselves to be part of a working class distinctly at odds with the exploiting classes . . ."; ". . . All thought of themselves as politically 'progressive' . . ." They entertained the feeling that despite their high incomes and access to the media "they are still part of a despised underclass, oppressed . . . by an Aryan ruling class of businessmen and others. This feeling was by no means confined to Jews."

Hostility toward businessmen and military was also reflected in the television programs the author, Ben Stein analysed. By contrast the poor and minority groups tend to be idealized: "If there is any sort of people who are unequivocally loved on television, it is the poor. They do no wrong, are always either heroes or victims . . . In an America riddled with flaws . . . the poor stand out . . . blameless and pure . . ."

Stein concluded: "The people who are in a position of creative authority in television feel very much at war with the power centers of American life . . . They see the businessman class, the heir class, the military officer caste, the people from Grosse Pointe . . . as their enemies."[54]

Lipset and Schneider reached similar conclusions regarding the nature and effects of the mass media: "Recent research has found a strong and direct link between political cynicism and exposure to negative information in the media."[55]

Another development that has signalled the gains made by the social-critical spirit in American life has been the growing entrenchment over the past two decades of Marxist academics.[56] As stated by two of them "A Marxist cultural revolution is taking place today in American universities." Among the gains made by this movement they noted the new spurt in the publishing of Marxist texts and textbooks by prestigious academic publishers and over 400 courses offered in Marxist philosophy, as well as the election of Marxists to head the organization of American historians and teachers of literature.[57]

There have been other indications of the persistence and revival of the radical-critical attitudes on American campuses and of the domination of the public political discourse by left-wing causes and groups. Free speech on the campuses has never completely recovered from the vicissitudes of the 1960s. Speakers disliked by radical groups—however small in numbers they might be—cannot as a rule make a presentation without disruption, be they officials of the U.S. Government (such as Jeane Kirkpatrick or Caspar Weinberger), or representatives of anti-Sandinista groups in Nicaragua (like Eden Pastora), or scientists studying heredity in intelligence (like Arthur Shockley and Arthur Jensen) or former radicals converted to Evangelical Christianity (like Eldridge Cleaver).[58]

Expressions of social criticism and the influence of the sensibilities of the 1960s is not limited to higher education. In an exhaustive study of the presentation of religious and traditional values in public school textbooks used by an estimated 60% of all American students taking U.S. history Paul Vitz found "a strong liberal bias demonstrated by their [the texts'] failure to even once introduce a typical conservative political or social issue . . ." Likewise the role models selected by the authors were predominantly associated with liberal political or social causes. The political bias of these texts was also reflected in their orientation to characterize recent American history in terms of three issues: minorities, feminism and ecology and in an anti-business attitude."[59]

I will summarize now the main themes of social criticism embraced, elaborated and disseminated by large numbers of American intellectuals between the 1960s and 1980s. Subsequently I shall attempt to explain the persistence of this phenomenon.

Generally speaking the social critics' sense of indignation is fuelled by discrepancies between ceremonial social values (as for example equality) and their limited realization. It is widely held among them that American society does not live up to its promises, beliefs and ideals.

The critiques of the 1960s, which continue to nurture those of the 1980s, focus on the ills and evils of capitalism: its impersonality, injustice and greed. At the societal level these evils are seen as breeding and maintaining a variety of institutionalized inequalities. At the personal or social-psychological level capitalism is blamed for the undermining of community and the impoverishment of personal relationships. Sexism and racism are considered by the critics essential parts of American culture—often but not invariably associated with capitalism. Capitalist technology is regarded as a particularly destructive force leading on the one hand to the despoliation of nature, on the other to the arms race and a possible nuclear war. Ever since the Vietnam war the United States has become for the social critics the major threat to world peace, a militaristic country which also seeks to maintain or expand its economic stranglehold over Third World nations, syphoning off their wealth and degrading their cultural traditions and independence. American policies in Central America have been especially strongly castigated and viewed as replications of the Vietnam policies.

Critics regard all social problems in American society as products of the entire social-political system and of the exploitative, selfish elite groups in charge of it. They see little hope for improvement without radical institutional transformations; there are differences of opinion among the critics whether or not such change can be accomplished without revolutionary violence or a further change in the global balance of power at the expense of the United States. Some hope that domestic economic difficulties may lead to such institutional restructuring.

In the words of Peter Berger, "There is a broad, probably growing consensus to the effect that the market economy is intrinsically evil, that the culture of the mass of the American people ('Middle America') is inferior and pathological, and . . . that the political system of liberal democracy is a corrupt sham."[60]

III.

The social critical temper and a strong sense of the flaws of society have for some time been an integral part of the identity of elite intellectuals in the West. As Czeslaw Milosz pointed out "A conviction of decadence, the rotting of the West, seems to be a permanent part of the equipment of enlightened and sensitive people for dealing with the horrors accompanying technological progress."[61] Technological progress and its questionable fruits have certainly been among the more recent factors accounting for the disenchantment of intellectuals. More generally speaking, modernization and its discontents, (as for example discussed by Peter Berger[62]) go a long way explaining the attitudes in question. The freedom, the cultural and political pluralism and the choices available in Western societies is another factor to be noted here. Milosz coming from a part of the world without such choices and pluralism observed more than three decades ago:

> . . . Western intellectuals suffer from a special variety of *taedium vitae;* their emotional and intellectual life is too dispersed. Everything they

think and feel evaporates like steam in an open expanse. Freedom is a
burden to them. No conclusions they arrive at are binding . . . The result
is constant uneasiness . . .[63]

Here Milosz brilliantly anticipated the identity problems of Western
intellectuals which were to achieve greater prominence in subsequent
decades. Comparing the position of Western with Eastern European
intellectuals he also noted that "What can be said openly is often much
less interesting than the emotional magic of defending one's private
sanctuary."[64]

A sense of purpose is not among the qualities Western, including
American intellectuals possess in abundance. As I argued elsewhere[65]
the lack of such purpose and the attendant discomfort have been
among the notable characteristics of many American intellectuals and
a principal source of dissatisfaction with their society, faulted for not
providing them with sustaining values. Under such conditions the
social-critical impulse can find few constructive outlets (except for
those who embrace some variety of Marxism) and moral affirmation
becomes difficult.

Paul Craig Roberts characterizes the resulting attitudes as a "fusion
of moral scepticism with the demand for moral perfection. . ." He also
points out that the high, moralistic demands on the part of intellectuals
are almost invariably directed at their own society, rarely at those
opposed to it: "The structure of this frame of mind causes cynicism to
be suspended in regard to the motives of foreign opponents . . .
focusing scepticism only inward . . ."[66] This mindset also helps to
understand the moral equivalence thesis discussed earlier and its
relatively benign treatment of the Soviet Union.

A similar double standard was observed by Aaron Wildavsky as
regards perceptions of domestic and foreign affairs:

. . . the very people who argue the best-case thesis in foreign policy also
argue the worst-case thesis in domestic policy. Harmony in domestic
policy, they claim, is the ideology of the oppressor. There are irreconcil-
able conflicts between the haves and havenots which cannot be compromised but only overcome by struggle. Foreign policy, apparently is
different . . . many of the people who hold a best-case belief about the
Soviet Union hold a worst case belief about capitalism.[67]

In other words, the intellectuals here discussed alternate between
moral absolutism and moral relativism. The former is reserved for
their own society which is judged by high and uncompromising standards; moral relativism and far more flexible and relaxed standards

apply to other societies, especially those adversarial towards their own. This attitude is often associated with "selective determinism." One must not be judgmental toward groups (or countries) designated as underdogs and objects of sympathy since their behavior is determined by forces beyond their control; by contrast the groups (or countries) viewed with hostility and seen as victimizers are not perceived as similarly shaped by their environment or history; they are in total control of their actions, they can make choices and hence deserve to be judged.[68]

Another way to highlight these contrasts is to note that American intellectuals, even the most severe social critics among them, harbor high expectations about their society, and it is the frustration of these expectations which often turns into bitterness and rejection. I had argued elsewhere, that the broad historical background against which such expectations are played out is that of secularization. As Roberts put it ". . . the secularization of Christian moral fervor . . . produced demands for the moral perfection of society . . . "[69]

In the final analysis alienation is, among other things a response to the frustration created by the lack of meaning in modern society. It has been pointed out often enough that politics takes on religious overtones when religion proper withers, at any rate among intellectualls. Along these lines Doris Lessing observed:

> There are certain types of people who are political out of a kind of religious reason . . . I think it's fairly common among socialists: They are in fact God-seekers, looking for the kingdom of God on earth . . . trying to abolish the present in favor of some better future—always taking it for granted that there *is* a better future. If you don't believe in heaven you believe in socialism.[70]

There is a close and obvious connection between the embrace of Marxist socialism and the social critical impulse. Marxism is a philosophy of intense moral indignation—a worldview that helps to organize and systematize moral passion and which provides a seemingly scientific foundation for protesting social injustice. Marxism performs additional religious functions by pointing towards a better future which will arrive as a combined result of both the inexorable forces of history and the freely chosen effort of individuals who achieved the proper understanding of social forces. Leszek Kolakowski concluded his monumental study of Marxism as follows:

> The influence Marxism has achieved, far from being the result or proof of its scientific character, is almost entirely due to its prophetic, fantastic

and irrational elements . . . Almost all the prophecies of Marx and his followers have already proved to be false, but this does not disturb the spiritual certainty of the faithful . . . for it is a certainty not based on any empirical premises or supposed 'historical laws', but simply on the psychological need for certainty. In this sense Marxism performs the function of religion . . .[71]

In addition to the more general conditions of contemporary Western intellectuals noted above, there are certain cultural-historical traits peculiar to American society which contribute to the trends here discussed. While I stressed above the susceptibility to the ideals of Marxism and their confluence with the social-critical impulses, now I will focus on the impact of an excessive individualism, a hallmark of American cultural and political tradition. This individualism combines an overly optimistic view of individual potentials with a similarly sanguine belief in the possibilities for their fulfillment. Such a conception of the individual with virtually unlimited innate potentials for self-realization—but needlessly handicapped or enslaved by social institutions—is another important source of social criticism in the United States especially since the 1960s. According to an American social scientist "One of the bewildering characteristics of much contemporary radical criticism in America is . . . a kind of overwhelming optimism . . . much radical thought in America partakes of the deeply conventional American belief in perfectibility, fundamentally a form of chronic optimism." Once such an inflated conception of individual potentials is entertained it is easy to exaggerate the limits society places upon the unfolding of such gifts and easy to feel indignant about *all* restraints: "The underlying feeling is one of outrage that society should have mechanisms . . . which inevitably restrict the movements of the individual within it. This outrage seems to derive from the truly radical belief in the sacredness of the individual, a belief which is of course typically American."[72]

Even Marxists not typically attached to the values of individualism have voiced similar sentiments. Bertell Ollman remarked that ". . . class, nation, religion and race remain prisons from which each individual must escape in order to establish truly human relations."[73] Ollman is far from singular among American academic Marxists linking individual liberation to a vast institutional transformation of capitalist society that would sweep away all confining social categorizations.

Thus the radical critiques of American society are nurtured not only by the discontents of modernity but also venerable elements of the American cultural tradition: high expectations about human and institutional perfectibility and a reactive anger when the hoped for improvements fail to materialize.

The persistence of the radical critiques of American society in the late 1970s and early 1980s also has more immediate and tangible social-historical explanations. Among them are the memories of Vietnam and Watergate, the most often cited symbols of corruption in recent American history. Vietnam, in the eyes of the critics was not only a wasteful and brutal war, or a serious political miscalculation, but also a revelation of the true nature of the entire political system, its rapacious, murderous quality. Since it was a destructive and poorly legitimated war, as self evidently wrong as the juxtapositions of great wealth and dire poverty, it provided a highly effective tool of social criticism.

The American involvement in the Vietnam war had another, less obvious but more enduring result. If the American conduct in that war signified evil, the defeat of the United States demonstrated that this evil power was no longer strong and certainly not invincible. Gabriel Kolko, another prominent social critic drew this conclusion while the war was still fought: "For the United States to fail in Vietnam would be to make the point that even the massive intervention of the most powerful nation in the history of the world was insufficient to stem profoundly popular social and national revolutions throughout the world. Such a revelation of American weakness would be tantamount to a demotion of the United States from its present role as the world's dominant superpower."[74]

Vietnam had indeed demoted the United States from its status of invincible superpower, a development which not only gave pleasure to the radical critics but has also contributed to a greater readyness to engage in nationwide self criticism and an increased receptivity to accept critiques from abroad. The defeat has also weakened trust in American institutions and contributed to a decline of collective self-esteem especially among elite groups. Failure always has a delegitimating effect whereas success even in the pursuit of the most debased goals tends to silence doubt and criticism. In this sense the domino theory was correct: a severe blow was dealt to the assertiveness and self confidence of the United States as Vietnam became the uncontested symbol of disgrace, weakness and loss of national will. A new isolationism was among the consequences of the failure in Vietnam, which had numerous manifestations and ramifications in many parts of the world.

Watergate in turn revealed and highlighted corruption in domestic politics and deprived the presidency of the aura of respect and legitimacy it used to enjoy. Watergate and Vietnam together have remained powerful points of reference for an enduring national self-denigration and doubt not easily dispelled even by a cheerful and optimistic president like Reagan.

In fact, Reagan's rise to power may be considered among the factors promoting the survival and renewal of social criticism in the United States in recent years. While his election might have been seen as a triumph of the social-political forces hostile to the disparagement of American society, it was actually an event that reinforced estrangement. With Reagan in the White House social critics could point with renewed confidence to the menacing ascendance of forces obstructing beneficial social change and to a resurgence of all trends and tendencies in Ameican life they deplored. While none of the ambivalently wishful predictions of an emerging police state, or American style fascism popular among radicals of the 1960s materialized, there was at least a conservative Republican president in the White House. He stood for everything the critics abhorred: vocal support for capitalism, unashamed American patriotism, a willingness to reassert American influence abroad, an untroubled identification with "Middle American" cultural values and an unapologetic anti-communist persuasion. His election therefore stimulated and reinvigorated the political energies of many adversarial groups and movements—on the campuses, in the churches, the media—which have been with us since the 1960s.

The recruitment of many former radical activists into academic teaching positions has been another development conducive to the persistence and virtual institutionalization of the radical critiques of American society. Their settling on the campuses and academic communities has been a major factor in the rise and consolidation of the subcultures of social criticism and estrangement. Estrangement thus institutionalized has become easier to bear than Marx had dreamt of in his philosophy.

To be alienated today in America means many things not associated with the state of mind or social situation the concept used to signify. It is compatible with holding of opinions both popular and fashionable, receiving social honors and recognition, belonging to a cohesive and lively subculture, having a secure position in important social institutions and being active in public affairs. Being estranged today may also mean access to new sources of self-esteem attendant upon the role of righteous social critic and the self-assurance that comes from the knowledge of exposing social evil. Increasingly the sense of identity of many humanistic intellectuals has become tied in with their self-conception as social critic and voice of secular morality in a corrupt and irrational society.

The sense of estrangement from society—that is to say, the strongly felt conviction that this society is altogether worthless and unjust—is also compatible with a reasonably cheerful personal disposition and the untroubled enjoyment of the available pleasures of life: material, social, aesthetic. It is easier today to be a social critic in the United States because the gloom, withdrawal, marginality and disadvantage earlier associated with alienation and sustained social criticism have largely receded.

The recollections of William Philips, a charter member of the New York intelligentsia help to grasp the differences between the quality of alienation among intellectuals in the present and at earlier times:

> . . . we enjoyed the benefits and disadvantages of being out of the mainstream of the culture . . .
>
> I was the member of five minority groups. I was a disaffected writer and an editor of an against-the-grain publication. I was a Jew. I believed in modernism, which at the time was outside the dominant culture. I had become an anti-Communist . . . which was not very fashionable.
>
> Literary life in New York in the thirties for me and the writers around *Partisan Review* seemed marginal to the main concerns of the city and the country. We felt completely outside the literary as well as the political establishment.[75]

In a similar spirit William Barrett a member of the same generation stressed the centrality and "special enchantment" of the avant-guard position for intellectuals to whom being an innovative and marginal outsider used to be a compelling need.[76]

In more recent times, while the outsider status (or marginality) can no longer be plausibly invoked, it still is occasionally claimed, due to its traditional association with moral and political autonomy and the exercise of independent critical judgement among intellectuals.

The current situation of estranged intellectuals in American society may thus be summarized:

> While intellectuals have become better integrated, structurally speaking, their estrangement persisted and acquired a certain respectability. Even the most vehement denunciations of the social order ceased to be viewed as acts of defiance, nor was any risk attached to them . . . On the contrary such critiques have become a badge of belonging to subcultures . . . Alienation and rejection of society could no longer be associated with non-conformity, dissent or innovative social criticism; estrangement itself has become a new subcultural norm, a new form of conformity . . .

> When hundreds of thousand . . . people act out jointly their "noncon-
> formity" it does become a new form on conformity as happened to many
> forms of social criticism, deviant values, "alternative life styles" and
> attitudes associated with the counterculture . . . [of the 1960s][77]

These changes in the substance, quality and context of estrangement and social criticism had numerous consequences. While critiques of American society have become increasingly standardized, repetitive and unoriginal, the groups and institutions devoted to their articulation and dissemination have multiplied. They include radical "think tanks" (such as the Institute of Policy Studies and its many auxiliaries), large segments of the academia, the media and the churches. Gradually much of radical social criticism has become transformed into an established part of our intellectual discourse and a form of conventional wisdom.

Radical social criticism has produced its own critics over the past decade or two, a group of prominent and active intellectuals usually called neoconservatives ranged around publications such as *Commentary, Public Interest, Policy Review* and to some degree, *The New Republic*. While visible and not without some friends in Washington, the influence of the neoconservatives within the intellectual community at large and especially in academic life has been quite limited.

Still, intellectual life in the United States has become more polarized and though the verities of the adversary culture no longer go totally unchallenged, much of it persists due to its successful institutionalization; more people than ever before make their living in occupations and institutions which permit and encourage the continued elaboration and expression of the themes of social criticism we have become familiar with since the 1960s.

Much of the foregoing discussion suggests that contrary to the conventional sociological wisdom the connection between socio-economic and political marginality on the one hand, and the propensity to radical social criticism on the other, has become tenuous, at any rate in American society. Marginality, defined in some more objective way, (e.g. with reference to income, education, social position and political affiliation etc) no longer provides a satisfactory explanation of the rejection of the prevailing social-political order; on the other hand *perceived* or *claimed* marginality can still be associated with such rejection.

The social history of the last quarter century in the United States thus makes it difficult to detect a link between the better structural integration of intellectuals and a rising moderation, or decline of the social-critical temper. On the contrary a reflexive critique or disparagement of American society has become firmly entrenched during a period of occupational prosperity for intellectuals (that benefied many of the most eloquent and impassioned spokesmen of social criticism). The critiques of American society have, over the past two decades acquired solid subcultural foundations and have become institutionalized—a process that assures their vigorous survival regardless of the (good) socio-economic fortunes and political freedom of the critics and regardless of the improvement or decline in the qualities of life in American society.

Notes

1. Reprinted with some modifications from Alain Gagnon ed,: *Intellectuals in Liberal Democracies*, New York: Praeger, 1987. Parts of this essay also appeared in "The Survival of the Adversary Culture, *Partisan Review*, 1986 No. 3.
2. Czeszlav Milosz, *Visions of San Francisco Bay*, New York: Farrar, Straus, Giroux, 1975, p. 114.
3. Peter L. Berger, "The Socialist Myth", *Public Interest*, No, 44, 1976. Summer, p. 3–4.
4. Robert J. Brym, *Intellectuals and Politics*, London: Allen & Unwin, 1980, p. 12.
5. Frank Parkin, *Middle Class Radicalism—The Social Basis of the British Campaign for Nuclear Disarmament*, Manchester: Manchester University Press, 1968, p. 30.
6. See for example Bennet Berger, "Sociology and the Intellectuals: An Analysis of a Stereotype", *Antioch Review* No 17, September; Lewis Coser, *Men of Ideas*, New York: Free Press, 1965; Paul Hollander, *Political Pilgrims—Travels of Western Intellectuals to the Soviet Union, China and Cuba*, New York: Oxford University Press, 1981, pp. 40–73; Karl Manheim, *Ideology and Utopia*, New York: Harcourt, Brace, 1936; Edward Shils, *The Intellectuals and the Powers*, chicago: Chicago University Press, 1972.
7. Michael Novak, *The Spirit of Democratic Capitalism*, New York: Simon & Schuster, 1982, p. 206.
8. Mary Douglas and Aaron Wildavsky, *Risk and Culture*, Berkeley: University of California Press, 1982, p. 159.
9. Joseph Epstein, "True Virtue", *New York Times Magazine*, 1985 November 24, p. 72.
10. Richard Hofstadter, *Anti-Intellectualism in American Life*, New York: Vintage, 1962.
11. Quoted in Ernest van den Haag, ed. *Capitalism, Sources of Hostility*, New Rochelle, New York: Epoch Books, 1979, p. 150.
12. TRB, "Dohrn Again", *The New Republic*, 1985, October 14, p. 4.
13. William Serrin, "Anti-Vietnam Activists Now Aids Workers as Lawyer", *New York Times*, November 29; Staughton Lynd, Letters in *New York Times*, 1979, July 2 and 1985 November 3.

14. Michiko Kakutani, "The Strange Case of the Writer and the Criminal", *New York Times Book Review Section,* 1981, September 20.
15. Leon Wieseltier, "Ideas in Season," *Partisan Review* No. 3., 1982, p. 420.
16. Christopher Lehman-Haupt, "Review of Gore Vidal: The Second American Revolution", *New York Times,* 1982, April 27.
17. Dorothy Rabinowitz, "A Report from the American Writers' Conference", *The Wall Street Journal,* 1981, October 16.
18. Richard Bernstein, "Nuclear Foes Ponder Fate of the Earth", *New York Times,* 1982 October 22.
19. Wallace Turner, "Tax Refusal Completes Prelate's Moral Journey" *New York Times,* 1982, August 19.
20. Noam Chomsky, "Some Thoughts on Intellectuals and the Schools", *Harvard Educational Review,* 1966, Fall, p. 485.
21. Quoted in Nathan Glazer, "The Fire This Time", *The New Republic,* 1985, December 30, p. 42.
22. Jerry Farber, *The Student as Nigger,* North Hollywood: Contact Book, 1969.
23. Priscilla Long, ed. *The New Left,* Boston: Porter Sargent Publishers, 1969, p. 426.
24. Susan Sontag, "Some Thoughts on the Right Way (for us) to Love the Cuban Revolution", *Ramparts,* April 1969; Loren Baritz: *Backfire: A History of How American Culture Led Us into Vietnam and Made Us Fight the Way we Did,* New York: William Morrow & Co., 1985.
25. Joshua Muravchik, "The Think Tank of the Left," *New York Times Magazine,* 1981, April 26, p. 42.
26. Fox Butterfield, " 'Vietnam is Not Over' Parley on War Learns", *New York Times,* 1983, February 11.
27. Chomsky, *Cited,* 1966, p. 498.
28. Noam Chomsky and Edward S. Herman, "Distortions at Fourth Hand", *The Nation,* 1977, June 25.
29. A. J. Langguth, "Someone is Watching", *The Nation,* 1980, February 16, p. 181.
30. Martin Tolchin, "For Blacks, Racism and Progress Mix", *New York Times,* 1983, March 11.
31. D. Stanley Eitzen, *Social Problems,* Boston: Allyn & Bacon, 1983, p. 90.
32. Michael Lewis, *The Culture of Inequality,* Amherst: University of Massachusetts Press, 1978, pp. 112, 88, 192.
33. Jerome H. Skolnick and Currie Elliott, *Crisis in American Institutions,* Boston: Little, Brown, 1985.
34. Katie Glaenzer, "Marge Piercy Speaks of History's Oppression", *Daily Hampshire Gazette,* 1983, March 3, p. 4.
35. E. L. Doctorow, "It's a Cold War World Out There, Class of 83", *The Nation,* July 2, pp. 6, 7.
36. Ira Glasser, *Circular from the American Civil Liberties Union,* 1984.
37. Walter Cronkite, "Orwell's '1984' Nearing?", *New York Times,* 1983, June 5, Op-ed page.
38. A. M. Eckstein, "An Orwellian Nightmare Fulfilled: an Eyewitness's Account", *Chronicle of Higher Education,* 1984, October 17, p. 72.
39. Walter Goodman, " 'Nineteen Eighty-Four' is Found All Too Relevant to Today', *New York Times,* 1983, December 30.

40. See for example Richard Barnett, *The Giants,* New York: Simon & Schuster, 1978.
41. *George Kennan and His Critics,* Washington, D.C.: Ethics and Public Policy Center, 1978, pp. 32–33.
42. Rachel C. King. "U.S., Not Perfect: Should Not Judge Soviet Morality", *Daily Hampshire Gazette,* 1984, October 6.
43. E. L. Doctorow, "On the Brink of 1984", *Playboy Magazine,* 1983, February, p. 160.
44. S. Plous and Philip G. Zimbardo, "The Looking Glass War", *Psychology Today,* 1984, November, pp. 59, 56.
45. Martin F. Herz, *How the Cold War Is Taught,* Washington, D.C.: Ethics and Public Policy Center, Georgetown University, 1978, p. 72.
46. Michael Novak, Jeane Kirkpatrick and Anne Crutcher, *Values in American Government Textbooks,* Washington, D.C.: Ethics and Public Policy Center, Georgetown University, 1978, p. 27.
47. Melvin J. Lasky, "The Doctrine of Moral Equivalence", *Encounter,* 1985, December, p. 29.
48. Seymour Martin Lipset, "The Academic Mind at the Top: The Political Behavior and Values of Faculty Elites", *Public Opinion Quarterly,* 1982, Vol. 46, pp. 144, 145, 146.
49. Robert S. Lichter and Stanley Rothman, "The Media Elite and American Values", *Public Opinion,* 1981, October–November, pp. 43–44.
50. Robert S. Lichter and Stanley Rothman, "What Interests the Public and What Interests the Public Interests? *Public Opinion,* 1983, April–May, pp. 46, 45.
51. Stanley Rothman and Robert S. Lichter, "What are Moviemakers Made Of?", *Public Opinion,* 1984, December–January, pp. 15, 16, 18.
52. Linda S. Lichter, Robert S. Lichter and Stanley Rothman, "Hollywood and America: The Odd Couple", *Public Opinion,* 1983, December–January, pp. 55, 57, 58.
53. Stanley Rothman, *Social and Political Change in the United States—A Proposal for Continuing Research* (Mimeographed), 1985, Northampton, Massachusetts, p. 6.
54. Ben Stein, *The View from Sunset Boulevard,* New York: Basic Books, 1979, pp. 12, 13, 28, 92, 93, 94, 134.
55. Seymour Martin Lipset and William Schneider, *The Confidence Gap,* New York: Free Press, 1983, p. 403.
56. Stephen H. Balch and Herbert I. London: "The Tenured Left"; *Commentary,* 1986, October.
57. Bertell Ollman and Edward Vernoff, eds., *The Left Academy-Marxist Scholarship on American Campuses,* New York: McGraw Hill, 1982, pp. 1–2.
58. See for example John H. Bunzel, "Campus 'Free Speech' ", *New York Times,* 1983, March 13; and David Brock, "The Big Chill—A Report Card on Campus Censorship", *Policy Review,* 1985, Spring.
59. Paul C. Vitz, *Religion and Traditional Values in Public School Text-Books: An Empirical Study* (mimeographed research report) New York University 1985; pp. 43, III–IV. 39, 67. See also Vitz: "Textbook Bias Isn't of a Fundamentalist Nature", *Wall Street Journal,* December 26, 1985; also Paul C. Vitz: *Censorship: Evidence of Bias in Our Children's Textbooks,* Ann Arbor, Mich.: Servant Books 1986.

60. Berger, *cited*, 1976, p. 2.
61. Milosz, *cited*, 1975, p. 114.
62. Berger, *cited*, 1976.
63. Czeszlav Milosz, *The Captive Mind*, New York: Vintage Books, 1955, p. 75.
64. Milosz, *cited*, 1955, p. 76.
65. Hollander, *cited*, 1981.
66. Paul Craig Roberts, "Alienation and U.S. Foreign Policy", *Modern Age*, 1977, Spring, pp. 153, 159.
67. Aaron Wildavsky, "Best-Case Thinking" Correspondence, *Commentary*, 1984, September 5, p. 4.
68. Paul Hollander, *The Many Faces of Socialism*, New Brunswick: Transaction Books, 1983, pp. 241–251.
69. Roberts, *cited*, 1977, p. 153.
70. Doris Lessing, "Doris Lessing on Feminism, Communism, and 'Space Fiction' ", *New York Magazine*, 1982, July 25, p. 26.
71. Leszek Kolakowski, "Marxism—A Summing Up", *Survey*, 1977–78, Summer, p. 167.
72. Thomas Kreilkamp, *The Corrosion of the Self*, New York: New York University Press, 1976, pp. 34–35, 43.
73. Quoted in Guenter Lewy, "Academic Ethics and the Radical Left", *Policy Review*, 1982, Winter, p. 39.
74. Quoted in Robert W. Tucker, *The Radical Left and American Foreign Policy*, Baltimore: Johns Hopkins University Press, 1971, p. 53.
75. William Philips, *A Partisan View—Five Decades of Literary Life*, New York: Stein and Day, 1983, pp. 294–295.
76. William Barrett, *The Truants*, Garden City: Anchor Press, 1982, p. 93.
77. Hollander, *cited*, 1983, p. 324–325.

PART III
Political Escapism

13
Model Prisons and Political Tourism Under Socialism*

Demagoguery and misrepresentation are inevitable among the Communist leaders since they are forced to promise the most ideal society. . . .

Milovan Djilar[1]

Why are Western liberals—who are often such smart people— such slow learners about Communism?
. . . the continuing appeal of each new variant to men and women of goodwill can be explained only by fundamental cultural predispositions that condition the response to the political world.

Jeane Kirkpatrick[2]

I

It may seem somewhat incongruous and unexpected that political deception and self-deception should emerge as significant phenomena in twentieth century politics and, especially, international relations. Our times have been associated with the ascendance of science and advanced technology, the expansion of higher education, the growth of rationality, the continuing process of secularization and the loss of illusions—developments which on the face of it are not congenial to the massive entry of deception into the political arena including, of course, the rise of propaganda as a major device in the struggle for power. Equally unexpected has been the propensity of many highly educated people in Western societies to engage in prolonged bouts of political self-deception.

While deception carried out by intelligence services has of late been recognized as a staple of contemporary political warfare, less dramatic

*Originally written for a volume entitled *Deception in East-West Relations*, edited by David Charters and Maruice Tugwell.

forms of it—such as those linked with political tourism and political hospitality—have often gone unnoticed.[3] This chapter explores the techniques of hospitality (or political hospitality) and the forms of deception associated with it and aimed at the calculated misrepresentation of the political systems using these techniques.

All countries, like individuals, strive to create a favorable impression of themselves especially in the eyes of foreign visitors. However, the policies and practices associated with the concept of political hospitality and political tourism are both quantitatively and qualitatively different from these conventional attitudes and impulses. These practices embody notable and consequential political innovations made possible by the institutional arrangements and prevailing ideologies of the countries which have introduced them.

It was in the Soviet Union—and the countries inspired, influenced or dominated by it—that the techniques of hospitality were most purposefully and elaborately developed in the service of clearly defined political objectives. These techniques were embraced by political leaders who believed both in the importance of ideas as weapons and in the moral-historical superiority of their societies. They were determined that the political system they presided over should be seen in the most favorable light. Given such a disposition, the task of persuading outsiders about the virtues of their regime became a high priority. Certain of the essential superiority of their new social order, they were to spare no effort to demonstrate its excellence. These leaders believed that any shortcomings were temporary and need not be allowed to intrude on the impressions of foreign observers or visitors; such shortcomings could be passed over, denied and concealed.

The principles and evolving practices of political hospitality came to resemble those of socialist realism, the official Soviet (and Soviet-inspired) theory of literary and artistic creativity. According to its tenets, the writer and artist must capture and present reality—in a socialist society, at any rate—in its emergent state. What he must portray is not some statistical average, not a mere reflection of the way things actually are, but the way they are becoming and are supposed to be. Thus the artist must grasp the 'typical' and in doing so eliminate the dividing line between 'is' and 'ought'. He must assess the relative importance of his subject matter, and decide if it represents moribund, decandent tastes or emergent, future-oriented phenomena. Social phenomena in the process of decline can be safely ignored while those pregnant with the promise of the future deserve attention. (It is of course the Party and its leadership that determine the criteria for such selectivity and enable the artist to recognize what belongs to the past and what to the future.)

In the same spirit the techniques of hospitality embody principles of selectivity: the visitors to the new society are to be shown those aspects which point ahead, which represent the highest achievements of the new social order, perhaps exceptional today but not so tomorrow. Hence the issue of deception is transformed into the purposeful display of the most impressive and, theoretically speaking, the essential and future attributes of the society the political tourists are exposed to. Although these techniques interact with the predispositions and anticipations of many visitors, they have an impact of their own. As a minimum they solidify favorable predispositions by providing apparent confirmation for them.

Since the techniques of hospitality were pioneered by the Soviet Union it is of interest to examine the major factors which led to their adoption. Historical antecedents must be noted: the concept of 'Potemkin Village' is after all an old Russian contribution to politically inspired make-belief:

> . . . Potemkin, creator of those renowned 'villages' which remain to this day the prime emblem of Russian *pokazukha* ('bull') and *ochkovtiratelstvo* ('eyewash'). They were mere two-dimensional stage props erected in sight of the River Dnieper, being designed to impress upon the touring sovereign, as she glided downstream with a flotilla of notables, the comforting illusion that the wilderness around her was a prosperous and densely populated province of her realm. Well might Michael Speransky. . . complain in another context that 'in no other State do political words stand in such contrast to reality as in Russia.'[4]

The techniques of hospitality represent only one of many paths the Soviet regime has followed to create favorable impressions of itself abroad; as such the technique is a part of a much broader global campaign intended to project expedient images of the political system as a whole.[5] The Bolshevik conspiratorial tradition and the habits of secrecy it has bred are relevant factors. To be effective, political hospitality presupposes a measure of secrecy, and secretiveness has been a legacy of the underground work that characterized the political activity of the pre-revolutionary Bolsheviks. Only a secretive society with a population at once intimidated and severely limited in its access to information can effectively introduce and maintain over long periods misrepresentations of reality which are part of political hospitality.

A certain patriotic pride and mistrust of foreigners has also made ordinary Soviet citizens responsive to policies which sought to shield foreign visitors from the less appealing sides of Soviet life. This has also been a long standing historical tradition: "The regime of Nicholas I has been described as cynical and seemingly based on the cultivation of a series of massive fictions: there were 'two images of Russian reality—the country as it actually was and as the authorities wished it to appear.' "[6] Hence withholding unflattering information from foreigners has for long been a practice accepted by many social strata in Russia, not just by the leaders. In turn, the beleaguered, besieged self-conception of the Soviet regime intensified these cultural-historical propensities, a trend that has also been evident in China.[7]

Thus, all requirements for successful political deception were present in the Soviet Union: the will to deceive on the part of the elite, a generally docile and compliant population, the belief—on the part of the rulers—in the importance of the political objectives served by the techniques of hospitality, and absolute control over the resources needed for the conduct of these policies. Last but not least, many of those to be deceived provided little resistance and were predisposed to accept the messages and impressions their hosts were anxious to convey. Deception and self-deception were, for the most part, highy integrated and mutually reinforcing. In the words of Jonathan Mirsky, a chastened pilgrim to Mao's China: "Throughout our trip. . . we sheathed the critical faculties which had been directed at our own Government and. . . humbly helped to insert the ring in our own noses." One of Mirsky's former guides agreed: "*We* wanted to deceive you. But *you* wanted to be deceived."[8] Mirsky's comment also illustrates the important fact that the favorable predisposition of these visitors is inseparable, in most cases, from their disenchantment with their own society. Rarely in the political psychology of groups and individuals has there been such an unmistakable connection between these two sets of attitudes: the rejection of one's own society and the endorsement of another. And the more defects the political tourist discovers at home, the more receptive he is liable to be to the attractions of the new society abroad. This pattern has established itself with great clarity beginning with the Soviet tours of the 1920s and still prevails at the time of this writing.

There have been four major waves of political tourism in this century: the Soviet, beginning in the 1920s and cresting in the mid-1930s, the Chinese between the late 1960s and mid-1970s, the Cuban throughout the 1960s and diminishing without ending through the 1970s, and the Nicaraguan in the early 1980s. Other destinations included North Vietnam during the war and communist Vietnam after the war, but these attracted fewer visitors. In each instance the pilgrimages and tours have been stimulated by conditions and developments within the societies the pilgrims came from. In the case of the Soviet tours the major impetus came from the Great Depression and the attitudes it generated among Western intellectuals, increasingly critical of their crisis-ridden societies and looking for alternatives to the waste, inefficiency and social injustice they witnessed. The resulting predisposition to admire and endorse what was then seen as 'the Soviet experiment' was so overpowering that the Soviet regime came to enjoy its greatest popularity among Western visitors when it was the most oppressive and most mismanaged economically, its people most deprived both materially and politically. It was during the Moscow Trials, the Purges, the collectivization of agriculture and the associated famines that the greatest number of enthusiastic Western intellectuals visited and praised most highly the Soviet system.

The pilgrimages to Cuba and China were also played out against a background of domestic crisis though this time the causes of social criticism were of a different nature. In the 1960s and early 70s it was not poverty or unemployment that stimulated the critiques and rejections of American (and Western) societies but rather 'emply affluence', the Vietnam war and the racial unrest in the United States. Once more other countries, this time Cuba and China, provided counter-models embodying sense of purpose, community and social justice, or visions of simple, good life uncorrupted by the evils of capitalism as they appeared in modern, Western industrial societies.

In turn, the discovery of Sandinista Nicaragua as the current haven of socialist ideals coincided with the election and re-election of Ronald Reagan and the alienation he inspired (or intensified) among the American intelligentsia and segments of the middle classes. There was also a feeling, as in the case of Vietnam, among the potential and actual political tourists, that Nicaragua deserved special sympathy if the Reagan Administration was opposed to it and tried to overthrow it— the enemy of a depised Administration was bound to be the friend of the social critics.

The major components of political hospitality varied little over time. Thus already in 1920 Emma Goldman observed during her visit to the Soviet Union that "The British Mission was entertained royally with theatres, operas, ballets and excursions. Luxury was heaped upon them while the people slaved and went hungry. The Soviet Government left nothing undone to create a good impression and everything of a disturbing nature was kept from the visitors." Half a century later Hans Magnus Enzensberger, the German writer, observed: "In Havana I kept meeting Communists in the hotels for foreigners who had no idea that the energy and water supply in the working quarters had broken down during the afternoon, that bread was rationed, and that the population had to stand for two hours in line for a slice of pizza; meanwhile the tourists in their hotel rooms were arguing about Lukacs."[9] A similar spirit of political hospitality made its appearance in Sandinista Nicaragua of the 1980s, judging by the report of a recent visitor: "In a private state dining room I ate a sumptuous meal with a *commandante* at a long table, attended by five servants. The image of the protruding stomachs of the 'spoiled ones of the revolution' intruded while we consumed our meringue pie."[10] Such observations spanning a period of sixty years draw attention to certain essential components of political hospitality.

The basic premises of the latter are quite uncomplicated. Since generalizing from personal experience is a universal and almost irresistible impulse, it is imperative to integrate such experiences with the political objectives pursued. The Soviet approach became widely imitated:

> In a sense . . . the whole of Russia . . . was converted into a giant simulated prestige project . . . such as the great Dneprostroy Dam, while a continuing propaganda campaign proclaimed . . . that these spectacular enterprises were typical, if not of the country's progress as a whole, at least of achievements so imminent that they could be claimed as actual. Perhaps the most striking example of such an enterprise has been the impressive Exhibition of Achievements of the National Economy in Moscow. Around this foreign tourists are traditionally freighted, and can observe a few spectacularly fecund cows, sheaves of super-corn and gleaming combine-harvesters, not as the glaring exceptions which they regrettably constitute.

By the same token, for those favorably predisposed the " . . . Dnieper Dam and underground [railway in Moscow], Soviet . . . polar expeditions . . . and Soviet flame-throwers assumed the fetish-character of a lock from the hair of the beloved."[11]

For intellectuals in particular, generalizing from personal (and often limited) experience is a characteristic activity. Bearing this in mind, one may understand why, for instance, John Kenneth Galbraith, after being shown the kitchen of a plant in Peking, was led to conclude that "if there is any shortage of food [in China] it was not evident in the kitchen."[12] While this was literally true, Galbraith intended to convey that such examples of abundance made a widespread food shortage in general unlikely, even absurd. In a similar spirit G. B. Shaw in the early 1930s, looking around in an elegant restaurant in Moscow, was led to scorn reports of famine, and Ramsey Clark, not having personally witnessed acts of violence in North Vietnam, went on record affirming the peaceful nature of that regime. More recently Billy Graham returned from the Soviet Union declaring that he had seen "no evidence of religious repression." Like Shaw and Galbraith before him, he too was impressed by the quality of provisions he received and was ready to recognize the broader significance of such experiences, noting that "the meals I had are among the best I have ever eaten . . . In the United States you have to be a millionaire to have caviar, but I had caviar with almost every meal [in the Soviet Union]." Visitors to Nicaragua, writing in the Amherst College magazine, provided yet another example of wishful generalizing from personal experience—or non-experience as happened to be the case—as they assessed Soviet influence in that country: "As for Soviet dominance, in all our travels we saw only two Russian-appearing civilian men."[13]

To make the generalization of personal experience politically useful, two conditions must be met. The visitor's exposure to such experiences must be selective and the circumstances of his visit generally pleasant. It is difficult for most people not to have a favorable impression of those who treat them with kindness. Likewise it is difficult to believe that those who are kind to us can be unkind to others. Even in the relatively rare cases when the political tourists were not favorably predisposed toward the country they visited, the generous and attentive treatment they received tended to produce a disarming sense of obligation. Being critical of one's generous hosts creates a sense of betrayal.

The mystique of personal experience, belief in the authenticity conferred by 'being on the spot' also works in favor of political hospitality. Everybody has a vested interest in the credibility of his personal experiences and the generalizations and judgments derived from them. It is devastating to entertain the possiblity of being reduced to the status of a gullible tourist on a conducted tour, at the mercy of guide-interpreters. Most political tourists succeed in convincing themselves that this is not the case. Moreover, few people are immune to attentive treatment.

Delightful banquets are addressed both to the stomach and to the ego; they enhance both a sense of general physical well-being and of self-esteem. Such treatment is likely to establish both gratitude and receptivity toward the sights and settings displayed for the benefit of the visitor. Combined with favorable predisposition, such techniques are likely to set into motion selective perception, the application of double-standards and contextual redefinition (the process whereby particular events or phenomena reevaluated by their overall context and not by their concrete attributes), all of which reduce the importance of the realities actually experienced. These mental processes were exemplified when a sympathetic American visitor to Cuba argued—after being told that 15 per cent of the patients in the Havana psychiatric hospital had lobotomies performed on them—that "we have to consider that under socialism lobotomy plays a different role. . . . These are socialist lobotomies." In a similar spirit a recent supporter of Nicaragua reported that "as for censorship, certain things are not allowed to be printed in the newspapers, but people can write or say anything as long as it is not printed."[14]

Not every visitor to socialist states gets the same treatment: privileges are usually allocated according to the perceived importance of the visitor. For instance in Cuba "Fidel controlled abundant resources that enabled him to regulate the treatment accorded to his guest . . . he used and measured out these resources with his customary skill." For the politically favored there were opulent suites or protocol houses; unimportant visitors received accommodations "where the air conditioning did not work and breakfast took an hour to arrive."[15] Making the important visitor feel pampered and enlarging his sense of well-being is the first step in the deployment of political hospitality. Next is the actual tour—the display of carefully selected sights, events, institutions, groups and individuals. The visitor is to be isolated from phenomena not conducive to a favorable assessment of the social system he is seeing. In Cuba, for example, standard sights included Ramon Castro's diary farm, the Isle of Youth, the Lenin Vocational School, the Alamar housing project and the psychiatric hospital in Havana.[16] Besides the itinerary, the pacing of the tour is considered important. Tours are generally over-organized and rushed, leaving little time for the visitor to reflect on what he has seen.

On the comparatively rare occasions when the tourists encountered sights contradicting the approved images of the New Society, the official responses were predictable:

> Most of the time the Cubans take us around in a tightly arranged schedule leaving little free time. But today . . . three of us decided to walk back through old Havana. We see it close up—rows of decaying guildings. . . . We take a photo of a typical line of citizens waiting to obtain rationed goods at a department store. Within a few moments, a uniformed officer appears. He signals us that we are to come with him.
>
> The next few hours are spent in the local police station. . . . Finally, an officer appears: 'You can go now. But you must understand that the revolutionary process is complex. We are a society emerging from

underdevelopment. Our struggle is difficult. You can take pictures of anything and go anywhere—but no pictures of rationing lines.'[17]

The techniques of hospitality were also revealingly captured in the observations of Susan Sontag, at the time a sympathetic visitor to North Vietnam: "We are truly seeing and doing a great deal: at least one visit or meeting is planned for every morning and afternoon, and often in the evening as well . . . we are in the hands of skilled bureaucrats specializing in relations with foreigners." She also noted the "constraint of being reduced to the status of a child: scheduled, led about, explained to, fussed over, pampered, kept under benign surveillance. Not only a child individually, but even more exasperating one of a group of children." Hans Magnus Enzensberger made similar observations of Cuba:

> The *delegate* is always cared for by an organization. . . . Usually he receives a personal guide who functions as translator, nanny and watchdog. Almost all contact with the host country is mediated through this companion which makes distinct the *delegate's* segregation from the social realities surrounding him. The companion is responsible for the traveller's program. There is no travelling without a program. The guest may express his wishes . . . however he remains dependent on the organization that invited him. In this respect he is treated as though he were still under age.[18]

Ronald Hingley called the guide-interpreters "officially licensed greeters or contact men . . . who bear all signs of having been drilled in the gentle art of manipulating foreigners."[19] It was their task on the one hand to isolate the tourists from aspects of their society that might yield unwelcome impressions and to forestall spontaneous, unplanned or accidental encounters with the natives. On the other hand, they were entrusted to interpret correctly the realities the visitors were allowed to see. These circumstances help one to understand the sentiments of an anonymous Nicaraguan citizen: "To ask in Nicaragua whether the Revolution benefits the people; whether one is in favor or against the Revolution; or whether one is for the 'contras' without taking into account the circumstances, the place where one is asking, who is present, the degree of trust that the person being interviewed has in the interviewer, is tantamount, in my view, of not being interested in an honest answer."[20]

In some instances the higher authorities undertook sweeping measures to prevent unauthorized contact between tourists and natives. No longer completely assured of the docility of their people, the Soviet government during the 1980 Moscow Olympic Games stationed both uniformed policemen and plain-clothes men at the hotels where foreigners stayed, to keep the natives out. In a letter addressed to the foreign visitors, a Soviet dissident warned how their every free moment would be filled with entertainment and hospitality. "Any Muscovite will tell you that you will be living not in Olympic villages but Potemkin villages. . . . All this construction is one gigantic con game as far as the Russian people are concerned. It has nothing to do with the way we actually live."[21]

In the following sections we shall examine a form of political hospitality which exemplifies the most far-reaching attempt to misrepresent the nature of the political systems concerned: the conducted tours of correctional institutions spanning a period of some sixty years.

II

It is perhaps understandable that oppressive political systems have made the most determined efforts not merely to conceal their coercive policies but the substitute for them make-believe penal institutions for the benefit of foreign visitors. While these forms of deception, as others, were pioneered in the Soviet Union under Stalin, similar practices also sprang up in China under Mao, in Cuba under Castro and in Vietnam in the 1980s. The obvious purpose of all such displays was to impress selected visitors with the humane treatment of prisoners and the policies of rehabilitation which were supposed to highlight the moral superiority of the political system as a whole. The success of these regimes in creating positive impressions of their penal institutions and practices—based on the inspection of the models presented to the visitors—demonstrates the outer limits of human gullibility (rooted in the wish to believe) as well as the influence of the refined techniques of hospitality.

An early deception in this category was worked upon G. B. Shaw. The playwright was taken to timber producing areas near Archangelsk to prove that no slave labor was being used. "The method of refutation was the dismantling of the barbed wire and sentries' towers, and the marching of the prisoners into the depths of the forests for a few days. . . . This proved effective."[22] In this case, Soviet deception was limited to dissimulation, the hiding of the real. A later and more spectacular deception was to involve both dissimulation and simulation, the creation of a false picture of reality. This was presented to Henry Wallace and his party when they visited the Soviet Union in 1944. We are fortunate to have records of his visit produced not only by him and his traveling companion, Owen Lattimore, but also one provided by a former inmate of one of the camps the Wallace party visited.

The setting was Magadan, in the Kolyma region of the Soviet Far East, one of the most notorious places of detention and forced labor.[23] Unlike Bolshevo (a model prison near Moscow), it was not designed as a model prison camp, therefore it had to be converted into one, or at least be made presentable enough for the benefit of the important visitors. Remarkably, Wallace and Lattimore throughout their visit remained unaware of being in the middle of a vast complex of labor camps. Wallace wrote:

> At Magadan I met Ivan Feodorovich Nikishov, a Russian, director of *Dalstroi* (the Far Northern Construction Trust), which is a combination of TVA and Hudson's Bay Company. On display in his office were samples of ore-bearing rocks in this region. . . . 'We had to dig hard to get this place going,' said Nikishov. 'Twelve years ago the first settlers arrived and put up eight prefabricated houses. Today Magadan has 40,000 inhabitants and all are well housed.'

Subsequently Wallace's party was "flown north along the Kolyma Road to Bereliakh, where we saw two placer gold mines. The enterprise displayed here was impressive. Development was far more energetic than at Fairbanks [in Alaska], although conditions were more difficult." He continued:

> We went for a walk in the taiga. . . . The larch were just putting out their first leaves and Nikishov gamboled about, enjoying the wonderful air immensely. . . . The Kolyma gold miners are big, husky young men, who came out to the Far East from European Russia. I spoke with some of them.

Wallace also recalled having been taken in Magadan to "an extraordinary exhibit of paintings in embroidery . . . made by a group of local women who gathered regularly during the severe winter to study needlework." He could not have guessed, given his level of information about the area and its inhabitants, that they too were prisoners. As to the NKVD troops (another incarnation of the political police) assigned to his party: "In traveling through Siberia we were accompanied by 'old soldiers' with blue tops on their caps. Everybody treated them with great respect. They are membes of the NKVD . . . I became very fond of their leader, Major Mikhail Cheremisenov, who had also been with the Wilkie party."[24]

Owen Lattimore's vision of Magadan was very similar to that of Wallace:

> Magadan is also part of the domain of a remarkable concern, the Dalstroi (Far Northern Construction Company), which can be roughly compared to a combination of Hudson's Bay Company and TVA. It constructs and operates ports, roads and railroads, and operates gold mines and municipalities, including, at Magadan, a first-class orchestra and a good light-opera company.

> At the time we were there, Magadan was also host to a fine ballet group from Poltava. . . . As one American remarked, high grade entertainment just naturally seems to go with gold, and so does high-powered executive ability.

> Mr. Nikshisov, the head of *Dalstroi,* had just been decorated with the Order of Hero of the Soviet Union for his extraordinary achievements. Both he and his wife have a trained and sensitive interest in art and music and also a deep sense of civic responsibility.[25]

It is hardly surprising that things looked rather different to the more permanent residents of these parts. Elinor Lipper, the former inmate, devotes several pages in her book to her recollections of the visit of Wallace and Lattimore, whose accounts she subsequently read.

> He [Wallace] does not mention, or does not know, that this city was built solely by prisoners working under inhuman conditions. . . . He does not say—or does not know—that this highway [which Wallace made admiring references to] was built entirely by prisoners and that tens of thousands gave their lives in building it. . . .

As to the exhibit of embroidery done by local woman on long winter evenings, she notes that " 'the group of local women' were female prisoners, most of them former nuns, who were employed to do needlework for such highly placed ladies as Nikishov's wife."

In regard to Lattimore's compairson of *Dalstoi* with TVA and Hudsons Bay Company, she remarks that, among other differences, neither of these two used forced labor or shot their workers if they refused to work.[26]

Wallace and Lattimore cannot be fully blamed for failing to notice the surrounding realities. Not only did they have no preconception of the Soviet penal system but their hosts made a determined and successful effort to remove the reminders of the true facts of life in Magadan and Kolyma. Their activities provide one of the best examples of the techniques of hospitality on record. Lipper writes:

> I do not know what he saw in the rest of Soviet Asia, but in Kolyma the NKVD carried off its job with flying colors. Wallace saw nothing at all of this frozen hell with its hundreds of thousands of the damned.

The access roads to Magadan were lined with wooden watch towers. In honor of Wallace these towers were razed in a single night.

At the edge of the city there were several prison camps, among them the large women's camp with its several thousand inmates. . . . Every prisoner who was there at the time owes Mr. Wallace a debt of gratitude. For it was owing to his visit that for the first and last time the prisoners had three successive holidays.

The purpose, Lipper continues, was to ensure that the visitors did not catch sight of prisoners in the camp yards: to keep them indoors, movies were shown continually. Wallace's group saw a play, but was unaware that most of the actors were prisoners. They visited well-stocked shops, filled for the occasion with rich merchandise. "Then Mr. Wallace went home and published his enthusiastic report on Soviet Asia. The watch towers were put up again, the prisoners sent out to work again, and in the empty shop windows were to be seen nothing but a few dusty and mournful boxes of matches."[27]

Subsequently Owen Lattimore was indignant about criticisms of his and Wallace's account of their visit to Kolyma. In his letter written in 1968 to the *New Statesman* he was in no mood to be self-critical: "Is it assumed that a visit of this kind affords an ideal opportunity to snoop on one's hosts?" he asked. "Should one return fully briefed to write an intelligence report 'exposing' what one had not seen?" He went so far as to imply scornfully that after all Nikishov, the camp commander, could not have been such a tyrant ("the 'unspeakable Nikishov' . . . must have slipped up in his control"), since Elinor Lipper survived to write her book. He seemed to suggest that being on a goodwill mission and allied to the Sovet Union were good enough explanations for the euphoric accounts he and Wallace produced. Finally, as if to forestall further criticism of those who had written such accounts, he invoked the spectre of "possibly [a] second wave of Joe McCarthyism"—a singularly inaccurate foreboding in the late 1960s.[28]

Further light is shed on the display of Soviet prisons by the unusual case of a Polish socialist who was exposed to both the staged view of the Soviet penal institutions provided for the benefit of foreigners and the inside view accorded to the inmates. Jerzy Gliksman visited the Soviet Union in 1935, a member of a tour group organized by Intourist. A few years later, after the German-Soviet treaty and the joint Nazi-Soviet occupation of Poland, he was one of tens of thousands of Poles sent to Soviet labor camps. Much of his book narrates his camp experiences, but there is one flashback to his 1935 visit which included an excursion to the model prison at Bolshevo, near Moscow. Gliksman may well be the only person who had a double exposure to Soviet prisons, first as a visitor and then as an inmate. His account is probably the only retroactively critical and analytical description of such a conducted tour:

> I awaited the trip to the prison-camp at Bolshevo with great impatience. Neither the Intourist nor the VOKS customarily included such visits in their excursion schedules. I was assured that I had been granted a special privilege.
>
> And indeed, I traveled to the camp with a distinguished group of people, which included correspondents of great foreign newspapers, several writers, artists, labor leaders, etc. . . . My immediate neighbor in the luxurious Intourist bus . . . was a noted Mexican painter. Most of the conversation during the ride concerned the good will shown by Soviet authorities in consenting to show to foreigners even the detention place of criminals. What other government in the world would as easily agree to such a visit?
>
> After a short ride we arrived at Bolshevo . . . our bus entered a lovely park containing numerous trees and flower beds. . . .

Gliksman's tour included inmates' spotless dormitories, white, clean bedding, workshops to accommodate all vocations, tasty and nourishing food in the dining hall. His party noted how used the inmates seemed to be to visitors, and remarked that the unguarded camp gate stood open. After listening to a speech by the tour guide, which stressed how self-government and voluntary activities permeated the institution, the author

> saw tears in the eyes of an elderly English lady. They were tears of appreciation and joy. 'Wonderful! Wonderful!' she kept repeating.
> 'How beautfiul the world could be!' a French movie director who happened to be sitting at my side whispered into my ear.

But his guide had more to offer. "I should like to convince you of the truth of my statement," he told us. "I should like to call a group of young people in the room and leave them here with you, all by themselves!" Needless to say, the inmates confirmed the guide's stories, expressing contentment and joy.[29]

Most foreign visitors of Soviet penal institutions in the 1930s had no subsequent occasion for disillusionment. They were impressed not only by the practices of the Soviet 'correctional system' but also by its spirit. The new terminology introduced also signaled lofty aspirations, as was reported by Dr. J. L. Gillin, a former president of the American

Sociological Society and "one of the leading authorities on penology in the United States": "In accordance with the spirit of the Revolution the terms current in capitalistic penology are discarded. There are no 'crimes'; there are 'wrongs'. . . . There is no 'punishment', only 'measures of social defence'. . . ."[30]

Ella Winter explained how crime, according to Soviet law, was the outcome of antagonisms existing in a society divided into classes; it was always the result of faulty social organization and bad environment. The word 'punishment' was not approved of: it had been replaced by the phrase: 'measures of social defense'. Soviet criminology seemed to assume that the 'criminal' was not a criminal. He was not to be treated as an outcast. This theory was carried out in practice in the communes run by the OGPU.[31]

D. N. Pritt, the British barrister and King's Counselor, wrote that terms of imprisonment were on the average shorter than in England and the treatment of prisoners was one of the most remarkable features of the whole system. The Russians applied fully and logically the theory that imprisonment must be reformatory, and not in the smallest degree punitive; and they regarded society as sharing with the criminal the responsibility for his crime.[32]

The famous British political scientist, Harold Laski, contrasted favorably the environmentalist, social-determinist approach prevailing in the U.S.S.R. with the state of affairs in Britain:

> The final principle . . . is the effort, through the creative organization of leisure, to prevent that deterioration of character which seems so frequent in our normal prison population through deprivation of the habits and opportunities associated with normal social relations.[33]

Anna Louise Strong, the famous American friend of the Soviet Union, wrote that Soviet justice "aims to give the criminal a new environment in which he will begin to act in a normal way as a responsible Soviet citizen. The less confinement the better; the less he feels himself in prison the better."[34]

Mary Stevenson Callcott, an American criminologist, concurred. "There had been a steady effort to remove what they termed the 'prison spirit'. There is, they tell you, no such thing as a 'captive' or 'prisoner'. The idea is to keep the person deprived of his liberty from feeling in any measure isolated . . ." In doing away with handcuffs, with solitary confinement, with any type of corporal punishment, and with any prison garb the enunciation of policy did its part, but in the approach of the immediate staff to the inmates "there is seen a wholesomeness that no [penal] code could account for."[35]

Sidney and Beatrice Webb, relentlessly trying to sound matter of fact even about their objects of admiration, reported that "the [prison] administration is well spoken of and is now apparently as free from physical cruelty as any prison in any country is ever likely to be." Some of their beliefs must have undoubtedly been based on their visit to Bolshevo which they described as "a remarkable reformatory settlement, which seems to go further, alike in promises and achievement, towards an ideal treatment of offenders against society than anything else in the world."[36]

Maurice Hindus, the veteran reporter on Soviet affairs, put it more strongly. "Vindictiveness, punishment, torture, severity, humiliation have no place in this system. The Soviets are acting on the assumption that it is not the criminal who is under obligation to society but that society is under obligation to the criminal . . . There were no chain gangs, no severe compulsions, no lockstep and no striped or other uniforms. The prison existed not for punishment but for ministration."[37]

George Bernard Shaw's vision of the successful Soviet rehabilitation procedures was even more vivid:

> In England a delinquent enters [the jail, that is] as an ordinary man and comes out as a 'criminal type', whereas in Russia he enters . . . as a criminal type and would come out an ordinary man but for the difficulty of inducing him to come out at all. As far as I could make out they could stay as long as they liked.[38]

Shaw was not the only one who believed that Soviet prisoners found conditions so pleasing that they were reluctant to leave after they served their sentence. "So well known and effective is the Soviet method of remaking human beings," wrote Anna Louise Strong, "that criminals occasionally now apply to be admitted."[39] Mary Callcott observed at the labor camp established on the site of the Moscow-Volga Canal that "I could never see what kept men in this camp unless they wanted to stay there. No convicts I have known would have any difficulty if they wanted to break away."[40]

Many of the institutions visited by the Western sympathizers seemed to have no walls, fences or watchtowers. Apparently the prison system was based on trust. G. B. Shaw, upon inspecting a prison for women, opined that "none of these women would have been better off as innocent persons earning their living in an English factory," and found being in a Soviet jail a "privilege" compared to those in capitalist countries.[41] Mr. and Mrs. Corliss Lamont met prisoners who informed them that they did not feel at all as if they were in a prison.[42] Lenka von Koerber, a German student of Soviet prisons, asked one of the prison officials she met: "Is there any dissatisfaction among the prisoners?" She was told that "Naturally there is a little sometimes but very seldom. Our prisoners have unlimited right of complaint."[43]

Mary Callcott saw inmates in the Sokolniki prison who were

> talking and laughing as they worked, evidently enjoying themselves. This was the first glimpse of the informal atmosphere that prevailed throughout, and which caused us to look in some amazement at occasional scenes such as encountered as we entered the auditorium where a good pianist was playing and other men stood beside him or leaned on the piano, at ease and absorbed in the music.

In the course of her visit she commented on the interaction between "attendants" (guards) and prisoners:

> There seemed to be no feeling of restraint in their presence, but on the contrary an existence of comradeship showed. . . . As we were leaving the yard an incident happened that impressed us greatly. From the flower garden, one of the men [a prisoner] came with an armful of flowers that he wished to present to a member of the party. . . . He did it with the air of one who brings a bouquet from a prized garden of his own.

Upon the suggestion of the prosecutor accompanying her party she proceeded to the auditorium where, once more,

> an informal atmosphere prevailed that it would be hard to give an impression of. The men talked in low excited tones, the music continued, the prosecutor and the prison director leaned against the piano. . . . It was difficult to believe that his was indeed a prison of a more serious type. It had all the earmarks . . . of a community affair of local talent about to start. The program was given with zest and enjoyment.

The same scenes and impressions repeated themselves in the Moscow Novinsky Prison for Women. The girls chatted and laughed gaily and were also "unrestrained by the presence of attendants or directress. . . . The parting word from our hostess was: "I wish I might visit a prison in America with the same freedom with which I have shown you this." At the Bolshevo Labor Commune Dr. Callcott was at a loss "what to call this place. To say that it is a penal institution is misleading." Here, even more than in other institutions that she visited, "the principle of 'trust' [was] held like a shining torch before the eyes of incredulous youngsters."[44]

Even at the prison of Tjumen, near Sverdlovak, Koerber found most of the prisoners . . . quite cheerful, which puzzled me because it is a closed institution and also a clearing house for prisoners . . . to be sent to far off colonies in Siberia. In spite of educational work and self-administration one inevitably finds some men in closed prisons who look depressed and who appear to suffer under their captivity. Perhaps the freedom from depression of the prisoners of Tjumen had something to do with the wonderfully clear, invigorating air.[45]

Harold Laski too applauded not only the underlying principles of penal policy but also their reflections in the living conditions of the prisoners he himself observed during his visit:

No one who has seen over a Russian prison, and compared that experience with a visit to one in England, can doubt that the advantage is all on the Russian side. The prisoners with whom I talked were . . . men who were conquering themselves. . . . They had not been disciplined into machines. . . . They had not been made to feel that they were cut off from the outside world. They had no sense of being under the continuous supervision of an unfriendly eye. There was neither furtiveness nor fear about them.[46]

There was virtually no aspect of the prison conditions and penal policies that failed to provoke the enthusiasm of such visitors. Cultural, educational and recreational facilities were among the most highly praised. For example, prisoners were reported to have absolute quiet in the reading rooms where they had a good supply of newspapers, periodicals and books. If a play bored the prison audience, the dramatic circle would be asked to choose more carefully in future.[47] Inmates enjoyed radio, classes in cultural and vocational subjects, gymnastics, books, dramatic performances, concerts both for and by the prisoners, and a prison newspaper, in which the right to make complaints was an essential feature.[48]

It will not be necessary to argue further that the Soviet authorities were successful in creating an impression among many visitors totally at odds with what we have learned about Soviet penal establishments from their former inmates.

III

The Chinese efforts to impress foreign visitors with the superiority of their penal institutions were less ambitious than Soviet undertakings in the Stalin era. Nonetheless they too displayed some institutions to good effect. Despite the precedent of Soviet misrepresentation, Western visitors did not come to China armed with greater scepticism; quite the contrary. Their readiness to be impressed and find a more advanced society was even more apparent than their predecessors in the Soviet Union. They seemed quite prepared to accept the Chinese official claims about the penal system and to regard what they were shown as representative.

On the whole, Western intellectuals perceived the Chinese penal policies in much the same manner as the Soviet ones were seen in the 1920s and 1930s, but in the light of what had since been learned about Soviet practices, the Chinese policies were regarded as superior. In China, by these perceptions, there were no bloody purges, no Gulags, no forced confessions, no show trials. According to Simone de Beauvoir, "the Chinese have carefully studied that precedent [the Russian Revolution, as a whole] in order not to repeat its mistakes . . . the dissimilarity to the Stalinist system is patent, since no administrative internment exists in China."[49]

The Chinese, like the early Soviet reformers, stressed rehabilitation, work therapy in place of enforced idleness, humaneness over punitiveness. Both Soviet and Chinese officials fervently claimed that the eventual reintegration of convicts into society was their ultimate goal, and that the prisons or labor camps did re-educate the inmates. Corliss Lamont had no difficulty in transferring his benign views of the Soviet correctional system to the Chinese: "In China," he wrote, "even though it remains a dictatorship, they don't shoot their dissenters; they 're-educate' them. And that procedure applies also to the highest officials. . . . The same spirit of re-education and rehabilitation governs the treatment of crimes and disputes among the Chinese people."[50]

While most Western visitors entertained a favorable view of the Chinese penal system, the majority had no direct experience of even selected aspects of it, as the Chinese were less anxious to display their penal institutions, especially in more recent times. Explorations of the system, and especially prison visits, became more difficult during and after the Cultural Revolution, except for the May 7 schools. Simone de Beauvoir's report and commentary is among the most detailed and deserves to be quoted at some length:

> I did personally see one prison. . . . This one in Peking was not a model prison. . . . all central prisons are the same in China. . . . Here, the prison is in the depths of a kind of park; two soldiers are on duty at the outer gate; but once you are inside it you see no wardens, no guards, no guides, only ununiformed and—a fact of some importance—unarmed overseers. They exercise the functions of foremen and political and cultural instructors. The inmates wear no special costume, they are

dressed like everybody else, and nothing distinguishes them from the employees who supervise their work. The shops are located in the middle of a big garden planted with sunflowers; were it not for the watchtower—unoccupied, furthermore—. . . one would take this for an ordinary factory. . . . They [the prisoners] have a field for sports at their disposal, a big courtyard with a theater where a movie is shown or a play presented once every week; the day I was there they were rehearsing a play of their own. There is also a reading room stocked with books and periodicals where they sit and relax.[51]

De Beauvoir's view that this was not a model prison was disputed by others. Her fellow countryman, Jules Roy, wrote: "It was a model prison. It was shown to all the newspapermen and all the television crews." Edgar Snow, who had stayed in this notable institution, Bao Ruo Wang (as well as in many others, unsung by visitors), wrote: " . . . Prison Number One is still one of the best attractions of the standard Peking tour for foreign visitors, and they react predictably. How many pages of emotional praise have I read since my release concerning the wisdom and humanity of the Chinese prison system, all of them due to the good offices of Prison Number One."[52]

Pierre Trudeau (former prime minister of Canada) and Jacques Hebert were evidently also taken to the same prison, where only one sentry stood guard and within the walls of which "a garden welcomes us, planted with greenery and fine fragrant trees. This is a prison?" They too reported the absence of bars and were informed of the details of the rehabilitation process.[53] Apparently James Cameron, the British journalist, too, was taken to the same prison in 1954. It was explained to Cameron that reform through production was the manner of inmates' redemption, and the governor of the prison averred that most of them responded well to such treatment. The few obstinate ones were administered a "Social Rebuke," defined as "a critical attitude taken up toward the offender by the more progressive comrades, which manifests itself in an atmosphere of disapproval." But if all else failed, privileges, such as gifts from relatives, could be revoked and sentences could be lengthened. There were no escapes from the prison. " 'As a matter of fact,' said the Governor . . . 'some don't want to leave. They ask to stay when their time is up,' "[54] a remarkable echo of G. B. Shaw's earlier perception of Soviet jails.

When Basil Davidson, the English journalist, and his party visited the jail in Peking and Shanghai in the early 1950s, he suggested that in China those accused of counter-revolutionary crimes of violence were more leniently treated than violent criminals would be in Britain. "Some of these prisoners were the opium gangsters of yesterday;

others were recalcitrant landlords. Little by little they will be drawn back into the everyday life of China.''[55] Peter Townsend's account of the Chinese policies of re-education was largely based on plays performed by the Pure River Corps dramatic group, composed of former Kuomintang secret service agents.

> The Pure River Corps had settled a tract of land between Peking and Tietsin at a place called . . . Pure River . . . Hundreds of men working eight or nine hours a day gradually turned the wasteland into a garden . . . There are three meals a day, with plenty of fish and grain, and meat once a fortnight. In season they caught crabs in the irrigation channels. . . . Some of the pleasures of the outside world were brought to them. There was plenty of entertainment. . . . Not all of those freed wanted to leave Pure River Corps. . . . But when a man was released every effort was made to provide him with a job and readjust him to society. . . .[56]

Felix Greene was another privileged Western visitor who was allowed some glimpses of Chinese penal institutions in the earl 1960s. He found "the Chinese doing what we had been trying to get the English authorities to do for years without success. Mainly, of course, to get the stigma, the moral stigma, out of imprisonment." He too was astonished and pleased to note the virtual absence of guards, the open gates, the low walls, no locks, no window bars and a generally relaxed, genial atmosphere.[57] Audrey Topping was one of the few Western visitors in the 1970s who had a chance to comment on the Chinese penal institutions and policies on the basis of firsthand impressions following a visit to Nanking prison. She reported that the "Chinese fought crime with the same vigorous, politically oriented enthusiasm with which they fought hunger" and went on to praise the rehabilitation program based on "political education and labor." Concerning prison security: " '. . . what if a prisoner tries to escape?' I asked. 'Escape!' he answered. 'Where would he escape to? If his ideology is no good, the people will turn him in again. There is no place to escape to.' ''[58]

The May 7 schools were introduced during the Cultural Revolution. Their purpose was the re-education through manual labor of officials, white-collar workers, teachers, managers, and other assorted members of the higher strata of non-manual workers. Given the earlier commitment to reform-through-labor, it is arguable whether these schools were innovative in that respect. Professor Fairbank saw them as a device to forestall "the dreaded revival of special privilege for a new ruling class divorced from the people" or a place "to which white-collar personnel . . . regularly repair in rotation for a spell of farm

work and Mao study.'' Bernard Frolic compared them to an ''adult
Boy Scout Camp, or maybe what the Civilian Conservation Corps was
like during the Depression.'' Harrison Salisbury described them as ''a
combination of a YMCA camp and a Catholic retreat.''[59] From the
official standpoint, being sent to these schools was not a punishment
but an opportunity for self-improvement for those who had lost contact
with the masses and were in danger of developing an elitist consciousness based on their superior skills and training. Manual labor was the
universal remedy for such tendencies. There was a strong religious
streak in the whole enterprise: humility was to be instilled through
some pain and suffering. Klaus Mehnert reported how, for example, a
woman doctor cleansed herself by immersion in the world of peasants
she had earlier despised as a city doctor: ''When one of the peasant
women was sick she moved in with her in order to give her better care.
Here she did some of the dirtiest jobs herself, and so she got rid of her
prejudices.'' Generally speaking, ''the most repellent jobs'' were considered the most therapeutic, above all the emptying of latrines. One
of the officials whose case was described to Mehnert ''had come to
understand . . . that emptying latrines is not a dirty job, but honorable
work.''[60] Macchiocchi sensed a ''strange fraternity, the unprecedented
humanity which permeates this school—where does it come from?''[61]

A more prosiac explanation of attitude change through such methods
was proposed by Jules Roy:

> Anyone even suspected of a lukewarm attitude toward the party was
> immediately sent to one of the people's communes for a period of re-
> education. It seldom required any great length of time, digging in the soil
> and carrying buckets of excrement, before the recalcitrant no longer
> thought of anything except returning home and gladly furnished all the
> required proofs of devotion to the revolution.[62]

IV

More recently the grotesque spectacle of well meaning Westerners
visiting Soviet or Chinese prison camps and judiciously praising their
humane and englightened aspects was repeated in communist Vietnam
on conducted tours of its 're-education camps'. As in the past the
visitors were critics of their own society (in this case the United
States), deplored its policy toward the host country—an especially
strong sentiment given the American involvement in the Vietnam
War—and were favorbly disposed toward its social system. Yet even
when such attitudes are taken into account the credulousness of these
visitors remains quite extraordinary, given the availibity of informa-

tion about such camps from former inmates (many of whom were among the boatpeople), and also in light of information accumulated over time about the characteristic treatment of political prisoners in communist countries.

The following quotations were taken from the statement of a group of American church officials testifying before a subcommittee of the U.S. congress. They included Dr. Paul F. McCleary, executive director of Church World Service, Midge Austin Meinertz, Director of Southern Asia, Church World Service, Dr. Harry Haines, Executive Director of the United Methodist Committee on Relief:

> Arrangements for our delegation's visit to a reeducation camp in Vietnam were made through the efforts of Vietmy, the Committee for Friendship and Solidarity with the American People, located in Hanoi, in cooperation with the Vietnam Fatherland Front Committee of Ho Chi Minh City, both of which applied to the offices of the Army for permission to see such a place. The request was made in connection with our stated concern regarding human rights violations reported by the press in relation to reeducation centers established following the war in 1975. We were accompanied by two members of the Vietmy Committee, including our translator . . . and two representatives of their Army, (one press officer). . . .

> At the camp itself, although there was a small open sentry stand at the gate, there were no guard towers, no barbed wire, none of the traditional 'prison' appurtenances. . . . we observed that the men appeared to be sufficiently fed and in general good health. . . .

> When asked directly about punitive measures for would-be 'escapees' the camp commanders indicated that there were none. . . .

> Although the camp commanders assured us that no punitive measures were employed . . . they did indicate that positive reinforcement for meritorious behavior was common (extra cigarettes, extra soap, towels, whatever). . . . As we walked into the u-shaped central area, the men were mostly sitting on their sleeping platforms in small groups talking, playing cards, playing guitars, smoking home-made water pipes. . . . When we asked as to the limitation on personal effects we were informed that there were none. . . .

> As we neared the closed end of the U near the volley ball court, we began to hear singing from one assembly hall. A camp chorus practicing, but certainly not surprised at our visit. When our visit was explained to those assembled, there was the group applause we had grown used to in orphanages, rehabilitation centers, any formal presentation.

Remarkably enough, these visitors could not grasp why a number of inmates (incarcerated because of their prior association with Americans) were unwilling to converse with them or ask any questions (". . . no hands were raised"). Thus, despite repeated promptings, no questions were addressed to the visitors eager to learn first hand from the inmates about the conditions in the camp. Instead, a group spokesman stood up and delivered a statement:

> The substance of both camp members presentation focused on the new government's policy of leniency, the realization that there had been no bloodbath, the value of reeducation and manual labor; statements recognizing that they were trying to understand mistakes of the past and learn skills to contribute to the new society so that they could be reunited with their loved ones. After we left the hall, the camp commander asked whether we wanted personal interviews which they would be glad to arrange.

Given the earlier fiasco, the visitors declined to converse with the English-speaking inmates, whom they delicately insisted on calling "camp members." Needless to say, the amenities of the camp included tool and furniture workshops, gardens, and dining halls. Small touches, flowers in a vase made of a painted can, caught visitors' eyes. "In some ways the camp looked as though it could have been a small tropical resort area. . . ." Indeed, it seemed to be Americans that "the entire process of reeducation is one reflecting the government's commitment to encouraging and enabling people to exercise their rights, restored as full participants in Vietnam's future." In the course of this fact-finding tour the visitors also consumed a "delicious chicken, pork, rice, fruit" lunch made "entirely of camp-grown produce and livestock prepared by camp members."[63]

There were other illustrations too of the highly patterned predisposition not to believe that the Vietnamese communist authorities could mistreat their prisoners. American critics of the war—usually sympathetic toward North Vietnam—refused to believe that American prisoners of war were mistreated. Richard Falk, for example, wrote that the concern with the condition of American prisoners was "the result of a deliberate and cynical effort on the part of the Nixon administration to exploit the plight of the POWs." In the same spirit another war protestor and social critic, David Dellinger, referred to the "Prisoner of War Hoax," and Richard J. Barnett of the Institute of Policy Studies pronounced "the evidence of mistreatment . . . highly suspect." North Vietnam authorities did everything they could to foster belief in their humane treatment of the prisoners, who were frequently displayed and questioned for the benefit of American delegations friendly toward North Vietnam. As a result, "Upon his return from Hanoi [Ramsey]

Clark assured a committee of Congress . . . that the prisoners he had met were well-treated, had exercise, got all they wanted to eat. . . ."[64]

Not all foreign visitors were so easily impressed. Reporter Craig Whitney for one noted that one of the "new economic zones" (in general rather inhospitable areas where urban people were forced to settle) "was obviously meant to be a showcase; the guest book showed a parade of foreign dignitaries. . . ." He also observed in the course of his visit to the country as a whole that ". . . I was officially off-limits for the Vietnamese. The people are forbidden to talk to any foreigner. . . ."[65]

V

A 1984 trip by the Rev. Jesse Jackson provided insight into the Cuban management of prison visits for the benefit of foreign dignitaries. A journalist reported:

> What the Rev. Jesse Jackson saw . . . was a clean, painted prison where inmates played baseball—a scene, one released prisoner says, is 'very different from the way of life in Cuban prisons.'
>
> . . . officials worked for a week cleaning and painting the outside of the prison in preparation for Mr. Jackson's visit. . . .
>
> The morning of Mr. Jackson's visit, 'common' prisoners were assembled hastily, given new baseball uniforms and equipment and told to play ball . . . 'as soon as he [Jackson] left, the balls and bats were taken away and the prisoners returned to their cells.'
>
> Such elaborate preparations, including special diets and 'extra things like Kool-Aid' are routine when foreign delegations visit Cuban prisons, Mr. Noble [a released prisoner] said.
>
> 'Jesse Jackson did not see the jail as it usually is,' he said. 'Many delegations come and believe the country is what they have been shown. . . .' For example, the inside of the prison has never seen any paint. And for those political prisoners left behind, there is no medical aid.
>
> Even when foreign delegations visit the prisons political prisoners . . . are kept in their cells in a separate part of the prison. Prisoners convicted of non-political crimes are those given extra food and allowed to play baseball. . . .

The prisoner also noted that "We are never allowed to play baseball except when visitors come. We call it 'the visitors' team'." On the day of the release of the prisoners "many of them were allowed to wear a shirt for the first time in nearly two decades. . . ."[66]

VI

A 1981 publication by the United Methodist Church saw Cuba as "a vision of the future,"[67] and the Rev. Jackson's 1984 journey to that country suggested that it still retained some appeal. However, the 1980 outpouring of 125,000 refugees, most of them poor, young and dark-skinned, reports about the persecution of homosexuals, the growing militarization of Cuba society and the stationing of tens of thousands of troops abroad had tarnished the earlier image. Indeed, by 1979 the supply of authentic, appealing and untarnished socialist regimes or revolutionary societies had, for all intents and purposes, ran out. Following the death of Mao in 1976, his successors' revelations about Chinese society largely demolished the worshipful accounts the pilgrims to China had brought back earlier. Mao himself ceased to be deified and the new Chinese regime moved towards freer economic conditions, later going so far as to reject Marxism as an infallible guide.

The Soviet Union had lost its attraction decades earlier as even its most ardent supporters were jolted out of their faith by the celebrated revelations of Khrushchev about the reign of Stalin. Vietnam, united under the victorious communist regime, remained a possible Utopia, but again there were some problems. It was one thing to celebrate North Vietnam during the war when American bombs rained down upon it and its heroic guerrillas seemed to defy American military might—it was something else to sing its praise after over a million people had escaped under extremely hazardous conditions from the southern portions of the newly united country.

Consequently, for Western radicals, the rise of Marxist-Leninist Nicaragua could not have been better timed. Here was a *small* country which had earlier been dominated by the United States, run by a corrupt pro-American dictator, and which had been redeemed by an authentic revolution—the culmination of years of guerrilla war. The new regime came complete with a youthful leadership, most of them former guerrilla fighters, intellectuals of sorts (among the top leaders Daniel Ortega Saavedra, Ernesto Cardenal and Sergio Ramirez Mercado had poetic-literary leanings or credentials); others among the leaders embraced liberation theology, thus combining lofty spiritual perspectives with pragmatic, humane concerns. There was something for everybody, including feminists who could admire Nora Astorga, the deputy foreign minister celebrated for helping to trap and kill a general of Somoza's. In the words of Susan Horowitz, "a political activist who champions liberal causes: 'Oh God . . . To try to get the guy to bed and then kill him! Fantastic. It's like a western. That's my dream, to do that to Reagan, George Bush, go right down the line.' ''[68]

In their statement renouncing their earlier New Left affiliations, Peter Collier and David Horowitz— two former anti-war radicals and co-editors of *Ramparts*—explained the Nicaragua phenomenon:

> Epidemics of radical chic cannot be prevented by referring to historical precedents. That perennial delinquent Abbie Hoffman will lead his Potemkin-village tours of Managua. The Hollywood stars will dish up Nicaraguan president David Ortega as an exotic hors d'oeuvre on the Beverly Hills cocktail circuit. In the self-righteous moral glow accompanying such gatherings, it will be forgotten that, through the offices of the U.S. government, more economic and military aid was provided the Sandinistas in the first 18 months following their takeover than was given to Somoza in the previous 20 years. . . .[69]

The pilgrimage to Nicaragua provides a textbook example of the attitudes and circumstances which converge and combine to create the phenomenon here discussed. All the factors forming favorable predispositions among potential political tourists are in evidence.

To begin with, there was a large number of people in the United States (and to a somewhat lesser extent in Western Europe) who regarded themselves as former activists of the 1960s or at least sympathizers with the values and causes of that period. Although by the early 1980s these causes and the movements promoting them were no longer vital or prominent, the attitudes and values giving rise to them did not disappear. Even after the so-called 'me decade' (the 1970s) there still was a great deal of free-floating residual political energy and propensity to radical social criticism. There was, in short, a reservoir from which sympathizers could be drawn towards a new socialist revolution, or revolutionary country.

The element of the opportune political holiday should also be added to the motives of the potential tourists. In the words of Charles Krauthammer it is ''. . . the thrill of the *political* holiday which offers not personal but social upheaval. It is a favorite recreation of what V. S. Naipaul calls the 'return ticket revolutionary', the comfortable Westerner who craves the whiff of social chaos and will travel to find it.'' Krauthammer explained how first we had the Venceremos Brigade, eager to swing a sickle at people's cane. ''Now we have the European and American kids who hang around Managua wearing combat boots and T-shirts that read NICARAGUA LIBRE.'' People of this type were, somewhat paradoxically, reinvigorated by the 1980 victory of Ronald Reagan. His election as president proved to their satisfaction how bad the system was. A participant in a demonstration protesting American policies in El Salvador said: "It's kind of a social thing. . . . It's a gathering of the left. It's a good chance for the left to unite on a common theme. Ronald Reagan is the best organizer we have."[70] Such was the intensity of this antagonism toward Reagan that anything he opposed almost automatically came to be favored by the new (and old) social critics. This became especially important in regard to Sandinista Nicaragua, since this was a country Reagan criticized and sought to destabilize. But by no means was this the only factor making the Sandinista regime appealing.

The image of Nicaragua as a small, victimized country, another authentic underdog confronting the might and malevolence of the United States, significantly added to its appeals. David Wald (three-time Peace and Freedom candidate for the U.S. Senate) said: "You see the victim of a bully being set upon, and the tendency of any decent citizen is to come to the aid of the victim."[71] Correspondingly, for many idealistic Americans, Nicaragua inspired the same kind of guilt as did Vietnam. Michael Harrington wrote: "I came back [from Nicaragua] far more ashamed of my country than at any time since the Vietnam war. The Nicaraguans are a generous people, a poor and often hungry people, who want to make a truly democratic revolution and it is we who work to subvert their decency. . . ."[72] The Sandinista regime quickly recognized the enormous political potential of such sympathies, making good use of the lessons of Vietnam. The main lesson was, of course, that public opinion in the United States has great influence on foreign policy. The media in particular were to play an important part, as were the campuses and the clergy.[73] The regime also learned to tailor its messages to different audiences. For example:

> To American visitors, frequently from church and university groups, the revolution is described as a humanist one, a struggle against misery. To other visitors, with left-wing views, the talk is of 'scientific change' with no interest in achieving 'perfect democracy', but a revolution aimed at a 'total social transformation'.[74]

There was an instant community of interest between American social critics predisposed to discover a new, authentic socialist regime unburdened by the mistakes and associations of the past and the Nicaraguan authorities intent on influencing American public opinion.

The tours and pilgrimages started immediately after the triumph of the revolution in 1979: ". . . now that the rebels are victorious, there is a new rush of assorted politicians, journalists, academics and 'revolutionary groupies' eager to witness . . . the first popular revolution on the continent in 20 years,'' reported a *New York Times* correspondent.[75] Throughout the early 1980s the tours gathered momentum: "So many Americans and Western Europeans have descended on Nicaragua to study and work with the Sandinista government that a word 'internacionalistas' has been coined to refer to them.''[76] A year later in 1983 it was reported that "over the past year the Managua Government has been a near permanent host to American fact-finding missions, ranging from church delegations to doctors, students and senators, who are warmly received, briefed and shown projects.''[77]

Nicaraguan government officials and their American supporters alike have been explicit about the objectives of the tours: " 'It is very important to us for Americans to know what is going on first hand,' said embassy spokesman Ricardo Esopinoza . . . 'It's really part of Nicaraguan foreign policy,' said Pamela Perry of San Francisco's Nicaraguan Information Center, another affiliate of the Washington based network.''[78] Many visitors volunteered to work on various projects such as picking coffee beans, like their predecessors in Cuba (the Venceremos Brigade), who cut sugar cane. However, the ". . . brigade's central thrust is what each volunteer does when he or she returns to the United States.'' In the words of Diane Passmore, national coordinator of the National Network in Solidarity with the Nicaraguan People, ". . . the major goal is to have them return and tell others about the country and their experiences.''[79] Following her ten day visit organized by the Council on Human Rights in Latin America, Republican State Senator Jeanette Hamby and her fellow women tourists had "the fervor of new converts.'' Their subsequent activities were not likely to disappoint their hosts: "In Oregon Hamby and her friends have been speaking regularly before political, civic and church groups. They are seeking to persuade people . . . that our policies there [in Nicaragua] are politically wrong and morally corrupt.''[80]

The Nicaraguan public relations campaign has been appropriately described as ". . . a low key but relentless sales job, subtle but effective, high in moral tone but aimed right at the guts of the Americans' conscience.'' Interior Minister Borge concurred: "Nicaragua's most important war is the one fought inside the United States. . . . The battlefield will be the American conscience. . . .''[81] An ambitious outgrowth of these efforts has been the so-called "resistance pledge'' to engage in civil disobedience "at Congressional field offices, the White House, or other pre-designated U.S. federal facilities, including federal buildings, military installations, offices of the CIA, the State Department and other appropriate places'' in the event that "the U.S.

invades, bombs, sends combat troops or otherwise significantly escalates its intervention in Central America."[82]

It is not being suggested here that Nicaragua in the early 1980s was a country like the Soviet Union under Stalin or China under Mao. Nor was it, however, a country such as depicted by its American admirers. Thus even when allowances are made for the overpowering effects of favorable predisposition and the inherent limitation of learning about a country through a brief conducted tour, the credulousness of the visitors remains staggering. This conclusion does not rest merely on historical analogies, on the lessons of past pilgrimages and political tours. There is by now sufficient information available about Nicaragua to cast serious doubt on the images projected by its rulers and foreign admirers. According to Octavio Paz, the Mexican writer, "the process of Sovietization is quite advanced" in Nicaragua today.[83] Much additinal evidence originates with Nicaraguans untainted by any association with the Somoza regime, who were in fact supporters of the revolution which deposed him.

Eden Pastora is one such promiment leader who fought first Somoza and then the Sandinistas. He wrote:

> Sadly, the revolution's bright promise has not been realized. The Sandinist directorate has replaced the Somozas with a totalitarian tyranny. . . .
>
> . . . the Government has emasculated the country's independent labor unions. . . . Freedom of the press has been practically extinguished . . . the directorate has set up a powerful secret-police apparatus with the help of . . . East German or Cuban agents. . . .
>
> . . . [The regime] remains silent in the face of the Soviet invasion of Afghanistan and acts as an apologist for the . . . crackdown in Poland. . . . Despite . . . loans and outright grants totalling over $1.5 billion, the economy is in shambles. . . . Living conditions are deteriorating. The real wages of Nicaragua's working class have plummeted 60 percent during last year. . . .[84]

Domingo Sanchez Delgado, "a dedicated Marxist-Leninist" and nominee of the Socialist Party for President, said: "We are not Sandinistas. . . . We don't want a country where the press is not free . . . where power is abused . . . where young people can't go to the movies because they are afraid they will be captured for military service. . . . There is arrogance and abuse of every sort. This is hardly revolutionary conduct. . . ."[85]

Virgilio Godoy Reyes had been Minister of Labor in the Sandinista government from 1979 until 1984. He reached the conclusion that "These five years have shown the great error we made in giving our confidence to those who think of nothing but the interests of their party. . . . After so many dreams, disillusion. Instead of liberty, new forms of oppression. To say that the workers and peasants are in power is a monstrous lie. . . . The only equality we are achieving is equality in misery."[86] Arturo Jose Cruz, former Sandinista ambassador to the U.S. and the most prominent democratic critic of the regime, wrote after the 1984 elections:

> . . . I badly underestimated the vigor with which the newly elected Nicaraguan Government would preceed to repress its opponents and militarize the state. The Sandinistas are evidently determined to ignore the democratic yearnings of the Nicaraguan people. . . . The problem of Nicaragua is not MIG's and assault helicopters. It is, fundamentally, the absence of liberty—the character of the Government that will put such weapons to use.[87]

There has also been criticism among some of the former foreign admirers of the regime. Robert S. Leiken, who by early 1985 had made six trips to Nicragua, deplored the treatment of the Indians but pointed out that this was not the only repressive policy pursued by the regime. Contrary to the claims of American sympathizers, the Sandinistas have, between July 19, 1979 and December 12, 1982, carried out over 8,000 political executions, according to the Nicaraguan Commission of Jurists. Such examples of political violence, religious persecutions and human rights violations have been extensively documented by Humberto Belli, who used to be a supporter of the Sandinistas and editorial page editor of *La Prensa*.[88]

Yet, in a statement addressed to the people of the United States, Gabriel Garcia Marques, Carlos Fuentes, Gunter Grass, Graham Greene, Julio Cortazar, William Styron and Heinrich Boell protested Ameican threats to the "modest but profound achievements of the Nicaraguan revolution."[89] It seems scarcely possible that these prominent men of letters would have endorsed such a statement had they not become the victims of deception.

Of all the groups supporting the Marxist-Leninist regime in Nicaragua, the churches and those affiliated with them have been the most active and dedicated. Such a widespread involvement of the clergy has been the most distinctive characteristic of the pilgrimage to Nicaragua. The support took many forms: there was substantial financial assistance, there were tours, proselytizing in the media, and political lobbying. Reportedly, Maryknoll nuns working in Nicaragua paid visits in Washington to House Speaker Thomas O'Neill influencing his outlook.[90] The Reverend William Sloane Coffin, who had earlier affirmed the decency of the North Vietnamese communist regime, now assured readers of the *New York Times* that the Nicaraguan regime could not possibly be Marxist-Leninist since it included Roman Catholic priests.[91] A reporter for the *Catholic Worker* sensed "an atmosphere of youth, vitality and hope throughout Nicaragua."[92] Father Richard Perston of Lansing, Michigan, reached the conclusion that "the reign of God has arrived in Nicaragua,"[93] echoing a 1928 discovery by the English Quaker D. F. Buxton that, in the Soviet Union, communist society "is a more Christian one than ours."[94]

Given the circumstances, it is perhaps hardly surprising that the Sandinistas, like the Soviets, Chinese, Cubans and Vietnamese before them, felt sufficiently confident that the combination of their determination to deceive and the visitors' willingness to be deceived entitled them to advance to the most far-reaching stage of political deception—conducted tours of correctional institutions.

American churchmen visiting Nicaragua in 1983 reported on the prison system there, saying that "The prison we visited was the first of seven prison farms. Former national guardsmen willing to cooperate are moved through a series of more and more relaxed prison settings. The prison we saw had 38 inmates, no armed guards, conjugal visits." One prisoner "had high praise for the government and said if freed he would go to fight for the FSLN in the north. Money made from the crops is put back into improvements for the prison . . . As part of the routine the men attend classes in literacy and agriculture. Many who previously had no skill but shooting a gun, now have plans to become farmers."[95]

Günter Grass, the famous German writer and one of the sponsors of the writers' appeal, was given a personal conducted tour by Tomas Borge:

> We have been able to read that there are political prisoners in Nicaragua. What is meant, of course, are the members of the National Guard, who perpetrated crimes against the people. . . . We asked about them, and Tomas Borge, a minister of state [state security, or police] . . . immediately proposed a visit to Tipitapa prison. . . . It differs from Somoza's torture centers by the humane way in which sentences are carried out. . . .
>
> Several hundred former national guardsmen live here and . . . have received sentences ranging from three to thirty years. There is no death penalty. Prisoners work from Monday to Friday, and they have built a hospital and two new prisons with larger cells. . . . Saturdays and Sundays are kept free for visitors who come each week and are allowed to stay for three or four hours. There exist rooms . . . for married couples who are permitted a so-called intimate visit.

"If we take revenge [said Borge], we destroy the purpose of the revolution. Our revolution represents the renunciation of revenge."

. . . in this tiny, sparsely populated land, where Christ's words are taken literally, the Sandinista revolution provides a different example.[96]

Clearly, the techniques of deception associated with prison tours have traveled well.

VII

Political tourism in general and visits to Potemkin prisons in particular illustrate the deceptive potential of carefully prepared hospitality The fact that these techniques are working so well in Nicaragua today illustrates the continuity and tenaciousness of a method of political warfare and deception that was introduced and institutionalized by the Soviet Union in the 1920s. The survival of political hospitality is all the more noteworthy since each successive pilgrimage has, to some degree, been discredited as each country it served to elevate and glorify— the Soviet Union, China, Vietnam, Cuba—came to be seen in a more realistic and critical light with the passage of time and the accumulation of information. Moreover, while each new generation of Westerners contains pilgrims eager to discover the attractions of some new putatively socialist state, their ranks are swollen by veterans of past pilgrimages, tireless seekers after social justice, hardened social critics and protesters.

Although tours to Nicaragua followed a well-established pattern, they appeared to have some unique characteristics too. The regime has been more candid than other socialist states about the specific political objectives that the tours were intended to promote; mass tourism seems to have received a higher priority than VIP treatment of selected prominent figures; the emphasis on creature comforts so evident in earlier pilgrimages seems to have given way to "roughing it," presumably to infect visitors with a sense of guilt at the United States' past and present responsibility for material underdevelopment.

The Sandinista regime in the first half of the 1980s has not achieved full, totalitarian control. Their aim, it would seem, has not been to present images of a communist society that leave visitors impressed with communism—the total redefinition of social realities such as was successfully attempted in the Soviet Union and China. Instead, the Sandinistas seemed anxious to prove that some pluralism had survived. The organizational and moral support of the American churches, so important for the popularity and legitimacy of the regime, apparently required that the Marxist-Leninist character of the ruling party be portrayed as something else—some kind of benevolent socialism compatible with Christianity.

In all the countries involved in these deceptions, the opening of model prisons to visitors has illustrated both the depth of the commitment to deceive and the success which really methodical, sustained efforts can achieve. The impact of these techniques on Western public opinion and foreign policy reaffirms the importance Marxist-Leninist regimes assign to ideas—including impressions and beliefs—in the struggle for political influence and advantage.

Notes

1. Milovan Djilas, *The New Class* (New York, Prager, 1957, p. 31.
2. Jeanne Kirkpatrick, *Dictatorships and Doublestandards* (New York, Simon & Schuster, 1983), p. 17.
3. There are a few exceptions. See for example: Sylvia R. Margulies, *The Pilgrimage to Russia: The Soviet Union and the Treatment of Foreigners, 1924–1937* (Madison, Wisconsin University Press, 1968); Paul Hollander (i), *Political Pilgrims: Travels of Western Intellectuals to the Soviet Union, China and Cuba 1928–1978* (New York, Oxford University Press, 1981 and New York, Harper & Row, 1983); Hollander (ii), "Sojourners in Nicaragua: A Political Pilgrimage," *National Catholic Register,* 29 May 1983. See also Enzensberger *cited* below.
4. Ronald Hingley, *The Russian Mind* (New York, Scribner, 1977), p. 94.
5. See Richard H. Shultz and Roy Godson, *Dezinformatsia—Active Measures in Soviet Strategy* (Washington, Pergamon Brassey, 1984).
6. Hingley, *cited,* p. 108–109; here Hingley quoted George F. Kennan.
7. A recent study of China noted: "The simple presence of a foreigner is usually enough to deter people from arguing loudly, brawling, or molesting others. . . . " David Bonavia, *The Chinese* (Harmondsworth, Penguin Books, 1980), p. 164, suggesting similar cultural dispositions in that country.
8. Jonathan Mirsky, "Back to the land of little red lies," *The Observer,* 28 October 1979, p. 9.
9. Emma Goldman, *My Disillusionment in Russia* (New York, Crowell, 1970), p. 59; Hans Magnus Enzensberger, "Tourists of the Revolution," in *The Consciousness Industry* (New York, Seabury Press, 1974), p. 152.
10. Robert S. Leiken, "Nicaragua's Untold Stories," *The New Republic,* 8 October 1984, p. 17.
11. Hingley, *cited,* p. 246; see also Arthur Koestler, "Soviet Myth and Reality," in *The Yogi and the Commissar* (New York, Collier Books), 1945, p. 130.
12. John K. Galbraith, *China Passage* (Boston, Houghton Mifflin, 1973), p. 54.
13. Quoted in Eugene Lyons, *Assignment in Utopia* (London, Harrap, 1938), p. 430; "Clark's Hanoi Comments," *New York Times,* 25 October 1974; "Graham Offers Positive View of Religion in Soviet," *New York Times,*

13 May 1982; see also "Billy Graham Rebuffs Criticism of Soviet Trip," *New York Times*, 18 May 1982; and "Billy Graham, Back Home Defends Remarks," *New York Times*, 20 May 1982; F. Shepherd and G. Shepherd, "On the ground in Nicaragua," *Amherst*, Winter 1982, p. 20.

14. Ronald Radosh, "Cuba: A Personal Report," *Liberation*, January 1974, p. 26; Thomas J. Crowe (as told to Isabella Halsted); " 'Witness for Peace' visits Nicaragua," *Daily Hampshire Gazette* (Northampton, Mass.), 9 May 1984, p. 33.

15. Jorge Edwards, *Persona Non Grata* (New York, Pomerica, 1977), pp. 210–211.

16. Vivian Warner Dudro, "Covering Cuba," Paper presented at conference on *The Media and the Cuban Revolution*, Washington, D.C., November 1984, p. 13.

17. Radosh, *cited*, pp. 26–27.

18. Susan Sontag, *Trip to Hanoi* (New York, Farrar, Straus & Giroux, 1968), p. 12; Enzensberger, *cited*, pp. 135–136.

19. Hingley, *cited*, p. 95.

20. "Letter from Nicaragua," *New America*, July 1984, p. 7.

21. Anthony Austin, "U.S. Tourists Tourists' View: Impressive, but Grim," *New York Times*, 23 July 1980, p. B9; "The Potemkin Olympics," *New York Times*, Op-ed page, 17 July 1980.

22. Robert Conquest, *Kolyma: The Arctic Death Camp* (New York, Viking, 1978), p. 204.

23. See Conquest, *cited*

24. Henry A. Wallace, *Soviet Asia Mission* (New York, Reynal & Hitchcock, 1946), pp. 33–35, 217, 84.

25. Owen Lattimore, "New Road to Asia," *National Geographic Magazine*, December 1944, p. 657.

26. Elinor Lipper, *Eleven Years in Soviet Prison Camps* (Chicago, Regnery, 1951), pp. 111–112, 113, 115.

27. Lipper, *cited*, pp. 266–269.

28. Owen Lattimore, "Letter to the Editor," *New Statesman*, 11 October 1968, p. 461.

29. Jerzy Gliksman, *Tell the West* (New York, Gresham, 1948), pp. 163–178.

30. J. L. Gillin, "The Prison Systems," in Jerome Davis (ed.), *The New Russia* (New York, John Day, 1933), pp. XI, 220.

31. Ella Winter, *Red Virtue* (New York, Harcourt, Brace & Co., 1933), p. 206.

32. D. N. Pritt, "The Russian Legal System," in Margaret I. Cole (ed.), *Twelve Studies in Soviet Russia* (London, Gollancz, 1937), p. 161.

33. Harold J. Laski, *Law and Justice in Soviet Russia* (London, Hogarth Press, 1935), p. 25.

34. Anna Louis Strong, *This Soviet World* (New York, Holt & Co., 1936), p. 254.

35. Mary Stevenson Callcott, *Russian Justice* (New York, Macmillan, 1935), pp. 161, 236–237.

36. Sidney and Beatrice Webb, *Soviet Communism: A New Civilization?* (New York, Schribner's, 1936), pp. 587, 588.

37. Maurice Hindus, *The Great Offensive* (New York, Smith & Hass), pp. 305, 306.

38. George Bernard Shaw, *The Rationalization of Russia*(Bloomington, Ind., Indiana University Press, 1964), p. 91 (first published in 1931).
39. Strong, *cited,* p. 262.
40. Quoted in Strong, *cited,* p. 258.
41. Shaw, *cited,* pp. 92, 73.
42. Corliss and Margaret Lamont, *Russia Day by Day* (New York, Covici, Friede, 1933), p. 142.
43. Lenka von Koerber, *Soviet Russia Fights Crime* (London, Routledge, 1934), p. 179.
44. Callcott, *cited,* pp. 186–187, 189–190, 192, 201, 221, 224.
45. Koerber, *cited,* pp. 17, 19, 197.
46. Laski, *cited,* p. 27.
47. Koerber, *cited,* pp. 40, 43, 44–45.
48. Laski, *cited,* p. 28.
49. Simone de Beauvoir, *The Long March* (Cleveland and New York, World Publishing Co., 1958), p. 388.
50. Corliss Lamont, *Trip to Communist China: An Informal Report* (New York, Basic Pamphlets No. 20–21, 1976), pp. 20–21.
51. Beauvoir, p. 385.
52. Jules Roy, *Journey Through China* (New York, Harper & Row, 1967), p. 53; Bao Ruo Wang, *Prisoner of Mao* (Harmondsworth, Penguin, 1976), p. 99. On Snow's visit to the same jail, see Edgar Snow, *Red China Today* (New York, Vintage Books, 1970), pp. 357–360.
53. Jacques Hebert and Pierre Elliot Trudeau, *Two Innocents in Red China* (Toronto, New York, London, Oxford, 1968), pp. 21, 21–23.
54. James Cameron, *Madarin Red: A Journey Behind the 'Bamboo Curtain'* (London, Joseph, 1955), pp. 96, 97, 99.
55. Basil Davidson, *Daybreak in China* (London, Cape, 1953), p. 183.
56. Peter Townsend, *China Phoenix: The Revolution in China* (London, Cape, 1955), pp. 318, 319, 320, 321.
57. Felix Greene, *Awakened China: The Country Americans Don't Know* (New York, Doubleday, 1961), pp. 55–56, 208–209.
58. Audrey Topping, *Dawn Wakes in the East* (New York, Harper & Row, 1973), pp. 66–67.
59. John K. Fairbanks, "The New China and the American Connection," *Foreign Affairs,* October 1972, p. 40; Michael Frolic, "Wide-eyed in Peking: A Diplomat's Diary," *New York Times Magazine,* 11 January 1976, p. 32; Salisbury quoted in Sheila Johnson, "To China with Love," *Commentary,* June 1973, p. 44.
60. Klaus Mehnert, *China Returns* (New York, Dutton, 1972), p. 63.
61. Maria Antoniette Macciocchi, *Daily Life in Revolutinary China* (New York, Monthly Review Press, 1972), p. 96.
62. Roy, *cited,* p. 164.
63. "Joint Statement by Dr. McCleary and Ms Meinertz," quoted in *Time for Candor: Mainline Churches and Radical Social Witness* (The Institute on Religion and Democracy, Washington, D.C., 1983), pp. 63–67.
64. Quoted in Guenter Lewy, *America in Vietnam* (New York, Oxford University Press, 1978), pp. 336–337.
65. Craig R. Whitney, "A Bitter Peace—Life in Vietnam," *New York Times Magazine,* 30 October 1983, pp. 61, 62.

66. Stephanie L. Nall, "Prisoner says Cubans fooled Jackson on jail," *The Washington Times*, 2 July 1984; Joel Brinkley, 70 Innings of Baseball, Then Freedom," *New York Times*, 30 June 1984; "Freed Prisoners look back in anger at long years in Cuba," *Los Angeles Herald*, 30 June 1984; see also Diego A. Abich, "Fidel Castro's Role Behind Jesse Jackson's Cuba Tour," *Wall Street Journal*, 2 November, 1984.
67. Rusty Davenport, "Cuba: A Land of Contrast," *Common Ground* (A Newsletter of the United Methodist Voluntary Service), Summer issue, 1981, No. 3/4, quoted in *Time for Candor*, cited, p. 83.
68. Art Harris, "Of Nicaragua—Nora Astorga's Revolutionary Journey," *The Washington Post*, 4 October 1984, p. B8.
69. Peter Collier and David Horowitz, "Goodbye to All That," *Washington Post Magazine*, 17 March 1985.
70. Charles Krauthammer, "Holiday: Living on a Return Ticket," *Time Magazine*, 27 August 1984, p. 52; Martin Tolchin, "Thousands March in Washington Protest on Salvador," *New York Times*, 26 March 1982.
71. *San Jose Mercury News*, 7, October 1984, p. 21A.
72. Michael Harrington, "Economic Troubles Besetting Nicaragua, *New York Times*, Op-ed page, 16 July 1981.
73. For an illuminating discussion of these parallels see Doan Van Toai and David Chanoff, "Learning from Vietnam," *Encounter*, September–October 1982; for an example of the sympathetic television coverage of Nicaragua, especially by public television, see John Cory, "Bringing Central America Into Focus," *New York Times*, Entertainment Section, 15 April 1984.
74. John Vinocur, "Nicaragua: A Correspondent's Portrait, "*New York Times*, 16 August 1983, p. A4.
75. Alan Riding, "A Reporter's Notebook: Managua Relaxes," *New York Times*, 23 July 1978, p. A3.
76. Raymond Bonner, "A Melting Pot Is Converging in Nicaragua," *New York Times*, 12 September 1982, p. 4.
77. Marlise Simons, "Nicaraguan Rebel to Seek Money in U.S.," *New York Times*, 19 September 1983, p. 3.
78. *San Jose Mercury News*,cited.
79. "U.S. Volunteers Help Nicaragua With the Harvest," *New York Times*, 16 February 1984.
80. Colman McCarthy, "The Other Side of the Sandinistas," *The Washington Post*, 8 July 1984, p. K2.
81. Juan Tamayo, "Sandinistas aim soft sell at activists," *Miami Herald*, 14 December 1983.
82. See for example, Gerry Scoppetuolo, "Resistance Pledge," in *River Valley Voice*, Winter 1985, p. 31.
83. Octavio Paz, "Which Latin America?", *Partisan Review*, No. 3, 1984, p. 381.
84. Eden Pastora, "Tyranny of Far Left or Far Right? Nicaraguan Sees Another Choice," *New York Times* Op-ed page, 14 July 1982.
85. Stephen Kinzer, "Marxist's Mission: Defeat Sandinistas," *New York Times*, 7 October 1984, p. 14.
86. Stephen Kinzer, "Nicaragua Party Fails to Stop Vote," *New York Times*, 23 October 1984.

87. Arturo Jose Cruz, "Managua's Central Problem," *New York Times*, Op-ed page, 6 December 1984.
88. Humberto Belli, *Christians Under Fire* (Garden City, Michigan, Puebla Institute, 1984), p. 129. This is not merely a record of religious intolerance but a far more comprehensive and thoroughly documented report on a wide range of Sandinista policies. For another account of developments in Nicaragua see Sister Camilla Mullay, O.P., and Father Robert Barry, O.P., *The Barren Fig Tree—A Christian Reappraisal of the Sandinista Revolution* (Washington, D.C., The Institute on Religion and Democracy, 1984).
89. "To the People of the United States," *New York Times*, 17 April 1983, p. 55.
90. See for example "Church Support for Pro-Sandinista Network" (Institute on Religion and Democracy Report, Washington, D.C., 1984); on the support among Catholic missionaries see Joan Frawley, "Revolutionists Win Converts Among Catholic Missionaries," *Wall Street Journal*, 7 October 1983; David Rogers and David Ignatius, "The Contra Fight," *Wall Street Journal*, 6 March 1985, p. 20.
91. William Sloane Coffin, "Nicaragua Is Not An Enemy," *New York Times*, Op-ed page, 31 July 1983.
92. Peggy Scherer, "Journey to Central America," *Catholic Worker*, January–February 1984, p. 8.
93. "the Reign of God Has Arrived in Nicaragua," *Catholic Weekly*, 25 March 1983, p. 7.
94. D. F. Buxton, *The Challenge of Bolshevism: A New Social Ideal* (London, Allen & Unwin, 1928), pp. 27, 85.
95. Mimeographed Report of Trip to Nicaragua by Fr. Bryan McNeil and Mr. Salvador Colon from the diocese of Houston, November 1983, p. 9.
96. Günter Grass, "Epilogue: America's Backyard," in Martin Diskin (ed.), *Our Backyard* (New York, Pantheon Books, 1983), pp. 246–247.

14

The Appeals of Revolutionary Violence: Latin-American Guerillas and American Intellectuals

Among these fully awake men, at the height of their powers, sleeping doesn't seem like a natural need, just a routine of which they had more or less freed themsleves . . . [They] exercise a veritable dictatorships over their own needs . . . they roll back the limits of the possible.

Jean Paul Sarte[1]

In Cuba hatred runs over into the love of blood; in America all too few blows are struck into flesh. We kill the spirit here . . . We live in a country very different from Cuba . . . You [Castro] were aiding us, you were giving us psychic ammunition . . . in that desperate silent struggle we have been fighting with sick dead hearts against the cold insidious cancer of the power that governs us, you were giving us new blood to fight . . .

Norman Mailer[2]

. . . we choose as a culture—and our press chooses as a profession—not to know of the blood of mothers and children spilled in the path of revolution and what is called progress . . . For these murderers on the left, there are always, in our universities and churches and entertainment and opinion industries, . . . lionizing folk eager to mythologize the cruel and violent as virtuous. Their reputations somehow remain untouched by the rivers of blood that flow right past them.

Martin Peretz[3]

I.

Norman Mailer's admiration of authentic political violence—such as he detected in revolutionary Cuba—aptly captures the emotions and approbation Latin American guerilla violence has evoked in many American intellectuals. Such violence was admired and approved of because of its passionate and spontaneous nature ("the love of blood") and because its revolutionary legitimation; for Mailer and other romantics, passion proved authenticity and good intentions, strong feelings were self-evident proof of a good cause. Perhaps, as the early Bolsheviks felt, "soiling one's hand" with violence provided the ultimate proof of authentic commitment (". . . he is indeed an 'egoist' who refuses the small sacrifice of dirtying his person for the sake of the salvation of humanity."[4] Cuban style (guerilla) violence stood in dramatic contrast with Mailer's vision of American repression: silent, cold, colorless, indirect, unspontaneous, inauthentic, routinized, lacking in passion.

It will be a major proposition of this paper that the appeals of Latin American guerilla violence and the associated idealization of the guerilla fighter are forms of social criticism directed at the United States. In the eyes of their American admirers the Marxist guerillas are surrogate avengers of the evils American capitalism perpetuates. The admiration of the guerillas is closely linked to the endorsement of the social-political values they represent and the political system they seek to establish. In turn the perceived authenticity of guerilla violence,—a major source of its attraction—reflects a more diffuse longing for authenticity on the part of the social critics. This longing for authenticity has in fact been a main theme of social criticism in American society since the 1960s. While it may be argued that Mailer expressed these sentiments in a more extreme and forceful way than entertained by other American intellectuals, such attitudes have been widespread and produced noteworthy double standards in judging political violence. While such double standards are not new—insofar as most people are always willing to condone questionable means to ends they consider laudable—the applause for Latin American guerilla violence is among the most striking expressions of this age old phenomenon in recent times.

Generally speaking estranged intellectuals tend to look upon revolutionary violence as invigorating and redeeming, or at least acceptable and justifiable, possibly a regrettable necessity but hardly a cause for moral indignation, let alone outrage. The appeals of violence and revolution are inseparable: non-revolutionary violence lacks the legitimacy while revolution without violence is inconceivable and would be inauthentic.

The myth of the revolution, as Raymond Aron observed well before the recent popularity of Latin American revolutionaries, consists in "foster[ing] the expectation of a break with the normal trend of human affairs . . . Revolution provides a welcome break with the everyday course of events and encourages the belief that all things are possible."[5] In the same spirit many American intellectuals since the 1960s have been searching for relief from what they perceived as the meaninglessness and the deadening routines of their modern, capitalist—industrial society. Visions of authentic violence appear to gratify such needs. Again as Aron pointed out: "He who protests against the fate meted out to mankind by a meaningless universe sometimes finds himself in sympathy with the revolutionaries, because indignation or hatred outweigh all other considerations, because in the last resort, violence alone can appease this despair."[6] Those applauding purifying violence from the distance rarely acknowledge, as Peter Berger cautioned, that "The reality of revolution, as against the romantic fantasies about it, is as ugly as the reality of war and in some instances uglier."[7]

That intellectuals supposedly dedicated to rational problem-solving and peaceful conflict resolution are attracted to and even fascinated by certain types of political violence suggests that the appeals of "good" violence are hard to resist. Even more striking has been that churchmen of many denominations have also been eager to condone revolutionary violence and sometimes barely able to contain their enthusiasm for it, as will be shown below. Their endorsement may even extend to non-revolutionary violence and coercion provided it is exercised by a revolutionary, or formerly revolutionary regime. Thus for example Bishop James Armstrong and Reverend Russell Dilley of the United Methodist Church wrote: ". . . there is a significant difference between situations when people are imprisoned for opposing regimes designed to perpetuate inequities (as Chile and Brasil, for example) and situations when people are imprisoned for opposing regimes designed to remove inequities (as in Cuba)."[8]

The appeal of the Latin American guerilla for American intellectuals can best be understood as part of the broader phenomenon of estrangement from American society which became widespread in the 1960s and has persisted into the 1980s notwithstanding certain political changes at the national level. The connection between the admiration of the guerilla and the rejection of American society is captured by an American social critic: ". . . an honest man today must consider the liberal as the true enemy of mankind . . . he must agree with Che Guevara that the only hope the peoples of the world have is to crush American imperialism by defeating it on the battlefield, and the only way to do that is to coordinate their attacks and launch them wherever

. . . men are suffering as the result of American interests . . . the poor and honest of the world must arise to launch simultaneous Vietnams."[9]

Correspondingly the idealized image of the Latin American guerillas and their brand of violence have reflected the political values and aspirations of estranged intellectuals and the spirit of our times. The culture heroes of the period—Che Guevara, Castro, Mao, Ho Chi Minh, possibly Franz Fanon—have all been associated with guerilla warfare.[10] Of one such culture hero, probably the foremost, it was observed that ". . . Che Lives—sprawled out in four colors across the paperback bookstand of your nearest Safeway . . . soon to be crucified by the Hollywood spectacle-mongers. Not even a communist revolution in Bolivia could save him from being a North American culture hero."[11] Even literary representatives of righteous political violence attracted a following as indicated by reports of professors of literature at an elite university who ". . . found that students respond to those works of authors such as Conrad and Dostoevski which are concerned with terrorists . . . they personally identify with and often admire terrorists."[12]

The guerilla shared attributes of other fashionable culture heroes of the times. In the words of Tom Wolfe: ". . . Radical Chic invariably favors radicals who seem primitive, exotic and romantic, such as grape workers who are not merely radical and 'of the soil' but also Latin; the Panthers with their leather pieces . . . and shootouts and the Red Indians . . ." The fashions of the times also mirrored the admiration for such culture heroes: ". . . middle class students . . . would have on guerilla gear . . . berets and hair down to the shoulders, 1958 Sierra Maestra style and raggedy field jackets and combat boots and jeans . . ."[13] Probably tens of thousands of posters of Che Guevara and an armed Huey Newton decorated the walls of college dormitories in the 1960s and 70s.

Latin American revolutions and revolutionaries also evoked associations of joyous fiestas for the North American onlookers. Tad Szulcz reported from the early days of the Cuban revolution: "The Cuban events . . . had an extraordinary impact . . . not only because they represented such an appealing social revolution but also because of their unusual, romantic, picturesque features. There was a touch of the glorious, inebriating fiesta about everything the victorious rebels did . . ."[14] The triumph of the Sandinista revolution likewise brought with it a "holiday mood" in Nicaragua as witnessed by an American social sicentist.[15] According to a reporter of *Playboy* magazine the festive mood persisted past the revolution: "Wherever we went, people were young, singing political folk songs and chanting 'Power to the People!' One night there was even a Pete Seeger concert in town!''[16]

Reaching out to admire and idealize revolutions and revolutionaries was part of a more diffuse quest for alternatives to a social system perceived as unjust, oppressive, inegalitarian, aesthetically deficient and generally unstimulating (". . . the talk of revolution offers a vicarious identification with adventure, strength and moral purity.'')[17] Focusing on the Latin American guerillas—concurrently with, or after the eclipse of the Vietcong—had its own logic. These guerillas and the social forces they supposedly represented could be regarded as victims of the United States and this made them all the more deserving of sympathy and support. C. Wright Mills was an important early representative of this school of thought. In the words of his biographer, Irving Louis Horowitz, "Latin Americans for Mills seemed . . . to represent the 'ideal-typical' oppressed region, whether in Spanish Harlem or in Playa Giron.''[18]

Particular embodiments of guerilla virtue and heroism—Castro, Che Guevara, Tomas Borge, Villalobos of El Salvador etc.—catered to the revolutionary romanticism of the critics of American society. Latin American guerillas were seen not only as fighters for the best of all possible causes, but also exceptional men, touched by the peculiar charm of Latin American culture, climate, language and tradition. They partook of exotic qualities which set them aside from other specialists of political violence. For example the Nicaraguan guerilla leader Omar Cabezas was said to personify ". . . both Quixote and Crusoe . . . Throw in a dash of existential anguish, two drops of Augustinian faith and Thomistic teleology, a measure of Marxist analysis . . . and a full ounce of Latin American, Nicaraguan, Sandinist brio and consciousness, and the result is strikingly humorous and forcefully dramatic . . .''[19]

It should be noted here that the propensity to idealize left-wing guerillas has not been limited to those of Latin America. During the Vietnam war similar attitudes were in evidence toward the Vietcong and its revolutionary violence. Occasionally anti-Israeli Arab guerillas also received respectful treatment if not outright admiration in the same circles. Nonetheless Latin American guerillas, since the rise of Castro and Che Guevara, have been embraced with a particular warmth and intensity and, for obvious historical reasons, for a longer period of time, up to the present. Their appeals had two major components: the guerilla way of life and violence on the one hand and their ideological orientation on the other especially their adoption of Marxism-Leninism. It was the combination of these elements—and especially the proper theoretical legitimation of otherwise less acceptable violence—that lent the guerillas their unique attraction (besides living in countries supposedly victimized by the United States).

The attitude of the same intellectuals toward the anti-Sandinista guerillas provides substantion of the point made above. The latter, as far as their brand of violence and way of life was concerned, were no different from the Marxist guerillas who fought Somoza or the guerillas operating in El Salvador. Yet the so-called "contras" have been held in contempt among these intellectuals since they were fighting *without* Marxist credentials and legitimation *against* a Marxist regime.[20] Jeffrey Hart also noted that ". . . guerillas . . . become fashionable only when they are communist and anti-Western."[21]

None of this is to suggest that the attributes and appeals of the Marxist-Leninist guerillas in Latin America had no historic precedent or parallel whatsoever. For example it has been argued that these guerillas had certain traits in common with the early Fascists of Mussolini's Italy, in particular the leader-worship and belief in the redeeming qualities of authentic violence. James Gregor wrote:

> When Lee Lockwood asked a survivor of the guerilla band that Castro led in the Sierra Maestra whether he had ever concerned himself with political ideology he could only respond with a guffaw. He replied that under the circumstances there was no time for that, and concluded "We let Fidel do our thinking for us."
>
> This was precisely the style of the Fascist *squadristi*, the street fighters of Mussolini. They were the vanguard of the Italian people, a "new and heroic generation," "unconditionally dedicated to the Cause," and "devoted to its supreme leader," . . . For *squadristi*, violence was the school of revolution . . . They were committed to the "moral regeneration" born of violence that would dissipate bourgeois apathy and egotism.

Pride in youthfulness and nationalistic self-assertion represented further shared attributes: "In the case of Castroism, the emphasis on youth, generational conflict, action as antecedent to thought, on the transforming function of military conflict, on the invocation of nationalist sentiment are all instances of Fascist *style*."[22]

It is important to point out that whatever the similarities between the styles of Latin-American guerillas and the early Fascist fighters, the appeals of Fascism for Western intellectuals was limited and short-lived whereas the appeals and idealization of Latin American guerillas has been tenacious and persisted over almost three decades and shows no sign of fading away. Instead each new wave of left-wing revolutionary violence is greeted with delight and rapidly gains an enthusiastic following and creates new, if temporary, culture heroes as American intellectuals move from the reverential identification with Castro and his guerillas to those of Nicaragua or El Salvador. For a while the admiration persists even after the conquest of power as the case of Cuba and Nicaragua suggest; the attributes of the guerillas continue to provide the revolutionary glow and legitimation to the new regimes.

Whether or not these intellectuals are more attracted to the guerillas fighting for power or securely entrenched and engaged with gusto in social engineering (or post-revolutionary violence) is not entirely clear. What is abundantly clear is that ". . . there has to be at least one approved insurgent movement on the Left at any given time . . ." and that ". . . the faithful do seem to need a place to which their faith can attach itself."[23]

A closer examination of the attractions of the Marxist guerilla, and his various contemporary Latin-American incarnations, will shed further light on the roots of the tenaciousness of the phenomenon here discussed.

II.

A more thorough examination of the appeals of the guerilla image is a useful guide to the dreams and frustrations of many contemporary American intellectuals. Such dreams have a venerable ancestry and echo the predicaments of intellectuals of other times and other societies as well.

Probably the single major benefit the attempted identification with the guerilla, and especially guerilla leader, yields to the intellectual is the resolution of the theory-practice dilemma. Intellectuals have traditionally been thinkers and not doers and often painfully aware of the distance separating their ideals from their fulfillment. Idealistic intellectuals at various times longed for effective political action but were incapable of moving from the plane of theory to that of action. The deeper their commitments to political change and social justice the more acutely their impotence is felt—whether due to social isolation, occupational segregation, lack of organizational experience and leadership or some flaw of personality. Many Western and particularly American intellectuals in recent times reached the conclusion that voicing social criticism, however eloquent, was an inadequate expression of their political commitment. Yet it has proved difficult to find practical opportunities, political allies or inspiring role models in their own society that would have made possible the transition from ideas to action. The American working classes have been notoriously unrevolutionary and repulsively contented with the status quo (from the standpoint of influential radical intellectuals such as Herbert Marcuse); black revolutionaries were small in number and unfriendly toward white middle class people, including the militantly estranged intellectuals.

By contrast Latin American guerillas were more successful in making a common cause with the masses and making ". . . the passive peasantry to understand the nature of the wrongs they [were] obliged to suffer."[24] The proper relationship between the guerillas and the masses has been a major preoccupation of both the theorists of guerilla war and their distant admirers: "The guerilla, who is often an educated man of middle class origins, will use his superior learning to enlighten the peasants, while the peasants will show him the *reality* of their social condition . . ."[25]

Latin American guerillas, beginning with Castro and Che Guevara possessed all the attributes radical American intellectuals in search of role models—or objects of idealization and identification—were looking for. Many of these guerillas, and certainly their leaders, appeared to be fellow-intellectuals of a vastly improved variety who heralded the end the baleful separation between theory and practice. That these guerillas were doers could hardly be doubted: Castro and his followers seized power and ran a state as did the Sandinistas twenty years later. Their colleagues in El Salvador controlled parts of the country and were active enough to engage the sympathetic attention of the news media; there was a good chance that they too would seize power.

C. Wright Mills was probably the first well-known American intellectual to discover, and testify to the authenticity of Castro and his fellow leaders and bring back the good news that they were not only fighters but also thinkers, true intellectuals who at long last succeeded in uniting theory and practice. They were exceptional individuals equally at home in the world of weapons and books. (Castro confided in Mills that his book *The Power Elite* "had been a bedside book of most *guerilleros* in the Sierra Maestra.")[26] Especially impressive were the accomplishments of Che Guevara, (even before his martyrdom), both a theoretician and accomplished practitioner of guerilla warfare. The intellectual credentials of the Sandinistas were also satisfactory as they included poets, writers, theologians, graduates of various universities (including Columbia in New York and Lumumba in Moscow).

The theoretical prowess of Latin American guerilla leaders rested on their Marxist-Leninist qualifications which enabled them to articulate their objectives and legitimate their methods in ways familiar and pleasing for American radical intellectuals. They were good Leninists zealously seeking theoretical guidance and legitimation for the actions they were going to take in any case.

The appeals of guerilla violence were also related to the social situation of its admirers. American intellectuals, and the academics among them in particular, have for some time been suffering from what might be called "excess security"—a condition that extended to the economic, political, and occupational spheres alike and led to a measure of discomfort and unease. Theirs was an unadventurous life free of any danger other than an automobile accident or delayed promotion. Deeply committed social critics found it particularly galling that their criticism did not bring persecution. It was difficult for American radical intellectuals to live dangerously in the service of a good cause. Guerilla violence meant living dangerously for a good cause; the attendant adventure and excitement was legitimated by higher purpose. A further attraction of this violence was its communal character: unlike the lone assassin, a more familiar embodiment of political violence in the United States, guerillas practiced their craft in cohesive, communal groups.

Guerilla authenticity—including the use of authentic violence—thus had several components; uniting theory with practice was perhaps the most important but not the only one. It was also important that these guerillas were not dogmatic and weighted down by the past and its mistaken "lessons." As C. Wright Mills put it, using a Cuban guerilla as his mouthpiece:

> We are revolutionaries of the post-Stalin era; we've never had any "God That Failed". We just don't belong to that lineage. We don't have all that cynicism and futility about what we're doing, and about what we feel must be done . . . We are without any of that ideological background; so we've had the courage for revolution; it wasn't destroyed by the terrible history of the world decline of the old left. We are people without bad memories.[27]

It is hard to know whether or not any empirical guerilla had said any such thing (given the structure of the book) but at any rate this is how Mills perceived the guerillas, their uniquely refreshing orientation and freedom from the guilt and the inhibitions of a chastened Old Left. Mills' guerilla doubled as a spokesman for the New Left Mills was propagating and projecting. Twenty years later the same refreshing spirit of youthfulness, undogmatic idealism and pragmatic quest for social justice was projected upon the Nicaraguan guerilla leaders by their American supporters.

In the same spirit John Gerassi, admirer of both the Vietcong and Latin American guerillas, praised "the spontaneity, existential commitment and will" associated with the "original barbudos."[28]

It should be pointed out that during the 1960s the action-orientation and apparent spontaneity of the guerillas were probably more important for their American supporters than their capacity to theorize. American intellectuals at the time were more interested in deeds than thoughts—which also helps to explain the attractions of guerilla violence. Throughout the period under discussion, from the late 1950s up to the present, two images and attractions of the guerillas vied with each other: the spontaneous noble savage and the thoughtful philosopher king, the latter usually projected upon the leaders, the former upon the rank and file.

Carlos Rangel's comments further clarify the attractions of the guerilla-image here discussed:

> . . . the emergence of revolutionary Cuba had a double meaning: it demonstrated the resilience of Leninism, and, more inportant, it briefly renewed the old socialist hope of a regime that could combine Communism and human decency. Old dreams were rekindled . . . [of] an island uncontaminated by civilization and original sin, peopled with noble savages free from ambition, cruelty, and envy . . . the revolutionary mystique as it had developed since 1917 . . . now assumed a new form. The noble savage became a virtuous revolutionary uncontaminated by Stalinism . . . And what more suitable cradle could this virtuous revolution have than a tropical island?[29]

The guerillas' bonds with nature have been a significant if implicit part of the noble-savage image. They were generally seen as children of nature, of the countryside. The guerilla was most readily envisioned as a denizen of impenetrable jungles and inaccessible mountains, at one with nature as he was with the simple people inhabiting such areas. He was both protected and nurtured by nature, its hardships steeled, energized and made him superior to the corrupt, enervated troops of the government he was fighting who lived in more comfortable settings. Guerilla warfare was primarily an outdoor activity involving a great deal of hiking, some mountain climbing, river crossing, hunting and fishing—a whole range of wholesome physical activities urban intellectuals were deprived of but heartily endorsed. The intimate relationship to nature was an important expression of the autonomy and authenticity of the guerilla fighter: it was a major source of his self-sufficiency.

The natural setting in which the guerilla operated was conceived by American intellectuals and rendered by reporters almost invariably as rugged but attractive and sometimes outright idyllic. The intimate contact with nature also made this mode of warfare more appealing— lurking in the jungles of Central America and scaling forbidding peaks was by itself a heroic activity even without fighting. It required good physique, toughness, determination, and survival skills urban intellectuals did not possess though secretly longed for. The harmonious relationship between the guerilla and nature fitted into the anti-industrial, anti-urban worldview of many North American intellectuals. The guerillas roamed the countryside like free spirits, they were not confined to suffocating and corrupting cities, they were free of the demeaning routines of urban and suburban life. Visiting intellectuals were invariably impressed by the purity and sparseness of such a way of life; the guerillas owned little, they carried what was necessary for survival and had no interest in objects viewed in Western society as important. The bonds with nature thus connected with the puritanical ethos of the self-denying guerilla fighter. Such puritanical attributes were the hallmark of the "New Man" the guerilla fighter represented: "These pure, ascetic revolutionaries, hardened by danger and privations, were expected after conquering power to exercise it with the same goodness, the same fervor they had displayed in gaining it; they were expected to communicate their fervor and altruism to the masses, and thus bring about 'the advent of the new man' through an unprecedented sociological mutation."—Rangel wrote.[30]

The self-conception of the guerillas was no less exalted. According to Omar Cazebas "The Frente Sandinista was developing . . . a spirit of iron, a spirit of steel, a contingent of men bound with a granite solidity, a nucleus of men that was morally and mentally indestructible . . . the genesis of the new man was in the FSLN . . . an open, unegotistical man . . . who sacrifices himself for others, who suffers when others suffer . . . The new man was born in the mountains . . ."[31]

The uplifting qualities of the guerilla way of life were also given expression by Regis Debray, the French theorist and occasional practitioner of guerilla warfare, himself much admired by American intellectuals as a personifier of the unity of theory and practice. Debray wrote:

> In the mountains . . . workers, peasants and intellectuals meet for the first time. Their integration is not easy at the beginning . . . Mistrust, timidity, custom have to be gradually vanquished . . . Since they must all adapt themselves to the same conditions of life, and since they are all participating in the same undertaking, they adapt to each other. Slowly the shared experience, the combats, the hardships endured together

weld an alliance having the simple force of friendship . . . Bureaucratic
faintheartedness becomes irrelevant. Is this not the best education for a
future socialist leader or cadre?[32]

The apotheosis of the veneration of the ascetic, saintly guerilla
leader was reached in the Che Guevara cult. I. F. Stone's recollections
were typical:

He was the first man I had ever met whom I thought not just handsome
but beautiful. With his curly, reddish beard, he looked like a cross
between a faun and a Sunday School print of Jesus.
. . . In Che, one felt a desire to heal and pity for suffering . . . It was out
of love, like the perfect knight of medieval romance, that he had set out
to combat with the powers of the world. . . .
In a sense he was, like some early saint, taking refuge in the desert.
Only there could the purity of the faith be safeguarded . . .[33]

Another admirer wrote of his image in death: "I remain with my
eyes fastened on the *guerrillero's* face, the magnificent face of this
Christ of the Rio Plata . . ."[34]

Not surprisingly Guevara also earned the praise of Sartre who
described him as " 'the most complete man of his time,' one who can
easily be compared to the giants of the Renaissance for the stupendous
many-sidedness of his personality: doctor and economist, revolutionary and banker, military theoretician and ambassador, deep political
thinker and popular agitator, able to wield the pen and the submachine
gun with equal skill."[35]

Guevara symbolized the transformation of political violence into a
more lofty calling: "The *guerillero* was the saint of the revolution,
superior to other men not only because of his personal worth and his
revolutionary conscience but also because of his charity and willingness to take upon himself the sufferings of the oppressed. A disciple
of El Che, the Colombian guerilla-priest Camilo Torres, went sofar as
to say that if Christ had lived in Latin America in our time he would
have been a guerilla fighter."[36]

It was of course easier to idealize (and virtually canonize) Guevara
than most other guerilla leaders due to his martyrdom—his capture
and execution in Bolivia. He was spared the moral ambiguities which
attend to the safe and durable possession of power, the transformation
of the guerilla fighter into party functionary.

While Guevara has become the most prominent embodiment of the
guerilla as saint, he himself had earlier popularized a saintly conception
of the guerilla. As one of his biographers put it: "Che gave an almost

celestial vision of his perfect hero as 'a sort of guiding angel . . .' Thus the guerilla fighter is nearly divine, an unearthly gift dropped from the heavens, a Robin Hood or a saviour, knight of chivalry who is magnanimous even to his enemies. If these visions are added to the technical, cultural, moral and ascetic qualities also defined by Che as necessary for the guerilla, then the image of the guerilla has replaced that of the saint."[37]

An important attribute and appeal of guerilla violence is its irregular, unconventional nature. Guerilla warfare and guerilla violence are not routine and resist routinization and thus present a welcome contrast to modern mass society and its bureaucratized violence Norman Mailer, among others denounced. The violence of the guerilla is an integral part of his way of life: it is more spontaneous, impulsive, exciting, adventurous and, again, authentic. The authenticity comes from the simple fact that the guerilla fights for a good cause, not for any personal gain, interest or advantage but for the liberation of others. For that reason the sympathetic intellectual can endorse this kind of violence without hesitation, it is virtually self-legitimating. Guerilla violence differs profoundly—in the eyes of these sympathetic beholders—from the warfare and violence standing armies engage in. For example two American scholars wrote: ". . . the government tries to vaporize the 'water', the people, through sheer terror. In contrast, the violence of the revolutionaries must be measured, clear, and precise."[38] Another apologist of guerilla violence, Philip Berryman, associated with the American Friends Service Committee also insisted that "there were clear differences in the way violence was used by the army and by the guerilla groups . . . the army practiced systematic torture and terrorism . . . and was largely indiscriminate in its violence whereas guerilla violence was targeted . . . [guerillas] made every effort not to endanger innocent bystanders."[39] It may be noted here that such views are no longer completely unchallenged even among those seeking sympathetically to understand guerilla violence, at any rate in El Salvador, as both NY Times reporters and the vice-chairman of Americas Watch noted a rise in the human rights violations committed by Salvadorian guerillas.[40]

The moral superiority of guerilla violence is also seen as connected to the pattern of recruitment. Becoming a guerilla is supposed to be truly voluntary: ideal-typical guerillas are neither conscripts forced to enlist, nor mercenaries who fight for money. (". . . unlike the government soldiers, the rebels weren't paid for fighting—they fought for something they believed in . . . their leaders were men of outstanding ability—inspiring, humane and master strategists . . ." according to

Leo Huberman and Paul Sweezey.[41] (Idealism does not always suffice to meet the manpower needs of guerillas. It has been reported recently from El Salvador that guerillas forced peasants to join them.) Still the basic image of the guerilla is that of a person who makes an existential choice as he decides to put his life on the line for a cause and thus demonstrates the authenticity of his commitment translating his political ideals into action.

American intellectuals rarely have this option: they must, as a rule confine themselves to the signing of petitions, writing articles or books, making speeches—however passionate, articulate and illuminating—or participating in demonstrations. Even if arrested for, say, blocking entrances to a military base, they are likely to be released on bail or perhaps detained for a short time—a far cry from the hardships, joys and risks of stalking the enemy with gun in hand. While few American intellectuals, including radical social critics would claim that the United States is ripe for guerilla warfare, they tend to sympathize with the handful of small groups,—Weathermen remnants, Black Liberation Army, Puerto Rican independence fighters etc. who seek to introduce guerilla war into the United States.

The appeals of guerilla violence are also the appeals of smallness against bigness, of a heroic, poorly equipped David against the Goliath of a technologically and numerically superior army. C. Wright Mills wrote: "So here's the story of the insurrection in one sentence: a handful of men on a mountain top, half starving at that, defeated a 12,000-man army paid by Batista and largely supplied and trained by Yankees . . . [the] truth is that guerilla bands, led by determined men, with peasants alongside them, and a mountain nearby, can defeat organized battalions of the tyrants equipped with everything up to the atom bomb."[42] In another account of distinctly religious undertones Castro and his small band are seen as sustained by their unshakeable faith in their mission: "With these 12 men on the top of the mountain that Christmas of 1956 Fidel Castro still believed he could make his revolution. He had every reason to despair . . . instead he was buoyant, optimistic, confident."[43] Similar notions dominated the perception of the Sandinistas: "The FSLN won the war not because of its military superiority, but because it was convinced of the rightness of its cause . . . The combination of a lean but well-trained and dedicated guerilla army and massive urban insurgency was more than Somoza's corrupt and demoralized army could withstand."[44]

The myth of the poorly equipped yet invincible guerilla has been popular ever since the Vietnam war. At the time Western sympathizers insisted that the Vietcong was hopelessly outgunned by the United

States overrating the importance of heavy weapons in guerilla warfare and overlooking the successful efforts of the Soviet Union and China to provide the Vietcong with all essentials of guerilla warfare. More recently Salvadoran guerillas and their American supporters have insisted that they were not supplied weapons from the outside and claimed that they were poorly equipped, relying primarily on captured weapons or those bought on the black market.[45] In each instance the myth of the under-armed guerilla facing a materially and numerically superior enemy has served the purpose of highlighting the heroism of the guerilla fighting seemingly overwhelming forces yet sustained by his spirit and superior values. Such a scenario also had the benefit of making possible the identification of the embodiments of good and evil respectively with the underdog and topdog and drawing on the sympathy generally reserved for the underdog.

The moral superiority of guerilla violence is predicated not only on the ends pursued but also its allegedly more humane character which is contrasted to the methods used by the adversary. Thus critics of the United States and its allies fighting Marxist guerillas are repelled by the uses of massive firepower—not only because of its potential threat to civilians—but also because of a deep-seated hostility to such applications of modern technology *and* a more general aversion to modern technology *per se*. The attitude here alluded to is part of the David versus Goliath syndrome combined with the preference for simplicity over complexity and the aversion to powerful machines of any kind. For example, much has been made of the repugnant impersonality of dropping bombs on people from a high altitude bomber, very much in the spirit of Normal Mailer who favored passionate, face to face confrontations with blows struck into the flesh over more impersonal modes of combat. Never was it made clear why, for instance it was morally preferable to kill in Vietnam one's enemies with concealed bamboo spikes smeared in excrement (to encourage blood poisoning) over burning them with napalm bombs, or why the assassination by communist guerillas of assorted civilians in the employ of the government was qualitatively different from the army killing civilians supporting the guerillas. As a rule these divergent judgements were rooted in the approval or disapproval of the objectives the violence claimed to serve. In general doubts were put to rest by pointing out that guerilla violence supported change whereas counterinsurgency sought to maintain the status quo.

As was noted earlier often even post-revolutionary violence could be assimilated into the moral universe of the intellectuals supportive of such regimes: it was often claimed that even the "worst criminals" opposed to the new regime were treated with consideration and humaneness.[46] Most frequently post-revolutionary violence came to be justified as defensive: Cuba defending against American subversion and Nicaragua resisting the "contras". Staughton Lynd, a former partisan of the Vietcong perceived Sandinista violence in such charitable terms: "That leadership was merciful to National Guardsmen captured during the insurrection. It abolished the death penalty and has not reinstated it. It has confessed error in its policy toward the Miskito Indians . . . Surely the best way to discover what these people [the Sandinista leaders] are really like would be to remove the external harrassment our Government has imposed on them."[47] In this, as in many other instances, the assessment of guerilla (or former guerilla) violence was based largely on misinformation and supportive sentiment; in point of fact the Sandinistas executed plenty of former National Guardsmen but succeeded in convincing segments of American public opinion that this was not the case.[48]

Generally speaking the information available on Marxist guerilla violence in the United States has been limited or justificatory; in turn there has been reluctance, on the part of the sympathizers, to process the available information that conflicted with their predisposition. There is little doubt that the idealization of Latin American guerillas and their violence has been made easier by the nature of the media coverage; this was also noted by Mario Vargas Llosa the Peruvian writer: "The violations of human rights that occur . . . in democracies like Peru and Colombia when they have to respond to guerilla actions or terrorism are always emphasized in the press, whereas one has to search long and hard in the same organs to find any comparable reporting on the violation of human rights in countries where they murder in the name of the revolution and openly proclaim that pistols and bombs—rather than ballot—are the appropriate instruments of political life."[49] The favorable media coverage itself results from a climate of opinion jointly created by journalists and academic intellectuals who share many political values and beliefs.[50]

The tradition of favorable media coverage of left-wing guerillas in the American mass media probably began with Herbert Matthews' glorifying accounts of Castro and his group in the Sierra Maestra in the late 1950s. Subsequently throughout the 1960s the Vietcong benefited from a similarly selective and benevolent coverage: guerilla violence, as far as most American reporters and TV cameramen were concerned, was virtually invisible and thus remained an abstraction for the American public including intellectuals. Many of the latter probably shared Mary McCarthys' stated preference to believe that only the United

States and its allies commit atrocities, as she made clear in her comments on the Hue massacre.[51]

The sympathetic media coverage continued in Nicaragua greatly benefiting the Marxist-Leninist revolutionaries seeking to influence American public opinion.[52] Shirley Christian, one of the few American journalists who did not invariably give the benefit of doubt to the Sandinistas wrote:

> . . . reporters covering the war saw Somoza's opponents, the Sandinistas, through a romantic haze. This romantic view of the Sandinistas is by now acknowledged publicly or privately by virtually every American journalist who was in Nicaragua during the two big Sandinista offensives, the general strikes and the various popular uprisings. Probably not since Spain has there been a more open love affiar between the foreign press and one of the belligerents in a civil war.[53]

Her study based on the scrutiny of several hundred news stories on Nicaragua published in the *NY Times* and *Washington Post* and broadcast over CBS during the period January 1, 1978 to July 21, 1979 established a clear pattern of selectivity in the reporting of revolutionary as opposed to counter-revolutionary violence. She wrote: "There were almost no reports . . . of unjustified or noncombat brutality by Sandinista forces against government supporters. One paragraph in a story mentioned a charge [of] . . . Sandinista . . . reprisals. . . but reported no investigation of it. There were also brief mentions of 'government informers' being killed or threatened."[54] Being deprived of visual images or detailed reports of Sandinista political violence strengthened the predisposition to take a benevolent, non-judgemental view of such violence. In the eyes of sympathetic American intellectuals there was little brutality committed by the guerillas and what there was had excellent justifications. In any event it was easier to overlook the unappealing aspects of guerilla violence when it did not have to be confronted on the television screen or through other detailed accounts.

The Salvadoran guerillas went to great length to influence American public opinion and representatives of the media by, among other things, taking journalists and various delegations on tours of rebel held territory. For example:

> As soon as the American visitors rolled into town . . . more than 300 peasants walked around a corner chanting slogans broadcast by two men with microphones reading from a script: "Bombs no, medicine yes, bombs no, schools yes."

The peasants followed along but one group got mixed up and began chanting "Bombs no, medicine no, schools no" until corrected by a leader.

Asked why they had walked in from all over the northern part of . . . Morazan, several peasants said they had been told by the rebels to demonstrate for the visitors.

. . . A rebel camera team filmed the peasants demonstration and the arrival of the American visitors, which one rebel with a loudspeaker called "a great gain" for the guerillas.[55]

It was also reported of the same visit that "The rebels spared no effort to impress the American visitors, providing ample meals of steak, fresh orange juice and baked bread, as well as beds, a video television screen and trucks for transportation. A well-known revolutionary priest, Miguel Ventura, offered mass in the local, bullet-pocked church. A rebel chorus sang hymns of liberation theology."[56]

In Nicaragua the guerillas had a long standing policy of deception aimed at outsiders as was shown by Douglas Payne.[57] These policies continued after the seizure of power as exemplified by the treatment of visitors from abroad often attended to by Tomas Borge himself. He made it a special point to take important visitors on tours of model prisons—in yet another demonstration of the humaneness of his regime. He also took the trouble to have a special office for receiving delegations from abroad as was reported by a former high ranking official in the State Security apparatus: "Borge has two different offices. One . . . is located in the Silvio Mayorga building where he meets religious delegations and delegations from democratic political parties. In this office Borge has photographs of children, gilded, carved crucifixes, and a Bible or two. Before Borge meets with religious delegations he usually memorizes Bible passages which he can quote . . . Borge's real office, where he fulfills his duties as Interior Minister, is located . . . in Bello Horizonte . . . In that office there are no crucifixes or Bibles—only Marxist literature and posters of Marx, Engles, and Lenin."[58]

Perhaps the best explanation of the favorable predisposition of both the media and intellectuals toward Latin American guerillas and the causes they were fighting for was offered by Jeane Kirkpatrick. She wrote:

One reason some modern Americans prefer "socialist" to traditional autocracies is that the former have embraced modernity . . . a profession of universalistic norms; an emphasis on science, education and progress . . . they speak our language.

Because socialism of the Soviet/Chinese-Cuban variety is an ideology rooted in a version of the same values that sparked the Enlightenment . . . it is highly congenial to many Americans at the symbolic level. Marxist revolutionaries speak the language of a hopeful future, while traditional aurocrats speak the language of an unattractive past. Because left-wing revolutionaries invoke the symbols and values of democracy . . . they are again and again accepted as partisans in the cause of freedom and democracy.[59]

She also observed an affinity between liberalism, Christianity and Marxist socialism displayed most vividly by " . . . left-leaning clerics whose attraction to a secular style of 'redemptive community' is stronger than their outrage at the hostility of socialist regimes to religion."

These attitudes have been most strikingly revealed by authors and "activists" associated with the American Friends Service Committee, long committed to the legitimation and support of revolutionary violence. Their justification rests on three premises: that 1) guerilla violence is restrained and selective; that 2) without violence no beneficial change is possible and 3) that guerilla violence is the violence of good intentions and laudable objectives. Such onlookers can neither imagine nor believe that guerilla violence too can be ugly, brutal and excessive; if given specific examples of its incidence they either question the credibility of the source reporting it or reduce its moral significance by asserting that such violence is atypical and rare, or results from exceptionally provocative and outrageous acts by the enemy. Above all, such sympathizers are morally disarmed by the claim that all acts of guerilla violence were designed to hasten the demise of a highly repressive and unjust social system As Philip Berryman put it: " . . . a Christian must see such regimes as embodying 'systems of sin'."[60]

That being the case taking up arms against it is easily justifiable. Once again the mystique of revolution and revolutionary violence offers legitimation albeit the terminology is different, appropriate to the religious discourse:

> . . . the signs of grace in a revolutionary *proyecto* would be that the life of the poor is enhanced, their dignity respected; that there is an overall movement toward equality, a willingness to accept austerity in the interests of all, a conscious effort to build a society on cooperation and common effort—all qualities that have their analogues in the ideal vision of the church and Christian life in the New Testament . . . Hence the revolution could be regarded as a bearer, or mediation, of grace . . . [61]

Other clerics went further claiming "To be a Christian is to be a revolutionary". Padre Gudalupe Carney wrote:

> We Christian Revolutionaries of Central America believe that the basis of the new Christian Socialist system will be a spirit of equality and brotherhood, rather than seeking personal gain. This search for personal gain, inculcated continuously by . . . structures of capitalism is a main cause of the injustices which we suffer at every level of life . . .
>
> We Christian Socialists want to help liberate people from this consuming drive for personal gain . . .
>
> I have a deep desire (which I am convinced comes from the Spirit of Jesus) to completely join the Honduran guerillas . . .
>
> There is no contradiction whatsoever between being a Christian, and a priest, and being a Marxist revolutionary.[62]

Such statements lead us back to ponder once more the attractions of revolutionary violence and especially the sources of the susceptibility to its appeals, and the attendant suspension of disbelief appropriate enough for clerics but less so for intellectuals (or clerics assuming the role of intellectuals) in full command of their critical faculties.

III.

Susceptibility to the attractions of revolutionary violence, at home or abroad, and the corresponding willingness to give every benefit of doubt to its perpetrators flourishes among those most thoroughly disenchanted with their own society that is to say, members of the intelligentsia. The admiration and legitimation of such violence is an integral part of the emotional support given to the goals the violence is supposed to bring about. However, as noted earlier, the use of violent methods in itself evokes admiration when viewed as proof of authentic commitment and personal courage. While in the 1960s American social critics envisioned the possibilities of the successful introduction of such cleansing, revolutionary violence in their own society, with the decline of such expectations there has been a shift to a greater identification with revolutionary movements and causes abroad and especially in nearby Latin America and its central regions. Since Cuba has ceased to be a revolutionary society and hence no longer a setting for the display of exotic revolutionary violence (though it may still be admired on other grounds), the Maxist-Leninist guerillas of Nicaragua and El Salvador came to embody the virtues of righteous revolutionary violence. Once again the ready acceptance of the claims, promises and methods of these movements raises questions about the deeper, possibly less political (or non-political) roots of their attraction. Could such factors play a part in the perceived attractiveness of revolutionary violence in addition to its putative role in bringing about a better society? There are a number of suggestive observations in Stanley Rothman's study of the radical youth of the 1960s that may have relevance to understanding the recurring admiration and sympathy guerilla violence evokes in many American intellectuals. Extrapolating from his findings it would appear that the appeals of guerilla violence here discussed are rooted in the pleasure of vicarious participation in righteous violence, or "the romance of cleansing violence":

> . . . feelings of shared oppression provided the contact point for identification with a revolutionary brotherhood. A young middle-class student [or not so young adult intellectual - P.H.] can thus consider himself the brother of oppressed peoples the world over, projecting his new-found feelings of solidarity onto peasants or proletarians . . . He becomes a self-chosen representative of the oppressed, a patron to the powerless. This identification helps to deny his own aggressiveness . . . By assuming the mantle of revolutionary agency, he gains self-aggrandizement . . . and achieves a sense of self-denial through his subsumption into a brotherhood of equals . . .

> For these middle-class students [and once more we might add, intellectuals - P. H.] revolutionary violence gradually came to be seem as logical extension of long and arduous effort to overcome their origins . . . This goal led them to . . . identification with the world's outcasts and victims, whom they viewed as sources of both moral and physical strength. [Rothman observes in another context that] For alienated quasi-intellectuals like Meinhof, terrorism represented a final opportunity to reject the seductive material advantages and the spurious moral standards of an evil system. Her new role as revolutionary outlaw combined self-denial with self-ssertion.[63]

The latter may be a crucial point: the irresistible appeals of a social role that combines ascetic, puritanical self-denial (Guevara style) with robust self assertion in the form of ideologically sanctioned release of aggression. Rothman argues that for the young middle class radicals—and we may add again, also for the not so young radical intellectuals—guerilla violence abroad (or Black violence at home) was attractive because of its compensatory aspects: the admirers felt powerless and were obstructed by both structural and psychological difficulties from embracing political violence.

The admiration of guerilla violence had much in common with the admiration of certain types of criminal violence and the idealization of some criminals in the United States—seen as Robin Hood types visiting retribution upon an immoral, flabby society, or culture heroes rebelling forcefully against an unjust system. The prototype apotheosis of the violent criminal turned social critic was, not surprisingly, provided by Norman Mailer's campaign for Jack Abbot the former convict turned author, who after a short spell of freedom and celebrity status in New York, was returned to prison for a new murder commited after his release.[64] The phenomenon had its equivalent in France where left-wing intellectuals embraced "another convict turned writer", "an outlaw hero, a poet, a kind of updated Francois Villion", Roger Knobelspiess, once pardoned by President Mitterand. He too insisted on being "a victim of the police and an unjust society".[65]

For those incapable of performing heroic deeds themselves but longing for masculine self-assertion, identification with the guerillas, and especially victorious guerillas held great attraction as for example Abbie Hoffman's comments on Castro's triumphant entry into Havana suggest: "Fidel sits on the side of the tank rumbling into Havana on New Year's day . . . Girls throw flowers at the tank and rush to tug playfully at his black beard. He laughs joyously and pinches a few rumps . . . The tank stops in the city square. Fidel lets the gun drop to the ground, slaps his thigh and stands erect He is like a mighty penis coming to life . . . "[66]

The support for guerilla violence among American intellectuals associated with hero worship also raises questions about certain alienating aspects of modern society that may create a more general predisposition to such hero-worship. Several decades ago Hans Speier addressed this issue drawing attention to the growing need, at least among some groups in modern society, for what he called, "freely chosen risk", that is to say, a form of adventurous and exciting self-assertion associated with physical combat. He argued that modern, urban, industrial and highly bureaucratized society makes life, for some, overly secure, predictable and boring, removing the possibilities of "elementary experiences of physical risk." Speier wrote:

> A truly bewildering specialization of work . . . has created a web of interdependence which all of us help to spin and in which each of us seems caught . . . We are divorced from the naive and full assertion of life . . .

> . . . it is in hero worship that he [modern man] betrays a deep need from the yoke of civilization.

> Modern hero worship is a safe and underhanded way of obtaining vicariously what life refuses to give freely. Hero worship is a worship of active unbridled life . . .

> . . . worship of the heroic may be a substitute for action from which they [the worshippers] are barred by circumstance, fear and convention.

Speier also noted among the components of modern hero worship: ". . . the primeval veneration of strength and freely chosen risks in defiance of Christian and middle class ethics . . . a life experience in which aspirations are curbed, desires censored . . . [and] the passivity which modern civilization promotes . . ."[67]

It is at the confluence of such generalized discontents of modern life and the more specific critiques of pluralistic capitalism that we find the breeding ground which nurtures the admiration of many American intellectuals toward Latin American guerillas and their political violence.

Notes

1. Jean Paul Sartre: *Sartre on Cuba*, New York, 1961 pp. 44, 102, 103.
2. Norman Mailer: *The Presidential Papers*, New York, 1968, pp. 69–70.
3. Martin Peretz: "Washington Diarist", *The New Republic*, May 2, 1983.
4. Nathan Leites: *A Study of Bolshevism*, Glencoe: The Free Press, 1953, p. 114.
5. Raymond Aron: *The Opium of Intellectuals*, London: Secker & Warburg 1957, pp. 35, 43.
6. Aron *cited* pp. 48–49.
7. Peter Berger and Richard J. Neuhaus: *Movement and Revolution*, New York: Anchor Books 1970 p. 51.
8. Quoted in *A Time For Candor: Mainline Churches and Radical Social Witness*, Washington, D.C.: Institute on Religion and Democracy, 1983 p. 81.
9. John Gerassi: "The Political Activist Pivot" in I. L. Horowitz, Josue de Castro and John Gerassi eds.: *Latin American Radicalism: A Documentary Report on Left and Nationalist Movements*, New York: Random House, 1969 p. 493.
10. See also Ronald Berman: *America in the Sixties*, New York: The Free Press, 1968, esp.Ch 11.
11. Steve Weissman: "The Prophet, Armed", *Ramparts*, August 24, 1968 p. 59.
12. David C. Rapoport and Yonah Alexander eds.: *The Rationalization of Terrorism*, Frederick Md.,: University Publications of America, 1982, p. 19.
13. Tom Wolfe: *Radical Chic and Mau-Mauing the Flack Catchers*, New York: Bantam Books, 1970, pp. 49–50, 152.
14. Tad Szulcz: *The Winds of Revolution*, New York: Praeger, 1963 p. 120.
15. Thomas W. Walker: "Images of the Nicaraguan Revolution" in his collection *Nicaragua in Revolution*, New York: Praeger, 1982 p. 82–83.
16. *Playboy*, September 1983 p. 58.
17. Berger *cited* p. 60. for an excellent update on these attitudes see "The Myth of Revolution", *The New Republic*, April 29, 1985 pp. 7–10.
18. Irving Louis Horowitz: *C. Wright Mills—An American Utopian*, New York: Free Press, 1983 p. 300.
19. Carlos Fuentes: "Foreword" to Omar Cabezas: *Fire from the Mountain—*

The Making of a Sandinista, New York: Crown Publishers, 1985 p. XI–XII.

20. See for example Alexander Cockburn and James Ridgeway: "Reagan's 'Secret War' in Jalapa—Eyewitness to Terror", *Village Voice,* July 12, 1983.

21. Jeffrey Hart: "Guerilla chic: what is and isn't fashionable", *Washington Times,* June 27, 1983.

22. A. James Gregor: *The Fascist Persuasion In Radical Politics,* Princeton: Princeton University Press, 1974, pp. 302, 308, 309.

23. Peter Shaw and S. M. Lipset: "Two afterthoughts on Susan Sontag", *Encounter,* June–July, 1982 p. 40; and Walter Goodman: "Hard to digest", *Harper's,* June 1962 p. 6.

24. Richard Gott: *Guerilla Movements in Latin America,* London: Nelson, 1970 p. 359.

25. Andrew Sinclair: *Guevara,* London: Collins, 1970 p. 35.

26. K. S. Karol: *Guerillas in Power,* New York: Hill & Wang, 1970 p. 58.

27. C. Wright Mills: *Listen Yankee—The Revolution in Cuba,* New York: Ballantine Books, 1960, p. 43.

28. John Gerassi: "The Spectre of Che Guevara", *Ramparts,* October 1967 p. 30.

29. Carlos Rangel: *The Latin Americans—Their Love-Hate Relationship with the U.S.,* New York: Harcourt, Brace Jovanovich, 1977 pp. 128–129.

30. Rangel *cited* p. 129.

31. Cabezas *cited* p. 85, 86–87.

32. Regis Debray: *Revolution in the Revolution?,* New York: Monthly Review Press, 1967, pp. 110–111.

33. I. F. Stone: "The Legacy of Che Guevara", *Ramparts,* December 1967 pp. 20–21.

34. Eduardo Galeano: "Magic Death for a Magic Life", *Monthly Review,* January 1968 p. 13.

35. Michael Lowry: *The Marxism of Che Guevara: Philosophy, Economics and Revolutionary Warfare,* New York: Monthly Review Press 1973, p. 7.

36. Rangel *cited* p. 129.

37. Sinclair *cited* p. 42.

38. James Kohl and John Zitt: *Urban Guerilla Warfare in Lain America,* Cambridge: MIT Press, 1974 p. 24.

39. Philip Berryman: *The Religious Roots of Rebellion,* Maryknoll: Orbis Books, 1984 p. 209–210.

40. Aryeh Neier: "Abuses by Salvadoran Guerillas," *NY Times,* Op-ed page, July 26, 1985; see also Lydia Chavez: "1500 in Salvador Flee Rebel Area", *NY Times* June 7, 1984; also Warren Hoge: "Rebel Tactics Enrage Some in El Salvador," *NY Times,* March 16, 1982; also James LeMoyne: "Salvador Rebels Reported to Execute 9", *NY Times,* November 4, 1984; also "Peace Hope Dies for Salvadorans", *NY Times* October 14, 1985.

41. Leo Huberman and Paul Sweezey: "The Conquest of Power", *Monthly Review,* November 1960, p. 63.

42. Mills *cited* p. 50, 114.

43. Huberman and Sweezy in *Monthly Review,* November, 1960, p. 55.

44. Thomas W. Walker: *Nicaragua—The Land of Sandino,* Boulder: Westview Press, 1981, p. 93.

45. See for example Edward Schumacher:" Salvador Guerillas, In Interview, Say They Are Short of weapons", *NY Times,* February 22, 1981; also Raymond Bonner: "With Salvador Rebels in Combat Zone, *NY Times,* January 26, 1982.

46. See for example Carleton Beals: "Terror in Cuba? . . ." *The Nation,* January 24, 1959 p. 64.

47. Staughton Lynd: "The High Cost of Fighting Our 'Contras' ", Correspondence Page, *NY Times,* November 3, 1985.

48. See for example Humberto Belli: *Christians Under Fire,* Garden City, Michigan: Puebla Institute, 1984, esp. pp 57–64, 132–137; also by the same author: *Breaking Faith—The Sandinista Revolution And Its Impact On Freedom And Faith In Nicaragua,* Westchester, Illinois: Crossway Publishers, 1985.

49. Mario Vargas LLosa: "Latin America—A Media Stereotype", *Atlantic,* February 1984 p. 22.

50. See for example: S. Robert Lichter and Stanley Rothman: *The Media Elite and American Values,* Ethics and Public Policy Center (Reprint), Washington, D.C., 1982; also by the same authors: "Personality, Ideology and World View: A Comparison of Media and Business Elites", *British Journal of Political Science,* No, 1, 1984; Leopold Tyrmand: "Media Shangri-la", *The American Scholar,* Winter, 1975–76.

51. Quoted in *Commentary,* January 1974, p. 36.

52. For a discussion of such manipulations see Paul Hollander: "The Newest Pilgrims", *Commentary,* August, 1985.

53. Shirley Christian: "Covering the Sandinistas—The Foregone Conclusions of the Fourth Estate", *Washington Journalism Review,* March 1982 p. 34.

54. Christian *cited* p. 37.

55. James LeMoyne: "The Rebels Give Show in Salvador" *NY Times,* July 8, 1985.

56. James LeMoyne: "Salvador Rebels Vow to Spread War", *NY Times* July 7, 1985; a discussion of similar Nicaraguan political hospitality, i.e. techniques for impressing visitors may be found in Paul Hollander: "Sojourners in Nicaragua: A Political Pilgrimage", (see page ...) and also by the same author: "Political Hospitality in Cuba and Nicaragua" (see page ...).

57. See for example Douglas W. Payne: "The 'Mantos' of Sandinista Deception", *Strategic Review,* Spring 1985.

58. "Nicaragua's State Security: Behind the Propaganda Mask—An Interview with Alvaro Jose Baldizon Aviles" *Briefing Paper, Institute on Religion and Democracy,* September 1985 p. 2.

59. Jeane J. Kirkpatrick: *Dictatorship and Double Standards,* American Enterprise Institute, Washington, D.C. 1982 pp. 44–45.

60. Berryman *cited* p. 382.

61. Ibid. p. 389.

62. Padre J. Guadalupe Carney: *To Be a Revolutionary,* San Francisco: Harper & Row, 1985 pp. 438, 439, 440. The author after moving from Honduras to Nicaragua wrote: ". . . I have been very restless here in Nicaragua . . . because there is no longer any persecution here. There is no need to denounce and fight against injustices here . . . in Nicaragua there are no repressive authorities . . ." p. 430.

63. Stanley Rothman: *Roots of Radicalism—Jews, Christians and the New Left,* New York: Oxford University Press, 1982 pp. 188, 166, 198, 365.

64. See for example M. A. Farber: "A Killing at Dawn Beclouds Ex-Convict Writer's New Life",*NY Times,* July 26, 1981; also Naomi Munson and James Atlas: "On Norman Mailer and Jack Abbott: The Literary Life of Crime",*The New Republic,* September 9, 1981.
65. John Vinocur: "Convict-Poet, Idol of France's Left, Is Fallen" *NY Times,* June 14, 1985.
66. Abbie Hoffman: *Revolution for the Hell of It,* New York, 1968, p. 13.
67. Hans Speier: *Social Order and Risks of War,* New York: Stewart, 1952, pp. 123, 125, 126, 127–128.

15
The Sojourners in Nicaragua: A Political Pilgrimage

Over the past half century, the Soviet Union, China, Cuba, North Vietnam and various other putatively socialist states have inspired a flood of reverential on-the-spot reports and travel accounts.

These accolades were often written by Western visitors,including intellectuals, artists, scientists, journalists, politicians, social workers—and also members of the clergy.

Ironically, the admiration heaped upon the Soviet experiment under Stalin peaked during the first half of the 1930s, exactly when the Soviet Union went through the most pathological state of its history, when its famous show trials were staged, purges carried out and—as if this were not enough—millions also died of hunger.

Such facts, however, rarely intruded on foreign enthusiasts, who arrived and left knowing little about these events or found ways to neutralize their moral impact.

In a similar way, Western and especially American visitors provided the most flattering portraits of life in Mao's China during the Cultural revolution which terrorized much of the population, brought higher education to a halt, disrupted the economy and created generally nightmarish conditions. Once again, there was an almost total divorce between the realities of the social-political landscape and its description by political tourists.

It's against this historical background that one must examine the recent upsurge in uncritical admiration of Nicaragua's Sandinista regime, exemplified by a recent (March 1983) issue of the Washington-based Christian magazine, *Sojourners,* and particularly by one of its articles by Joyce Hollyday and Jim Wallis entitled "A Fragile Experiment."

Summarizing similarities in the literature of political pilgrimages is easy. Much of this literature, in fact, (including recent reports from Nicaragua) is interchangeable to an astonishing degree. Underlying the pilgrims' highly patterned positive impressions is a routinely favorable predisposition. This in turn rests on the visitors' estrangement from their own society which prompts the quest for appealing alternatives elsewhere.

In Nicaragua as in the Soviet Union, China and Cuba, the authorities make sure that visitors are exposed to sights and individuals conducive to favorable impressions—for example, schools, playgrounds, clinics and citizens supportive of the regime. Since the Marxist government in Nicaragua has not yet fully consolidated its power, leaving a few pockets of dissent, it did not (or could not) insulate Hollyday and Wallis from contact with a few people representative of such attitudes.

For the most part, however, the *Sojourners'* authors met supporters and officials of the regime (and in any event, they were not in the mood to give much credence to critical comments, as will be seen below). Even an official of the fisheries industry contributed to the list of Sandinista accomplishments, noting that while under Somoza the shrimp population was overharvested, "Now the shrimp grow to their full size: 'We might say that the revolution has also been good for the shrimp' " (p. 11). The literacy campaign also had a favorable impact on the visitors who failed, however, to ponder the range of printed matter the newly (and already) literate would have access to.

The predisposition of *Sojourners* toward the regime is most tellingly revealed in the willingness of these visitors to accept without any trace of skepticism official explanations which the less committed would find objectionable.

Thus, Hollyday and Wallis echo the regime's line regarding the Miskito Indians: "The relocation was a political necessity" (p. 11). They also assure us that "no one had any evidence of 'massacres' of the Miskitos during the relocation . . ." (p. 11). If such evidence *had* been presented, would they have found it "solid" or convincing enough? Or would they have dismissed it as counter-revolutionary propaganda? Given the reluctance of Marxist regimes to invite cameramen to record their coercive operations, their sympathizers are saved from having to confront such issues.

True, the authors learned of "isolated incidents of violence." Such incidents, however, did not stimulate their moral indignation or spark their critical faculties. On the contrary, they believed that even the armed enemies of the revolution received humane treatment:

"Each National Guard member received a three-year prison sentence; additonal years were added based on the testimonies of eyewitnesses to their crimes. All cases are currently under review. Unlike most revolutions, this one carried out no mass reprisals or executions.

The government's commitment has been to try to reintegrate the guard into society, working to change the conscience of these men who under Somoza had received psychological training for killing and torture". (11).

Such confident assertions were apparently made in ignorance of other reports, such as the one in *The New York Times* which stated that "during this period of chaos [in 1979], officials now concede several hundred prisoners were summarily executed." The same article also quoted Jose Estaban Gonzales, the now-in-exile secretary general of Nicaragua's permanent human rights commission, who said that "the Sandinista regime applies methods of torture and repression very similar to those applied . . . by the Somoza dictatorship" *(New York Times,* March 5, 1981).

Criticism of the Sandinistas' refusal to hold elections "shows lack of understanding of the Nicaraguan situation," according to one Sojourners source (p. 13). The article explains:

"Elections are expensive to carry out and more pressing needs demanded the country's scarce resources . . . The Sandinistas wanted first to educate the people so they could be better prepared to make choices about their political future" (p. 13).

One wonders if the *Sojourners* visitors have ever heard of other Marxist states where "too pressing" needs either prevented elections from being held, or, more commonly, simply transformed them into rituals of endorsing the single list of official candidates by a population presumably so well educated that it no longer felt the need to make any choice.

In any event, who needs elections in a country where people have such easy access to their leaders? Case in point: ". . . All Nicaraguans have a great deal of access to the Sandinista leaders. We were convinced of this the evening we met with Daniel Ortega. After each member of our delegation had stepped forward to shake the hand of the chief of state and the television cameras had stopped rolling, Gilberto Aguirre of CEPAD (the Evangelical Committee for Aid and Development) stepped up, smiled, and said 'Daniel!' and the two embraced. We explained that we do not have such a relationship with Ronald Reagan" (p. 12).

Such were the proofs of the democratic and open nature of the Nicaraguan regime—recorded, for the most part, by television cameras of the government.

The visitors also disclaimed that Marxism was a significant factor influencing the policies of these accessible and humane leaders:

"We did not discover the 'Marxist totalitarian regime' that is reported in the U.S. Several government leaders admitted that they have been influenced by Marx . . . However, many of the leaders with whom we talked are Christians and stated that Jesus Christ has had the far greater influence'' (p. 12).

Another example of the credulity of the authors is provided by their description and interpretation of one of the clearly anti-religious actions of the regime:

"In retaliation for this anti-revolutionary posture, 30 of these churches [of the Jehovah's Witnesses and the Seventh Day Adventists] were taken over . . . by Sandinista youth who attempted to turn them into early childhood centers, libraries and health centers. Hoping that the problem would settle out [sic] the Sandinista leadership did not interfere, and this was seen by the conservative churches as tacit approval of the takeover, and a sign of religious repression. The situation escalated and threatened to get out of hand. The government realized that it had made a mistake, and reopened the churches'' (p. 12).

So after all, the government *was* involved in the incident, if as the authors admit, it made a "mistake" and had the power to rectify that mistake. In any event, the authors can understand these policies since, as they noted earlier, "the Nicaraguan evangelical Churches were *infected* [my emphasis] with anti-communist ideology . . ." (p. 12). They also can sympathize with press censorship "given the history of conservative papers in Latin America" (p. 13).

Historical parallels are also employed to universalize deficiencies:

"Like any nation, especially one in the years following a revolutionary triumph, Nicaragua is not exempt from the problem of individuals and groups vying for position and influence in the new regime. That certainly was the experience after the American revolution . . . In such an atmosphere charges and counter-charges tend to fly. [So much for criticism of the regime]. Most countries just need time to sort out those internal problems without inferference from the outside'' (p. 13).

The misapprehension of political developments in Nicaragua conveyed in the March issue of *Sojourners* follows a well-worn path. As other political pilgrims before them, the authors seem determined to believe that the grass is greener in yet another revolutionary society. In conclusion, they write, "We believe that something unprecedented in Central America is happening in Nicaragua'' (p. 13).

One wonders if it would have made any difference had they known that many similarly hopeful travelers before them also believed that something unprecedented was happening in the Soviet Union, China, Cuba, Albania, Bulgaria, Mozambique or many other countries of a similar political inspiration. Whatever was "unprecedented" in these countries was not what the visitors had in mind.

It is, of course, also possible that Hollyday and Wallis *know* the history of such countries—to which Nicaragua looks for inspiration and support—and find little in them reprehensible to their Christian-humanistic sensibilities. Or, on the contrary, they know and deplore the distortions of revolutionary idealism in these countries, but believe that Nicaragua can avoid them if only the United States will let this new crop of revolutionary idealists proceed unhindered.

Given the history of countries calling themselves socialist or Marxist-Leninist, it is discouraging to witness this unfolding repetition of a discredited chapter in Western intellectual history, the latest addition to the already overabundant documentaries of human credulity.

16
Political Tourism in Cuba and Nicaragua

*We saw . . . a country where the great majority of people believe
they are the makers and the beneficiaries of a new society . . . we
were inspired. Cubans are characterized by . . . a burning desire
for the rest of humanity to gain the freedoms that Cubans have so
recently won . . . We returned hoping that our communities can
lead America in developing humility we need to learn from Cuba.*

Newsletter of the United Methodist Voluntary Service[1]

*In Havana I kept meeting Communists in the hotels for foreigners
who had no idea that the energy and water supply in the working
class quarters had broken down during the afternoon, that bread
was rationed, and the population had to stand for two hours in
line for a slice of pizza; meanwhile the tourists in their hotels
were arguing about Lukacs.*

Hans Magnus Enzensberger[2]

*. . . you can see people full of smiles . . . There is joy and
enthusiasm for life and for work . . . We wanted to create in
Nicaragua a joyful people who would sing and dance and this has
been achieved. . . . Nicaragua is the only country in the world
which publishes the poetry of the police.*

Ernesto Cardenal[3]

*Nicaragua's most important war is the one fought inside the
United States . . . The battlefield will be the American conscience
. . . When they (the visitors) return to the United States they have
a multiplier effect on the public opinion of your country . . .*

Thomás Borge[4]

True Believers

A group of senior citizens from Northern California, members of a
coffee bean-picking brigade, gladly exchanged (for three weeks), the

comforts of middle class life for the harsh realities of the Nicaraguan countryside. One of the volunteers explained: ". . . it is a privilege, an invigorating, rewarding experience . . . It is a joy to be doing something worthwhile."[5]

An attorney from a small town in Virginia reported—after a three day visit to Nicaragua undertaken "to form first-hand impressions"— "an exciting and vibrant spirit of independence."[6] Michael Harrington, the democratic-socialist author, wrote: "I came back (from Nicaragua) far more ashamed of my country than at any time since the Vietnam war. The Nicaraguans . . . want to make a truly democratic revolution and it is we who subvert their decency."[7] The Reverend William Sloan Coffin considered the foremost objective of the Nicaraguan regime "to stop the exploitation of the many by the few . . ." A group of religious citizens testified to ". . . a gentleness in the Nicaraguan nature, as exemplified by the words of Tomás Borge, Minister of Interior."[8]

Richard Barnett, a leading member of the Institute for Policy Studies in Washington said that "To defend the right of the Nicaraguan people to conduct their experiment . . . is . . . an obligation of U.S. citizenship." Richard Falk, professor at Princeton University suggested that ". . . it seems imprudent for a progressive interpreter of Central America to dwell on the deficiencies of the Nicaraguan revolution. . . . "[9]

Such and many similar statements indicate that in the early 1980's Nicaragua was highly popular with many Americans of different backgrounds, both as a country to visit and as a political system to defend in the United States. The significance of these attitudes transcends Nicaragua; they reflect recurrent susceptibilities in American (and Western) society toward Marxist-Leninist systems which the latter carefully nurture and seek to enhance by the techniques of political hospitality.

Political hospitality consists of highly organized and purposeful efforts on the part of governments to display their political system and its various institutions in the most favorable light to foreign visitors; it is but one expression of the determination to persuade outsiders, and especially the elite groups of various countries, of the superior virtues of their society. While political hospitality is a matter of degree—all governments naturally prefer to be seen in a positive light and take *some* steps to attain this objective—fully developed forms of it can only be found in countries where the government has a monopoly of political power, as in the Marxist-Leninist one-party systems of our times.

There are a number of preconditions for the unhindered exercise of political hospitality. The first is the determination of the rulers to shape the image of their country in accordance with well-defined political objectives and ideological principles. Such a determination and the policies flowing from it rest, in turn, on the belief that they preside over a historically superior social system and are engaged in a collective enterprise the ends of which justify virtually all means including those used to increase its appeals among visitors and public opinion aboard. These power-holders being Marxists-Leninist, generally believe in the importance of ideas as weapons in the political struggle, including the ideas people—and especially influential people—abroad entertain about their society.

Secondly, the rulers of the country that extends political hospitality must have control over the material-economic resources of the country in order to make the kind of allocations the techniques of hospitality require. There must be state control over resorts, hotels, means of transportation, the training of guides and interpreters, funds for prestige or show-case projects (e.g., model prisons, farms, housing, clinics, schools, child-care centers, etc.). As a former supporter of Cuba, the Chilean Jorge Edwards observed: ". . . the socialist economy could concentrate its efforts on a small sector and obtain marvelous results, which were visible and highly suitable for impressing foreign visitors. . . ."[10]

Thirdly, political hospitality greatly benefits from a docile or intimidated population that will not question publicly the "definitions of reality" foreign visitors are given by the authorities; people who know that unauthorized contacts with foreigners are inadvisable and criticisms of the regime communicated to them even more so.

A Cuban citizen wrote: "Here we have no human rights, no peace and not even the right to subsist, if you are not . . . ready to play their comedy trying to show the world that we are free and owners of our decision and future; thousands . . . had played this play during twenty one years. . . Here everybody is afraid of everyone and you can't believe in anyone. . ." Another observer noted: "Fearing denunciation, Cubans are . . . reluctant to reveal themselves to an inquiring foreigner or even to friends . . ."[11]

Given the preconditions noted above, it is not surprising that the techniques of political hospitality reached their highest level of development in the communist societies of our times. (I am using the term "communist" to refer to one-party systems which legitimate themselves by ideas derived from Marxism-Leninism and share many institutional characteristics especially in areas of political and economic controls.) These techniques were pioneered by the Soviet Union as early as the 1920s and adopted by every successive communist regime. Besides the Soviet Union and China, Vietnam and Cuba and most recently Nicaragua, are the most notable historical examples of the implementation of these techniques.[12]

It should be noted that political hospitality serves not only political but also economic purposes. Every communist country—with the possible exceptions of Albania and North Korea—has been eager to improve its economy by acquiring Western currencies through tourism. This is not to say that these countries would allow economic considerations to override political ones; communist countries place limits on tourism and prefer group tours; they concentrate tourists in particular areas, resorts or hotels; sightseeing activities are restricted to approved sites and large parts of the country remain closed to tourists. David Caute, the English author wrote of his visit to Cuba: ". . . the tourist . . . is dispatched in pursuit of factories, schools, universities, housing projects and research institutes . . . his holiday is not treated as an escape . . . but as a chance to penetrate the virtues of the socialist model."[13]

It is important to point out that despite the magnitude of the efforts and resources devoted to political hospitality, its impact has always been dependent on the climate of opinion prevailing in the countries the tourists came from and on their predisposition or receptivity to the messages conveyed to them by their hosts. Political hospitality by itself rarely changed the minds of people or created enduringly favorable images of the countries which dispensed it. There has always been an interplay between the expectations and attitudes of the visitors and the experiences and impressions they acquired in the course of their guided tours. Heberto Padilla commented on such tourists "disillusioned by the arthritic socialist experiences in Europe, they imagined they had found spontaneity here in a budding revolution . . . Every revolution, however remote, personified for them the ideal which their nation lacked . . . "[14] It was also observed of the visitors to Nicaragua that "for many, travelling here confirms an already solid belief in what the Sandinistas are trying to do."[15]

Correspondingly, the propensity to visit countries boasting of putatively superior social arrangements almost invariably emerges at times when social, economic or cultural conditions in the countries of the tourists become problematic or unsatisfactory. Thus the great waves of tourism or pilgrimages to the Soviet Union arose when Western countries, including the United States, were beset by the economic difficulties and disorders of the Depression in the late 1920s and early 1930's; trips to Cuba, Vietnam and China became popular in the United

States during the 1960s and early 70s, when, besides the Vietnam war, domestic problems surfaced (i.e. racial conflict and a malaise associated with "empty affluence") and persuaded some groups that alternatives to what they regarded as unjust and oppressive social-political arrangements of their own country must be found. Most recently, the upsurge of sympathy toward Nicaragua has been closely connected with the aversion the Reagan administration has inspired among segments of the American public and with the conviction that if his administration was opposed to the Sandinistas, this by itself proved that they deserved the support of right- thinking citizens.

Given the general decline of the attractiveness of the Soviet model— long ceased to be seen as a revolutionary vanguard or "new experiment" in establishing an authentic socialist society—and given the political changes and revelations following the death of Mao in China, neither of these countries remained capable of evoking the sympathy and admiration they once inspired. While their techniques of political hospitality are unchanged the number of favorably disposed Western visitors has sharply declined and reverential travelogues about them now rarely appear.

Newly united Vietnam too lost its earlier, war-time glamor due to the exodus of over a million boatpeople, its continued militarization and close ties with the Soviet Union. It was easier to idealize it as an opponent of the United States and an apparent underdog fighting under the banner of national unity and socialism, than today as an impoverished garrison state invading its smaller Cambodian neighbor.

While the appeals of Cuba have also substantially declined, it has not yet been totally discredited either on the media, or among the intellectuals, or church groups. Cuba has retained an enthusiastic if small following among academics and church people who continue to be impressed by its perceived achievements and have remained recipients of Cuban political hospitality. Curiously enough, despite its police state aspects, severe shortages, religious repression, the outflow of over one million refugees, the persecution of homosexuals (among others), the maintenance of an enormous military establishment and its unhesitating support for Soviet policies, Cuba's reputation suffered much less, although the range of opinion on Cuba is divided, even in liberal-left circles. It is likely that Cuba's relative success in preserving a positive image has been largely due to Castro's continued presence and predominance—he represents, at least in the eyes of the sympathetic beholders, revolutionary continuity and personifies the revolutionary mystique, and remains a charismatic figure. The animosity of successive American administrations toward Cuba has also contributed to the persistence of a measure of support for Castro among those whose political sympathies are shaped, above all, by their own adversary positions; for them the enemy of their enemy is invariably a friend.

In view of what was said above, the rise of Nicaragua to preeminent status among the countries to be idealized is easy to understand. Here was at last a *new* revolutionary socialist regime, a *small* country earlier victimized and dominated by the United States, now ruled by a group of idealistic young revolutionaries locked in mortal combat with the United States. Here was a new regime untarnished (at least in the eyes of its supporters) by association with the Soviet Union, or the mistakes and excesses of other socialist systems. An enormous reservoir of goodwill has been available for the Sandinistas facilitating their projection of a favorable image of their policies and institutions. Political tourism to Nicaragua soon became a major expression of support for that regime. The Nicaraguan authorities well aware of the political importance of public opinion in the United States developed an ambitious program of political hospitality. They greatly benefited from the lessons of Vietnam.[16]

Cuban and Nicaraguan political hospitality aimed essentially at the same goals and used the same techniques. It had two major components: first, the creation or strenghthening of favorable attitudes among visitors by "ego massage", that is, by making the tour a pleasant experience both physically and psychologically, by attending to the needs of the visitors and catering to their self-esteem. Such treatment creates or contributes to a sense of obligation or indebtedness toward the generous host; it also helps to stifle or defuse critical sentiments.

The second major component of political hospitality is the screening of reality, the controlled presentation of what there is to see, the selective display of the features of the country—human, social, institutional. Political hospitality seeks to minimize chance encounters and experiences and generally succeeds in excluding unfavorable impressions.

To these generalizations it should be added that the basic principles of political hospitality here outlined are not uniformly applied; the more important the visitors, the greater efforts will be made to make them feel well liked, comfortable, etc., and to expose them to the most carefully selected encounters and sights, the most inspiring experiences.

The obvious premise of these methods—personal attentiveness and selective display—is that people generalize from personal experience; hence, it is desirable to make such experiences both pleasant and politically instructive. Thus, even if the tourists arrive armed with critical anticipations or a sound knowledge of the political system and its shortcomings (which is rarely the case), there will be few opportunities for them to confirm such anticipations by what they see or hear. (Nicaragua as of this writing is a partial exception to this: since the rulers are somewhat constrained to tolerate a residual pluralism or symbolic opposition, visitors may still have experiences which will not support all the claims of the regime and will find people willing to voice criticism. However, as the power of the regime expands, there will be fewer and fewer discordant voices contesting the messages the authorities seek to convey.)

I will in the following first examine Cuban political hospitality and its potential contribution to the images held about that regime in the United States.

Techniques of Control

Political hospitality is not only a series of measures designed to make conspicuous the attractive aspects of a society—it is also a system of prevention, filtering and censorship. It begins with efforts to ensure that the impressions of the visitor will not be contaminated by unauthorized and uncontrolled contacts and experiences. In the efforts the guide-interpreters play a crucial part. An English journalist wrote:

> Visitors to Cuba are normally assigned a guide and if they travel outside Havana they are expected to take a Cuban chauffeur and hire a car . . . Cuban guides alloted to western visitors are invariably highly sophisticated party persons . . .

> Controls over the visitors' movements are facilitated by the official provision of transportation:

> Every taxi journey is logged at a special office inside each major hotel. You are required to give your destination and your name and hotel room. These are then copied into a log. These logs are openly examined at regular intervals by the police.

> . . . Visitors also need to take good care of the hotel cards they are given when they register . . . These give the visitor's name, hotel and room number. Without these cards it is virtually impossible to do anything.[17]

These observations were corroborated by another visitor describing arrangements at the Hotel Habana Libre: "The police stop any unauthorized Cuban who tries to slip into this palace of imperialist delights.

Another cop waits at the foot of the grand staircase questioning anyone who looks suspect"[18]

The pervasiveness of the controls is further illustrated by the following observations:

> The delegate . . . receives a personal guide who functions as translator, nanny, and watchdog. Almost all contact . . . is mediated through this companion, which makes distinct the delegate's separation from the social realities surrounding him. The companion is responsible for the traveller's program . . . The combination of being spoiled and impotent is reminscent of an infantile situation.[19]

The presence of the guide-interpreter is not the only obstacle to frank exchanges between natives and visitors. As a recent report noted, "Cubans understand full well the rules . . . and most obey unquestioningly. They know who is authorized to speak with foreigners . . . "[20] Carlos Ripoll, a former Cuban citizen, commented: "One can easily imagine the disdain and frustration with which Cubans look upon foreign reporters—often officially escorted and always friendly toward the regime—who stop them to ask naively: 'Amigo, are you happy with the revolution? What do you think of Fidel Castro?' "[21] Sam Farber, another former citizen of Cuba and specialist on pre-revolutionary Cuban history, said, after revisiting his native country that "no Cuban who is really discontented will talk to a stranger."[22] He also pointed out that restrictions intensify "before a big international get-together", that is, when opportunities for meeting foreigners are the most abundant. Controls over foreign correspondents and reporters are especially tight and the attempts to influence them predate their actual arrival. As revealed by a former Cuban intelligence agent Juan Vives:

> In the subtle process of influencing the news nothing is left to chance. Extensive files are kept on all significant newpapers and periodicals around the world . . . Whenever a foreign correspondent applies for a visit to Cuba, his entire personal career is reviewed for any sign of vulnerability or weakness of character. His hotel room is bugged . . . and whenever he leaves it, he is followed by surveillance experts . . . Any document or photograph that the foreign reporter obtains that might be damaging to Cuba is retrieved by arranged assault or fake robbery . . .
>
> In fact police control within Cuba is so severe that there is virtually no circulation of typewritten copies of unauthorized literature such as occurs in Eastern Europe and Russia . . . [23]

Vivian Warner Dudro, in her study of the American press coverage of Cuba, (based on interviews with journalist) found much to support the above. For example, "Every journalist agreed that one of the major obstacles to investigative reporting in Cuba is the tightly controlled transportations system." She also learned that "many people . . . will not be interviewed without permission from their local Committee for the Defense of the Revolution." Sometimes journalists were taken on officially sponsored sightseeing tours without realizing it, as was the case of "One journalist . . . taken to Ramon Castro's farm [a standard way-station of many itineraries] when he asked a cab driver to take him to a farm."[24]

Frances Fitzgerald reported over a decade ago that she and other journalists" could not arrange a trip of more than an hour outside Havana." She also bore witness to the connection between the generous political hospitality received and a diminished journalistic willingness to press for particular targets of reporting:

> It was embarrassing for us to make demands [regarding itineraries] since the government insisted on treating us as guests and keeping us in a style to which even Cuban officials are not acustomed. Each of us who stayed behind after the [Anniversary] Celebrations was given a car and driver, and at the Capri we had air-conditioned rooms, meals with beer and wine and as much meat each day as the Cuban rationing system allows an individual for a week.[25]

When tourists deviated from the officially arranged itineraries and activities the authorities had no hesitation to intervene:

> Most of the time the Cubans take us around in a tightly arranged schedule leaving little free time. But today . . . three of us decided to walk through old Havana . . . We take a photo of a typical line of citizens waiting to obtain rationed goods at a department store. Within a few moments, a uniformed officer appears. He signals that we are to come with him.

> The next few hours are spent in the local police station . . . Finally, an officer appears: "You can go now. But you must understand that the revolutionary process is complex . . . Our struggle is difficult. You can take pictures of anything . . . but no pictures of rationing lines."[26]

Following in the Soviet tradition of political hospitality Cuban guides would sometimes plead ignorance of the location of particular sights, or difficulty of access to them:" . . . when we ask to see the largest synagogue in Havana, our guide says he does not know where it is and forgets to find out . . . "[27]

As noted earlier, a major thrust of political hospitality, in Cuba and elsewhere, is to make the visitor feel appreciated and comfortable, materially as well as psychologically. The techniques for accomplishing this vary according to the importance of the visitors or the type of the group. The reception given to members of the American Venceremos Brigade, a pro-Castro group volunteering manual labor, obviously made a deep impression:

> People were standing on the deck of the ship coming toward us wearing orange sweatshirts with the Brigada Venceremos insignia. The ship circled us . . . Everywhere along the harbor people stood watching us come in. The Cubans were smiling, waving and giving us the clenched fist symbol of revolutionary solidarity. We had arrived: revolutionary Cuba, a dream in progress in the Western hemisphere We were ecstatic.

Arrival by air could be equally festive:

> . . . a shout of joy and triumph as the plane touched down . . . and we stepped out. The first free soil I had ever known . . . Smiles everywhere, bright lights as the Cuban newsmen filmed our joy . . . A trio of singers played Latin music and "Che" smiled from a portrait on the wall as daiquiris and hors d'ouevres were offered Singing, talking, drinking together in José Martí airport in Havana, in Revolutionary Cuba.[28]

Another group of enthusiasts from Australia received similar treatment:

> Much was made of the fact that we were the *primera brigada* from Australia and after a month of being feted and honored we began to feel like Princess Di.
>
> . . . We arrived at the Julio Mella Campamento Internacional in some style. A police motorcycle escort, a police car with blaring siren and an ambulance accompanied us all the way from the airport (and were to escort us in similar fashion for the rest of our stay) . . . The fact that it was midnight had not deterred the entire staff from lining up at the entrance to applaud our arrival.[29]

An American businessman travelling in a group of six (including a U.S. senator) described his arrival:

> The grand design of our tour . . . became clearer some two hours out of Havana when we arrived at our lodgings. The Cuban government had selected a marble-floored seaside villa at Veradero Beach once owned by the Barcardi family of rum fame. Assured that the Bacardi's no longer planned to use the house, we settled in with a small platoon of foreign

ministry personnel, chauffeurs, waiters and kitchen staff. An official welcoming dinner awaited us . . .

. . . The cornerstone of all arrangements was the "hot line" telephone in our villa, which seemed to be in constant use, day and night. Via this life-line, Havana could monitor our progress through housing projects, schools, national shrines, cattle-breeding farms and recreational centers.

. . . When we forayed into public restaurants . . . The lead car would disgorge several security men who would enter the restaurant, check out the restrooms and tables and then lead our entourage to a secure dining location in the corner of the room.

. . . In administrative matters . . . one finds a lightness of spirit more reminisc⌐ .t of an East German border post. Hotel elevator operators . . . function effectively as wardens, checking passengers' room identifications before permitting access to each floor.[30]

Some of the distinguished visitors evinced at least a fleeting unease upon encountering the luxuries heaped on them. Thus Sartre remarked on his "millionaire hotel room" in a veritable "fortress of luxury." Angela Davis, the American communist party funtionary (and vice-presidential candidate) calmed her conscience by recalling that "the Habana Libre, formerly Havana Hilton [was] now freed from the veined fingers of decadent old capitalists. This was the first time I had stayed in such a fancy hotel . . . "[31] On the other hand, Ernesto Cardenal (who was to become a member of the Nicaraguan revolutionary government) noted without any apparent unease, the "sumptuous dining room" of the National Hotel in Havana, where he was offered, among other things, "lobster thermidor, frog legs, French wine" and where the 'uniformed waiters were not servile but companionable; they didn't call you 'sir' but 'comrade' "—a change in terminology that for Cardenal seemed to have a momentous significance, compensating for the fundamental assymetry of the situation he described.[32] He was not the only admirer of Cuba who commented on the excellence of the provisions: Andrew Salkey, a West Indian author making his home in the United States made reference to items such as "delicious criollo pork, rice and wild salad" and other joyous meals cooked to perfection.[33]

International conferences always put Cuban political hospitality into high gear. In 1979 for instance, participants at the Conference of the so-called Non-Aligned Movement, were provided with no fewer than 117 new Mercedes automobiles, among other vehicles.[34] Salkey, a delegate at the 1968 Cultural Congress admitted to a "certain amount of uneasiness" upon contemplating his privileges as compared with the way the average Cuban lived. (Mercifully this uneasiness "wore

off".) The privileges included " . . . the free, all-in luxurious hotel
. . . four enormous dining rooms to choose from, an international
cuisine (changed daily), free laundry service, free telephone . . . free
taxi cabs and Congress cars and buses . . . free entry to the city's
theatres and exhibitions . . . added to all that, my return air ticket . . .
plus my overweight also paid . . . Too much, too much to accept." But
in the end, he accepted it all perhaps in part because he persuaded
himself that the lavish hospitality was "little inspired by ideological
gain": There were also "going away presents" for the delegates:
books, records, posters, cigars, numerous bottles of rum of various
size and type, etc.[35]

Even regular tourists (as distinct from politically important delegates) were given privileges: " . . . foreigners can now jump the
perennial lines for taxis and restaurants . . . 'Cubans don't mind'
insisted Jesús Jiménez, the vice president of the Cuban Tourism
Institute."[36] There have also been special shops established where
tourists (and members of the Cuban elite) can buy scarce consumer
goods and food for foreign currency.

In Cuba as in other similar societies the leaders themselves played
an important part in political hospitality. Castro in particular took it
upon himself to meet and befriend an important visitor—politicians,
businessmen, journalists, selected intellectuals—a part he played with
great skill and considerable success. Meeting Castro was by itself an
event that made the chosen visitors feel important and appreciated.
Sometimes Castro took the visitor on whirlwind tours of inspection all
over the country, often himself driving. ("Barbara Walters recounted
that he [Castro] offered to take her any place on the island.")[37] One of
the first to benefit from such attentions was the famous American
sociologist the late C. Wright Mills, who spent three and a half days
with Castro "devoting an average of 18 hours in every 24 to discussions"; he was informed by Castro that his *Power Elite* "had been a
bedside book of most of the *guerrilleros* in the Sierra Maestra."[38]

Castro also charmed and overwhelmed Sartre, who came to see him
as a renaissance man, a charismatic hero, who "exercise[d] a veritable
dictatorship over [his] needs [and] . . . roll[ed] back the limits of the
possible."[39] Senator McGovern was equally impressed—following a
personal sightseeing tour with Castro—especially by Castro's knowledge of "almost any subject from agricultural methods to Marxist
dialectic to American politics."[40] He left Cuba convinced that "from
all indications, Castro has the support and outright affection of his
people."[41] Castro apparently also succeeded in establishing a close

personal relationship with Pierre Trudeau, prime minister of Canada, which benefited his regime.[42]

While Castro has been in the forefront of such encounters, Ernesto "Che" Guevara also used to meet important visitors as did Castro's brother Ramón. Members of the Australian brigade reported being "taken to visit a 'genetic' dairy farm. There shaking hands with each of us . . . was a tall sturdy figure in olive green army fatigues, green cap, grey-black beard, dark glasses and smoking a huge cigar . . . It was only after we'd all been greeted that we discovered he was Fidel's big brother, Ramón. He won our hearts immediately with his avuncular good humor, his naturalness and his willingness to answer all questions."[43]

Occasionally political hospitality extended to the display of prisons, or model prisons, or parts of prisons spruced up for the benefit of important visitors:

> What the Rev. Jesse Jackson saw . . . was a clean, painted prison where inmates played baseball—a scene, one released prisoner says, is "very different from the way of life in Cuban prisons." . . . Officials worked for a week cleaning and painting the outside of the prison in preparation for Mr. Jackson's visit . . . The morning of Mr. Jackson's visit 'common' [i.e. non-political—] prisoners were assembled hastily, given new baseball uniforms and equipment and told to play ball . . . as soon as he [Jackson] left, the balls and bats were taken away and the prisoners returned to their cells."

Such elaborate preparations, including special diets and 'extra things like Kool-Aid' are routine when foreign delegations visit Cuban prisons, Mr. Noble [a released prisoner] said.

> Jesse Jackson did not see the jail as it usually is. . . . Many delegations come and believe the country is what they have been shown . . . For example, the inside of the prison has never seen any paint. And for those political prisoners left behind, there is no medical aid. Even when foreign delegations visit the prisons, political prisoners . . . are kept in their cells in a separate part of the prison. Prisoners convicted of non-political crimes are those given extra food and allowed to play baseball.[44]

Another unusual event that occurred during the Jackson visit was a special church service for the obvious benefit of Jackson attended by Castro himself.[45] If the Reverend found it strange that the head of a militantly atheist state would attend such a service, there is no public record of it. (The incident may remind the reader of Brezhnev's attempt to impress President Carter by remarking at their summit meeting in Vienna, that God would never forgive them if they had not reached an agreement on disarmament—a comment that made at the time, a deep impression on Mr. Carter.)

Predisposed Political Tourists

It should be stressed again that the effectiveness of political hospitality depends greatly on the predisposition of its recipients. The suspension of critical faculties and the wish to believe are crucial. If so, even political imprisonment may be viewed as excusable—redeemed by its goals, as it were—by those sympathetic toward the regime. Thus Bishop James Armstrong and Rev. Russell Dilley wrote, in their "Statement of Church Persons after Visiting Cuba, June 19–28, 1977: ". . . there is a significant difference between situations where people are imprisoned for opposing regimes designed to perpetuate inequities (as in Chile and Brazil, for example) and situations where people are imprisoned for opposing regimes designed to remove inequities (as in Cuba)."[46] Underlying this justification is the belief that the Cuban system has in fact removed the inequities and political prisoners are jailed for opposing such policies (!), and, most importantly, that ends justify means—a view especially remarkable when taken by churchmen. In the same spirit Richard Falk, well-known social critic and protester of American policies abroad, said of the current leaders of Nicaragua: "They may be brutal, they may be imprudent in certain ways, but I think they are basically trying to create a much fairer social and economic order for their people."[47] Good intentions thus remove the moral stigma of questionable means.

Another time honored method of rationalizing the restrictions on personal and political freedom in Cuba (and elsewhere) has been to define them as luxuries, or ethnocentric Western values of no interest to the ordinary citizens of the countries concerned. Andrew Zimbalist, a professor of economics at Smith College in Massachusetts pointed out that "Cuba should . . . be judged by different standards of personal freedom . . . Cuba does not have the luxury of allowing the kind of political openness that we have in the U.S."[48] Knowing little about the specifics of such restrictions and about the political violence used by the regime made it easier to take this position. As early as in 1961 a street protest by poor women near the Cuban beach resort of Varadero was brutaly crushed next to this popular tourist town. Carlos Franqui recalled: "On my way back to Havana I passed through Varadero and wondered what sort of Cuba the visitors were seeing while ten minutes away there was a carnival of persecution in full swing. These people saw a stage-set Cuba, not the reality we had to live in every day, and they took the part for the whole.''⁴⁹

When favorable predisposition combines with ignorance and lack of imagination, the visitors' capacity for absorbing the messages of political hospitality greatly expands. It would not occur to a retired physician from a small New England town on a conducted tour (member of "a religous study group") that he might have been taken to the same farmhouse and the same old lady as countless others before him, regaled with the same story ("We sipped straight rum while we listened to the elderly woman tell how before the revolution she had often been hungry and how after the revolution, even though old, she had been taught to read and write."⁵⁰) It may also be noted here that such "before and after" presentations by old people have been standard fares of political hospitality not only in Cuba but also in the Soviet Union, China, Vietnam and similar countries. The contrived nature of such visits was vividly described by a former Cuban guide-interpreter in the film "Improper Conduct", including the practice of stopping, in a seemingly random manner, at the same apartment in the same (model) housing project with group after group, where the (same) residents extended their hospitality to the foreigners offering provisions generally unavailable to the public.

Another example of the combination of credulousness and ignorance can be found in the reaction of sympathetic foreigners to the giant rallies and marches, taken to be evidence of the popular support enjoyed by the government: ". . . imagine thousands upon thousands of people slowly moving forward, five, six, sometimes ten steps at a time and then waiting . . . sometimes in the shade but most times under the punishing . . . sun." Another supporter wrote: ". . . the March of the Fighting People had mobilized five million Cubans, including the stunning procession of some two million in Havana that marched . . . for eight hours . . . in a show of disciplined strength that has little rival in history . . . [There have of course been many rivals: in Moscow, Peking and especially in Nurenberg during the Nazis.] There was serenity and order to the streets . . .''⁵¹

A former citizen of Cuba had no difficulty explaining the phenomenon: "People are always amazed how Castro gets half a million people to show up . . . Basically when he talks they shut down certain parts of the factories, shut down the schools, bus half a million people to Havana and don't let them leave until he is finished".⁵²

While, as noted above, the effectiveness of Cuban political hospitality cannot be assessed without taking into account the predisposition and political beliefs of the visitors, it doubtless has made a contribution to the maintenance of a relatively favorable image of the regime. This is all the more noteworthy since the Cuban propaganda efforts have been counterbalanced by the presence of hundreds of thousands of Cuban exiles in the United States who have no illusions about the character of that political system. Nonetheless many myths and illusions about Cuba continue to find receptive audiences among those estranged from and hostile to American society. Cuban political hospitality has been successful in comfirming and solidifying the beliefs of those who were susceptible to its messages in the first place.

The New Political Mecca

It is not surprising that political hospitality in Nicaragua has much in common with its Cuban counterparts since Cuba has served in general as the model for the new regime. (The Nicaraguan leaders had a longstanding relationship with the Cuban authorities, receiving training, advice and material assistance from Castro while in the underground.) Like in Cuba, as little as possible is left to chance. A former Nicaraguan offical of the Interior ministry, Alvaro Baldizon explained: 'Security agents pretending to be photographers, journalists or relatives of people in the region to be visited frequently join the delegations . . . on their trips . . . They report to the Ministry on the groups' itinerary. Using advance notice . . . Borge [minister of interior] sends teams of people to be on the routes used and in the localities to be visited. These are called 'casual encounter' teams . . . pretending to be local residents . . . They describe alleged contra atrocities and the benefits of the Sandinista revolution . . .''[53]

The Nicaraguan policies of political hospitality have possibly been even more ambitious than those of Cuba, more explicit and specific in their political objectives. The goal of the Sandinistas was not merely to create a generally favorable image of their regime in the United States—their carefully calculated propaganda campaigns (of which political hospitality was but one manifestation) were aimed at particular political targets. Above all they were seeking to persuade American public opinion and policymakers to cease all support for the Contras and for the remaining pockets of peaceful opposition. They were seeking to project the image of a small, poor, victimized country, beset by economic difficulties caused by the guerilla war (and the United States), of a government committed to political and economic pluralism, leaders who were flexible egalitarian idealists inspired more by religion than Marxism-Leninism and who were most unhappy about diverting scarce resources to warfare. They also claimed to pursue a blend of (true) Christianity and form of socialism untainted by the mistakes of the older Soviet-type regimes. They vocally asserted their independence from the Soviet Union except for the necessity of accepting assistance refused by the United States. The hostility of the United States left no alternative but pushing Nicaragua closer to the Soviet Union and Cuba—a myth identical to that surrounding Castro's relationship to the Soviet Union. (According to Susan Kaufman Purcell, director of the Latin-American program at the Council on Foreign Relations, Shirley Christian, in her *Nicaragua: Revolution in the Family,"* provides convincing evidence that the Sandinista leaders intended to establish a Leninist system from the day they marched into Managua".)[54]

Another distinctive goal of Nicaraguan political hospitality has been to convey an impression of political pluralism not claimed by other similar regimes.

A strategy of deception or "manto" (the Spanish word for cloak) had deep roots in the political history of the FSLN (Frente Sandinista de Liberacion Nacional). As traced by Douglas W. Payne:

> The *manto* is one of . . . [the] basic tenets of guerilla war and revolutionary strategy with which Sandinista leaders and cadres became engrained under political-military training that began in the Soviet Union and Cuba during the late 1950's . . .
>
> . . . As a political weapon over and above the more generally recognized tactical techniques of disinformation. It [i.e. the manto or deception] is central to the success and survival of any Marxist-Leninist revolutionary group that aims to secure and expand a foothold in close proximity to its perceived and powerful enemy.[55]

Thus the Sandinista deceptions have in some ways been more purposeful and carefully thought out than those encountered in other similar systems which at least did not seek to misrepresent to the same degree their basic policies and institutional patterns. The Sandinistas were also adept at tailoring their messages to the proclivities of different audiences as reported by an American journalist: "To American visitors, frequently from church and university groups, the revolution is described as a humanist one, a struggle against misery. To other visitors, with left-wing views, the talk is of 'scientific change' with no interest in achieving 'perfect democracy', but a revolution aimed at a 'total social transformation.' "[56]

The policy of maintaining a facade or semblance of political pluralism led to the survival of minor opposition groups and one (heavily censored) opposition newspaper *(La Prensa)* for the benefit of foreign visitors and public opinion abroad. (The principles of censorship were identical to those found in all communist systems. Thus for example " . . . censors objected to the publication of a story [in *La Prensa*] about a 96-year old woman who had committed suicide, charging that the story was 'an attack on the psychic health of the people and, therefore, an attack against the security of the state.' "[57]

Many of the techniques for utilizing supportive foreigners resembled those employed by Cuba. Thus while Cuba set up the Venceremos Brigade, composed of sympathizers to assist in the harvest of sugar-cane as an act of revolutionary solidarity, Nicaragua attracted groups to harvest coffee beans; volunteers from abroad were also used in other projects and in various advisory capacities.[58]

In contrast to Cuba, Nicaragua did not have a preeminent figure, like Castro, to impress visiting foreign dignitaries; on the other hand, all members of the junta made themselves readily available to visitors. Thus it was noted that "Almost any visiting American official, no matter how low his rank, can now expect to meet with at least two of the nine comandantes . . . Non-official American visitors . . . can count on at least one . . ."[59] The legal director of the Texas Civil Liberties Union, James C. Harrington wrote: "We met Sergio Ramirez [member of the junta], two department directors . . . Vice-Foreign Minister, Nora Astorga (a charming heroine of the revolution) . . . the Minister of Culture (Father Ernesto Cardenal) and . . . two of the three Electoral Commission members . . . We broke mid-day bread with three Supreme Court judges . . ."[60] Even a reporter for *Playboy* magazine, hardly a revolutionary publication, found the leaders very accessible: "After the interviews were under way, some of the Nicaraguan leaders began inviting Marcelo [the photographer] and me, well, to hang out with them. Things we did in Managua: go with Borge to a prison farm for Mosquito Indian counter-revolutionaries; watch father Cardenal put on all all-day Latin-American song festival . . . dinner at Ramirez house."[61]

Tomas Borge, the minister of internal security, (political police) was particularly active meeting important visitors. He had a special office for receiving delegations from abroad:

> "Borge has two different offices. One . . . is located in the Silvio Mayorga building where he meets religious delegations and delegations from democratic political parties. In this office Borge has photographs of children, gilded, carved crucifixes, and a Bible or two. Before Borge meets with religious delegations he usually memorizes Bible passages which he can quote . . . Borge's real office, where he fulfills his duties

as Interior Minister, is located . . . in Bello Horizonte . . . In that office there are no crucifixes or Bibles—only Marxist literature and posters of Marx, Engels, and Lenin."[62]

Borge also seemed to specialize in taking important visitors on tours of (model) prisons (such as mentioned by the *Playboy* reporter) including Gunter Grass, the famous German writer who was suitably impressed: ". . . in this tiny, sparsely populated land . . . Christ's words are taken literally."[63] By contrast the "Representatives of the committee [Lawyers' Committee for International Human Rights] were refused permission to visit El Chipote, the main security police detention center in Managua. The report says that 'Minister Borge explained that the presence of a stranger could interrupt the process of interrogation and persuasion'."[64]

Nicaraguan political hospitality and the political tourism it catered to benefited to an unusual degree from domestic political conditions in the United States. These included the hostility to President Reagan and his various policies (including his attempts to put pressure on the regime in Nicaragua), the isolationism inspired by Vietnam and the eagerness of former Vietnam protesters and social critics to find new, but similar causes to champion. For such groups—just as Vietnam in the 60's provided, in the words of Susan Sontag, a key to the systematic critique of the United States—Nicaragua in the 1980's offered similar possibilities. No wonder that prominent figures in the anti-war movement—and vocal critics of American society—found it congenial and natural to become supporters of the Sandinistas. Their ranks included William Sloan Coffin, Benjamin Spock, Alan Ginsberg, Linus Pauling, George Wald, Eqbal Ahmad, Noam Chomsky, Harvey Cox, David Dellinger, Richard Falk, John Gerassi, Robert McAffe Brown, Pete Seeger, Adrienne Rich, Jessica Mitford, the Berrigan brothers, Abbie Hoffman and many other Vietnam era protest-celebrities.

There was a tendency in some instances to project upon present day Nicaragua the atmosphere of American college campuses of the 1960's. For example: "Here was a place seemingly run by the kind of people who were Sixties radicals. Wherever we went, people were young, singing political folk songs and chanting, 'Power to the People'. One night there was even a Pete Seeger concert in town!"[65] As a more detached observer put it: "For . . . the backpacking 'sandilistas', Nicaragua seems to be a way station on a trip back through the 1960's."[66] The Sandinistas were able to rely on a vast network of support groups and organizations within the United States which helped to prepare and funnel tour groups to Nicaragua. Those specialising in the organization of tours—as distinct from the even more numerous support groups of more diffuse purpose—included Marazul, Inc., The National Network in Solidarity with the Nicaraguan People, Nicaragua-Honduras Education Project, the Nuevo Instituto de Centro America, The Guardian Weekly, Tropical Tours, Tur-Nica (the official Nicaraguan agency), United States Out of Central America and Witness for Peace (associated with the American Friends Service Committee). All these organizations had many local chapters nationwide.[67] The scope of the phenomenon (of political tourism) may be glimpsed from a listing of tours advertised and organized by Marazul Tours (*one of the tour operators*) for the period November 1984 and April 1985.

The groups listed included: the Marazul Study Tour, Mining Conference, Witness for Peace-West Virginia, Harvest Brigade (six of them), Pan American Nurses Conference, Witness for Peace-Arizona, New Orleans Study Tour, Boston Nicaragua Study Tour, Christian Theological Seminary, Teachers College Study Group, NICA Spanish Language Program, Health Pac Study Tour, OXFAM America Group, Witness for Peace-Kansas, Guardian Study Tour, Witness for Peace-Baltimore, Bengis Social Service Group, Militant/Perspective Mundial Tour, Vassar College Study Group, and many others. Such tours have been complemented by the speaking tours of various representatives of the Nicaraguan government within the United States, energetically visiting campuses and making use of the American media.[68]

According to the Nicaraguan Minister of Foreign Trade 100,000 Americans visited Nicaragua since the revolution in 1979. Many tours have been organized by the Protestant Committee for Aid and Development[69]—highlighting the important part played by American churches in fostering political tourism to Nicaragua. While past political tours, including those of Cuba, have also benefited from the cooperation and sympathy of churchmen, the support extended to the Nicaraguan regime by the Churches has been exceptionally warm and wide ranging. It included not only fund raising and organising tour groups but also lobbying politicians. House Speaker Thomas O'Neill, influenced by Maryknoll nuns, reached the conclusion that American non-intervention and withdrawal of support for the guerillas would " . . . allow them [the Nicaraguan people] to make their own free choice of government."[70] Personal influences of another kind were also at work in the case of Senator Tom Harkin of Iowa, "a long time friend" of Miguel D'Escoto, foreign minister of Nicaragua. Harkin, with Senator Kerry of Massachusetts visited Managua and subsequently lobbied forcefully against aid to the guerrillas.[71] Harkin and Kerry bolstered their pro-Sandinista position with a study prepared by the

Institute of Policy Studies in Washington, an organization specializing in the production and dissemination of the critiques of the United States and capitalism.[72]

Hollywood celebrities have been another group attracted to the Marxist-Leninist regime in Nicaragua and successfully enlisted in its support. For example, it was reported that

> Two years ago at a conference in Mexico City, Rosario Murillo, the wife of . . . Daniel Ortega Saavedra, asked a well-connected American, Blase Bonpane, to organize delegations of prominent American celebrities to Nicaragua . . .
>
> Mr. Bonpane, a former Maryknoll priest and professor of Latin American history at the University of California at Los Angeles, is a liberation theologian sympathetic to the Sandinistas. He understood . . . the impact Hollywood stars could have on American public opinion. . . .
>
> Many of the most visible critics of U.S. Policy come from Hollywood— celebrities like Ed Asner, Mike Douglas and Susan Anspach.
>
> Much of Hollywood interest in Nicaragua can be traced to Blase Bonpane who helped organize a nine-city tour with singer Jackson Browne, actors Mike Farrell and Diane Ladd, former Georgia State Senator Julian Bond and others. The tour was aimed at rallying opposition to U.S. intervention in Nicaragua."[73]

Another interesting example of pro-Sandinista lobbying (linked to political hospitality extended by the Nicaraguan authorities) was provided by the Washington law firm of Reichler and Applebaum, an officially registered agent of the Nicaraguan government. The firm organized a team of Americans to investigate within Nicaragua the alleged atrocities of the guerrillas with the assistance of the government (and its resident sympathizers) which gave them ". . . in country transportation, boarding, housing, office space, staff and, one can assume, the witnesses themselves . . ."[74] The timing of this inquiry coincided with the Congressional vote on aid to the guerrillas.

Thus the Sandinista regime has built up a large and influential lobby in the United States adept at influencing both the media and public opinion and members of the Congress and highly successful in diverting attention from the substantial human rights violations committed by the Nicaraguan authorities.[75]

As in the case of political tourists in other communists countries, the visitors' apparent suspension of critical faculties enhanced the quality of their experiences in Nicaragua. A professor of computer studies (at Hampshire College in Amherst, Mass.) was struck by "the comfortable presence of government soldiers. Nicaragua is a country where nobody is afraid of the soldiers . . . They are people. You can walk up and talk to them."[76] Poet Adrianne Rich described revolutionary Nicaragua as a "society that took poets seriously" and approvingly quoted someone who told her that "You'll love Nicaragua. Everyone there is a poet".[77] Father Richard Preston of Lansing, Michigan reached the conclusion that "the reign of God has arrived in Nicaragua", as well as the "reign of truth, hope and justice".[78] With good reasons did Karen Martin-Schramm (of the Center for Global Services and Education of the Lutheran Church in Minneapolis) observe that "many Americans journey to Nicaragua as 'a matter of faith' ".[79] Sergio Ramirez Mercado, a member of the junta put it in a more understated way: "Religious, social workers, actors, writers. They all come to resolve their doubts."[80]

Not surprisingly Jaime Chamorro Cardenal, an editor of *La Prensa,* the hard pressed opposition newspaper saw it differently: "Some honestly come to investigate, but most come to confirm what they already believe . . . They are sent down here by groups that are partial to the Sandinistas, and once they get here they are quite ingenuous. They believe everything they are told."[81]

Not all conducted tours produced the desired results. At least two participants of what seemed a typical tour (organized by the Center for Global Service and Education of Augsburg College, in Minneapolis) returned disillusioned. They provided revealing details of the techniques of political hospitality they experienced. They wrote:

> During the two week period our group was subject to incessant thinly disguised indoctrination . . . We were exposed to a total of 45 speakers of which only 7 spoke from a pro U.S. perspective and we were conditioned to distrust them before and after they spoke to us. . . .

> The Center organized full itineraries for each country [Mexico and El Salvador were added to Nicaragua] which allowed only short periods of time on our own. However the language barrier and unfamiliar environments still kept us dependent on the staff.

> . . . Another technique was . . . setting aside a period in the evenings for what they called 'reflection time'. During these sessions they always encouraged discussions putting emphasis on our 'feelings' rather than on facts. These seemed to be directed conversations. . . .

> . . . Throughout the trip they tried to get us emotionally involved.

> . . . We visited the state-owned Helanica Textile Factory where a spokeswoman appealed to us to tell the people in the U.S. that they did not want war.

. . . The same no war theme was repeated by the Minister of Education, Fernando Cardinal . . . During his session, Cardinal told us he sometimes spoke to groups like ours two or three times a day and that nine out of ten of them represented protestant churches.

The forced relocation of the Moskito Indians was 'justified' by another priest Justinian Liebl . . .

. . . the travel seminar is designed, organized and conducted to overwhelm the participants with information which supports the anti-U.S., pro-Sandinista bias of the Center for Global Service and Education.[82]

Since they were *not* uncritically disposed to begin with, these two visitors managed to learn some facts about Nicaraguan life their hosts had not intended to bring to their attention, as for example the threat of the loss of ration cards as an inducement to vote in the (1984 Fall) elections. They nonetheless concluded that ". . . it is extremely difficult to maintain a balanced perspective after being exposed to these combined techniques for a period of two weeks. If we had not had each other to talk to we might have begun to question our own position . . . We felt it is virtually impossible for anyone who is naive and uninformed, and trusting of the Center, not to succumb to this type of brainwashing."[83]

Robert Leiken, another former American sympathizer reacted negatively to the culinary manifestations of political hospitality: "In a private state dining room I ate a sumptuous meal with a comandante at a long table attended by five servants. The image of the protruding stomachs of the 'spoiled ones of the revolution' intruded while we consumed our meringue pie."[84] He observed with dismay the rise of "A Sandinista *nomenklatura*" benefiting of hard currency stores, luxury restaurants and the former mansions of the Somoza dynasty, called "protocol houses" (as in Cuba). A recent *New York Times* report confirmed his observations: ". . . the most striking is the emergence of what one diplomat here calls 'the Sandinista *nomenklatura*'—a new revolutionary bureaucratic elite of *commandantes* and other high officials, insulated from the hardships and privations endured by the rest of the populace. They live in homes expropriated from the old bourgeoisie . . . They can shop at special 'dollar stores' reserved for diplomats and enjoy privileges ranging from reserved box seats at the baseball stadium to unlimited supplies of rationed gasoline and water."[85] (The expensive tastes of the leaders was also illustrated by the purchase of $3500 worth of designer glasses by Daniel Ortega and his wife on their visit to New York in 1985 at Cohen's Fashion Optical store on the Upper East side.[86]) At every level political criteria exerts influence on living standards as in the case of allocating housing for the poor: "Managua's squatters . . . feel they are being passed over in favor of Sandinista activists. In particular their complaints are directed toward a showplace housing project . . . in southwest Managua. There, 860 new homes have been built and occupied by families chosen through a system in which . . . political loyalties were one of the principal criteria."[87]

Such news items rarely reach the political tourists and if they do they are likely to dismiss them as either untrue, or atypical, or insignificant; their beliefs will not be eroded by information at variance with their convictions[88] as long as they remain committed to a vision of a superior alternative to their own corrupt society.

It may thus be concluded that political tourism brings no greater enlightenment—and probably far less—than ordinary tourism does in our times: "It was once believed that as international travel and communications became easier, international understanding would grow. It has not . . . Western tourists . . . return, in spite of their bulging photograph albums, as ignorant as when they set out."[89]

Although I emphasized throughout this article the importance of favorable predisposition on the part of political tourists as a major determinant of the success of political hospitality, the latter continues to play an important part in confirming such predispositions and providing experential support for hopes and longings which—as contemporary history has shown—can be projected upon a number of different societies at different times.

Notes

1. Rusty Davenport: "Cuba: A Land of Contrast"; *Common Ground*, (A Newsletter of the United Methodist Voluntary Service), Summer 1981, quoted in *A Time for Candor: Mainline Churches and Radical Social Witness*, Washington, D.C., Institute on Religion and Democracy, 1983, p. 85.
2. Hans Magnus Enzensberger: "Tourists of the Revolution" in *Consciousness Industry*, New York, 1974, p. 152.
3. Ernesto Cardenal: "The Revolution is a Work of Love", *Nicaraguan Perspectives* (Berkeley), Fall 1981, pp. 6, 7.
4. Tomas Borge quoted in Juan Tamayo: "Sandinistas Aim Soft Sell at Activists, *Miami Herald*, December 14, 1983.
5. "Americans Work Free in Nicaraguan Fields" AP Report, *Daily Hampshire Gazette* (Northampton, Mass.), January 24, 1985, p. 40.
6. Larry Hoover: "Attorney Visits Nicaragua", *Daily News Record* (Harrisonburg, Va.) January 3, 4 1986.

7. Michael Harrington: "Economic Troubles Besetting Nicaragua", *New York Times*, Op-ed page, July 16, 1981.
8. William Sloan Coffin: Nicaragua is not an Enemy", *New York Times*, Op-ed page, July 31, 1983; Nicaragua Visited", *The Churchman*, April–May 1984, p. 16.
9. "The U.S. Left and Nicaragua", *The Nation*, April 20, pp. 456, 458.
10. Jorge Edwards: *Persona Non Grata*, New York, 1977, p. 198.
11. "A Cuban's Letter: No Human Rights", *New York Times*, Op-ed page, December 3, 1980; Edward Gonzales: *Cuba under Castro: The Limits of Charisma*, Boston: Houghton Mifflin, 1974, p. 9.
12. For a book length study of political hospitality and its major recipients see Paul Hollander: *Political Pilgrims-Travels of Western Intellectuals to the Soviet Union, China and Cuba, 1928–1978*, New York: Oxford University Press 1981 and Harper and Row 1983.
13. David Caute: *Cuba Yes?*, New York, 1974, p. 49; on recent Cuban efforts to expand tourism see M. A. Moore: "Cuba Strives to Increase Tourism", *The Miami News*, October 16, 1981.
14. Herberto Padilla: *Heroes are Grazing in My Garden*, New York: Farrar, Straus, Giroux, 1984, pp. 121, 122.
15. Edward Cody; "Americans Pay Homage to a Revolution", *Washington Post*, July 23, 1985.
16. For an illuminating analysis of such parallels see Doan Van Toai and David Chanoff: "Learning from Vietnam", *Encounter*, Sept–Oct. 1982.
17. Ian Mather: "Even the Taxi Driver Spies on You", *Business Traveller*, Nov–Dec. 1979, pp. 36, 37.
18. William Scobie: "In Castro's Havana, Life is Waiting for Hours for ice cream", *Florida-Times Union*, August 23, 1985.
19. Enzenberger *cited*, p. 135–136.
20. "Castro's Cuba: Progress but at a High Price", *U.S. News and World Report*, August 20, 1984, p. 34.
21. Carlos Ripoll: "The Price of Socialist Riches", *New York Times*, January 19, 1975, Op-ed page.
22. "A Look at Cuba Today", *Changes*, July–Aug. 1980, p. 14.
23. Cord Meyer: "But Spies and Agents Cloud Castro's Intentions", *The Evening Sun* (Baltimore), May 7, 1982; see also Juan Vives: *The Masters of Cuba (in French)*, Paris, 1981.
24. Vivien Warner Dudro; "Covering Cuba", Paper delivered at the conference on The Media and the Cuban Revolution, Washington, D.C., November 1984, pp. 11, 13.
25. Frances Fitzgerald in *The New Yorker*, February 18, 1974, p. 41; see also Ronald Radosh, ed.: *New Cuba*, New York, 1976, p. 144.
26. Ronald Radosh: Cuba: "A Personal Report", *Liberation*, January 1974, pp. 26–27.
27. Suzanne Garment: "Cuban Politics: Living with the Lies", *The Wall Street Journal*, April 19, 1985, p. 29.
28. Sandra Levinson and Carol Brightman, eds.: *Venceremos Brigade*, New York, 1971, pp. 74–75.
29. Meredith Bergman: "The Australian Brigade", *The National Times (Sydney)*, March 1, 1984.
30. Ned W. Bandler Jr.: "Taking the Cuban Tour", *Freedom at Issue*, Nov–Dec. 1977, pp. 6, 8, 9.

31. *Sartre on Cuba*, New York, 1961, p. 47; Angela Davis: *An Autobiography*, New York, 1974, p. 203.
32. Ernesto Cardenal: *In Cuba*, New York, 1974, p. 4.
33. Amdrew Salkey: *Havana Journal*, Harmondsworth, England, 1971, pp. 195, 218.
34. Flora Lewis: "Havana Parley: Long on Oratory", *New York Times*, September 5, 1979, Op-ed page.
35. Salkey *cited*, pp. 25 and 210.
36. Alan Riding: "Castro Offers to give His All", *New York Times*, June 23, 1982.
37. Charles Bartlett: "The Castro the T.V. Specials Don't Show Us", *The Washington Star*, June 15, 1977.
38. K. S. Karol: *Guerillas in Power*, New York, 1970, p. 58.
39. Sartre *cited* pp. 102, 103.
40. George McGovern: *Grassroots: The Autobiography of George McGovern*, New York, 1977, pp. 267–77.
41. Quoted in Carlos Ripoll: "Did Fidel Seduce McGovern?", *The Washington Star*, April 13, 1977.
42. John B. Harbon: "Trudeau, Castro: Pals for 25 Years", *The Miami Herald*, December 31, 1983.
43. Meredith Burgman *cited*.
44. S. L. Nall: "Prisoners Say Cubans Fooled Jackson on Jail", *Washington Times*, July 2, 1984; Jole Brinkley: "70 Innings of Baseball. Then Freedom", *New York Times*, June 30, 1984; "Freed Prisoners Look Back in Anger at Long Years in Cuba", *Los Angeles Herald*, June 30, 1984.
45. Dudro *cited* p. 24.
46. Quoted in *A Time for Candor, cited*, p. 81.
47. "The Confessions of Richard Falk", *Prospect*, November 1983, p. 9.
48. Mark Averit: "Smith Professor Describes Life and Economy in Cuba". *Daily Hampshire Gazette*, July 11, 1984.
49. Carlos Franqui: *Family Portrait with Fidel, A Memoir*, New York, 1984, pp. 144–145.
50. Edward Manwell: "City Traveller Finds Country Vastly Changed", *Daily Hampshire Gazette*, April 4, 1984.
51. William Lee Brent: "The People's March", *The Black Scholar*, July–Aug 1980, p. 50 and Robert Chrisman: "Cuba: Forge of the Revolution" *Ibid*. pp. 60–61.
52. Modesto Maidique: "Fidel's Plantation", *The Stanford Magazine*, Winter 1983, p. 31.
53. "Nicaraguan Defector Details Sandinista Repression", *Newsletter*, Council for Democracy in the Americas, Washington, D.C., 1985, p. 6.
54. Susan Kaufman Purcell: "Behind Revolution", *New York Times*, July 20, 1985. Similar evidence can also be found in Humberto Belli: *Christians Under Fire*, Puebla Institute, Garden City, Michigan, 1984 and in his *Breaking the Faith: The Sandinista Revolution and its Impact on Freedom and Christian Faith in Nicaragua*, Westchester, Ill.: Crossway Books, 1985.
55. Douglas W. Payne: "The 'Mantos' of Sandinista Deception", *Strategic Review*, Spring 1985, pp. 9–10.
56. Jon Vinocur: "Nicaragua: A Correspondent's Portrait", *New York Times*, August 16, 1983, p. A4.

57. Joel Brinkley: "Nicaraguan Urges U.S. to Rein in Rebels", *New York Times*, January 4, 1985 p. A3.
58. See example for Raymond Bonner: "A Melting Pot Is Converging in Nicaragua", *New York Times*, September 12, 1982; "U.S. Volunteers Help Nicaragua with the Harvest", *New York Times*, February 16, 1984; "Senior Citizens Planning to Help Nicaragua Harvest" (AP), *Daily Hampshire Gazette*, January 9, 1985.
59. *Miami Herald cited.*
60. James C. Harrington: "Countering Nicaragua's Contras", *The Texas Observer*, June 15, 1984, p. 17.
61. "Playboy Interview: The Sandinistas", *Playboy*, September 1983, p. 58.
62. "Nicaragua's State Security: Behind the Propaganda mask—An Interview with Alvero Jose Baldizon Aviles", Briefing Paper, *Institute on Religion and Democracy*, Washington, D.C., September, 1985, p. 2.
63. Gunter Grass: "Epilogue: America's Backyard" in Martin Diskin, ed.: *Our Backyard*, New York, 1983, p. 247.
64. Shirley Christian: "Nicaragua Police Criticized on Rights", *New York Times*, April 5, 1985.
65. *Playboy cited* p. 58.
66. Cody *cited* in *Washington Post.*
67. See for example Jack Foley: "Nicaragua is Invaded by American Visitors", *San Jose Mercury News*, October 7, 1984; for an account of the influx of Western European visitors see Warren Hoge: "Nicaraguan Scene: Fiery Slogans, Designers Jeans", *New York Times*, January 6, 1982.
68. See for example "Nicaraguan Official on Campus Today" *Massachusetts Daily Collegian* (Amherst), May 7, 1985 (this refers to the visit by Ernesto Cardenal); and Athleen Elington: "Visiting Student Activists Outline Views", *Daily Hampshire Gazette*, October 17, 1985.
69. Stephen Kinzer: "Sandinistas' Visitors: Motives touch off dispute", *New York Times*, July 4, 1985.
70. Margaret Shapiro: "The Roots of O'Neill's Dissent", *Washington Post*, June 5, 1985.
71. See for example Loring Swaim: "Betrayal for Those Who Seek Freedom", *Daily Hampshire Gazette*, April 29, 1985.
72. Shirley Christian: "Nicaraguan Week in the Capital", *New York Times*, April 19. 1985.
73. Marshall Ingverson: "From Actors to Advocates, Americans Are Flocking to Nicaragua", *Christian Science Monitor*, November 23, 1984, p. 6; for further references to this nine city tour see also "Radical Chic. . . . Returns" in Review and Outlook, *The Wall Street Journal*, October 12, 1984.
74. Jim Denton: "Contra Atrocities or a Covert Propaganda War? A Lobbying Drive Began in Managua". *Wall Street Journal*, April 23, 1985.
75. See for example Fred Barnes: "The Sandinista Lobby", *New Republic*, January 20, 1986.
76. "Computer Teacher Felt 'At Home' in Nicaragua," *Daily Hampshire Gazette*, February 6, 1985.
77. "Poet Adrienne Rich Mixes Poetry, Politics in Talk at U. Mass.", *Daily Hampshire Gazette*, September 29, 1983.
78. "The Reign of God has Arrived in Nicaragua", *Catholic Weekly*, March 25, 1983, p. 7.

79. *San Jose Mercury News cited.*
80. Quoted in AP Report "The 'Other Side' of Sharpening Confrontations," *Daily Hampshire Gazette,* September 30, 1983.
81. Kinzer *cited, New York Times,* July 1985.
82. "Report on Travel Seminar Conducted by Center for Global Service and Education, Augsburg College, Minneapolis, MN", *Congressional Record—House,* April 16, 1985, pp. H 2043, 2044, 2046.
83. *Ibid.* p. H 2044.
84. Robert S. Leiken: "Nicaragua's Untold Stories", *The New Republic,* October 8, 1984.
85. Larry Rohter: "Managua Rule seen As Leftist Hybrid", *New York Times,* March 3, 1985, p. 3; for another discussion of such inequalities see Carlos Rangel: "The Double Life of Nicaragua's Comandantes", *Wall Street Journal,* December 1, 1984.
86. Maureen Dowd: "Reporter's Notebook: Ortega Chic", *New York Times,* October 25, 1985.
87. "Nicaragua Squatters Increase but the Outlook Looks Grim", New York Times, February 18, 1985, p. A6.
88. For example Robert Leiken's recent "The Nicaraguan Tangle", in the *New York Review of Books* (December 5, 1985) prompted a sympathizer I know to seriously consider ending his subscription to the magazine rather than contemplate the information put forward. Those favorably disposed are also likely to dismiss "Comandante Bayardo Arce's Secret Speech before the Nicaraguan Socialist Party" published by the State Department in March, 1985 either as a questionable document, possibly forgery, or a statement of no importance.
89. Michael Howard: "The Bewildered American Raj", *Harpers,* March, 1985, p. 58.

17

A Neglected Destination for Political Tourists

Some years ago I wrote a book entitled *Political Pilgrims*[1] which dealt with the susceptibilities of Western intellectuals toward political systems such as the Soviet Union under Stalin, Mao's China and Castro's Cuba. The book also examined their experiences in the countries concerned, including their exposure to what I called the techniques of hospitality, or political hospitality.

Subsequently I wrote several articles on the revival of the same phenomenon in Nicaragua, that has become the most popular destination of political tourists and pilgrims in recent years.[2] In all these instances my work was based on published materials: primarily the reports of the visitors, and various other sources on the conditions of life in the countries concerned. I myself have never been on a conducted tour of any kind, much less on a political tour or pilgrimage.[3] My own travel interests have always been separate from my political sympathies, or interests or from my social-scientific fact finding impulses. Last but not least I was saved from the temptation of embarking on a political pilgrimage (or tour) by the fact that most countries providing such services are ruled by political systems I find singularly unappealing; political hospitality is the most highly developed in countries where ideas are treated as weapons, that is to say, in Marxist-Leninist systems. Not only was I not favorably predisposed toward the countries most apt to dispense political hospitality—thus lacking in the basic qualification of a potential pilgrim—I was also an unsuitable candidate from the standpoint of the appropriate authorities.

Thus I had good reasons for resigning myself to remain deprived of the experience of political hospitality, although over the years I was often told that as a student of political tourism I ought to experience it first hand.

Last summer an unusual opportunity presented itself, which I thought, might give me at least a partial exposure to the situations and experiences in question. I was invited to attend a conference (on recent developments in Mainland China) and to be a guest of the Government Information Office of the Republic of China on Taiwan. In the latter capacity I was to take part in unspecified sight seeing activities and give a lecture or two. The idea that I should visit Taiwan came from two American academic friends who had been there many times and thought it was an interesting country to visit. They suggested to the appropriate authorities that I be invited.

I should say something about my attitude toward Taiwan up to that point, i.e., prior to my visit and the prospects of a visit. The fact of the matter is that I did not give much thought to Taiwan. I knew little about it and had no strong feelings about it. It was not a country I had ever expected to visit, or had great interest in—either touristic, or political, or social scientific. Nor was it a country I viewed as a shining example of beneficial social engineering, or model of any type of social-political rectitude. In other words I had a reasonably open mind about Taiwan, somewhat "tainted" by a mild sympathy since it was a Western-oriented country which came into existence by virtue of the opposition of its rulers to communist China which under Mao became one of the most repressive totalitarian systems of our times. Also relevant here is the fact that I subscribe to the belief that there are significant differences between authoritarian and totalitarian systems which are both morally and politically consequential and can be detected without undue intellectual exertions. My visit certainly helped to further clarify these distinctions as will be noted below.

What were the Taiwanese practices of political hospitality and how did they resemble, or differ from those I had written about in the context of communist systems?

There was an obvious irony to the situation that could not escape me. Here I was, the author of a lengthy study critically dissecting the gullibility of pampered visitors to communist countries, and the techniques of hospitality they received, ready to expose myself to what I expected to be somewhat similar treatment dispensed by government officials who obviously wished that I absorb highly favorable impressions. While I wanted to learn about the effects of such a conducted tour I also felt uneasy about it. To be sure the Taiwanese authorities never approached the heavy-handed determination conveyed, for instance by Tomas Borge, minister of interior (state security, that is) of Nicaragua, who said: "Nicaragua's war is fought inside the United States . . . The battlefield will be the American conscience . . . When they [the visitors] return to the United States they have a multiplier effect on the public opinion of your country."[4]

Assuming the role of respectfully treated political tourist and guest of the government, (of any government) was certainly a novel experience. It took some getting used to to have a large black air-conditioned American car at my disposal from 9 a.m. until the evening hours with a chauffeur and guide/interpreter, to have doors opened in front of me and umbrellas held over my head and be accommodated in a large and quite luxurious hotel. My young guide, a part-time graduate student in American studies, was anxious to please and solicitous about my safety and wellbeing. There was a written schedule for my eight days in Taiwan. I was very well fed both in and outside the hotel and was given a number of small presents (a small tea set, tea, books about Taiwan, a large basket of fresh fruit, cuff links and tie clip with the insignia of the Republic of China).

What I described sofar I called the ego-massage in *Political Pilgrims:* being well treated and provided with ample creature comforts—good food, excellent accommodation, comfortable transportation etc. A further component of ego-massage is to make the visitor feel important by more subtle means, such as the company of important officials. I had a one hour interview with the head of the Government Information Office (Ph.D. Columbia University), an office of some importance as it is attached to the prime minister's office and compound; I shook hands with the Prime Minister (all the Conference participants had a chance to do so) and I was also met by a high official of the ruling Nationalist party (Harvard Ph.D.) in his office. On all these occasions pictures were taken.

So much for the similarities between the political hospitality I had written about and that experienced in Taiwan.

The differences begin with the itinerary that was devised for me and the responsiveness to my requests to change it. Most striking was its apolitical character. There was little effort to show me showcase projects reflecting favorably on the economic, social or cultural accomplishments of the regime. Also, unlike in communist countries, where the itineraries are typically packed, making it difficult for the visitor to have unsupervised time and wander around freely, I had ample free time to do as I pleased.

Here is an example, day one:

9:30 a.m.: Visit Confucian Temple; 10:30: Lungshan (Dragon Mountain Temple); 11:30: Chiang Kai-Shek Memorial Hall; 14.00: "Window on China" (small scale reproductions of historic and contemporary buildings similar to Madurodam near the Hague in Holland). All these were in Taipei, except for the "Window on China" about one hour drive.

In the course of my entire visit I was not taken to a single factory, farm, clinic, hospital, new housing project, construction site, kindergarten, or school (except the Chinese Opera School that was combined with attending a student performance). I was not introduced to outstanding and satisfied workers, peasants, or office workers telling me how much their life changed since the new political system was established; I was not taken to any mass meeting or rally. On one drive (returning from "The Window on China" display) we stopped at my request at a hydroelectric plant and reservoir which I noticed on the map. My guide had little to say about it. (Evidently, in Taiwan, as in Western countries, such things are taken for granted and treated as ordinary utilitarian installations, rather than semi-sacred legitimating objects proving the spiritual superiority of the political system.)

We made another unscheduled stop at a Wildlife Safari Park where we observed wild animals while driving through—there were no suggestions from any quarter that such an exhibit testified to the wisdom of the government and its solicitousness toward the recreational needs of the citizens. Likewise no self-congratulatory remarks were occasioned by our drive on the recently completed superhighway, linking the north and south of the Island. And when we saw the aboriginal, non-Chinese inhabitants (they number about 200,000 out of a total population of almost 20 million)—performing dances at their cultural center, my guide did not seize the opportunity to instruct me about the benevolent cultural-social policies of the authorities allowing the preservation of their ancient customs and ways of life.

The most explicitly political sight on the trip was the Chiang Kai-shek memorial (a giant building with a large museum) and a military shrine dedicated to various martyrs. The most explicitly economic sight I was taken to was the Taiwan Trade Center, a huge modern exhibition hall where virtually everything made in Taiwan is displayed under one roof for the convenience of foreign buyers or businessmen.

In the entire course of our sight seeing activities my guide made no attempt to impress upon me the enlightened policies and accomplishments of the government. He responded eagerly to my questions but did not always have the answer; for instance I had many questions about various shrines and temples and the religious beliefs they catered to, as well as somewhat esoteric geographical inquiries about heights of mountains, or distances between various points.

The schedule, as already noted, allowed for plenty of "unchaperoned" activity. Of course one's freedom of movement is always circumscribed in a strange country and especially by the language barrier; it was advisable to have little cards written by the hotel employees informing taxi drivers of one's intended destination. I did explore Taipei by myself (on foot and by taxi) but out of town I went with the guide.

While there is a visible military presence—railroad bridges and some public buildings guarded by armed troops, honor guards at places like the Chiang Kai Shek Memorial and the Martyrs' Shrine, plus many barracks and other military installations in and around Taipei—to my knowledge no part of the island is off limits to visitors (except military bases) and those renting cars can come and go as they please without guides and without officially approved routes. I never encountered any warning against taking pictures anywhere (which can be found even in such "liberal" communist countries as Hungary). And unlike on Soviet airlines (at any rate in Soviet airspace) passengers on the domestic flight were not warned against taking pictures (nor on the international flight of the official Taiwan airline as we approached the island).

The schedule was changed several times at my request. For instance, having read about a natural wonder of Taiwan—(while waiting for my visa in what amounts to the Taiwan consulate in Boston)—a huge gorge in the East-Central part of the island—I expressed interest in looking at it. The trip required a whole day hence the earlier scheduled activities were cancelled. We took a very modern electric train, traversing a scenic coastal route to the area and continued by car; flew back by plane to Taipei. While I thoroughly enjoyed viewing the marble cliffs, waterfalls and temples on mountain sides, the trip could not be conceived of as substantially contributing to my appreciation of government policies, or serve any other political purpose. On the other hand the pleasant outing was bound to put me in a genial frame of mind, creating a generally sympathetic disposition toward the authorities who arranged it. Certainly it would be naive to suggest that only explicitly and heavy handedly political tours can influence the outlook of the visitor.

Generally speaking I was not hindered in the slightest from behaving like a regular tourist seeking out the natural wonders and other sights of apolitical interest (e.g. old temples). All this was quite different from the policies of communist countries, for example Cuba, where, in the words of an English author, ". . . the tourist . . . is dispatched in pursuit of factories, schools, universities, housing projects and research institutes . . . his holiday is not treated as an escape . . . but as a chance to penetrate the virtues of the socialist model."[5]

Actually the temples and shrines, both old and new, while representing an appropriate tourist sight, (exotic, colorful, intricately decorated) did have political significance. (Only two were originally included in the itinerary but I wanted to see more and did). These shrines were not showpieces saved and maintained for the benefit of tourists (like the handful in Mainland China). They were well patronised places of worship, found everywhere, in the city as in the country, they came in all shapes and sizes and were usually thronged by the natives performing religious rites,—praying, making food offerings, lighting candles and incense—in short, practising their religion. They were among the reminders of the difference between authoritarian and totalitarian systems, between systems which legitimate themselves by some variety of Marxism-Leninism and those which do not.

It may be argued that apolitical as it was, my itinerary skipped not only the prototypical political-economic sights but also spared me of contact with the seamy sides of life. Did I have a chance to see poor neighborhoods? Could I learn about the restrictions on free speech which have been established by the officially proclaimed state of siege since 1949? Did I speak to critics of the regime, to the discontended, to opposition politicians?

While inspecting slums was certainly not part of the planned itinerary, there was no discernible attempt to shield me from them either. In the course of the many drives in and around Taipei I did see poor neighborhoods and dilapidated housing but no people sleeping on the streets, or lieing in the gutter, no emaciated children, or derelicts scrounging in garbage cans. Nor did I see open sewers, or people going to some communal well or water-faucet. I did see from the train one group of women doing their wash in a stream.

Whatever material shortages may exist were not reflected in lines of people in front of food or other shops. I have seen hundreds of shops of all kinds, as well as street markets—it is hard to avoid them, the place is full of commerce. Crowds there were but not lines.

Did I see beggars and poorly dressed people? I did not, but then, as I noted in *Political Pilgrims,* beggars can be removed from the street by authorities who do not view begging as a basic human right. People on the street and especially women, were well dressed in Western style. The street scenes in general testified to the kind of prosperity the statistics reflect. (More of those later.) Taipei (as well as the two large provincial cities I saw, Hualien on the East coast and Keelung in the North) is busy and vibrant, and displays an impressive range of goods and services. There is heavy traffic, cars, buses, trucks and an especially a vast number of motorbicycles and motorscooters, which apparently are accessible to the less prosperous elements of the population. Hardly any bicycles were seen and no horse drawn carts.

I did not speak to any opposition politician nor did I make such a request hence I don't know what response I might have gotten. I understand from American specialists of Taiwan that such contacts are not difficult to make. It is a reflections of my limited fact finding zeal rather than official policy that this source of information had not been tapped.

What of substance did I learn about Taiwan? Did political hospitality achieve its objectives? Did I come back with favorable impressions and if so, is it possible to separate those created by the tourist pleasures (and the ego massage) from more substantial truths learned independent of such attentions and the intentions of my hosts?

There is no doubt that (as I argued in *Political Pilgrims*) kind, generous and attentive treatment, such as I had been given, tends to create a sense of indebtedness toward one's host and can soften even a searchingly critical disposition. On the other hand given a high degree of self-consciousness on my part about these matters and the opportunity to discuss Taiwan at some length with a number of old China and Taiwan hands (who were at the conference and had been to both Chinas many times) and by doing some outside reading, it was possible to learn things about Taiwan which my itinerary did not cover.

It should also be noted here that Taiwan invites many of its critics and allows social scientists and journalists from abroad to conduct independent inquiries and studies, hence government figures and statistics are subject to independent verification and challenge and therefore quite reliable. Not only can foreigners come and go but the Taiwanese too can travel abroad without difficulty (except to Mainland China).

The most unexpected conclusion I came away with was that Taiwan is the kind of country the political pilgrims discussed in my writings should greatly admire. It is a country Western intellectuals concerned with material progress, economic development and beneficial modernization should make their favored destination. Taiwan meets many of the criteria Western intellectuals used to justify their sympathy toward Marxist-Leninist systems of far more modest material accomplishments and far worse record on political and personal freedoms. Moreover Taiwan is a country where the venerable and generally dubious rationalization offered to explain the denial of civil rights (in many Third World countries and Marxist-Leninist systems) has some validity. In Taiwan, it can be argued, limits on civil rights and political opposition has made a contribution to the kind of political stability which in turn made significant material progress possible.

Indeed few countries in the world today can claim a more impressive record in material progress than Taiwan. Between 1953 and 1984 the average annual growth rate of its economy was 8.8%; per capita GNP increased from $100 in 1952 to $3067 in 1984 (as against approx. $300 in Mainland China). With one of the highest population densities in the world and without any significant natural resources (and only 25% arable land area) it has become an exporter of food.[6]

Those who regard the campaigns against illiteracy in countries like Cuba and Nicaragua as most heartwarming achievements of these regimes should also be impressed by the fact that in approximately three decades illiteracy in Taiwan has been reduced from over half of the population to under 7%. Moreover ". . . life expectancy has increased from 44 years in 1949 to 72 years today."[7] According to the most recent figures 83% of the homes have telephones, 98% refrigerators, 101% motorcycles, 12% automobiles, 78% washing machines, 97% color television sets and 30% air conditioning.[8]

Such feats of modernization were accompanied by a more egalitarian income distribution: "Whereas in the early 1950s the ratio of the average family income of the top 20% of the population and that of the lowest 20% was approximately 15 to 1, by 1984 it had narrowed to about 4 to 1."[9] 90% of farmland is held by owner-farmers due to the land reform of the early 1950s.

Such progress has been made under difficult political conditions which necessitated the maintenance of a large military forces draining the economy. It should also be noted that American economic assistance ceased in the mid 1960s. These gains are even more striking when compared with those of Cuba, a country of comparable size and resources though with only half the population to support and the beneficiary of significant and continuous Soviet aid.[10]

Thus by any standard Taiwan has been one of the few great success stories of modernization in the post World War II period yet it has attracted little attention among Western intellectuals supposedly concerned with efficient and humane policies of modernization.

Why has this been the case? And why, by contrast, were the many failed experiments of regimented, coercive modernization in putatively socialist countries given every benefit of doubt, and often fulsome praise, while the successes of Taiwan were ignored, or if noted not given any moral credit?

I think a major part of the explanation is that those proclaiming the blessings of modernization in Marxist-Leninist systems had other agendas, other interests, over and above material progress and economic development. As I emphasized in *Political Pilgrims* their underlying interest was not so much economic-developmental but rather spiritual-ideological. The main appeals of the countries endorsed by the political pilgrims were their (perceived) sense of purpose and sense of community. Material accomplishments in themselves, without being ennobled by a great ideological-spiritual design were of limited interest. Thus for example "For Beatrice and Sidney Webb (as for many other Western intellectuals) what mattered was not so much the specific institutional accomplishments but the underlying higher purpose: 'The marvel was [wrote Gertrude Himmelfarb] not that there should be parks, hospitals, factories . . . [in the Soviet Union, that is]; after all these could be found in England as well. The marvel was that they should, as the Webbs thought, be inspired by a collective ideal, a single moral purpose.' "[11]

For Western intellectuals disposed to the admiration of Marxist-Leninist societies there was always a qualitative difference between identical material objects found in the admired "socialist" as opposed to the despised capitalist setting. Thus ". . . Soviet construction projects symbolized a transcendence of the human condition . . . Pablo Neruda wrote . . . : 'I shall never forget my visit to that hydroelectric plant overlooking the lake, whose pure waters mirror Armenia's unforgettable blue sky. When the journalists asked me for my impressions of Armenia's ancient churches . . . I answered them . . . : The church I like best is the hydroelectric plant, the temple beside the lake.' Many similar comments were made about the miracles of Soviet industrialization. Many Western visitors seemed to forget that they were describing inherently ordinary objects—factories, hydroelectric plants, bridges, schoolhouses . . . which under capitalism would provoke little excitement. All such inherently ordinary or prosaic objects . . . were transformed, in the eyes of the beholders, by their purpose and context."[12]

The indifference, or aversion to Taiwan on the part of Western liberals confirm the points made above. The material achievements of a political system that is both pro-American and largely capitalistic do not appeal to the moral-ideological sensibilities of a large portion of the Western intelligentsia; such systems cannot be given moral credit for their accomplishments. This applies not only to Taiwan but also to Japan, South Korea, Hong Kong, Singapore, Malaysia.

Thus even if it is granted that Taiwan has a high standard of living this can be dismissed as yet another example of empty affluence or corrosive consumerism conferred by a capitalist economy undeserving of moral support or sympathy. (Many Western social critics seem to believe that material deprivations under socialism are preferable to material fulfillments under capitalism.)

The material achievements of Taiwan are not the only basis upon which it could claim the sympathy of Western intellectuals. As some readers may recall, I had found in my earlier work that a victimized, underdog vision of several Marxist-Leninist countries was another of their attractions: the Soviet Union in its devastated early years (also historically victimized by foreign aggressors); China exploited by the Western powers through much of its recent history and painfully backward from the material standpoint; little Cuba kept under American political-economic domination and now small Nicaragua "bullied" by the United States. The economic underdevelopment of these countries also conferred an aura of innocence, while the huge obstacles to be overcome in their path to progress lent a heroic touch to their exertions.

Taiwan could certainly claim the underdog status and the sympathy that goes with it. It is a small country (not much bigger than Holland) confronting a giant, hostile power, communist China eager to gobble it up. Not only is it small in land area and population, its armed forces too are dwarfed by those of communist China which ". . . has almost 10-12 superiority over ROC [Taiwan] in personnel and is superior in most categories of major military equipment. In 1981 [it] had about 4.7 million men under arms . . . [its] navy of some 2650 vessels . . . [including] 100 fully armed attack submarines . . . the ROC [Taiwan] maintains about half a million men under arms. Its navy has about 340 combatant units including . . . 2 unarmed submarines . . ."[13]

As these authors point out Communist China has been in a position to impose a naval blockade on Taiwan that would economically strangle and thus politically undermine the system. Hence the Taiwanese are genuinely threatened and their sense of threat has as much, or far more plausibility than that routinely invoked by communist regimes, both to urge on their population to greater exertions and to justify drastic restrictions of personal and group freedoms. Moreover Taiwan has lost much of the American military umbrella that protected it before the United States reestablished diplomatic relations with Mainland China and it has also become diplomatically isolated as other nations too broke off relations.

But even if some credit were to be given to Taiwan's material progress, and even if it is allowed that it is indeed a small and beleagured nation, Western intellectuals intent on rejecting it can fall back on deploring its undemocratic domestic policies. They can argue that it is a right-wing authoritarian system dominated by the remnants of the former Nationalist regime which does not tolerate political pluralism and meaningful opposition.

This brings us to yet another noteworthy paradox and double standard. Western observers inclined to give the benefit of doubt to most Third World dictatorships allegedly determined to modernize and improve the material well being of their people explain and excuse *their* human rights violations and undemocratic practices by arguing that: a) it is unreasonable and ethnocentric to expect that all countries of the world adopt "Western style democracy"; b) that such countries have more important tasks than to worry about the niceties and luxuries of such democracy; c) that the maintenance of political stability is vital for economic progress hence the necessity to limit competition for political power; and finally d) that many such countries including the Soviet Union in the 1920s or 30s, or more recently Cuba and Nicaragua, face external threats which further justify the restrictions on civil liberties and free expression.

On all these counts Taiwan's authoritarianism can be viewed with a similarly benign, understanding attitude. Why should it have "Western style democracy" when most of the world does not? Why, given its beleagured position and diplomatic isolation should it not feel threatened? Given these threats why should it be as tolerant of its domestic critics and enemies as the authorities of the secure and well established Western democracies are? And why should the argument not apply to Taiwan that securing positive freedoms—i.e. economic benefits and progress, such as employment, better public health, access to education, social mobility, a more egalitarian income distribution, etc.— sometimes requires a trade off in tighter political controls? Moreover as Gregor and Chang point out in their study of human rights in Taiwan, "The citizens of the Republic of China on Taiwan enjoy far more of the social and economic rights . . . than citizens of any Marxist regime and more than those in some authoritarian regimes in Asia and Africa. But more important, they enjoy those human rights along with more abundant civil and political freedom."[14] (Moreover since my visit in the summer of 1986, the elections in December resulted in the emergence of a significant opposition party; in the words of an American observer, "Taiwan is moving steadily toward a more representative government and a two-party political system.")[15]

There is little doubt that the human and civil rights violations in Taiwan have been far more limited than those institutionalized by communist regimes and "nothing remotely akin to the mass murders and expulsions that have figured so prominently in the post-revolutionary history of Marxist regimes."[16] It is also of some significance that the high degree of coercion and regimentation citizens of communist systems generally experience is not balanced or mitigated by impressive gains in their standard of living, in some instances not even by political stability. Mainland China has not only been exceptionally repressive under Mao, (and plagued by shortages)—it also used to be a "chronically unstable" political system.[17] My visit to Taiwan was instructive on several counts. For one thing it deepened the realization that the distinction between authoritarian and totalitarian systems is neither an empty abstraction nor a weapon in the cold war but a social-political reality that is clearly reflected in the way people live.

The trip also confirmed that the attraction of political systems exercise has less to do with their tangible accomplishments than with the desires and expectations of those attracted to them. To say the least, Taiwan is on no count morally, politically or economically inferior to the societies which charmed the political pilgrims and elicited the accolades of Western intellectuals and other political tourists; nor can most member nations of the United Nations (from which Taiwan was excluded) boast of superior political, economic or cultural accomplishments. That Taiwan's progress has received so little recognition is more a reflection of the predisposition of Western intellectuals and opinion makers than an accurate measure of the defects or injustices of its social-political system.

Notes

1. *Political Pilgrims: Travels of Western Intellectuals to the Soviet Union, China and Cuba*, New York: Oxford University Press 1981; New York: Harper & Row 1983.
2. "Sojourners in Nicaragua", *National Catholic Register*, May 29, 1983; "The Newest Political Pilgrims", *Commentary*, August 1985; "Political Tourism in Cuba and Nicaragua, *Society*,May 1986.
3. The distinction between them is slight: political pilgrims, as I used the term in the book, refered primarily to intellectuals of some distinction who visited the certain countries with highly positive anticipations and were given VIP treatment; political tourists are similarly disposed but more numerous, less fervent and lacking in personal distinction. To put it more simply, pilgrims are more devout than tourists. Like all tourism, political tourism is a mass phenomenon, as in Nicaragua today.
4. Juan Tamayo: "The Sandinistas Aim Soft Sell at Activists", *Miami Herald*, December 14, 1983.
5. David Caute: *Cuba Yes?* New York, 1974, p. 49.
6. *Republic of China 1986 - A Reference Book*, Taipei and New York, 1986 pp. 193, 199.
7. A. James Gregor and Maria Hsia Chang: *The Republic of China and U.S. Policy—A Study in Human Rights*, Washington D.C. 1983 pp. 31, 64.
8. *Free China Journal*, May 18, 1987 p. 4.
9. *Republic of China - A Reference Book*, cited p. 99; for an American study

of such and other accomplishments see John C. H Fei, Gustav Ranis and Shirley W.Y. Kuo: *Growth with Equity: The Taiwan Case,* New York 1979.

10. Gary S. Becker: "Cuba's Record Can't Compare With Taiwan's 'Miracle' " *Business Week,* June 16, 1986.
11. *Political Pilgrims* cited p. 121.
12. *Political Pilgrims* cited p. 137.
13. Gregor and Chang *cited* p. 41.
14. Gregor and Chang *cited* p. 90.
15. Harvey J. Feldman: "Taiwan Moves Toward a Two-Party System", *NY Times* December 17, 1986, op-ed.
16. Gregor and Chang *cited* p. 95.
17. See for example Alan P.L Liu: "How can we evaluate the political system on Mainland China", Paper presented at the "15th Sino-American Conference on Mainland China", Taipei, Taiwan, June 1986.

EPILOGUE:

Growing Up in Hungary-
Connections Between
Life and Work

Epilogue
Growing Up in Hungary—Connections
Between Life and Work[1]

Well before the editor of this volume suggested that I make a contribution to it I had given a fair amount of thought to the influences which the circumstances of my life exerted on my choice of an occupation. I had also indulged in occasional reflections about the factors that shaped my particular professional interests as a sociologist. While such speculations are bound to be inconclusive, they were difficult to resist; I was predisposed to take fewer things for granted than those who spend their entire life in the society where they were born. As a matter of fact, I took explicit notice of the biographical elements in my work in two books.[2] On both of these occasions I also provided information to the reader to enable him to make his own judgments about some of the influences which shaped my work.

One thing is clear: the choice of sociology as my profession was not the culmination of a long-standing desire, the fulfillment of carefully nurtured aspirations, or the fruit of disciplined planning. When at the ripe age of twenty-four I enrolled as a first-year undergraduate at the London School of Economics to pursue a degree in sociology, I had just learned about the existence of such a course of study. In Hungary where I grew up there was no such thing and insofar as something remotely resembling sociology existed (it went under the name "tarsadalomtudomany," or the "science of society"), it was tainted by its association with the official cultivation of (the prevailing versions of) Marxism-Leninism. "The science of society" in Hungary was in effect a higher form of "agit-prop," inextricably tied to the provision of ideological guidance to the population and the legitimation of the political system. I did not aspire to become initiated into such skills and acquire certification in them, nor would I have been found acceptable for such a calling by the authorities. My political dependability was questionable. More of that later.

Shortly after my arrival in England in late 1956 I was shown the catalogue of the London School of Economics which included course descriptions in sociology complete with the assigned readings. The degree program in sociology entailed courses in classical theory, ethics and social philosophy, social psychology, criminology, English social history and others which looked interesting in their own right, though I had no idea what these courses would add up to. I was not sure precisely what I wanted to study when I arrived in England. (When I left Hungary a few weeks earlier I did not anticipate becoming a university student; my aspirations were more modest.) While growing up I was attracted to some kind of literary occupation, but once in England I thought it would be unrealistic and somewhat presumptuous to study English literature, which had been one of my priorities in Hungary. (I knew some English before I left, but it was mostly reading knowledge.) Given my vague humanistic and political interests, I had also considered, after my arrival in England, contemporary history and journalism as fields of study. But then, as noted above, I learned about the existence of sociology and given these somewhat amorphous interests it appeared a good choice, especially at LSE since I preferred living in London to the possibility of being sent to a provincial university. (Having spent involuntarily a number of years in the Hungarian countryside, big-city life held great attractions.)

When I began my studies in sociology in early 1957 I did not give much thought to what I would do with my B.A. and I barely knew what graduate schools and higher degrees were. I did not have a very strong attachment to the discipline as such, and, as a matter of fact, I have not developed one in subsequent years either, notwithstanding the various forms of certification I acquired in it. I have always felt that my life and work would not have turned out very differently if instead of sociology I had chosen political science, or social psychology, or cultural anthropology, or modern European hstory. Being a sociologist as such has never been a major defining factor of my identity, professional or personal. I felt and still do that there are many interesting things one can do as a sociologist, but the same was true in other disciplines such as I mentioned above. I never had any fantasies about becoming a scientist of society or about sociology being or becoming such a science.[3] Nor did I look upon it, unlike many of my humanistic and equally unscientific friends and colleagues, as a powerful, or potentially powerful tool of social change and improvement. By taking this position I had cut myself off from the two most common sources of attachment to sociology and from the groups representing them: the positivist-empiricist, scientific wing on the one hand, and the idealistic, cause-oriented, social-critical camp on the other.

If a sociologist is, or can become, an intellectual and if intellectuals do indeed emerge from the kind of social context Karl Mannheim had proposed, then of course I was a good candidate for becoming a sociologist. I was certainly "free floating" and in more than one sense, especially after my departure from Hungary on November 19th, 1956. I was at that point in time removed from my native country, family and friends, detached from any particular ethnic subculture, without any occupational qualifications, and unequipped with any religious-metaphysical worldview. To be sure, leaving Hungary was not the only factor creating this state of affairs; rather, it was a culmination of the "free floating" status adding another important, perhaps decisive, dimension to it. In Hungary itself I was not firmly anchored in any social-cultural context. My family was Jewish but neither practicing Jews nor involved in Jewish community life. Being Jewish for me meant mostly a memory of past persecution (in 1944) and a vague pride in the intellectual accomplishments of Jews. Socially or sociologically speaking, my family was steadily losing status and financial security while I was an adolescent; we were downwardly mobile by political design. After I finished high school, until leaving Hungary, I was a manual laborer of one kind or another, as well as a political exile and private in the Hungarian People's Army (more of that later). Both while in Hungary and after leaving it, the unfriendly Soviet appellation "rootless cosmopolitan" was readily applicable to my station in life. To be sure, it was a lot better to be considered such a person in England and the U.S. than in Soviet-controlled Hungary.

It is an important fact that I spent my life in three countries: the first half in Hungary, the second in the U.S. and in between three years in England. The proposition may thus be entertained that I became at least in part a sociologist as a response to marginality or uprootedness, this being a congenial discipline for the study and perhaps also the experience of this state. In addition to the theoretical plausibility of such a connection some confirming evidence may also be found in my first voluntarily chosen sociological investigation I undertook while an undergraduate at LSE (discounting seminar papers) which was a study of the adjustment of Hungarian students to life in Britain, that is, a study of my peers. While findings of this study eventually formed the basis of my M.A. thesis for the Univeristy of Illinois, I undertook it for no academic credit but out of personal interest and because the University of London underwrote the modest expenses as it was curious to learn something about the attitudes and condition of its charges. (This was also my only study that some of my colleagues would call "empirical" since it was based on mail questionnaires.)

The other obvious consequence of having lived in three countries may be found in the development of my comparative interests which have informed, in various ways, each of my major works.

It may be easier to point out what factors did not enter into my choice of sociology than to specify very clearly why the choice was made. Thus it had nothing to do with parental advice or suggestion since my parents were not around; it was not made on account of my perception of the study and practice of sociology as a lucrative or especially prestigious calling; the decision was not made through a process of elimination because nothing else was available; and there was no peer or group pressure urging me to make the choice. Perhaps there was (after all) a measure of submerged parental influence, that of my father, who used to talk wishfully about my becoming a writer. Well, sociology—as other academic disciplines—allowed one to write, even exerted some pressure to do so, although when I chose it I was not fully aware of this.

Besides the accidental circumstances involved, my becoming a sociologist also had some of the hallmarks of the contemporary quest for doing something important, meaningful or creative, insofar as there is a choice in one's occupation. Upon my arrival in England I had an unexpectedly wide range of choices. I don't think that anybody would have objected if I had insisted upon embarking on a degree program in astrophysics or microbiology or Islamic scriptures or British colonial history. I was unaware of any pressure being brought upon our selection of the course of study. Naturally it was assumed that we would opt for subjects or programs which provided some continuity with our past academic endeavors and interests; many of the Hungarian students in England had been college students in Hungary at various stages in their academic careers. (I never attended college in Hungary for the reasons to be discussed below.)

In the final analysis my choice of sociology is best explained by my perception of it as an intellectually stimulating and vaguely creative discipline, involving one with significant issues of human life and social existence, a pathway to a better understanding of the many painful and puzzling situations we find ourselves in through life. Becoming a sociologist reflected a desire to address some important problems though it was far from clear what concrete problems I was going to investigate.

While I was growing up in Hungary and thinking ahead of possible occupations, my interests and aspirations were decidedly humanistic-literary. By the time I was in my teens attending the gymnasium (selective academic high school), I wanted to become a writer or literary historian, critic or translator—occupations far more closely related to one another in Hungary (and Eastern Europe in general) than in the United States. From a practical point of view this would have meant taking a degree course in Hungarian and English (or Hungarian and Russian) language and literature, possibly in combination with the study of translation. Most people with this type of specialization (language and literature) became high school teachers, yet such qualifications were also useful if one sought to pursue the literary-journalistic activities I aspired to. Since at the time when my academic plans were formulated (1950–51) the study of English in Hungary was extremely limited (due to its gradual elimination from secondary school curriculum) I was channelled by the relevant authorities to the Russian-Hungarian language and literature program. I would have preferred English but the important thing was to gain admission to *any* faculty of any university in order to avoid being drafted. (If admitted one could get away with ROTC style military training with summer camps instead of the dreaded 2–3 years the draftees had to serve.) Although my admission to the University of Budapest was officially recommended by the high school branch of the official youth organzation (called at the time The Alliance of Working Youth)—which was a precondition of gaining entrance—and my grades were also good enough to qualify, the notification of acceptance did not lead to my entering the university. A number of events interfered, first and foremost the delivery by the police of a notice from the Ministry of Internal Affairs. We were informed that as relatives of my maternal grandfather (a former businessman) who shared the apartment with my parents and myself, we were to be exiled from Budapest to a particular village in Eastern Hungary. The latter was designated as a "compulsory dwelling place" which we were not permitted to leave past a radius of six kilometers measured from the village center.

I have often thought that this event might have represented a point of departure, or at least marked the incubation period of my future interests in sociology—not so much because it obliterated the prospects of studying Russian and Hungarian (or any other kind) of literature, but because it resulted in my being placed in numerous problematic and thought-provoking social contexts and situations. These in turn inspired questions about the nature of the social world and especially the relationship between the individual and society and various social institutions. Even further back in my life there were other historical-political events and situations apt to stimulate interest in social order and conflict and the social forces which so obviously impinge on personal lives. I have in mind the Nazi era (short as it was in Hungary, lasting from March 1944 until January 1945) and its impact on my life. Being Jewish, my family and I stood a very good chance of being killed and at ages 11–12 I was well aware of that and properly concerned with such a prospect. While the events of 1944–45 did raise my level of "political consciousness" and enhanced my interest in politics it did not occur to me (until decades later) that there might be occupations within which one could pursue such concerns, or, if there were, such pursuits could be independent of the reigning political authorities. Nor did the experience and threat of Nazism have a noticeable impact on my professional interests and motivation once I became a sociologist. Rather than incorporating and reflecting professionally and intellectually those truly traumatic events, much of my sociological work focused on Soviet totalitarianism and its more recent variants and on the ideological appeals such systems exerted in the West. Undoubtedly my personal experience in communist Hungary between 1948–56 (recounted below) contributed to my preoccupation with and critical disposition toward Soviet-type regimes and their ideological legitimation. Why did similar, and far worse, experiences under Nazism not lead to a similar preoccupation with Nazism, in or outside my work? This is all the more curious since Nazism represented a life-threatening experience (and also subjected me and my family to physical violence) whereas the communist regime did not. A close friend of mine, the late Stanley Milgram, who read an earlier draft of this paper noted with justification:

> . . . what the Nazis and their Hungarian collaborators did to the Jewish population of Hungary could easily engender a life-long hatred of fascism and a life-long preoccupation with . . . its character. Your own family suffered immensely from the Nazi onslaught. The facists were, in fact, trying to kill you, your mother, father, sister and grandparents. You lived in a cellar to escape them. You and your father were taken out and were within minutes of being shot.
>
> For all this you retain an almost cheerfully detached and objective view of the Hun, showing little academic interest in fascism and directing all your professional bile against the second tidal wave that swept over you, the Reds. For all the communists' failings . . . they nonetheless did not try to ferret you out for the sole purpose of pushing you and your family into gas ovens. And yet, on an emotional level, it is the communist system that became the only form of tyranny that engaged you professionally. . . . There is an interesting question here of why one and not the other was singled out in your case, while in many other people I know it is the holocaust and the Nazi experience that dominates and energizes their professional lives. I pose this as a kind of mystery . . .

I may also add, to further deepen the mystery, that I have never forgotten these experiences (nor tried to) which occurred at an obviously formative period of my life at age 12–13.

I agree with Stanley Milgram that on the face of it my attitude in this matter does seem peculiar, perhaps even irrational. I can nonetheless offer some explanations.

It appeared to me, as early as in my teens while still in Hungary that morally as well as historically speaking the issue of Nazism had been basically settled. No sane, decent, respectable or intelligent person, nobody of any significance or merit, defended the Nazis or had anything good to say about them, or tried to minimize their misdeeds. The condemnation of Nazism seemed, and still does seem, universal and total. The word itself became a synonym for evil (along with "fascist"). Nobody, or nobody that mattered, needed to be convinced about the enormity of the moral outrages this political system had committed—on this one issue virtually all schools of political thought and persuasion were in agreement. Not only was there a firm and widespread rejection of Nazism, it was also a well documented evil; information of every kind was widely available: visual, written, social scientific, statistical. Even more important (as far as my motivation was concerned) was that it did not take great intellectual discernment or political courage in the Western (or Eastern) world to condemn Nazism; nor did it require any special capacity for insight. At last there was the fact that this most self-evidently evil phenomenon of our times was defeated and destroyed, utterly extinguished. (As a 13–14 year old I attended the public trials in Budapest of Hungarian war criminals and approved of the death sentences they were given; on one occasion right after the siege of Budapest I attended a public hanging in a main square of Budapest of two Hungarian SS guards guilty of many murders and tortures of Jews; I also approved of the proceedings as did my father who was one of the most gentle persons I have ever known.)

By contrast, the debate over the nature of communist systems and ideologies is far from settled, certainly not in Western countries, and least of all among Western academic intellectuals, who became my peers. This was a somewhat shocking discovery that instantly confronted me after my arrival in England. The attitudes I encountered—and still do—both in England and in the United States ranged from stunning ignorance, to ambivalance, wishful thinking and outright sympathy. Moreover, I found little significant change in the course of the quarter century I had spent in the West. To be sure, there have been shifts of attention and affection over time from the Soviet Union to China, from China to Cuba, from Cuba to Nicaragua. The quest for the authentic embodiment of socialism still continues among people who represent, structurally speaking, the subculture to which I belong (as well as some other groups such as many churchmen).

I ought to add here that my disputes over the nature of communist regimes have a long history and had preceded my arrival in the West in 1956. Already in the late 1940s and early 1950s I began to harbor critical sentiments toward such systems observing the evolution of the Hungarian regime headed by Matthias Rakosi who used to be described in the official publications as the "most faithful Hungarian disciple of comrade Stalin." Most of my friends and peers at the time were still pro-Soviet and hence pro-communist; their disillusionment was not long in coming (a matter of another year or two), but there was nonetheless a period when I felt somewhat isolated and uncomfortable on account of my political views. This may represent some kind of a pre-history of the predicament I felt in my more mature years in Western academic settings, once more among friends, peers or colleagues whom I liked or respected to various degrees yet who saw the world in ways very different from the way I did.

Hence I have been intellectually and professionally "energized" (as my friend Milgram put it) through my entire academic career by what seemed to be the obtuseness, ignorance or inexperience of my fellow intellectuals, by an ongoing need to dispel their illusions in some measure. Or, to put it more simply, the lingering leftism of so many Western intellectuals (and what struck me as a good deal of associated self-deception) has remained an enduring source of irritation and motivation. Possibly if most of these people had agreed with my assessment of contemporary Marxist-Leninist regimes and movements I would have been less likely to bother writing about them. I would have been far less motivated to write about such societies if there had been a moral consensus about them similar to that about Nazi Germany, South Africa or some right-wing regimes like that of Chile in recent years.

To this day I believe that this issue has not been settled, neither morally nor intellectually; that many Western intellectuals and other people of good will and idealism remain prey to illusions and wishful thinking in these matters as well as seriously uninformed about the nature of political systems they choose to idealize and admire. Moreover, I have also harbored some apprehension to the effect that this kind of ignorance leading to the support of these regimes and movements could, in the long run, constitute a threat, that these naifs could unwittingly contribute to the spread of the type of political systems I wished to get away from when I left Hungary in 1956.

Another minor paradox may be noted here. I have been back to Hungary several times (though it took me a long time to make the first return trip in 1974, 18 years after I had left) and I found these visits quite pleasant. I have experienced little if any hostility toward the regime in Hungary. Nor have I written anything about matters Hungarian (with the exception of one short, impressionistic travel report).[4] Matters Hungarian, or Hungarian-communist, never preoccupied me either professionally or personally. Was I making an exception for my native country? Possibly so, but on the other hand it seems that I have never been particularly involved with matters Hungarian since I left, either negatively or positively. Compared to my fellow Hungarian refugees of the same generation, I seemed to have had a healthy detachment: I neither romanticized all things Hungarian from food to music (though I certainly like Hungarian food and Bartok) nor was I harshly critical of the Hungarian regime or people in the manner of the disappointed lover. I never maintained ties with Hungarian groups, organizations or subcultures in the West though I kept up my friendship with my old Hungarian friends, some dating back to grade school, most to high school.

In summing up my differing professional and personal attitude towards Nazism and communism, it rests on the conviction that the moral-intellectual (as well as historical) battle against Nazism had been won decades ago. The conflict with Marxism-Leninism and the political systems it inspires (or which use it for legitimation) still goes on. I also believe that the Soviet Union in particular despite, or because of its internal problems and weaknesses, remains a more specific threat. One cannot look around the world today without noticing that the number of countries with domestic political arrangements similar, in various degrees, to those of the Soviet Union—and in any event, anti-Western and anti-democratic—have multiplied in the last three decades. Having twice experienced rapid, repressive political changes sweeping through a country where I grew up I cannot dismiss out of hand the possibility of such changes occurring at some unspecified time in the future in Western countries, although the precise circumstances under which they might occur are hard to predict. By contrast I am far less susceptible to the currently fashionable images of nuclear apocalypse.

As regards the impact of the years between finishing high school (in 1951) and entering the LSE (in January 1957), I had made a connection only after the facts, as a student of sociology. During those five unpleasant years I gave little if any thought to the relationship between what I had experienced and the larger and more theoretical questions about social forces and personal lives or the intersections of the public and private spheres and so forth.

The rural exile itself is perhaps worth a few comments, as it was an experience I trust none of the other contributors to this volume share with me. The point to make is not that it was the most terrible experience one can have, or the most punishing form of confinement. After all, prison, labor camp, psychiatric hospitals, interrogations and physical abuse by the political police are far worse and many East Europeans had experienced these under Nazi or Soviet supported regimes. The institution of exile imported to Hungary from the Soviet Union was a somewhat unusual form of deprivation as it combined relative freedom (within the six-kilometer radius) with enforced idleness, physical-material deprivation, loss of social status, political stigmatization and uprootedness. The government decided to scatter a few hundred or a few dozen former residents of Budapest (the capital city) in dozens, probably hundreds of villages in the eastern part of Hungary. This was done in part to alleviate the housing shortage in Budapest (the apartments of those exiled were instantly given to other allegedly more deserving groups and individuals) while at the same time the removal of the politically undesirable elements from the capital was also supposed to raise the tone of public life and "purify" the capital city. Furthermore, as the authorities put it, such a removal also struck at the existential-class roots of the exiled—it was a weapon and a stage in the class struggle. What they meant was that the exiles would find it difficult to make a living in the rural areas, which was true enough. They were also punished for their imputed socio-political sins by the imposition of primitive and unpleasant rural living conditions.

I suppose that there were two major sociological lessons or insights implicit in both the experience of Jewish persecution and the Soviet style exile—not that I grasped them at the time. One was simply the fact that human beings regardless of their personal qualities or characteristics are often forcibly assigned to broad categories: racial, ethnic, political, socio-economic—and treated accordingly. In effect the authorities practiced an applied sociology; they acted in some situations at any rate as believers in a strict socio-economic (earlier racial-ethnic) determinism. They made a serious attempt to predict attitudes, values, even behavior from relatively abstract sociological criteria. Thus I was classified as politically unreliable (after 1951) solely on the ground that my maternal grandfather had been a capitalist. My actual behavior was of no importance. Thus did the regime demonstrate its belief in a far-flung social determinism extending over three generations. Others were exiled because they, or their parents or husbands (or sometimes even former husbands) owned businesses, big or small, used to be civil servants (in the pre-communist regime), had been officers in its army or police or could look back upon a prosperous law practice. Thus a systematic attempt was made to weed out groups of people who were seen as supportive of or implicated with (economically or politically) the former socio-economic system. Of course, as much historical evidence has shown, political values and attitudes are formed and shaped in all sorts of ways and neither one's own occupation, or income, nor that of one's parents' (let alone grandparents!) offer any clear-cut guidance to how such values will shape up. "Class interest" in particular has proved to be a nebulous concept. Thus for example after World War II. as a teenager I was active in the communist youth organization,[5] had vigorously rejected the worldview and political outlook of my parents and grandparents (for instance, it was unthinkable that I would in any capacity get involved with my grandfather's enterprise, a possibility he briefly entertained as a distant prospect before his business was taken away from him), and was on the verge of becoming a Party member.

The early attractions of the communist regime and youth movement are easy to explain. My Jewish friends and I felt deeply grateful to the Red Army for bringing about our survival; it was the arrival of these forces in Budapest, in January 1945, that made it possible for the remaining Jews—whether in the ghetto or hiding (like my family and myself)—to survive. For this we felt indebted to the Soviet troops and the country which sent them. The same sense of gratitude was extended to the Hungarian representatives of affiliates of the Soviet Union, the Hungarian Communist Party, its leader, Rakosi, and its youth movement. (I recall that in some instances this went so far that two of my friends, whenever they encountered a portrait or bust of Rakosi or Stalin, bowed their heads; this was not a joke, they were totally serious about it.) This pro-Soviet fervor was so intense that it even survived for a few years my experience of Soviet soldiers raping women in the same air-raid shelter where my family and I stayed for a while after the end of the fighting in Budapest. While I could not *see* what was happening I could hear the screaming of the women involved and saw the soldiers looking for women. I also recall my sister hiding under pillows and other bedcovers when Soviet soldiers were combing the shelter looking for women. The same sense of gratitude also explained the support of Hungarian Jews of more mature years for the

Soviet Union and the political party it sponsored in Hungary. Generally speaking, in those years (1945–1949 or thereabouts) Hungarian Jews looked at the Soviet Union as the slayer of the dragon of antisemitism and their protector.

My political disillusionment with the Communist Party and regime was gradual and had preceded the deprivations for which I could blame the regime (such as the exile, military service and loss of opportunity to go to college). I became disillusioned, generally speaking, because of my growing perception of the deepening gulf between what the new regime had promised and what it delivered; because of the startling divergence between theory and propaganda on the one hand and practice or reality on the other. I found particularly repellent both the tone and substance of the official propaganda, its repetitive self-righteousness, its transparent lies, its brutal distortions of reality, and the regime's growing reliance on coercion and intimidation. On my way to school I could observe, over several years, the physical expansion of what then was the Hungarian equivalent of the KGB, as one building after another was taken over in a residential area to accommodate an ever-growing apparatus of coercion. As an unintended irony, the nucleus of this complex of buildings used to be the headquarters of the Hungarian Arrowcross (Nazi) Party.

It may be conjectured that the experience of such phenomena provided the stimulus for the subsequent development of my sociological interests in the relationship between "ideal" and "actual" in various spheres of social and political life and more specifically in the practices and institutions of political propaganda, public relations, commercial advertising, and the conducted political tours (in which the putatively socialist countries like the USSR, China and Cuba excel). I have in general retained a morbid fascination with the various institutional (and also personal) attempts at misrepresenting reality; such concerns have found substantive expression in my work.[6]

Among the external-institutional influences on my outlook on life and possibly also on my professional interests I must also mention the experience of military service. The latter was at the time, and still is, universal in Hungary and it can only be avoided, as noted earlier, or limited in duration, by attending university as a full-time student. Since I could not attend university, I was duly inducted into the Hungarian People's Army in the Spring of 1953 shortly before Stalin deceased. Due to my unfavorable political rating as deportee or an exiled person (I was drafted while living in the village) I was automatically assigned to what was called "construction units" set up for the politically unreliable elements of the population who were not given military training. We were, however, not deprived of all pleasures of socialist military life: we too were provided with regular political instruction and spent at least one hour every day with drills (before and after our work shifts). About half way through my military career, these units, due to general political changes, were disbanded and I was given a chance to savor the life of the infantryman, including extended guard duties carrying a rifle or submachine gun.

What did all this have to do with my sociological interests? Like the exile, but more so, military service was an experience of deprivation. Not only was there the standard hierarchy and system of subordination, but it was of an unusually rigid and mindless kind, such as most American servicemen are unlikely to experience. The Hungarian armed forces at the time seem to have embraced the most disagreeable military traditions deriving on the one hand from the Austro-Hungarian Monarchy (in turn influenced by the Prussian style) and the Soviet forms of punitive authoritarianism and commitment to the minute regulation of one's life. For instance, our hair was removed at the moment of induction and we remained totally shorn for the entire first year of our service. Leaves were rare and a special privilege and none given in the first six months or a year. The food was worse than (from what I read) what inmates of maximum security prisons consume in this country. The work was quite hard and there was a system of general harassment by the NCOs and political commissars. For instance, our bed linen and "mattress" (stuffed with straw) were almost daily thrown off by the NCO[7] and not infrequently we were ordered on lengthy marches or drills during the night. But we were not beaten though verbal abuse was common. Above all, we were utterly deprived of control over any aspect of our lives however trivial. Serving in the Hungarian People's Army (as it was called) was better than being imprisoned (depending on the prison) but not by a wide margin. Moreover, our deprivations were not cushioned by the development of "social solidarity": we were largely "atomized"—at least initially, as the authorities sought to prevent any group formation and often deliberately tried to set us against one another. (For example, the political officer suggested that we beat up those who did not pull their weight at work and thereby make the "Collective" as a whole suffer. His suggestion did in fact inspire occasional nocturnal beatings which were truly revolting to witness.) Life in the army also offered abundant examples of mindless regulations, crude and subtle inequalities and status distinctions, the use of naked power and the relationship between physical-material deprivations and one's outlook on life. To sum up the probable impact of the army on my later interests and involvement in sociology: it sensitized me to the pervasiveness of the inequalities of power and the possibilities of large-scale regimentation and intimidation.

Among the political-historical events which probably influenced my sociological leanings were World War II, especially as it was fought in Budapest, and the Hungarian Revolution of 1956 (and its defeat). They both helped to impress on me the endemic nature, the normalcy of conflict, of bloody political violence in human affairs. Perhaps both experiences implanted the seeds of skepticism toward theoretical approaches in sociology that emphasize value consensus, normative integration or the part played by constructive rationality in the settling of human disputes. The defeat of the Hungarian Revolution in particular was an all too obvious lesson in "might is right" and a reminder that force can resolve conflict with enduring results and ideas can in fact be silenced by naked power—perspectives on social-political life generally uncongenial to most Americans, including intellectuals and social scientists. Nevertheless, my experience of political violence and coercion did not make me a "conflict sociologist," as the term is generally understood and used in current American sociological discourse.[8]

There remains the important matter of the influence of particular academic settings and courses of study.

I tend to think that as far as my overall intellectual development and aspirations are concerned, the gymnasium and its milieu was the most important. Within that setting my cohort, my classmates should be singled out as the most significant influence. It should be noted here that "classmates" in this context had a different meaning than in the United States. It was a cohesive group (of about forty) which stayed together for the entire eight years of the high school experience as well as in particular classes or courses since we had virtually no electives. While it is always tempting to romanticize one's youth, it cannot be denied that my classmates constituted quite an impressive group, especially in the light of their subsequent accomplishments. Many of them proceeded to distinguished careers. My closest friend in Hungary, George Konrad, became a well-known writer not only in Hungary but in numerous Western countries as well. Every one of his books have been translated and published in English (and most other major European languages) and favorably reviewed in major Western publications—a highly unusual achievement for a Hungarian writer, however well appreciated in his own country. Another friend, who did not stay until graduation, went to Israel in his teens and eventually became not only a general but also commander of artillery of the Israeli armed forces and subsequently of logistics. The current head of Hungarian television was a classmate, also active in producing plays, films and even operas. Of some note has been another friend of my teens who attended university in the Soviet Union and subsequently became a widely traveled foreign correspondent, interviewing in their own languages several world leaders. Others, less prominent, ended up pursuing successful professional careers in medicine, the sciences, architecture, engineering and the humanities or social sciences in academia either in Hungary or abroad. In my estimation at least one-third of my class (of about forty) left in 1956 and completed their higher education abroad: primarily in England, Canada, the United States or France.

My classmates, or at any rate those who belonged to the bookish Jewish group, exerted a subtle but profound infuence on my overall intellectual development and aspirations. I am quite certain that if and insofar as I had become a card-carrying intellectual, it started in Madach Gymnasium in the years 1943–1951. There is no question in my mind that the tone of intellectual discourse in and outside the classes was well above that which can be found among undergraduates on many, possibly most, American campuses. Our interests were primarily literary-humanistic, philosophical and also political. My classmates often read books more advanced and demanding than those which were required readings.

It may also be noted that my high school was sex segregated as were all schools at the time in Hungary and this too contributed to a certain intellectual-male-bonding, or a tone of seriousness which might otherwise not have been present. We missed the company of girls badly but their absence made us in some ways more bookish or monkish. We had no interest whatsoever in sports and especially team sports.

While the gymnasium exerted much influence by way of providing a general predisposition to some form of intellectual activity, my formal training in sociology obviously shaped my more specific interests within the discipline and the type of sociologist I was to become. Having attended first a British university and then Princeton helped to make me more of a humanistic-qualitative than "scientific" empiricist sociologist. There have been a number of teachers who made significant and favorable impressions on me—few of them were quantitatively oriented. At the same time I don't think that any of them have decisively influenced my professional interests. In most cases they had little to do with the kind of work I later undertook. From LSE Tom Bottomore, Hilda Himmelweit and Ernest Gellner were noteworthy (though I often did not fully understand what Gellner was saying in his lectures), as was the gentle, nineteenth-century rational humanism of the late Morris Ginsberg. At the University of Illinois in Champaign-Urbana the graduate seminars of the editor of this volume and of Joe Gusfield beckon from the distance as instances of memorable intellectual stimulation in areas which had much to do with my later work: Gusfield taught political sociology (I recall writing a paper for him about the *disenchantment* of a group of formerly pro-communist Western intellectuals) and Bennett Berger gave a course on intellectuals or the sociology of knowledge; his remark that it is only the intellectuals who are truly alienated has stuck in my mind over decades. At Princeton (where I hastily transferred largely because of my dislike of the countryside in Illinois) the most memorable course (perhaps because its product, a seminar paper, eventually became my first published article)[9] was one I took with Harry Eckstein in the political science department, thought I cannot recall its title. There was much congenial intellectual discourse with Charles Page, Melvin Tumin and Morroe Berger, in and outside the classroom, as with Allen Kassof who provided my first and only formal exposure as a student to Soviet studies. I felt far less congenial with Marion Levy, yet, as is often the case, in retrospect it appears that his demanding seminars were a useful educational exercise and a possible incubation period and source of encouragement for my later comparative work. I recall having written seminar papers in which I compared something or other in countries such as East Germany, the Dominican Republic, Yemen and Tasmania. Such fanciful geographic choices reflected my interests rather than Levy's, but he did not mind which countries we picked as long as we gathered some information on the basis of which certain institutions could be compared. Here I also recall with some pride that I read virtually everything Princeton library had on the social structure of Tasmania (it was a modest collection).

Although, as described earlier, I drifted into the study and subsequent practice of sociology in a somewhat casual and unpremeditated manner, my commitment to certain basic values and my work as a sociologist have become closely intertwined. Correspondingly, there has also been something of a political focus and value basis for much of my work which I never tried to hide.[10] But, unlike so many of my fellow sociologists concerned with and committed to uncovering and exploring the injustices and defects of American society, I was more interested in exploring the injustices and deformities of other political systems, namely those of the Soviet variety inspiration. Such an orientation followed quite transparently from my background but also from my experiences in the West. Somehow I managed to retain over all these years a naive astonishment (and occasional indignation) over the fact that Western intellectuals, including perhaps most American social scientists, show so little appreciation of or support for the intellectual and political freedoms they have and for the political institutions which sustain them. Having come from a part of the world which has always been, and certainly was in my lifetime, quite intolerantly repressive, I could not sufficiently appreciate or share the estrangement of many of my fellow intellectuals and academic colleagues; I could not warm to their radical social criticism—a circumstance which circumscribed my otherwise reasonably harmonious adjustment to the academic-professional subculture.

For better or worse my views and values changed little over the years. A recent reviewer of a collection of my essays (which span a period of twenty years) remarked upon the consistency of my views revealed by these pieces.[11] I am not sure if this is a cause for pride or embarrassment, celebration or unease. Perhaps I ought to be troubled by the lack of significant change in my views and sense of identity over the years: it might signify an alarming absence of "personal growth." For better or worse, I probably finished "growing" quite a while ago; moreover, given my Eastern European background, I consider the process more limited in duration and potentialities than my more optimistic fellow Americans.

These concluding reflections may show that despite my professed reluctance to identify closely with my chosen discipline I adopted some of its deterministic perspectives even though I do not find beliefs in either social or historical determinism congenial and compatible with an optimistically open-ended view of human destiny.

Notes

1. Originally written for a collection of writings by American sociologists dealing with the relationship between life and work, this essay itself is an illustration of the connections between life and work. Most of it was written in an idyllic setting conducive to a more willing acceptance of one's life and work. It is quite likely that had I written this piece under the usual working conditions at home I might have been less indulgent but also less informative in lingering over aspects and details of the relationship between my life and work than was the case.
   The place in question was the Study and Conference Center of the Rockefeller Foundation (Villa Serbelloni) located in Bellagio, Italy. These remarks should also qualify as an expression of appreciation and thanks to the Foundation for providing such unusually pleasant living and working conditions which also led to other written work.
2. In the Preface to *Soviet and American Society: A Comparison* (pp. xi–xx) and in the Introduction to *The Many Faces of Socialism* (pp. 1–12).

3. My teacher Marion Levy, Jr., at Princeton University when I was a graduate student there once asked me: if I had a choice would I be a great scientist or a great artist? I did not hesitate to opt for the latter, confirming his dark suspicions.

4. "Public and Private in Hungary: A Travel Report" in *The Many Faces of Socialism,* cited, pp. 175–185.

5. In that capacity I occupied myself, among other things, with plastering the blackboard in school with stickers issued by the Hungarian Communist Party demanding that "reactionary" teachers be removed from the schools—this, needless to say, preceded the communist takeover after which the authority of teachers was fully restored in line with the overall strengthening of authority at all levels.

6. Above all in *Political Pilgrims—Travels of Western Intellectuals to the Soviet Union, China and Cuba.*

7. For not looking exactly like a matchbox. This ideal, given the soft straw stuffing, was almost impossible to attain. We would get up an hour before we had to in order to have sufficient time to smooth or sharpen the edges and arrange everything with the utmost symmetry. Nonetheless, the shape of beds remained the most common source of harassment and pretext for punishment.

8. In the Introduction to *The Many Faces of Socialism* (cited above) I have written: "Having such an enlarged awareness of conflict in human affiars did not, however, make me a 'conflict sociologist' as the term is used these days, meaning 'Marxist,' particularly since I also believe strongly in the causal importance and autonomy of ideas in social and political life." I noted in the same introduction other reasons for not becoming, or later assuming a Marxist stance as a sociologist. One was being "force-fed in school . . . a watered down Marxism (which nevertheless had something to do with the more genuine article). Forced intellectual diets produce strong reactions of distaste and nausea as do most diets administered under compulsion. . . . Second and more importantly, Marxism was discredited for me (and the vast majority of the population, intellectuals included . . .) by the vivid contrasts between promises, ideals, propositions and values derived from it (both from the esoteric and watered down versions) and its discernible applications in daily life." (p. 2 *cited*)

9. It was published in *Problems of Communism* in 1963 (and reprinted in *The Many Faces of Socialism*) under the title "Privacy, a Bastion Stormed" and addressed Chinese official morality under Mao (based on translated official texts).

10. See Preface, 1973, *cited,* and Introduction, 1983, *cited.*

11. See Ivan Szelenyi's review of *The Many Faces of Socialism* in *Contemporary Sociology,* May 1984.

Bibliography of Major Works

(Editor) *American and Soviet Society: Readings in Comparative Sociology and Perception.* Englewood Cliffs, N.J.: Prentice Hall, 1969.
Soviet and American Society: A Comparison. New York: Oxford University Press, 1973; Chicago: Chicago University Press, 1978 (paperbound).
Political Pilgrims: Travels of Western Intellectuals to the Soviet Union, China

and Cuba 1928–1979. New York: Oxford University Press, 1981; New York: Harper & Row, 1983 (paperbound).
The Many Faces of Socialism—Essays in Comparative Sociology and Politics. New Bunswick, N.J.: Rutgers University, Transaction Books, 1983.
In progress: *Conformity and Criticism in American Society—Varieties of Estrangement since the Late 1970s.* (for Oxford UP)

Education

High School (Madach Gimnazium), Budapest 1943–1951
London School of Economics, University of London 1957–59; B.A. in Sociology (1959)
University of Illinois (Champaign-Urbana) 1959–60; M.A. in Sociology (1960)
Princeton University 1960–63; Ph.D. in Sociology (1963)